BOOKS BY RICHARD HARRIS

The Real Voice
A Sacred Trust
The Fear of Crime
Justice
Decision
Freedom Spent

Freedom Spent

Freedom won
Freedom lent
Freedom gone
Freedom spent.
— Anon.

FREEDOM SPENT

by
Richard Harris

LITTLE, BROWN AND COMPANY BOSTON / TORONTO

FIRST EDITION

T 10/76

Most of the contents of this book appeared originally in *The New Yorker,* in somewhat different form.

The author is grateful to Oxford University Press, Inc., for permission to quote from *Origins of the Fifth Amendment: The Right Against Self-Incrimination* by Leonard W. Levy. Copyright © 1968 by Clio Enterprises Inc.

LIBRARY OF CONGRESS CATALOGING IN PUBLICATION DATA

Harris, Richard, 1926–
Freedom spent.

Includes index.

1. Civil rights—United States. I. Title.
KF4749.H35 342'.73'085 76–21634
ISBN 0–316–34824–4

Published simultaneously in Canada by Little, Brown & Company (Canada) Limited

PRINTED IN THE UNITED STATES OF AMERICA

For Hal Scharlatt

A man of wondrous spirit and
generosity and kindness and
decency and laughter, a man
who had no meanness in him —
a good man.

Acknowledgments

I want to thank Professor Thomas I. Emerson, of the Yale Law School, for his critique of my history of the First Amendment right to freedom of expression; Professor Yale Kamisar, of the University of Michigan Law School, for his critique of my history of the Fourth Amendment right to be secure against "unreasonable searches and seizures;" and Professor Leonard W. Levy, dean of the graduate faculty of history at the Claremont Colleges, for his critique of my history of the Fifth Amendment right against compulsory self-incrimination. I am additionally and deeply indebted to Professor Levy for his monumental works *Legacy of Suppression: Freedom of Speech and Press in Early American History, Origins of the Fifth Amendment: The Right against Self-Incrimination,* and *Against the Law: The Nixon Court and Criminal Justice,* which I used extensively in this book. Finally, I am endlessly grateful to Burt Neuborne, professor of constitutional law at the New York University Law School, for his wise counsel at crucial points in this long project.

I also want to thank Robert Lescher, my literary agent, who has been unflaggingly diligent on my behalf; Sara Spencer, Evan Cornog, and Patti Hagan, of *The New Yorker* checking department, for their invaluable assistance; Robert Bingham, my editor at *The New Yorker,* for his boundless good will and invaluable editorial aid; and William Shawn, editor of *The New Yorker,* who has made this book and many, many others not only possible but inevitable.

Acknowledgments

Contents

Prologue

The Sacred Fire of Liberty

The preservation of the sacred fire of liberty, and the destiny of the republican model of government, are justly considered as *deeply,* perhaps as *finally,* staked on the experiment entrusted to the hands of the American people.

— George Washington
First Inaugural Address

When President Washington spoke of "the sacred fire of liberty" being "entrusted to the hands of the American people," neither he nor any of them could have foreseen that this great social conflagration, which had been ignited by the Declaration of Independence and then placed inside that ingeniously wrought furnace the Constitution, would go untended almost from the start. The simple and overwhelming truth is that the most fundamental parts of the American Constitution — above all, the guarantees of personal liberty contained in the Bill of Rights — have rarely been enforced. The myth of freedom has been driven into us incessantly almost from birth, but the reality of freedom eludes us to this day.

For the first century and a half of this nation's existence, the only kind of liberty that mattered to most people, and to government on every level, was economic liberty — the unhampered freedom to acquire and protect property. More simply put, having money meant being free. A great and abundant continent lay before the new Americans, and the hope of riches, or for many of them simply survival, drove this nation to a frenzy of exploitation and plunder. Even so, America offered more freedom than other nations of the world, for it was a place of nearly endless social plurality and economic opportunity, and anyone who didn't like the way life was going in one community could pick up and go somewhere else to start anew. But with the disappearance of the frontier and the full settlement of the land came the arrival of "mass society" — immense government, huge businesses and labor unions, and an intricate network of nearly total communications that could be used to manipulate the great majority of the people as never before. At the same time, society has become more and more intolerant of differences within it and more and more uncertain of its purpose and of the meaning of "the American dream." In addition, Congress is today blind to the people's needs, the Presidency contains the power to bring about a personal form of despotism, and the judiciary nearly always serves the interests of the state rather than its citizens. In sum, the possibility of there being a true tyranny of the majority on a national scale has become ominously real for the first time in the nation's history, for mass society has created all the elements necessary to make the individual in America extinct.

In 1788, the year that the United States was established as a nation, Thomas Jefferson wrote to a friend, "The natural progress of things is for liberty to yield and government to gain ground." That progress has been inexorable in America, and of all the tyrannical threats to the individual today none is more powerful or menacing than the threat posed by his oldest enemy: government. One of the truths that was so self-evident to the Founding Fathers — that all governments everywhere are always opposed to the needs and interests of their citizens — has been forgotten by succeeding generations of Americans. Also forgotten has been the basic purpose behind our Constitution — to create a government that would be strong enough to protect the people but not strong enough to destroy their freedom. This truth and this purpose have been forgotten because the rhetoric of freedom has been so unceasingly dinned into American ears by our leaders in every station that most of us have become deaf to the resounding proofs of tyranny that we hear every day. In fact, we are deaf even to the rumbling, imminent threats to our own most immediate and most precious freedom — those inalienable rights to life, liberty, and the pursuit of happiness.

Prologue

The rights that lie closest to the heart of one's individuality are the right to express oneself freely, the right to be secure in one's home, and the right not to be forced to tell government what one may have said or done. Once we are deprived of these rights, we cannot be free even to think. And without thought we cannot be free to develop ourselves as we see fit – surely the purpose of democracy. The stories that follow are about six ordinary American men and women who recently fought to preserve these irreplaceable rights – *our* rights – against government usurpation from the bottom to the top in this country.

Part One

A Scrap of Black Cloth

I

"We live by symbols," Justice Oliver Wendell Holmes said. For many people, symbols provide the only means of expressing their deeper feelings, and the visible manifestation of the invisible – an engagement ring, a flag, a beard, a Cadillac, a gun, a crucifix, a pair of bluejeans, a monogram – often expresses more in an instant for and about them than their words or acts ever could. Words or acts must first be stated or committed, then interpreted, and finally understood, but symbols immediately convey meaning through a kind of emotional shorthand. And while a statement that is embodied in words or acts lasts only as long as it is remembered, a symbolic statement exists for as long as it is visible.

In the political and social worlds, symbols command attention in a way that only the cleverest words and the boldest acts do. In fact, such words and acts rarely have a comparable effect unless they become symbolic – as, for instance, in words like "We shall overcome" or "the silent majority," and in acts like burning draft cards or standing in the schoolhouse doorway. In totalitarian states, leaders use this power of symbols (the swastika, say) to instill obedience through terror. In democratic states, leaders use this power of symbols (chiefly the national flag or anthem) to instill obedience through faith. And in the United States people use this power of symbols to fulfill their peculiar need to express to every passerby their views on everything from love of country (a flag decal on the window of a car) to belief in God (a plastic figure of the Virgin on the dashboard). For such people, reliance on symbols probably reflects simply the desire of the speechless to speak. But that reliance may also create and exacerbate discord within a nation, for the innate power of symbols that can arouse the most passionate feelings of reverence, hope, and love in one person can arouse equally passionate feelings of scorn, fear, and hatred in another.

War inevitably produces symbols. Ordinarily, they are aimed at one goal – unity of purpose – but the war in Vietnam produced a great abundance of them, because the pro-war and the anti-war factions kept trying to best each other symbolically as well as practically. In the end, they did little more than aggravate their mutual hostility, and at times this led to acts of revenge – mostly on the part of the supporters of the war, who defended, and often possessed, authority and power on various levels.

No one can tell how many people were ostracized, or persecuted, or dismissed from their jobs, or prosecuted on trumped-up charges, or run out of town because of their opposition to the war, but there undoubtedly were many thousands of them altogether. Those who paid for standing up for their unpopular beliefs probably lived mainly in places where people were generally unaccustomed to dissent from political and social orthodoxy. Of course, America has always been a basically conservative country, and such places abound, particularly in rural and semi-rural areas, where suspicion of anyone who seems different and under outside, or alien, influences is an essential feature of the social structure.

A few people began arriving at the Quaker meetinghouse just off the corner of Main and Sixth Streets in a quiet, lower-middle-class neighborhood of Elmira, New York, at a little before eleven o'clock on the morning of Sunday, November 9, 1969. Although the Elmira Meeting of the Religious Society of Friends had fewer than a dozen members at the time, they had contributed enough money to buy a new meetinghouse, and this was their first use of it. Formerly a Methodist chapel, it lacked the dour appearance which so often characterizes that denomination's houses of worship; it was a small, inviting place with gray shingled siding and white trim and, in front, a defiant little square tower with a mock battlement top. Altogether, the building suited its new owners, who were also modest, friendly, determined, and, by general standards, a bit odd. That autumn Sunday, they passed through the front door into a dark, wood-panelled vestibule and climbed a flight of stairs to a door that gave onto a room of twenty-five by fifteen feet — bare except for a small table and a couple of dozen folding chairs lining its walls — which the Quakers were going to use for their weekly meetings instead of the large room downstairs. As the members came in, they quietly took seats and sat meditating. Now and then, one of them suddenly spoke out — to tell a story that illustrated a moral or religious principle, or to make a brief declaration of spiritual belief, or to confess a personal failure of conscience. That morning, an unusual number of remarks concerned the effects of the war in Vietnam on the life and spirit of man.

The religious meeting ended at noon, and afterward the members turned to a discussion of worldly topics that involved them collectively, such as arrangements for making monthly payments on the mortgage for their new quarters, and a decision on the kind of advice that should be given to a local boy who opposed the war and had appealed to a member of the Meeting for help in staying out of the Army. Once these matters were disposed of, the clerk of the Meeting — a square-faced middle-aged man by the name of Werner Salle, who owned and ran a refrigeration-and-air-conditioning business in town — brought up the forthcoming protest against the war, which was generally known by the title Vietnam Moratorium, or, more often, simply the Moratorium. (Either designation was somewhat inaccurate, for both properly belonged to a protest held the previous month throughout the country under the auspices of various radical student groups, which tended to put off generally conservative people like the Quakers. Officials of the Nixon Administration had predicted a small and violent turnout for the October event, but it had been an unexpectedly large and peaceable success, and subsequently the idea and the name were taken over by more acceptable anti-war sponsors, who planned similar demonstrations for the following months.)

The local Moratorium was to be held on the fourteenth and fifteenth – the coming Friday and Saturday – and now Salle asked for suggestions about what members of the Meeting who wanted to participate might do for the cause of peace. He said that he had met with a few people from various church and community groups who were trying to organize a small anti-war movement and they had made various proposals: placing a pro-Moratorium advertisement in the local newspaper; putting up pro-Moratorium posters and distributing pro-Moratorium leaflets and handbills in certain heavily travelled places in and around Elmira; keeping the meetinghouse open Friday and Saturday for a vigil; joining a major march and rally in Washington on Saturday; and wearing black armbands as symbols of mourning for those who had been killed in the war. These suggestions were unanimously agreed to by the members, and a couple of them volunteered to arrange for the newspaper advertisement and to find out more about plans being made by some students at Elmira College for bus transportation to Washington. Then the coming Wednesday evening was set for a work session at which members and outsiders who might want to contribute to the anti-war effort would make posters, leaflets, and armbands.

Although the people at the meeting felt that such attempts to add to the growing public demands for peace in Southeast Asia were, at best, frustratingly modest, they felt that as a religious group there was little more they could do to express their opposition to the war. Division over the war was again approaching the point of crisis in the nation, with anti-war leaders vowing to drive President Nixon out of office, as they had driven President Johnson out of office, unless the war was ended at once, on practically any terms. And Nixon, vowing that he would not be "affected whatever" by such protests, had turned Vice-President Agnew loose on the Administration's opponents after the success of the first Moratorium. Agnew called the demonstrators – several million of whom had marched and rallied in hundreds of large and small protests across the country in October – "merchants of hate" and "parasites of passion," and warned that the rest of the American people could "afford to separate them from our society, with no more regret than we should feel over discarding rotten apples from a barrel." Since the threat to separate the Administration's adversaries from society clearly implied the use of force – either government force, which would have required suspension of the Constitution, or vigilante force, which would have brought anarchy and an official excuse for repression of dissidents in the name of order – some people feared that if the protests were too successful they might prompt President Nixon to strike out at his enemies more forcefully than he already had.

Despite this danger and the personal risk that anyone who stood up to the Administration took, millions of people across the country seemed to feel that they had to act in some way to show their revulsion against the war. The handful of Quakers who got together in Elmira, for instance, hoped that the name "Quaker" itself would reassure local citizens, who were generally conservative and inclined to support the President, that it was not radical to oppose the war. Once people got over the fear of behaving like radicals, this theory went, they might be willing to speak out against the war locally and thereby add their numbers, however small, to the growing public protests against the Administration's policies.

"At the time, there was almost no overt opposition to the war in this area," a member of the Elmira Meeting explained later. "Most people here are accustomed to trusting and obeying authority, wherever it resides. Everybody seemed to be asleep in their consciences, but we believed that a good many of them were deeply disturbed about the war. Our hope was that we could waken the pro-life spirit in some of them."

At the same time, none of the Quakers expected much to come of their efforts. "The work we did," Salle said afterward, "was an attempt to express through our own actions what we thought God would want us to do – without our thinking of ourselves as agents of God and without our thinking that this was going to end the war or have any large effect. We believed that we could change things, but only gradually, as each individual expression of conscience must in time."

A few days before the Quakers made their plans at the meeting in Elmira, President Nixon delivered a nationally broadcast speech in which he appealed to "the great silent majority of Americans" to rally to his support on the war issue, and vast numbers of his listeners – seventy-seven per cent, according to a Gallup poll – responded favorably to his plea. That set the stage for a confrontation between the anti-war and pro-war sides, and it was widely feared that there would be an uncontrollable eruption of violence, with terrible consequences for the nation. To a large extent, the Administration created this fear and then used it to persuade citizens to stay away from Washington during the November protest there. In the early part of that month, a Department of Justice spokesman, John W. Dean III, announced intelligence reports on plans by the Weathermen, by ultra-conservatives, and by street gangs organized by both sides to have a showdown in the capital. And as people like the members of the Elmira Meeting were getting ready to support the Moratorium, pro-war groups were getting ready to oppose it. About that time, the American Legion, the Veterans of Foreign Wars, and the Young Americans for Freedom announced that they would rally and march by the tens of thousands in demonstrations to be held across the country in the coming days. Tuesday was to be Veterans Day, and it was to highlight Honor America Week, a patriotic event deliberately designed to drown out the pleas for peace.

On Wednesday evening, half a dozen members of the Elmira Meeting got together as planned in a tall buff-colored Victorian house next door to their meetinghouse (both of which they had purchased for ten thousand dollars) and set to work making posters, leaflets, and armbands. During the course of the session, they were joined by eight or ten non-Quakers, most of them Elmira College students, and the group turned out a large number of appeals to their neighbors in the area to support the Moratorium. A couple of the women who were on hand spent the evening cutting armbands out of a few yards of black silk that

Salle had bought that morning at J. C. Penney. One of them remarked on the fine quality of the material, and Salle apologized for buying anything so expensive for such brief use. "I was in a hurry, and didn't pay any attention to the cost," he explained.

Among those present at both the Sunday meeting and the Wednesday work session was Charles James — a tall, very thin man of forty-one with dark hair, a long, rather troubled-looking face, and an unexpectedly cheerful manner — who had moved to the area a few months before to take a job teaching eleventh-grade English at a high school in Addison, a small town about fifteen miles west of Elmira. When James left the Wednesday meeting, he took along a batch of mimeographed leaflets and two armbands, and drove to his home, in Horseheads, just north of Elmira. James and his wife, Neva — a graceful, good-looking woman in her late thirties, with shoulder-length black hair parted in the middle and heavy black brows — had supper after he got home, and he spent some time with their four daughters, who ranged in age from seven to sixteen. Then he and his wife sat down in the living room to talk about what they should do to support the Moratorium. Both of them were reluctant to do anything that might make them stand out unduly and give them a reputation for being troublemakers, and, as former residents of upstate towns that were much the same as Horseheads and Addison, they knew that almost any noticeable divergence from accepted models of conduct would be looked upon with suspicion.

As it happened, the bus company that had agreed to rent a bus for the trip from Elmira to Washington sponsored by students from Elmira College was unable to provide a driver, because its regular drivers were so alarmed by F.B.I. warnings about violence during the Moratorium that they refused to make the run. James wanted to drive his family's Volkswagen bus in its place, but his wife said, "You'll get in trouble with the school. Don't do it." After thinking it over, he finally agreed with her, and accepted her suggestion that they demonstrate where they stood on the war by spending the coming Saturday at the Quaker vigil in Elmira. Still, James felt guilty about doing so little for the cause of peace – no more, he pointed out, then joining others who felt the same as they did already – and proposed that Neva and he wear the armbands he had brought home. At least, he said, that gesture might compel those they worked with to stop and think about whether they were actually supporting the war by not openly opposing it. Neva James said that it would be pointless for her to wear an armband to her job – at Elmira College, where she was in charge of student financial aid – because she knew it would have no positive effect on her co-workers, and she saw no reason to be stared at and talked about for no purpose.

At that, James realized that he, too, was reluctant to cause a stir among the people *he* worked with by making an essentially pointless gesture. "The main question on my mind at the time was how willing was I to take the stares and cracks from other members of the faculty," he recalled. "I viewed wearing an armband as the most restrained way possible to make a statement about the war. It certainly didn't seem to be a cataclysmic thing to do."

Mrs. James agreed. "We were determined not to do anything rash," she said. "The Quakers felt that any illegal or extreme act would frighten local people, as well as violate our beliefs and defeat our purpose. We had to be very careful not to do *anything* that could seem radical to *anybody*. So the armband looked like the best solution – a symbol more than an act." She paused for a moment, and then added, "But even that much wasn't easy for Charles to do. It has always been extremely difficult for him to do things that might make someone else disapprove of him. He's always found it very hard to take unpopular stands. And yet he holds some unpopular views, so he's had a great conflict in being himself and dealing with society at the same time. Those moments when he *has* stood up for himself have been very traumatic for him."

Small as the gesture of wearing a black armband to work seemed to both the Jameses, he put off his decision about it throughout the evening and the next day. A television program that the Jameses had intended to watch that night was preëmpted by a live broadcast of another Agnew speech — this one attacking the major television networks for having allowed their commentators to deliver "instant" analyses of the President's silent-majority speech the week before and for being controlled by an "unelected élite." Agnew warned, "It is time that the networks were made more responsive to the views of the nation and more responsible to the people they serve."

Under the circumstances, James was alarmed by the unmistakable message of the speech: Conform or be silenced. And he was unsettled by the realization that if the Administration was prepared to take on giant corporations like those owning the networks — which, he strongly believed, had said far too little rather than too much about its shortcomings — there was even more danger facing the individual who spoke out against the President's policies than people like James had thought. "Even so, I considered wearing an armband a very small way to protest," he said. "In fact, I was kind of ashamed of myself for not doing more."

When James woke up on Friday morning, the fourteenth, he saw the piece of black silk lying on the dresser and knew that the time for him to make up his mind was at hand. Still, he put off his decision for the moment, and went to have breakfast. He and his wife didn't discuss the subject at the table, and when he got ready to go to work he forgot about the problem. But as he was knotting his necktie in front of the mirror on the dresser, he glanced down and saw the armband.

"I was suddenly held by the feeling that the armband lying there symbolized a life-and-death question," he said. "I was struck by the awareness that after at least twenty-five centuries of civilization men still find within themselves the will to deliberately and, when possible, carefully kill each other. And often this killing occurs while they look at one another, face to face, and willingly behold dying and death. I considered my wearing the armband — considered its value and considered the possible glares and frowns of colleagues at school. Then I was staggered all over again at the thought of man's willful killing of man. I realized that I could not responsibly leave the armband behind and go through even another day. If my wearing it could bring someone, anyone, to consider that some people do believe in the preciousness of life and dare to say so, then our world would have a better chance of survival. Our Quaker Meeting had made the armband for this purpose. The rest was up to me. Those years of writing letters, preaching, speaking, arguing, and marching against the war would be rendered hollow if I didn't wear it. I wore it."

James was born and brought up in the small upstate town of Hornell, where his father owned a prosperous florist business that had been in the family for two generations. Young Charles was the only son, and was expected to take over the business someday, but even after he flunked out of horticultural school at Cornell in his first year for bad attendance and worse grades, he couldn't bring himself to disappoint his father by announcing that he didn't want to spend his life selling flowers and shrubbery, and he went back home and dutifully entered the florist business.

"As a kid, I wanted to believe in things — I was a believer by instinct — and it was important for me to stand up for what I believed in," he said. "One belief I had was that a man has a right to his own life. But I was constantly subjected to pressure to live someone else's kind of life and go into the family business. I had a terribly strong desire to be my own person, and I had a very deep faith in Christ. I wanted to be a minister, but I was afraid to go ahead and become one."

Seven years after he left Cornell — including three years in the Air Force during the Korean war and close to five years in the family business — Charles James, married and the father of two children, was still working for C. G. James & Company, Florists. But that year, 1955, he decided to make the break at last and enter the Methodist ministry. Making the decision was easier than announcing it, though, and when he finally got up the nerve and blurted out the news to his father, Charles fainted and was unconscious for two hours.

For eight years, James was an undergraduate or seminarian, and during this period he also served as a full-time parish minister. "I was so conservative that my fellow-ministers kidded me about it," he said. "I carried the Bible with me all the time, and they thought I was overdoing it. I guess I was — from their viewpoint, anyway. It was a long time before I came to feel that many of them no longer believed in what the church, or Christianity in general, stood for, and that they had turned into bureaucrats in clerical clothes. I guess that often happens to people who set out to do good and then discover that it can't be done in the system they're a part of. When I finally realized that, I was ready to get out."

Neva James, who had been strictly raised as a Methodist, had strongly supported her husband's decision to enter the ministry, and she even more strongly opposed his decision to leave it. "I thought we could keep working inside the church for what we believed in," she said afterward. "From childhood, I had been taught, and had believed, that the church was the true way to goodness, and that if one was really committed to the church one could help relieve suffering in the world."

As James listened to his wife describe her feelings during that period, he nodded, and said, "For those first few years, I believed that the members of the church felt as we did. But then I began to see that it was all a fraud. They didn't believe in the words of the church — those were merely sermons to be sat through on Sunday, not words to live by. In my innocence and naïveté, I hadn't realized that in reality I was just presiding over a social club."

Neva James was unwilling to give up all they had worked for, and begged him to reconsider his decision to leave the church. Then one day she was reading "Walden," and ran across a famous passage — "I learned this, at least, by my experiment; that if one advances confidently in the direction of his dreams, and endeavors to live the life which he has imagined, he will meet with a success unexpected in common hours. . . . If you have built castles in the air, your work need not be lost; that is where they should be. Now put the foundations under them." The realization that she might retain her hopes even if her way of life changed gave her some encouragement, but she wasn't ready to give up the church yet, and clung to the belief that her husband would change his mind. Then she had her fourth child, at a time when she was exhausted by overwork in the parish and at home and weakened by her fear of leaving the church. Finally, she collapsed and had to be hospitalized for a week. "When I came home, I stayed away from church one Sunday while Charles was holding services," she said. "I lay there on the sofa, and as I listened to the organ music I picked up the hymnal and started reading the words that went with the music. The difference between those lovely thoughts and the disappointing practices of the church made me decide then to go along with Charles."

In the course of training for the ministry, he had picked up a bachelor's degree in education, with a major in English and history, and shortly after he resigned from the church he got a job teaching English in a public high school in Bainbridge, a small upstate town. The Jameses spent four years there quite contentedly, but then they decided that perhaps they were rusting away and might enjoy city life more — at least as a change. In the summer of 1967, they moved to New York City, where James got a job teaching English to non-English-speaking Puerto Rican children at the Arturo Toscanini Junior High School, in the Bronx. The Jameses settled in a quiet section of Flushing, where the schools seemed fairly placid and safe for their children, and before long they got used to, and even enjoyed, the pace and demands of city life.

After a year, James began to feel that they had made the right choice, but then, just as he got into his second year's work, there was a citywide teachers' strike — the ugly Ocean Hill-Brownsville dispute concerning decentralization of control over public schools — which lasted more than two months. He refused to join the great majority of teachers who supported the strike against decentralization, because he felt that it was largely motivated by racism and was harming the school-children without helping anyone else. As a result, he was called a "scab" by other teachers and a "nigger-lover" by white parents, and his children, who attended daily demonstrations against the strike, were taunted and harassed by pickets.

"We were very naïve, and I suppose that if we had known the

danger we faced we wouldn't have done what we did," Mrs. James recalled. "Where we had come from, people are very polite, and if they disagree with you they rarely tell you so. But in the city people aren't like that. They just let you know – right out – that they hate you. I had never seen that kind of hostility before, and I wasn't prepared for the abuse and obscenities and threats. The area we lived in in Flushing was all white, and when we went to a community meeting there about the strike we were the only people out of eight hundred who opposed it. When the moderator asked for a show of hands of those who were against the strike and we raised ours, the audience booed and screamed and cursed us. I was called on by the moderator to express the opposite view from the majority, and when I stood up to speak they screamed and booed some more. I was terrified. It was like a newsreel of some South American dictatorship or of Germany in the thirties. I hadn't really realized until then what was meant by 'the tyranny of the majority.' Anyway, I clenched my hands and swallowed, and said that they all claimed there wasn't any intimidation in the strike but that I felt very intimidated at the moment. I said that when I was escorting some black children to school that morning one of the pickets had leaned over to the nearest child and said, 'You black bastard!' At that, a woman in the audience screamed, 'You liar!' and began running down the aisle. They stopped her before she got to me. Afterward, people wrote 'nigger-lover' on our garage door, and telephoned us with threats and obscenities. We were so innocent – foolish, really. We invited blacks into our apartment for strategy meetings, and before long not a person on the block would speak to us. It got so bad that a woman friend met me every afternoon at the subway stop when I came home from work and walked with me the few blocks to where we lived."

Despite the hostility and fear the Jameses experienced, they look back on their two years in New York with some fondness – chiefly because of the friends they made there. One of them was a black minister by the name of Timothy Mitchell, who was one of the leaders of the anti-strike minority. "He had a profound influence on us," James explained. "He showed us how to be very sure of what we believed in before we went out and took a stand. That was something I had never learned to do, and Tim taught me how. He showed me that once you commit yourself to a position with intelligence and enlightenment, it doesn't matter how others respond to you. You don't try to convince your opponents or trick them to win. All you do is tell what you think is the truth – always." The Jameses also made a few close friends among other teachers who opposed the strike and among members of the Flushing Meeting of the Religious Society of Friends, which they began to attend during that period. Both of them found the friendly and sympathetic outlook of the Quakers far more congenial than the personally distant traditional attitude of the Methodists.

James, in particular, was irresistibly attracted by the Quakers' belief in nonviolence. His parents had believed, and taught him to believe, in the inevitability of retribution and in unquestioning patriotism. "Maybe that's why I enlisted in the Air Force after the terrible slaughter of American troops in Korea in the summer of 1950," he said. "But I had a problem even then about reconciling Christianity with killing, although I never was in combat. I didn't resolve the conflict at the time, but afterward I became increasingly convinced that no man has a right to violate another man through war, any more than he has a right in civil society to murder someone. I felt that it was the fault of leaders everywhere who hadn't really tried to find other ways of resolving quarrels. In the end, the people had to go off and kill and be killed because of their leaders' mistakes. But in this country right and wrong seldom get discussed except as abstract moral principles, and when I was young I could never find anybody to talk this over with. If you are serious about serious things, I learned, you are disliked. You are supposed to be serious only about unimportant things, like baseball and beer. Most American men probably know who the second baseman on the Yankees is, but most of them probably don't know who their congressman is. Anyway, after I got out of the service I read a lot about American history and foreign affairs, and came away convinced that our foreign policy has been the same as our domestic policy toward minorities ever since the Indians were driven off their land. When I saw that, I decided I couldn't participate in the manly business of killing any longer. It was the first time in my life that I had had anything more than an abstract moral feeling to base my actions on. By the time we moved to New York, my mind was fixed. And as soon as the Vietnam war became real to me, in 1966, so did my position on it. That was the beginning. All my life, I had been unable to take a position and stick to it. I didn't have the courage or the conviction to make my views clear. I needed a way to stand up – even if it was a small, maybe futile, way."

Late in the spring of 1969, the Jameses got ready to move again. New York City was not their kind of place, they agreed – its rage and violence and turmoil were too much for them – and they decided to move back upstate to the kind of community they felt more at home in. But they made their decision with some uneasiness, for they knew that in such places any failure to conform to the prevailing outlook and general mode of living could cause trouble, too. Still, they wanted to put down some roots at last, and to bring up their children in comparative safety and peace. There were several openings for high-school English teachers upstate, and James finally took one at Addison High School, a few miles from Elmira. Before driving to Addison for his interview with the principal of the school district, James had his hair, which he had let grow rather long, cut very short. He wore a dark suit, a white shirt, and a plain, narrow tie for the interview, but on his way to it he was so nervous about his appearance that he stopped off and had his hair cut again. He got the job without any difficulty and then the Jameses rented half of a two-family house in Horseheads, which was over twenty miles from Addison and in another school district.

"We didn't want to live in the same community where Charles taught, because we knew that some of our less orthodox views would be sure to get back to the school, and might cause some ill feeling," Mrs. James explained recently. "Also, we didn't want the children to go to school in the same system where their father worked. We'd had enough trouble with that in the city."

As for James, he didn't want *any* kind of trouble. "What I

want," he told his wife, "is to be not a teacher but a man who is teaching."

Addison, a bleak village of some two thousand inhabitants, is situated in the pleasant low hills of what is known as "the southern tier" of upstate New York – just above the Pennsylvania border. The business district of the town is a block long and is mostly made up of two- and three-story buildings of red or rust brick. There are a few drab shops, the Ritz Café, a gas station, and the Central Cigar Store, which has a large sign hanging out in front that says "Billiards – Guns – Ammo." One block off the main street is Addison High School, a fairly imposing structure designed in what might be called Grecian Academic. The main section, which was built forty-odd years ago, is a two-story red brick building with a peaked roof; in the center is a broad, buff-colored wood portico supported by six columns; and on top of the roof above that is a two-tiered clock tower. Directly across the street, on the lawn in front of a small shingle house, is a painted wood Uncle Sam holding a flagpole.

At a little before eight o'clock on the morning of November 14, 1969, Charles James drove through Addison, parked his car in a large lot beside the school, and hurried in to his homeroom to get ready for the arrival of his students. Almost as soon as he had taken off his topcoat and sat down behind his desk, the high-school principal – a bald, bespectacled, middle-aged man named Carl Pillard, who had been a math and gym teacher before he became a school administrator – came into the room and sat down in a chair beside James's desk. "Some of the students will be wearing armbands today," Pillard told him. "Just act like nothing has happened. Pay no attention to them."

James nodded, and at that moment Pillard noticed the armband on his sleeve. He seemed startled, but he said nothing, and a minute later he left the room. Five minutes afterward, a woman teacher hurried in and told James that if students wore armbands to school the teachers were instructed to ignore them. James merely nodded again, and said that he understood. "When nothing more happened immediately, I figured that was the end of it," he said later. "If students who wore armbands were to be ignored, it seemed likely that faculty members who wore armbands would be ignored, too."

James's homeroom period lasted about twenty minutes, after which he had a free hour to finish preparing for his first class — poetry for students who were not going on to college. "They were a particular challenge to me, because I was convinced they could do very well with poetry if given a chance," he said. "That morning, we were comparing certain aspects of poems by Matthew Arnold, Karl Shapiro, and Ogden Nash, and the kids were really going at it."

Suddenly the wall telephone buzzed, and James answered. It was Pillard, who told him to come to his office immediately, and hung up. James was uneasy about leaving his class unattended — the previous year, he had stepped out into the corridor for five minutes at his school in the Bronx and returned to find that a desk had been thrown out the third-floor window — but since he had been ordered to report at once, he asked his students to behave themselves for a few minutes and left.

When he entered the principal's office, Pillard demanded, "Why are you wearing that armband?"

James was stunned. "I felt as if I had just been flung onto an ice floe," he said later. "I couldn't believe that I was expected to describe a lifetime of development and belief in one answer." He looked at Pillard for a time, and then turned his head and stared out the window. Finally, he looked back at Pillard and said, "Because I am against killing."

The answer didn't satisfy Pillard, who told him that if he continued wearing the armband parents and other members of the community — who vote on the school budget — would become incensed at the school for not disciplining him, and said that by noon everyone in Addison would know about the armband. "There could be serious trouble," he added.

At that, James smiled and asked, "You mean they'd be upset by my asserting my rights but they wouldn't be upset if you took my rights away?"

Pillard ignored the question and accused James of "taking a political position" by wearing the armband. That interpretation had never occurred to James, and again he stared in disbelief at the principal without answering the charge. Finally, Pillard said, "I'm going to have to ask you to remove the armband."

James was having difficulty controlling himself and was trembling nervously. He later said, "I always get severely agitated when there is a confrontation that involves a collision of principles and when, at the same time, it's obvious that there's no possibility of really talking things over sensibly. That was the kind of situation it was, and I felt great anxiety." To put Pillard off long enough to give himself some time to recover from the shock of what was happening, James asked to be allowed to think it over. "I have a wife and four children to consider."

"If you know what you're going to do, you know right now," Pillard retorted.

James had meant more than his responsibility for supporting his family, but he didn't explain what he had in mind, because he was sure that Pillard wouldn't understand. "I knew that my children would stand in disappointed wonder if I let a man take from me my statement of belief, my simple protest against killing," James said later. Then, with a self-deprecating smile, he added, "And after that thought there were images of sermons I had preached and prayers I had offered for people like Socrates, Antigone, St. Joan, George Fox, Daniel Berrigan, and I asked myself, 'Where is the reality? What can possibly be real at this moment?' "

Finally, Pillard demanded a decision from him, and James said, "I choose to leave the armband on."

Pillard ordered him to go to the office of the principal of the school district, Edward J. Brown, which was in the same building. James replied that he had to check on his class first, and left. The students there seemed to be behaving themselves, and after asking them to carry on James walked slowly down the long corridor to Brown's office. Brown had had limited experience as a teacher, having spent two years teaching mathematics and fifteen years as an administrator. A tall, slender, middle-aged man with deep-set eyes, a thin, clamped mouth, and the stern demeanor of a person who was not accustomed to being crossed, Brown was obviously expecting him. "Why are you wearing that armband?" he demanded.

Since the question was the same as the one that Pillard had first asked him, James concluded that the reason for the delay before he was summoned was to give the principals time to devise a common strategy for dealing with him. By this point, he was determined to stick to his decision not to take off the armband, and was now more sure of himself and more relaxed than he had been when Pillard confronted him.

Looking at Brown, James answered him as he had answered Pillard: "Because I am against killing."

"You are not being responsible toward the students," Brown said.

"I think I am," James replied, and went on to explain that for years educators had urged that school faculties contain various kinds of teachers, with varied viewpoints, since youngsters learn from their teachers not only about the world but about people. "Children get their first ideas about character and personal relationships outside the family from observing their teachers in contact with themselves and with other students," James told him. "It's the whole atmosphere, with its many stimuli, that helps inform and excite children about the world. If all teachers were the same, and had the same attitude and the same approach, there would be no excitement and little learning."

Brown looked at him as if to say that James was not there to deliver a lecture on pedagogy, and said, "I am responsible for these children."

"I guess he meant that exposing them to me any further would be irresponsible of him," James said afterward. "I could see almost at once that Brown was fully prepared to dehumanize me by not letting me stand up for myself, and to humiliate me for stepping even this tiny bit out of line by letting my students and my colleagues and my family know that I had backed down. I don't believe he cared about the students. What he cared about most was that his authority had been challenged."

"This is a political act," Brown said. "It is an illegal act. You are acting against the President of the United States, Mr. Nixon."

Concluding from this that Pillard's similar charge had been devised by Brown, James denied that he had any political motive, and added that, as both Brown and he knew, President Nixon had not been responsible for the war. Brown ignored the point, and asked why he hadn't worn the armband when he applied for the job.

Taken aback by the foolish nature of the question, James answered, "For the same reason that I didn't come in then with a chalice and a wafer – it wasn't the right day." By this stage, he observed later, it was clear to him that they "were just bartering phrases, not exchanging ideas," and that any chance of talking over the issue sensibly was lost, probably for good.

Brown stated that in his opinion the Moratorium was a political event and that James's use of the school as a forum for expressing his political views was both unethical and illegal for a teacher; that while teachers could properly raise a controversial issue in class if the subject was relevant to the course being taught, they were obliged at the same time to present "objectively all known points of view on the issue;" that the armband could have a disruptive effect on the students and a divisive effect on the faculty; that as principal of the school district he would get legal advice on the propriety of a teacher's wearing an armband to express his opposition to the war; and that in the meantime James would either take off the armband or leave the school.

James refused to remove the armband, whereupon Brown told him that he was suspended, and ordered him to go back to his classroom, pick up his personal belongings, and leave the building. James asked if he should go at the midday break, and Brown shook his head angrily. "Oh, no," he said. "Right now. I want you to get your things together and leave the building right now."

While James was packing his belongings, the teacher who headed the English Department came in, and he told her what had happened. On a number of occasions, she had praised him for his teaching skills and his hard work to make his classes a success, and now her eyes filled with tears. "I don't understand," she said. "What could they be thinking of? What are they trying to do?"

James comforted her, and then said that he had only one request. Several weeks before, Brown had given him permission to assign one of his classes some plays by O'Neill and Miller and a novel by Faulkner — a rather surprising approval, since not long before Brown had denied another teacher permission to take an English class to see a performance of *Romeo and Juliet,* on the ground that it was too suggestive for impressionable young minds. Now James asked the department head, "Just promise me that the kids will get a chance to read those new books when they come in."

He had packed and was about to leave when Pillard hurried in and told him to march his class to the cafeteria, even though it was not the lunch period. "I assumed that the idea was to get me to disobey an order that didn't involve my basic rights, and provide other grounds for firing me," James said later. "So I marched the kids to the cafeteria, and then I marched myself on out of the school."

Dazed by his superiors' reaction to a scrap of black cloth on his sleeve, James drove absentmindedly back toward Elmira on his usual route, which took him through Corning. Suddenly he decided that the best thing he could do would be to take immediate constructive action to give himself a feeling of hope, and he drove directly to the local board of education and filled out an application form for a teaching job in the Corning public-school system. Cheered and emboldened by this act, he then stopped off at a street-corner telephone booth and called the American Civil Liberties Union, in New York City, which, he knew, had often given legal advice and help to people who got in one kind of trouble or another when they opposed the war in Vietnam. The person on the other end told him to get in touch with the nearest A.C.L.U. chapter in the area, which was in Ithaca, and gave him a name and a telephone number.

Up to this point, James had not thought about the act of wearing an armband as embracing any specific legal right. In fact, in his discussions with his wife and his thoughts on the subject, he hadn't considered the legal aspects of his act at all. "I just assumed that I had some kind of a right to express my conscience," he explained. "All I meant to do was express my belief in the primacy and the preciousness of life. When I was thrown out of school for that expression, I took it for granted that I would be vindicated."

James put off making the call to Ithaca for the time being, and resumed his drive to Elmira, to join the vigil being held at the Quaker meetinghouse, where he was to meet his wife after work. He knew that he should call and tell her what had happened, but he couldn't bring himself to just then. He suspected that she viewed the armband as an ineffective protest and would be appalled that he had lost his job for it, so he decided that he would sort out his thoughts before he spoke to her. At the outskirts of Elmira, James changed his mind about going directly to the vigil and turned onto the road to Big Flats, a small town where an old friend was the Methodist minister. James had a long, intense talk with the minister, who strongly supported the stand he had taken. Relieved and encouraged by his friend's words, James went on to the vigil.

Only half a dozen people were present, and, after meditating for a time, James broke the silence in the room. "Guess what happened to me for wearing the armband," he said. "I just lost my job."

Two members who were also wearing armbands gasped, and Salle, who had bought the material for the armbands and was wearing one, too, looked shaken. He asked what had happened, and James described the events of that morning. When he finished, Salle said, "This is a serious, frightening situation in a democracy. We can't just sit here and let it happen." After the group discussed what might be done, Salle suggested that he get in touch with a local newspaper reporter whom he knew, in order to inform people about the episode and generate some public pressure on Brown to reinstate James. But James disagreed with the proposal, because he feared that it might be a mistake to publicize the matter and perhaps antagonize Brown further before he had a chance to think over the case and see that he had behaved improperly. But then James decided that he had better take Salle's advice. As he explained afterward, "I realized that Brown had already blown things up way out of proportion to their real meaning, and that if I didn't react quickly and effectively he would get away with what seemed to me to be basically a tyrannical act."

James and Salle went to the Quakers' house next door, where some members and outside volunteers were finishing a last batch of posters urging local participation in the nationwide series of rallies and marches the following day. A woman was on the telephone lining up people who might want to join the group that was going to Washington early the next morning for the march to be held there. When she paused between calls, Salle used the phone to ring up the reporter he knew, a woman called Peg Gallagher, of the Elmira *Star-Gazette,* who listened to his account of James's suspension and promised to come right over. James then telephoned the representative of the Civil Liberties Union in Ithaca — Jules Burgevin, a professor of education at Ithaca College — and told him what had happened. "They can't do that!" Burgevin cried, and promised to get in touch immediately with his chapter's legal adviser and call back.

James was deeply anxious about his wife's reaction when she learned about the official reaction to his armband, and he told Salle that he wanted to know as soon as she arrived at the vigil, so that he could be the one to tell her. But when she came into the meetinghouse, James was next door being interviewed by Mrs. Gallagher. Salle quickly went up to Mrs. James. "I've got bad news for you, Neva," he said. "You'd better sit down." Before she had time to, he went on, "Charles has lost his job."

She swayed, and quickly sat down. "I couldn't imagine what Charles had done," she said afterward. "We had both been so careful. Then, when I learned why he had been fired, I was just indignant. I decided that if something like a little black armband was that offensive to these people, it was useless to be careful, so why try?" She hurried next door to find her husband, who was stricken by a sense of guilt when he saw her and realized that she knew what had happened — that, once again, he had brought difficulty and pain into her life. Approaching him, she took his face in her hands and kissed him gently. Then she smiled and said, "Now that you're unemployed, why don't you drive our bus to Washington?" James grinned and said that he would.

Not long afterward, Burgevin called back and told James that the adviser to the local A.C.L.U. chapter — Harrop Freeman, a professor at Cornell Law School — felt that Brown had violated James's constitutional right of free speech. Surprised by this conclusion, James pointed out that he had worn the armband to make his religious conviction and his moral conscience known, and asked if the issue wasn't more properly one of freedom of religion. Burgevin explained that in Freeman's opinion the Supreme Court and other federal courts had interpreted acts like wearing armbands to constitute what was called "symbolic expression," which was akin to "pure speech." James was a little perturbed by being told why he had done what he had done, but he didn't press his point. Burgevin went on to say that Freeman and he had drawn up a letter, which had just been sent to Brown, and read it to James. The key paragraph stated:

> Students and faculty in high schools have the right to wear armbands to show their stands on issues. This is an expression of free speech. The local school cannot rule on length of hair, clothing worn and other similar matters. The local school cannot regulate this for students or faculty.

The trouble with the letter was that it was wrong — or at least debatable — on one crucial point. Although the Court had ruled that students did not lose their right of free speech "at the schoolhouse gate" — including the right to wear black armbands — no precisely relevant ruling on teachers' right of free speech while they were in school had ever been handed down by the federal courts. It was several months before James learned about the possible misinterpretation, and today he is by no means sure that he would have gone on fighting for what he believed, and had been assured, were his legal rights if he had known that the question he had raised had never been judicially resolved. "I felt then that because I was legally in the right I had to be reinstated in my job, and that while things would undoubtedly be awkward for me in school from then on, at least I could go on teaching and being myself to some degree without being shoved all over the place," he said. "When I drove our bus out of Elmira bound for Washington early the next morning, I was jubilantly singing 'We Shall Overcome' with eight or nine students from Elmira College who were on board. And I really thought I *had* overcome. I had stood up, and I had won. I didn't dream then how wrong I was, or how long and bitter and agonizing my fight would be."

An article on James's suspension appeared in the Saturday-morning edition of the *Star-Gazette*. That day, the Addison school board met in a special session to discuss the case. While the board members talked about James, he was marching along Pennsylvania Avenue in Washington with more than five hundred thousand fellow-citizens. It was the largest gathering of people in the capital in history, but it got surprisingly little attention. President Nixon showed his lack of interest in the mass pleas of his constituents by watching a football game on television while the great chanting, singing crowd passed by outside. In Horseheads, Mrs. James, who was worried about violence breaking out during the march, kept switching her television set from channel to channel in an attempt to get some news about what was happening in Washington. ABC and CBS didn't even have live cameras on the scene. All three major networks covered the event briefly on the evening news, but only NBC interrupted, even briefly, the day's television schedule to report what was going on in the capital. Although the Administration had been unable to stop the mass protest from taking place, or to noticeably reduce its size, Agnew's anti-network speech two nights before had apparently succeeded in scaring the networks out of covering the Moratorium as a major news event, thus considerably reducing its effectiveness throughout the country.

Finally, Mrs. James switched off the television set and turned on the radio, which was presenting live, if somewhat spotty, coverage of the demonstration, and soon learned that almost no violence had occurred. She relaxed a bit then, but shortly after dark, while she was washing the dinner dishes, there was the clumping sound of heavy footsteps on the front porch and loud pounding on the door. "I was terribly frightened," she said. "After what had happened, I thought it might even be night riders. But I went to the door and opened it. Standing there were two men in black raincoats. They scared the wits out of me. They asked if Mr. James was there. I said no, he was in Washington. Then they gave me a letter for him from the Addison Board of Education, and I closed the door."

The letter, from the president of the local board, was dated that day and stated:

> The Board of Education of Addison Central School District has conferred with counsel and very thoroughly discussed the facts of your situation. The Board has, unanimously, confirmed the action of District Principal Edward J. Brown regarding your suspension on Friday, November 14, 1969.
>
> The Board deems your action to be a political act. As such, it is prohibited in the school. It is, also, deemed unethical action on the part of a teacher to engage in such activity.
>
> You may return to class on Monday, November 17, 1969, with the understanding that you engage in no political activities while in the school.
>
> Of course, the Board recognizes fully your absolute right to express outside of the school any beliefs that you may have.

When James read the letter, after returning from Washington the following day, he was outraged by its conclusion – that his act had been purely political in nature. He had hoped, and expected, that the school board would be more than a rubber stamp for Brown's decision. "The board failed, or refused, to see that the fundamental difference between a religious act and a political act is that in committing a political act you're only seeking to gain secular advantage in a contest between two or more secular forces," he explained. "A religious act, on the other hand, can be political in style but it is essentially not aimed at a political end. A religious act, to some extent, has its end within itself, because it says something about what it means internally to the person who commits it but it doesn't have a specified result. Each person can react or not, as he or she chooses, to that act. If I wear an armband only to protest a particular war and ally myself with a particular group that thinks this war is a bad way to behave internationally, then that is a political act on my part. But if I wear a black armband because I'm horrified that this is the way men are solving their problems — by destroying themselves purposefully — and I believe that war and killing are wrong in themselves, then that is a religious act. However, if that war is also a political issue at the time, you cannot avoid becoming politically entangled, in the minds of others, when you object religiously. Some people can't understand that difference, because for them religion is something that is supposed to make life easier, as if man had created God. For the Quakers, religion usually makes life harder, though infinitely more precious, because in their view it is the spirit of God in man that counts, not the formalities of an artificial society that man has set up, more or less arbitrarily, to make the impossible task of people living together a bit more easy."

As James thought over the board's letter that Sunday evening, it occurred to him that neither Brown nor the board had formally rejected the A.C.L.U.'s position and that neither had demanded a promise from him that he would not wear the armband again in school. "Since I did not, and could not, agree with the board that wearing an armband to protest killing was a political act, I felt free to return to school the next day without being bound in any way by their restriction," he said. "That the armband was political was their assumption, not mine, and they had yet to prove it. My assumption was that Brown had acted illegally and that neither he nor the board had any authority to limit my right to express my conscience. So I decided to go back to work." He did not decide then what he would do when the next Moratorium was held, in mid-December.

In the next couple of days, the Jameses learned that several teachers in nearby school systems had also worn armbands on the previous Friday – some of them black and some red-white-and-blue – without being so much as officially reprimanded. "I concluded that the school board couldn't fire Charles, and knew it," Mrs. James said. "After the A.C.L.U. told Brown that he couldn't do that to Charles and the school board didn't respond, I was convinced that the board's members were merely bluffing, to try to save Brown's face."

Bluff or not, there was a lot of support locally for the board's position. On November 20th, the Addison Teachers Association considered the issue, and voted twenty-seven to fifteen in favor of the board's position. Stories about the affair in the *Star-Gazette* and the Corning *Leader* created some interest in the case, and if the letters to the editors of both papers were any measure of public sentiment, most readers also supported Brown and the school board. So did the managing editor of the *Star-Gazette,* Burt Blazar, who observed in a column he wrote, "While James may think his armband means one thing, the context in which he's wearing it implies another. It implies opposition to the Vietnam war – a political thing."

Again James was offended by the attempt to interpret his motives. And when he read Blazar's observation that "political statement has no place in the school system – unless it is accompanied by equal views from the other side," James threw the paper aside. The standard requirement in New York State schools that all sides of any controversial issue must be presented if one side is presented had always struck him as a piece of absurd hypocrisy on the part of school authorities. "The entire public-school system in this country is geared to parroting traditional views," he said. "That is the only side one can find in almost any history or civics textbook. In the history texts my children have used here, it's claimed that the Spanish-American War broke out when Spain declared war on us. I looked through several textbooks at Addison High and couldn't find anything resembling a fair view of, say, Castro. All of them are so terribly biassed that they don't attempt to teach one side of an issue fairly, let alone both sides. And that's true not just of history and civics courses. Anyone who teaches literature unavoidably gets into all kinds of social and political issues in the course of discussing plays and novels. It would be impossible, in terms of the time available, to present all sides, even if the teacher knew what they were. But the main point is that the farthest thing from the minds of those who run the school system is to have all sides of controversial issues presented to students. What the authorities want is what the school system was designed for — to turn out obedient, subservient young adults. If the schools' aim were to turn out imaginative, creative kids, they would at least get a chance to hear some radical viewpoints to balance the deeply conservative bombardment that they are constantly subjected to on the outside."

Subsequently, a couple of students at Addison High stated that they had been unaware that there was any sensible way to look at the war in Vietnam except the President's way. In fact, they said that most students in the school hadn't known what James's black armband stood for until he was suspended and the case got into the newspapers. Of course, they knew that people opposed the war, but they thought such opponents were largely hippies and crazies. When James was thrown out of school for standing up against the war, some of these students apparently realized for the first time that a serious and sincere man could be against what they had been taught to believe in. In the end, then, it wasn't James who taught them this lesson, it was Brown, who showed them, however inadvertently, that there was another side to this issue.

Neva James's confidence that Brown would take no further action against her husband gradually weakened as the time for the next Moratorium, in mid-December, grew closer. "I figured there would be some kind of trouble, because I knew that the school had a tacit policy of getting rid of people who didn't fall into line," she said. "I didn't want Charles to wear the armband again.

And yet I didn't feel I could urge him not to wear it, since I believed that the school board and Brown had been so wrong. All I knew at the time was that I didn't want another hassle with another community and be forced to pick up and move all over again."

During the month between the two Moratoriums, James's greatest concern was his wife's growing anxiety. "I was very defensive about it," he said. "Nothing was clear-cut in my mind. I wasn't acting out of certainty that I was doing the right thing. It wasn't as though I had the assurance that the morality of such an act as wearing an armband was clear. I don't think that acts of conscience have anything to do with traditional ideas of right and wrong, morals, or values. I was way out there at sea, and I had only my own mind and heart to steer by." A couple of days before the December Moratorium, his concern about his wife's reaction and the effect on his family if he wore the armband again became so unnerving that finally he drew back from that problem and retreated into an examination of his own motives, to make certain that at least he had not been corrupted by the attention he had received. "I don't know how fairly I treated Neva during that time," he said later. "All I knew was that it was a private decision."

Mrs. James wondered if a man was entitled to make an entirely personal judgment about such a matter once he had a family. "Charles acted for himself, but the children and I have to assume the consequences of his action," she explained. "It wasn't my conscience or my children's consciences that were at stake. If you choose something personally, that's one thing. But if you have to go along with the choice someone else makes, that's quite a different thing."

The December Moratorium began on the twelfth, and the Jameses woke that morning before dawn. Both of them were thinking about the armband, which was again lying on the dresser, but neither spoke of it. James thought briefly about what might happen if he wore it to school again. He suspected that Brown would prefer to ignore it rather than to get embroiled in an unpleasant legal fight, which, it seemed then, he was certain to lose —

above all, a fight that might make him look rather foolish in the end. Still, James believed, Brown could not abide disobedience or a public defeat. Finally, James decided that he could not base his actions on what Brown might or might not do. "I saw then that I had to act as I would have acted if I hadn't been suspended," James said. "I couldn't let the suspension intimidate me in my behavior insofar as my behavior was evidence of what I believed."

As he started to get dressed, his wife came into the bedroom from the kitchen and asked, "Are you still sure you want to wear it?"

"Yes," he said.

She said nothing more, but she kept hoping that he would change his mind. James didn't change his mind, and a few minutes after he appeared in school wearing the armband Brown suspended him again. A month later, the local school board fired James.

James was confident that his dismissal would quickly be countermanded by an administrative or judicial office of the state, and that he would be back teaching at Addison High School within a few weeks at the most. His involuntary idleness made him more aware than he had ever been of how much he liked his work — most of all, the persistent challenge of introducing students to the world outside their rather narrow lives — and he began planning new approaches to his task. He assumed that Pillard and Brown would resent his return and might make life difficult for him, but he also assumed that in time they would forget about the trouble and let matters go back to normal. Enduring a few trying weeks or months of that sort, he decided, would be better than pulling up and moving his family again, so when he was approached about a teaching job at a public school in Batavia, New York, a few days after he was fired and the case was reported in local newspapers, he didn't explore the possibility. If he had known how long the armband case would drag on and what deprivation lay ahead for him and his family, he has said, he would have immediately taken any other teaching job that was offered. "I could have gone on fighting from a distance," he explained. "But I wanted my rights *and* my job back, and I thought it would all be settled soon."

If James had also known about the doubts that were initially entertained by some of the lawyers who became involved in his case, he might have given up his fight altogether right then. As it happened, when the representative of the A.C.L.U. chapter in Ithaca called the New York City office of the Civil Liberties Union, a lawyer there had too hastily assured him that James's constitutional rights had clearly been violated. Another A.C.L.U. lawyer, who ended up handling the James case, later said, "I guess the response was the automatic one often given here – what should be right is right – but when we finally sat down and discussed the matter we had some serious misgivings. What we were worried about most was the 'slippery slope' question – that is, if you allow someone to wear an armband, where do you stop? Do you then have to let others wear swastikas or Nazi uniforms or the white sheets of the Ku Klux Klan wherever and whenever they want to? That question was particularly unsettling when it was asked in the context of a public school. After all, if schools weren't run with some authority and discipline, the entire educational system might collapse. Where does one draw the line?"

In the end, the staff decided to draw the line where the Supreme Court had seemed to draw it in the case that James's first legal advisers relied on as a binding precedent – Tinker v. Des Moines Independent Community School District, which the Court had ruled on a year before. That case involved a girl who was suspended from the junior high school for wearing a black armband to protest the war in Vietnam. The Court decided that her act constituted symbolic expression, and was constitutionally protected under the free-speech clause of the First Amendment. One sentence in the Court's opinion – "It can hardly be argued that either students or teachers shed their constitutional rights to freedom of speech or expression at the schoolhouse gate" – had persuaded Professor Freeman that the ruling extended to teachers, too, and the lawyers at the A.C.L.U. were inclined to agree. Still, they weren't convinced that the statement had to be read that way.

In fact, the Tinker decision circumscribed students' First Amendment rights so narrowly that all one could say with any certainty about it was that Mary Beth Tinker had a right to wear a black armband to her school at the particular time and under the particular circumstances that existed when she wore it.

During this period, the A.C.L.U., like other civil-liberties outfits, was severely limited by lack of money and personnel, and the James case was turned over to its most active volunteer, a private lawyer by the name of Jeremiah Gutman, who at any given time handled a caseload of a hundred clients, half of whom he represented for little or no fee. Gutman agreed to take on the James case — at least through the administrative course of remedy, which seemed to him the simplest, quickest, and cheapest method. All that it required was an appeal, in the form of a legal petition, to the New York State Commissioner of Education, Ewald B. Nyquist, who was generally regarded as a fair man and a defender of individual liberties within the school system. Gutman had argued a number of civil-liberties cases before Nyquist, and had always prevailed. He was sure that he would this time, too. "With Nyquist's record," he said later, "there was every reason to believe that he would be in our corner all the way."

The opening argument in the petition to the commissioner was that James had been denied the ordinary safeguards guaranteed by the constitutional phrase "due process of law." As James stated in an affidavit about his first suspension, "I received no notice of the charges against me, no advance notice of the board's meeting at which my case was to be considered, no opportunity to contest the action taken against me, no right to be confronted by the evidence against me, no right to present evidence on my own behalf, no right to cross-examine hostile witnesses or to call friendly ones, and no right to be represented by counsel, nor was I afforded any other means of presenting my position and views to the board." After that, the petition claimed that since James's assertion of his rights had not impinged on or restricted anyone else's rights, his superiors had exceeded *their* rights in firing him. The third, and final, point in the petition was the crucial one — the specific right that James had asserted and been denied. While Gutman was working on the petition, James became so nervous about this point that he drove down to the city to discuss it with him, and to make sure that his motive was clear — that he had acted out of religious conviction and had expressed his religious conscience by wearing the armband.

Gutman — a rather flamboyant, friendly man with curly gray hair and a full beard — heard James out, and essentially agreed. But then he pointed out that an expression of religious conviction was still an expression and, as such, fell under the free-speech rather than the freedom-of-religion clause of the First Amendment. Once more James was distressed by the willingness of others to interpret his motives for him, but he didn't object or press his point, because he realized that the lawyer was merely doing a lawyer's job — trying to defend a client as best he could. As for Gutman, he later explained, "I wanted to emphasize speech, because I thought the Supreme Court's decision in Tinker was absolutely determinative. My impression was that the issue James was raising had already been settled. It looked to me like a sure thing — a clear First Amendment run-through."

James was distressed by the legal approach, because he felt that the misleading nature of his defense might ultimately seem to alter the character of what was being defended — his reason for wearing the armband. Still, he never expressed his dissatisfaction to Gutman. "I guess I lost control of my own fate at that point," he remarked not long ago. "I turned myself over to the lawyers, and gradually my goal changed from the moral vindication of my religious conscience to the practical business of getting my job back."

To many lawyers, James's objection would have seemed legally and historically irrelevant, since freedom of religion and freedom of speech have always been inextricably entwined philosophically and practically. And, according to one of the lawyers who later worked on the case, "James's objection was personally irrelevant as well, because what mattered once he raised this issue was not *his* right as he saw it but rather *every* man's right as the *law* saw it. In our view, and ultimately in the view of the courts, the issue was freedom of speech."

On February 5, 1970, Gutman submitted to the State Education Department in Albany the petition contesting James's dismissal on the grounds that he had been denied due process of law and the right of freedom of speech. Copies of the petition were sent to Brown, Pillard, and the school board, and the lawyer who represented all of them, a private practitioner from Corning named Harry Treinin, submitted a response. It claimed that as a probationary teacher James had no vested rights under state law to a hearing or to be told why he was fired; that his failure to present a balanced view of a controversial issue to his students was unprofessional and unethical; that he had committed a political act by wearing the black armband to work at a time of national discord over the war in Vietnam; that he had been insubordinate in refusing to take it off; and that the issue of free speech was in no way involved.

At the hearing—held on Tuesday, March 10th, at the State Education Department headquarters, in Albany—Gutman and Treinin elaborated on the positions taken in their legal papers, and from time to time Nyquist asked each of them questions. For instance, when Treinin—a white-haired man with silver-rimmed glasses and a rather dramatic manner—repeated the charge that James had committed a political act in wearing the armband, the commissioner asked whether it could be looked upon as anything but a political act. "No!" Treinin cried. At another point, Gutman argued that since everyone was unavoidably biassed in some ways, teachers should merely make their biasses clear at the outset of any classroom discussion of a controversial matter, so that their students might know where they stood. Treinin was aghast at the suggestion, and excitedly described what would happen in public schools throughout the country if this viewpoint and James's act were upheld. One could envision the time, he warned, when fifty teachers would show up for work at a school like Addison High with twenty-five of them wearing black armbands and twenty-five of them wearing sashes of red-white-and-blue. "It would be a standoff—a terrible situation," he said. "It would turn our classrooms into a battleground of opposing political forces."

In view of what had been happening in some colleges in the

United States — student takeovers of administration buildings, barricades, riots, arson, bombing, sniping, and heavily armed policemen and troops patrolling campuses — an armband-and-sash confrontation by opposing groups of public-school teachers in a small-town high school seemed a comforting prospect. Nyquist suppressed a smile, and not long afterward he ended the hearing with the observation that since "important philosophic considerations" were involved in the case, his decision on it might take some time.

James left the hearing in a state of exhilaration. "It was great — it really was," he told reporters outside. Part of his reaction was due to his delight at listening, for the first time, to a discussion of the issues in the case — even if the freedom-of-religion issue was dealt with only in passing by Gutman. But a larger part of James's reaction was due to the positive impression that Nyquist had made on him. "I saw that he was intelligent and enlightened," James explained. "After the calm, detached way he behaved, I was certain that he wouldn't rule against me."

And Gutman was equally confident — largely because of the negative impression that Treinin had made on him. "He had no legal basis for his case whatever," Gutman observed.

The Elmira *Star-Gazette* and the Corning *Leader* gave the James case extensive coverage, which soon stirred up a good bit of controversy among local citizens over the act and the result of wearing a black armband. On one side, James was defended in letters to the editor as a hero crushed by systematic repression ("He had the audacity to buck the establishment; the principal gave an order, the order was not obeyed. The teacher was fired. This is once again an example of how authoritarian the public school system has become") or a target of the far right ("Too terrified of freedom of thought, speech, and action to tolerate [dissent], they . . . are self-styled Christians and patriots who pretend to defend freedom by advocating its suppression"). On the other side, he was attacked for being either dangerously misguided ("To allow everyone to do exactly as he pleases under the guise of constitutional rights will not only create chaos but destroy the democracy that has provided so much freedom") or an outright traitor ("Hitler knew the way to power was in gaining control of the minds of the young. Are our schools, churches, and courts being infiltrated by a clever group seeking to undermine the great principles our nation was built on and eventually to overthrow our government?").

For his own part, James was more offended by the continuing attempts to describe his motives than he was by either the strident tone or the often silly content of such letters. "As I have repeated over and over, I acted out of religious conviction, to demonstrate my opposition to killing—any and all killing—of human beings," he wearily told a reporter. "But others keep telling me that my act was political, it was an attempt to influence students unfairly, it was unpatriotic, it was even treasonable. At the start, it was *my* act. But now it seems as though it wasn't mine at all."

James was also exasperated by the outright refusal, on the part of many of his acquaintances and even members of his family, to believe that he had been fired merely for wearing a black armband. "Everybody keeps asking me in private, 'What did you *really* do?' " he said. When his sister's husband, who worked for the federal government, learned about the incident, he telephoned from Washington to ask James what he had really done, and clearly didn't believe the answer. And James's mother called to lecture him on how he must trust the government, as she did, and then to beg him to desist from whatever he was doing so that his brother-in-law would not be fired by the government for being related to him.

As the days passed, it became clear to James that the growing controversy over what he had done would make it far more difficult now for him to return to work comfortably, and that it would both encourage Brown to oppose his reinstatement and discourage other possible employers from giving him a job. Whichever way Nyquist's decision went, James began to fear, he would be tagged at worst as a troublemaker and at best as a person who would not accept injustice quietly. "People may claim to like a man who stands up for himself," he said, "but they don't want to hire him." One local exception to this rule was the director of the adult-education department at Corning Community College. Two weeks after James was fired, the director offered him a part-time job teaching English literature one evening a week, at a salary of six hundred dollars for the term. James accepted at once, and shortly after he began conducting the course, early in February, he was told that he could stay on during the summer term with a three-course teaching load, at three times the salary. He accepted that offer, too, and then a little later he was asked if he wanted to stay on as a full-time instructor the following fall. That meant he could not go back to Addison High, but the chance to teach on the college level and to read and study was so attractive that James tentatively agreed to the proposal. Even so, he intended to go on with his case until he was vindicated.

About this time, Neva James decided to give up her job at Elmira College. It paid so little that it hardly seemed worth the expenses and inordinate difficulty it involved. James had to drive his wife to work in the morning, spend the day scouting around for part-time work, pick her up and take her home, and then drive into Corning and back for his evening teaching schedule. Some days, he put more than two hundred miles on the car. In any case, her resignation meant that they had less money to live on, and James began to look for higher-paying odd jobs than the few he had found so far. One Sunday, after attending the Quaker meeting in Elmira, he happened to mention to some members who went over to the adjoining house for coffee and a visit that he was looking for work to tide him over the next few months. Salle, the clerk of the Meeting, offered him a job helping to deliver and install commercial refrigeration units, at a wage of three dollars an hour. James went to work the next day.

Late that April, South Vietnamese forces, supported by the United States, invaded Cambodia. The anti-war movement, which had been quiet since the December Moratorium, was revived by this unexpected expansion of the war. This time, the kinds of people who had usually not participated before in opposition to the war — ordinary middle-class and middle-aged citizens, business and social leaders, and even Wall Street lawyers — joined the demonstrations that swept the country. Students again rallied and marched, and at Kent State University, in Ohio, National Guardsmen shot and killed four of them. Stunned and sickened by that tragedy, more and more citizens joined the anti-war cause. One of them was the president of Corning Community College, who appeared on campus the next day wearing a black armband. Several local residents who had suspected his liberal tendencies took the opportunity to denounce him and to call for his ouster. That move failed, but early that summer they discovered that James was employed by the college, and pressed the school administration to get rid of such a notorious radical. In the end, the plan to take James on full time was quietly shelved — so quietly, in fact, that he himself didn't hear about it until nearly the end of the summer.

In the meantime, the Jameses had made some plans that were based entirely on the promise of a full-time job in the autumn. The plan was to buy a derelict farmhouse and some thirty-five acres of scrubby, worn-out farmland that went with it, for a total price of twelve thousand five hundred dollars. At the time, the Jameses were paying a monthly rent of a hundred and seventy-five dollars, and they figured that if they could raise the down payment for the farm — fifteen hundred dollars — James could get a G.I. mortgage, and they would end up paying only ninety-odd dollars a month for a place to live. Once again a member of the Elmira Meeting came to their aid — a woman who gave them a check for the down payment.

The farm was near the small town of Pine City, on a rural lane called Christian Hollow Road, about five miles from Elmira. The house itself — a dilapidated one-and-a-half-story clapboard structure — was uninhabitable, and anyone with less determination and enthusiasm than the Jameses would probably have concluded that it should remain so. But they went to work fixing it up at once. They scoured and disinfected, patched and painted, mended the roof and repaired the plumbing, and within a few weeks the house was almost fit to live in.

"We were really jubilant," Mrs. James recalled a couple of years later. "At last we had a home of our own — and even land to roam on." They planted a garden of late vegetables and pruned some scraggly grapevines and a neglected orchard of apple, pear, and plum trees that James found on the property, and they canned and froze whatever they grew but couldn't eat.

Mrs. James had become increasingly concerned about the children, who were beginning to show signs of being adversely affected by their father's case, and part of her reason for giving up her job had been that she wanted to spend more time with them. "The kids bear scars from all we've been through," she said recently. "We were absorbed, we were away a lot. When you never know if you're going to have money to eat next week or a place to live next month, it's hard to pay the attention to your youngsters that they need. When all they hear is talk about the case, when everyone talks about their father, the telephone is always for their father, the papers have stories about their father, they suffer. Also, it made them too adult too soon. They should have had a better chance to be children and to grow up more slowly. I know they thought their father was right, and were proud of him. But I also know – I can see it in their faces sometimes when they look at Charles – that they're thinking, If it wasn't for your armband, we could have some new sneakers."

James tried to make up for the lost income by taking on every job he could find, no matter how menial or low-paid, and he worked especially hard preparing for his evening classes, so that his record would encourage the school to keep him on, as it had promised, in the fall. All in all, it was a difficult period, but the Jameses were hopeful that their troubles would soon be over. "We didn't know it then, but we were just embarking on our long experiment – to see how little money a family of six could live on," Mrs. James recalled months later. "We didn't dream when we laid out and planted the garden that it would be our salvation during the coming winter."

The "important philosophic considerations" that Nyquist faced in resolving the James case were apparently more intractable than he had imagined, for the spring and summer passed without any word from him. Mrs. James kept Gutman informed about the family's situation, and in April he wrote Nyquist to tell him that the family had incurred some medical expenses and to ask that the school board be required to make James's health insurance retroactive when he was reinstated. An aide of Nyquist's replied a month later that James would have to file an amended petition including such a request and that the school board would have to be given an opportunity to respond to it. That procedure, of course, would have delayed the decision even longer, and since Gutman didn't want to impose any more hardship on his client, he dropped the matter. By mid-August, there still was no word on the case, and then James learned that the full-time job at the college wasn't waiting for him after all. Although it was too late for him to get another teaching job for the coming school year, he applied to all the nearby school systems for a full-time post and for substitute teaching on the off-chance that an opening would turn up. Nothing came of either effort, so he turned to the want-ads in the *Star-Gazette* and the *Leader*. There was no work of any kind that he was qualified for; the recession that spread across the country that summer and fall hit the Corning-Elmira area rather hard, and many people there were unemployed. On a couple of occasions, James later learned, teachers with qualifications inferior to his were taken on by schools that he had applied to, and he began to wonder if he had been blacklisted – not officially but simply because he had come to be regarded as a troublemaker.

By the end of August, James had no job and no prospect of a job. His classes at the college had ended, and the family had reached the end of its meagre resources. If he didn't get money immediately, James realized, they would lose the farm, and have neither shelter nor food. "We thought and thought and talked and talked," Mrs. James recalled. "Finally, we saw that there was only one way out for us – welfare. We decided that if society denies you a livelihood when you can and want to work, then it's up to society to provide you with enough to live on. After all, we had both been paying into the unemployment-insurance fund for years, so it wasn't as if we were asking for a handout."

When James went to the local welfare office to apply for assistance, a member of the staff told him that he had to take the first job offered to him, whatever it was. If he went to work on a ditchdigging crew and then took a day off for a substitute teaching job – the kind of chance that might lead to a full-time post – and was fired from the crew for being absent, he would lose his welfare rights at once. That meant no food stamps and no Medicaid as well as no money. James told the man who gave him these instructions that since the rule discouraged, or sometimes prevented, welfare recipients from getting the kind of work they were qualified for and could support their families on, it was "asinine." The man said, "That's right," and handed him a paper stating that he promised to pay back all the welfare money he received. This raised the possibility – or, in the case of a man, like James, who would probably never earn more than a very modest salary, the likelihood – that he would be crippled by debt for years. But James knew that he had no choice. "If I had refused to sign the paper, he would have let us starve," he explained to his wife.

Before the welfare office would give the Jameses any money or food stamps, it dispatched a woman inspector to see how they lived and whether they actually had the number of children they claimed for their allowance – three hundred dollars a month. Once satisfied on these scores, the inspector asked to see their wedding license. "As if people like us were out there in the woods raising a houseful of bastards!" Mrs. James said. "I couldn't find the license, so I told her where we'd gotten married and said she could write and verify our legitimacy herself. That meant some work, so she said she'd take our word. And *that* meant there wasn't any strict rule on the matter after all, and that they were just trying to humiliate us."

In time, the Jameses got the impression that the welfare agency often used such demeaning tactics to discourage middle-class people from applying for aid. "When we first went to them," Mrs. James explained, "they acted horrified, and implied that no middle-class person with a college degree had *ever* come to them for help before." But the Jameses discovered that a fairly large number of such people had been forced to the same resort as they had. When the James children joined the federally supported free-lunch program at the schools they attended, a number of other children from middle-class families who were living on welfare but were too embarrassed to admit it were emboldened to join the program, too. Several of the youngsters confided to the James girls that they hadn't had a decent hot lunch for many months.

The humiliations that the Jameses — and, presumably, all other families living on such assistance — endured seemed endless and wholly unnecessary. For instance, James had to report to the welfare agency whatever he earned from odd jobs, and those sums were subtracted from his welfare check — a standard procedure that inevitably persuades all but the most independent-minded people who are driven onto welfare to stop looking for part-time work, since they are almost certain to receive the same amount of money without working. But the most unsettling revelation about the welfare system as the Jameses saw it was their discovery that the worst welfare chiselers were the people who manned the welfare agency. When the agency made a mistake in tabulating the Jameses' income, for example, it made up for the error retroactively for only one month, whereas if the Jameses had made a mistake in reporting income or in calculating what was due to them, they had to pay back all the money, no matter how far back the mistake went. "It was as if *they* would go hungry if they didn't get their money," James said. And when he finally got a part-time job teaching, the agency tried to limit his travelling expenses to two or three dollars a month. He argued and threatened to appeal to the state headquarters, and finally the agency grudgingly paid him forty dollars a month.

The agency also insisted that it was obliged to pay only the interest, and none of the principal, due on his mortgage on the farm. Since James had worked for a summer in a welfare office in New York City, he knew that the law required the agency to pay both the interest and the principal for temporary recipients — otherwise, of course, many homeowners on welfare would face foreclosure — but when he pointed this out the agency supervisor said that they had always done it that way. "He acted as though a bad habit was all right if it went on long enough," James remarked. "I demanded a hearing, so then they backed down and paid the principal. That happened only because I knew the law. God knows how they chisel people who don't."

"It's appalling what the welfare system does to people," Mrs. James said. "You go to the welfare office to apply for aid or to straighten out some mess they've created through bungling or indifference or meanness, and you have to sit there for hours waiting, waiting, while the welfare 'workers' drink coffee and talk and laugh together — and pointedly ignore you. The waiting room there was very warm in the winter, but I noticed that the people who came in never took off their coats. Some of them were young men who had always supported themselves but now just couldn't find work. They were so humiliated by necessity that they sat there clutching their coats to them, as if they were protection against the cold, unfeeling system. Anyway, the experience we had while on welfare was the second step leading to our awareness of how people suffer in our country. It made us a lot more radical than we had ever dreamed we could be."

Late that August, Gutman wrote a letter to Nyquist describing the Jameses' desperate plight and asking for a decision on the case. There was no answer. Outraged by this example of the state's neglect of and disdain for its citizens, Gutman wrote an angry letter to the State Education Department on September 17th, demanded a decision within a week, and threatened to take the matter to federal court if one wasn't forthcoming within that time. He also released the letter to reporters in Albany, and told them that James had clearly been blacklisted and that he, Gutman, meant to get to the bottom of it and find out who was behind the unwarranted delay and the persecution of his client. Precisely at the end of the time that Gutman stipulated, September 23rd, Commissioner Nyquist's office let it be known that a decision would be announced that day.

Gutman alerted the Jameses, and they spent most of that morning discussing what it would be like for both of them when James went back to his job — as they were sure Nyquist would rule he was entitled to do. Around noon, James opened a bottle of Riesling that he had been saving for more than six months for this occasion, and the two went out into the yard to sit in the sun and wait for the telephone to ring. Before long, it did. Mrs. James hurried inside, and James poured out a glass of wine and waited. When she came back through the door into the yard, he grinned and raised his glass in a toast.

She took a few steps toward him and stopped. "The decision went against you, Charles," she said.

He stared at her for a minute without speaking. Then he flung the glass into the woods and burst into tears.

The commissioner's eight-page decision began by disposing of the Addison school board's contention that under state law probationary teachers were entitled to neither a formal hearing nor an explanation for their dismissal; this rule, he pointed out, governed only cases where basic rights were not at issue. Similarly, he disposed of the argument that James's refusal to remove the armband constituted insubordination; if the order to take off the armband was an attempt to deprive James of his legal rights, Nyquest observed, he had not been insubordinate in disobeying it. The prior, and basic, question, he went on, was whether indeed James's rights had been violated. "The real issue before me, then," Nyquist wrote, "concerns the right of a schoolteacher in class to wear a black armband, which is expressive, though only symbolically, of a specific viewpoint."

To explore that issue, Nyquist turned to the Supreme Court decision in the Tinker case. Like Gutman, he noted that the Court had stated that neither students nor teachers "shed their constitutional right to freedom of speech or expression at the schoolhouse gate." But, unlike Gutman, he added that the Court, in Tinker, had concluded that the Constitution permitted "reasonable regulation of speech-connected activities in carefully restricted circumstances." Since the Tinker holding applied only to students directly, Nyquist moved on to another recent federal case concerning the First Amendment rights of teachers in class – Goldwasser v. Brown, in which the Court of Appeals for the District of Columbia had ruled the previous year that a government employee who had been hired to teach English to foreign military officers studying at a United States Air Force installation was properly dismissed for devoting classroom time to airing his views on American foreign policy and race prejudice; Goldwasser had appealed the ruling to the Supreme Court, which refused to review it.

Then Nyquist continued, "It is a matter of fundamental educational policy that whatever subject of instruction may be involved, the teacher must present the entire range of information available in relation to such subject . . . so that the student may have complete access to all facets and phases of the subject." Since James had given his students "only one point of view on an important public issue," Nyquist noted, he had clearly violated this policy. Citing the joint code of ethics adopted by the State Teachers Association and the State School Boards Association, Nyquist pointed out that the code made it unethical for either teachers or members of school boards "to promote personal views on religion, race, or partisan politics;" the term "partisan politics," he added, was not "limited to the politics of political parties, but embraces any political subject on which differing views exist." In conclusion, he ruled that James's act violated "sound educational principles" and was not "constitutionally protected."

Since James had meant his act to express a moral conviction that, to his mind, had nothing to do with politics, he could not see how it was partisan, even under Nyquist's exceedingly loose definition. When reporters called to get James's reaction to the decision, he told them, "It was a political decision on a moral act." Later, he clarified his position in a letter to the *Star-Gazette:*

> How much tyranny and injustice have been wrought because frightened authorities of state and frightened citizens have misconstrued religious statements for political ones! This misconstruction sees religion as a political threat. So Meletus with Socrates, Herod and Pilate with Jesus, New England Puritans with Roman Catholics and Quakers, Southern United States [Protestants with] Jews and Roman Catholics, and Protestant Ireland's present response to Roman Catholics, to name a few.
>
> What happens when a nation begins to tell a man what he

> means by the symbol he wears — what he means by the ashes, the Cross, the Star of David, the flag, the button, or the armband? What happens if the state or the community can say: "Oh, no! That's not what your armband means, that's not what your ashes mean, that's not what your Star of David means. What they mean is . . ."

Mrs. James put the decision in a more immediate context. "One teacher has asked if he must present the positive side of drugs as well as the negative," she wrote Gutman around the same time. "And we are all thinking of the fun in sex-education courses of presenting the positive side for premarital sex as well as the negative. And at Christmas we are going to demand that they present the atheist view along with the Christian approach. The irony of the situation is that quite likely Charles, for the first time in Addison, presented the other side of the issue of war and peace. I wish there were some way to force them to abide by this decision in their day-to-day teaching."

Brown admitted to the press that he was elated by the decision. Treinin predicted that the case would end up in the Supreme Court — an eventuality that he was reported to be anticipating with delight. And Gutman, who had not considered the case to be of any great significance when he took it on, agreed that it now might be crucial. "It wasn't important until we lost it," he said. "Then it became clear that if the ruling was allowed to stand, it would be a terrible precedent — a long step backward in the slow progress toward freedom of speech." Finally, the Civil Liberties Union announced that it would take the case to the federal courts.

By this stage, the Jameses had begun to feel that some measure of personal vindication among their neighbors was nearly as important as legal vindication in the courts. They realized that court action was unlikely to change the attitudes of suspicion and contempt they often met. In fact, a favorable court decision might well make matters worse for them, since the people who berated courts for "coddling criminals" were inclined to view radicals and even protesters against the war as being among the worst criminals of all – traitors. To counter this viewpoint, the Jameses saw that they had only one weapon – more free speech. Accordingly, when a reporter for *Milady,* the *Star-Gazette's* Sunday supplement, telephoned Mrs. James and asked for an interview she agreed to talk to him, and he came out to the farm one afternoon.

The article appeared as the centerfold in a mid-October issue of *Milady,* and included a large photograph of Mrs. James looking serenely gracious as she sat on the lawn before the farmhouse while a couple of dogs and cats lolled nearby. After a brief recounting of the Jameses' legal contest, the article went on, "One thing has changed—the James family's style of living. Early this summer they moved from a rented two-family house in Horseheads to a 35-acre farm they bought in Southport. One reason was Mrs. James' reluctance to spend the summer in the confines of 'the city.' Surrounded by apple trees and grape vineyards, she spends considerable time gathering fruit, baking pies, and making apple sauce or working in a thriving garden and corn field. Three affectionate hounds and two possessive cats are usually lying in the yard." The James family, the article mentioned at several points, was living on welfare aid.

Residents of the community were incensed. They wrote innumerable letters to the local newspapers and repeatedly telephoned a local radio talk show to demand that the Jameses be taken off the welfare rolls at once. Finally, the host of the talk show telephoned Mrs. James, on the air, to get her response. "If they're so worried about our being on welfare, why don't they let Charles teach?" she asked. Within the next few days, he got two offers of one-day substitute teaching jobs, and took both of them. After that, there were no more offers.

Not long afterward, the A.C.L.U. asked James for a description of his family's hardships, in case it was decided to ask the courts for damages. Mrs. James answered the request, and wrote:

> When it comes to damages, I suppose we could add the wild stories that have circulated relative to our purpose for being in Addison. It seems that there is "sure" info that we were "sent" to

organize the western part of the state for a takeover. Presumably for some subversive group which remains vague – depending on who is repeating the story, it is the Weathermen, the Panthers, or the Communists. The most common attachment for us is the Communist one, which up here covers anyone who thinks differently than the person talking. . . .

We are frequently recognized in the grocery stores, and dirty looks as well as obvious remarks are made about our food stamps. It has reached the point where I really prefer not to shop with food stamps, despite the fact that I do so with gusto to keep them from feeling that they are in any way intimidating me.

Yesterday, our daughters Amy and Honey, both juniors at Southport High in Elmira, had to sit in their English class and listen while their teacher read an article from some time ago which placed all the blame for student unrest and riots on Communism, and compared our current dissent to what occurred in Cuba prior to Castro's takeover. And so they must hear this one-sided presentation even while they know that Nyquist has said that this is bad educational practice. This is the kind of atmosphere in which a black armband becomes a threat.

About that time, Amy stopped going to the Quaker meetings in Elmira, and told her parents that she could no longer accept for herself their nonviolent, turn-the-other-cheek approach to life, because it had prompted most people to walk all over them. And their eleven-year-old daughter, Laurie, decided that she would no longer pledge allegiance to the flag in school assemblies, because her father's case had proved to her that the guarantee of "liberty and justice for all" was a sham.

That fall, James enrolled at Elmira College and continued working toward a master's degree, which he had to have to qualify for tenure in the public-school system and which he wanted so that he could move on to college teaching someday. Members of the Elmira Meeting, who felt partly responsible for his predicament, paid his tuition and helped the family out in various other ways. "The Quakers made it possible for us to stay here and go on fighting," Mrs. James said. "I knew that if an emergency arose, I could go to them. They understood better than anyone else what was happening to us, and they appreciated what we were doing. That September and again in December, a woman from the Meeting with whom I'd had no close association sent us checks for a hundred dollars each time. That money enabled us to stay here. With it I could buy clothes for the children, who wouldn't have been able to go to school otherwise."

At the beginning of 1971, James's fortunes improved for the first time since he was fired. That winter, he was made an instructor in education and philosophy at Ithaca College, assigned three classes, and paid a salary of three thousand dollars for the term. That was more than he had earned altogether since losing his job, and it enabled the family to go off welfare. James happily began teaching again, and one of his courses, called "The Problem of Evil," was among the most popular on campus.

In March, the A.C.L.U., which had been concentrating nearly all of its efforts and resources on combatting the Nixon Administration's direct onslaught against its most voluble and active critics on the national scene, went to work on the James case. It was turned over to Burt Neuborne, a thirty-year-old alumnus of the Harvard Law School, who found the practice of property law so dull that he had given it up and joined the A.C.L.U. legal staff five years before. He prepared a complaint for submission to federal court, and sent copies of it to James and his earlier legal advisers in Ithaca. James was delighted by the document, for it put primary emphasis on the claim that he believed most accurately reflected his position – that his constitutional right to freedom of religion had been denied him. Neuborne also contended that his client's right of free speech had been violated; that the school board's failure to give him a formal hearing abrogated the constitutional guarantee that due process of law be observed; and that since other teachers at Addison High School had been allowed to wear such symbols as crucifixes and Masonic pins and, in one case, to affix the sign "Peace with Honor" on a classroom bulletin board, James's dismissal had also violated his constitutional right to equal protection of the laws, as assured by the Fourteenth Amendment. Neuborne asked the court to reinstate James in his job and to award him damages of twenty-five thousand dollars.

The complaint was filed in the U.S. District Court for the Western District of New York, in Buffalo, on April 14, 1971. On June 4th, Treinin answered for Pillard, Brown, and the school board with eleven defenses: that whether or not the plaintiff's statements were true, defendants had done nothing illegal; that the complaint raised no substantial federal question; that the Commissioner of Education's decision was final under the law of New York State; that James had not exhausted state remedies, as required by federal-court precedents; that his dismissal was entirely lawful; that he had accepted the school board's condition after his suspension, requiring him to abstain from engaging in political activities within the school, but had then worn the armband again; that both acts were political and violated the principle that students must be shown all sides of controversial issues; that James had thereby violated his professional code of ethics; that he had betrayed his "commitment" to the public; that he had ignored a memorandum sent out by the State Education Department asking all school officials and teachers to remain neutral during the Moratoriums; and, finally, that by practicing his religion within the school he had violated the principle of separation of church and state. Once all the legal papers were submitted, Neuborne told the Jameses that it would probably be several months before the District Court would hear the case and several more months after that before it would hand down a decision.

That same week, James got his master's degree from Elmira College, and he hoped that he would be asked to stay on at Ithaca College as a full-time instructor that fall. But several members of the faculty and the board of trustees who had long argued that Ithaca College should upgrade its standards and standing by requiring that all of its teachers possess Ph.D.s finally prevailed on the school administration, and when a recent Ph.D. graduate from Yale applied for a job he got James's. With the end of the spring term, James's income from the college stopped, and the family had to go back on welfare. As it happened, the social worker who was in charge of the James case was away for a few days, and the agency refused to help the family even by advancing it some food stamps until she got back. As a result, the family had to subsist on what was ripe in the garden for nearly a week.

Late that spring, Neuborne happened to discuss the legal and personal implications of the James case with a friend who was a prominent Quaker teacher. After listening to the account of what James had done and what had followed from his act, the teacher observed that, to his way of thinking, James's sacrifice of his family for the sake of a symbol verged on idolatry. Entirely by coincidence, Mrs. James was beginning to question the meaning and value of her husband's act – not on theological but on personal grounds – at exactly the same time.

Her doubts began to surface in her mind toward the end of April, when she and her husband took the two youngest girls and drove to Washington to join the huge, and almost entirely peaceful, rally that was held there just before the Mayday Movement's mass demonstrations. The Quakers had organized, and obtained an official permit for, a prayer vigil in Lafayette Square, across from the White House. The Jameses attended the vigil, and joined a group of some two hundred Quakers who then crossed Pennsylvania Avenue to picket, as planned under another permit, on the sidewalk in front of the White House. After a time, the police ordered the pickets to disperse or face arrest – permit or no permit. The Jameses decided that Charles should leave with the children, so that his legal case wouldn't be complicated by an arrest, and Neva would stay and go to jail.

"I wasn't really worried," she said. "The Quakers had promised to take care of us. Anyway, I was in jail just long enough to be processed. I paid my ten dollars and came out, because we had to go home that night. It would have been more effective to stay in jail, as many of the other Quakers did, but I'd had enough, and we couldn't afford even the cost of my bond, let alone the cost of

Charles and the girls staying in Washington for several days. We needed the money to live."

In a discussion of the episode some months later, James talked about it less as a personal matter than as an example of the difference between the Society of Friends and other religious organizations. He explained, "Institutionalized religions are paying very high prices – losses in membership and losses in public respect – by concentrating on immediate concerns, such as what people will think of them if they don't conform to society's narrowest concepts of propriety, instead of concentrating on ultimate concerns, such as what is right. The little bit of thinking done by the heads of organized religions is controlled by the status quo – practicality, common sense, security – whereas true faith must have the character of ultimacy and be a total risk. This seems to be the dividing line. Nietzsche said that one should be willing to build one's house at the base of a volcano. Well, you won't find many ministers building houses there."

As James spoke, his wife listened intently, and then shook her head reluctantly and with a deepening look of sadness. "This is where you and I have a conflict – in how we see ourselves and the world," she said quietly. "My anxieties about what has happened come from the threat to the sense of security that I need. It's one thing to discuss philosophically what we believe in and what are the roles of the church and religion in our society. You can do that when you have a steady job and an adequate income. And you can go out and act, within philosophical and social limits, to bring about what you believe in."

She paused for a few moments, and then turned to an acquaintance who was sitting with them and said, "We have been terribly limited from the very outset because Charles hasn't been practical. So we don't have the freedom that we might have. Basically, I'm not a materialistic sort of person, but ever since Charles wore the armband I've thought of little besides food, clothing, and shelter for my family. I'm not sure where you draw the line so that you don't cripple yourself socially and emotionally, but I *am* sure that you have to draw it somewhere sooner or later. When you have no financial resources — and we've never had any — you're very limited in what you can do. Except for that one trip, we couldn't afford to go to Washington to demonstrate against the war that was destroying the country and all of us. We couldn't afford to join Common Cause or give five dollars to the anti-war movement. In fact, at one point we couldn't even afford an eight-cent stamp to write our congressman and urge him to oppose the war. Maybe the course that Charles chose — and that I accepted — was better for us than if he had kept silent and held on to his job. I don't know. All I know is that if something like this came up again, I would pray that Charles wouldn't do what he did before. You could spend your entire life in court, as a pauper, fighting injustice. I guess that in the end I'm more a political person than a religious person."

James did not say whether he would wear an armband again under the same circumstances. Instead, he looked at his wife and said, "But your responses to life are very religious."

"Maybe, but they are also very personal to me," she replied. "You make beautiful general statements, while I want to think about *us*. I'm very practical."

"Yet you got yourself arrested in Washington on purpose."

Mrs. James shrugged and looked away. "I knew there was no risk," she said. She was silent for a few moments, and then looked at her husband and added, "Besides, that act was far more effective than wearing an armband."

Early on the morning of September 27, 1971 — nearly two years after James first wore the black armband — he and his wife drove to Rochester, where a hearing on his case was to be held that day in federal District Court. Neuborne had flown in from New York City the night before, and they joined him for breakfast at the motel where he was staying. A deceptively pugnacious-looking man, with fluffy black hair, black-rimmed glasses, and a gentle manner, Neuborne had become fond of the couple, somewhat to his surprise, in the course of an earlier visit to them to get the basic facts of the case and during innumerable telephone conversations he'd had with them since. "Despite my profession, I'm not very contentious myself, and a lot of the people I represent — those who go out and fight for their rights regardless of the cost — are too belligerent for my taste," he said recently. "While I may admire them, just as I admire someone like John Lilburne or John Peter Zenger for what they did to secure human rights, I wouldn't want to have them over for dinner. But the Jameses seemed different to me. They hadn't sought out contention — they had been forced into it unwillingly and were hanging on more than they were fighting."

At breakfast, Neuborne sensed that James, at least, had changed in the months since they had last met. He seemed more radical in his general outlook and more pessimistic about his chances before the bar of American justice. And he had adopted some of the standard earmarks of the "Movement" — namely, long hair and a full, drooping mustache. For his own part, James knew that these attributes were the kind of symbols that were bound to antagonize the same sort of people who would object to a black armband, and he wore them with a sense of amused defiance. But as the time for his appearance in court drew nearer, he became rather nervous about the prejudicial effect his appearance might have on the judge. Finally, he asked Neuborne if he should get his hair cut short and his mustache shaved off before going to court.

Neuborne smiled and shook his head. "No, that's why you're here — because you want to be yourself," he said. "I'll get *my* hair cut."

The courtroom was crowded — mostly with people to be arraigned in minor criminal cases involving such federal offenses as rifling mailboxes, forging small checks, and driving stolen cars across state lines — and few of the defendants were accompanied by lawyers. The judge, an elderly man named Harold P. Burke, sat slumped at the bench, barely seeming to listen as one case after another was hastily called. "The Judge's clerk went through the rigmarole of telling them they had a right to have a lawyer present and asking if they wanted one, and all of them looked uncomprehending and said no," Mrs. James recalled. "They were run through there like animals through a slaughterhouse. It scared us. We'd had no idea this was the way that citizens, even the lowliest citizens, were treated by *their* government. And we'd had no idea that a man who had stood up for his beliefs by wearing a black armband would be thrown into a situation where he was made to feel that he had committed a crime. But that apparently was what we had waited nearly two years for."

Although Judge Burke had been known to show leniency toward young men who resisted the draft because of moral opposition to the war in Vietnam, he was still generally regarded as a rather harsh conservative whose unpredictable legal behavior often led to reversals by the Court of Appeals, frequently on grounds that his rulings violated elementary constitutional safeguards. Neuborne hoped that his freedom-of-religion defense of James's act would indirectly persuade the Judge, who was a Catholic, that if one teacher was forbidden to wear a Quaker armband to school, other teachers might be forbidden to wear crucifixes, and that this defense would also avoid introducing the nonreligious aspects of the slippery-slope problem. In any event, by the time the James case was called — more than three hours later — the courtroom was nearly empty, and the comparative silence after all the hubbub created a semblance of judicial calm.

Neuborne was first to present his side. He had prepared well for the case, and felt that he was singularly in tune with his subject. In fact, he later said that he had delivered the best oral argument of his legal career that day, despite one major drawback — about halfway through his presentation, he suddenly got the feeling that the Judge wasn't listening. During the questioning from the bench afterward, Neuborne's feeling became certainty, for several times the Judge mentioned that the youngsters in James's class had been "eleven-year-old students." Once when Neuborne corrected him by saying, "No, Your Honor, they were eleventh-*grade* students," Judge Burke nodded and replied, "That's right — eleven-year-old students." Neuborne's performance may have been wasted, he learned later from a fellow-lawyer, for the Judge was hard of hearing.

When Treinin got the floor, he repeated his favorite argument

– that if James was upheld, someday fifty teachers would turn up in a school like Addison High with twenty-five of them wearing black armbands and twenty-five of them wearing red-white-and-blue sashes, and the result would be a spreading dislocation of the nation's public schools and probably violence. Then he talked for a time about insubordination – namely, that James had disobeyed both the school-board letter and the State Education Department memorandum asking teachers to avoid taking sides in the Moratoriums. But his main point was that the case was *res judicata* – that is, it had already been judged and thus could not be legally raised again.

Neuborne listened to these contentions with a mounting sense of incredulity. "First of all," he said afterward, "those two documents told people to waive their constitutional right of free speech. And, second, the *res-judicata* theory was legally laughable, because the only judge of the issue so far had been Nyquist, who isn't a judge."

Three days before Christmas, Judge Burke delivered his decision, a two-page opinion that concluded:

> The questions raised by the complaint in this action are *res judicata*. The plaintiff in wearing the black armband in the classroom was effectively presenting only one side of an important political issue. In so doing he chose to ignore the expressed policy of the State Education Department calling for neutrality and objectivity in dealing with "Moratorium Days" on the part of teachers and administrators. . . . His actions in this respect amounted to insubordination. His actions were not constitutionally protected. Plaintiff's dismissal did not violate his rights under the First Amendment of the federal Constitution, nor any of his federally protected rights. He was not entitled to a hearing prior to his dismissal. The complaint is dismissed on the merits.

News of the ruling plunged the Jameses into despair. When they went to bed that night, Mrs. James kept saying to herself, "If only I don't wake up, I'll be happy."

James was hurt and angry, and he was also baffled by a telephone conversation he had had that day with Neuborne. The lawyer called to tell them about the decision and to promise that he would take the case to the Court of Appeals, which would certainly reject at least some of Burke's findings – most of all, his inane support of the theory of *res judicata.* Unknown to James, Neuborne had mistakenly got the impression after the hearing in District Court that his client disapproved of the freedom-of-religion basis for his defense, and would have preferred that the case be based on freedom of speech. Now Neuborne, thinking that he would please his client and also end up with a stronger defense, told James that he intended to switch his emphasis from religion to speech in the papers he submitted to the Court of Appeals. Dismayed by this switch, James nonetheless didn't express any objection to it – in part because he was too numb right then to react, and in part because he was reluctant to tell a lawyer whom he couldn't even pay what to do on his behalf. "I still wanted my case to rest on freedom of religion, but the basis for it was changed back to the original defense," he said later. "I wasn't asked if that was all right. It just happened."

James's failure to state his preference, which Neuborne would have accepted and followed unhesitatingly, may have reflected the conviction that often overcomes people who go through such experiences – that they can do little, and perhaps nothing, to determine their own fate. As the case moved on through the courts in a protracted and complicated fashion, James came to feel that he had less and less to say about what happened to him. At times, he even felt that he was the helpless victim of a mindless and remorseless legal system that he could influence no more than he had been able to influence the personal whim of a school principal, the rubber-stamp actions of a school board, the delay and neglect of a state official, or, for that matter, the strategy of his own lawyer.

In a way, James had missed the point. Although he had worn a symbol to express himself and only he could tell what he had meant to say by it, once he had put the piece of black silk on his sleeve *he* became a symbol, too. Now it was up to society to determine what that symbol – a citizen and teacher wearing a black armband – meant to it. And there was no way for society to do this except through the blind and lumbering processes of the law.

II

In the late nineteen-sixties, Justice Hugo L. Black delivered a lecture on the First Amendment, which he called "the heart of the Bill of Rights." Black, one of the few men ever to sit on the Supreme Court who took the declarations in the Bill of Rights literally, said at one point, "Since the earliest days, philosophers have dreamed of a country where the mind and spirit of man would be free; where there would be no limits to inquiry; where men would be free to explore the unknown and to challenge the most deeply rooted beliefs and principles. Our First Amendment was a bold effort to adopt this principle – to establish a country with no legal restrictions of any kind upon the subjects people could investigate, discuss, and deny. The Framers knew, better perhaps than we do today, the risks they were taking. They knew that free speech might be the friend of change and revolution. But they also knew that it is always the deadliest enemy of tyranny. With this knowledge they still believed that the ultimate happiness and security of a nation lies in its ability to explore, to change, to grow, and ceaselessly to adapt itself to new knowledge born of inquiry free from any kind of governmental control over the mind and spirit of man."

Justice Black's appraisal of the Framers' intent was undoubtedly correct. But perhaps a more pertinent viewpoint is to be found in an observation made by Mark Twain (who happened to marry a woman from Elmira and to spend his summers there), when he said of later generations of Americans, "It is by the goodness of God that in our country we have those three unspeakably precious things: freedom of speech, freedom of conscience, and the prudence never to practice either of them."

Having imprudently practiced both of them at once, James assumed that what he took to be the traditional safeguards of liberty in America would be quickly and decisively raised in his defense. He failed to understand, as almost all Americans have failed to understand, that those safeguards are, and always have been, largely rhetorical. While America may have allowed its citizens freer expression of belief and conscience than most other countries, it has usually granted this latitude because of public lack of interest, not because of legal obligation or devotion to the basic principles of freedom. When words have counted – most of all when they have alarmed the leaders of the nation, of a state, or of a municipality – there has been as little freedom of speech as in the meanest tyranny. In short, freedom of speech does not exist, and never has existed, in the broad way most Americans have assumed.

In the place of that freedom, there has been a popular belief that it exists, which has occasionally persuaded those who have been tempted to suppress speech to leave it alone. And in recent years there have been a number of judicial attempts – so far, fumblingly tentative – to apply some kind of definition that would set down the proper extent of, and limitation on, speech. Most of these attempts have been forced on the courts by people who, like James, thought they were merely asserting an inalienable and long-acknowledged right when they spoke out and who have gone to law when it was denied them. It is almost entirely because of such people that this nation has any legal precepts at all governing expression of belief and conscience. Unfortunately, the precepts that it has are exceedingly narrow, both in theory and in practice, and their main effect has been to limit rather than to enlarge freedom.

A Scrap of Black Cloth

Like many popular myths about America's heritage, the notion that freedom of speech was one of the fundamental goals of the Revolution and since then has been one of our proudest rights in this country has done more harm than good, because blind acceptance of the myth by the public has permitted government on all levels to restrict this right under the guise of protecting it. Also, the belief that colonial Americans fought for the right of all men to be free to speak their minds has been given overwhelming weight by the standing of those who shared the belief – until very recently, almost all of the nation's leading historians, lawyers, and jurists. In fact, it was not until 1960 that this deeply entrenched myth was seriously questioned by even the most skeptical and sophisticated chroniclers of American history and American law. In that year, Leonard W. Levy, dean of the graduate faculty at Brandeis University, published *Legacy of Suppression,* a historical and legal analysis of freedom of speech and the press, which demolished the myth – intellectually, at least – once and for all. "I have been reluctantly forced to conclude that the generation which adopted the Constitution and the Bill of Rights did not believe in a broad scope for freedom of expression, particularly in the realm of politics," Dean Levy began his book.

It was small wonder that he was reluctant, for his work flew in the face of all accepted scholarship and established wisdom, and, even more risky, it repudiated more than a century of liberal dogma. Since the book appeared, some libertarian writers who seem to believe that we cannot have freedom unless we have a heritage of it – most notably Irving Brant, in his book *The Bill of Rights* – have gone to frenzied lengths to refute the idea that Levy presented. They have not succeeded. On balance, Levy's conclusions (and the fact that he did *not* want to reach them) have persuaded most of the nation's leading historians and legal scholars that he was right. Of course, the popular myth has scarcely been dented. Its survival is far more dangerous than its death would have been, for the people are not going to demand what they believe they already have.

For several centuries, the rulers of England justified suppression of speech and writing on the basis of a doctrine known as "seditious libel" – in effect, any criticism of the form, laws, officials, symbols, conduct, policies, and virtually every other aspect of the existing government. With elaborate documentation, Dean Levy demonstrated that all the great philosophers and defenders of liberty of speech "from the time of Milton to the ratification of the First Amendment substantially accepted the right of the state to suppress seditious libel." He added:

> I find also that the American experience with freedom of political expression was as slight as the theoretical inheritance was narrow. Indeed, the American legislatures, especially during the colonial period, were far more oppressive than the supposedly tyrannous common-law courts. The evidence drawn particularly from the period 1776 to 1791 indicates that the generation that framed the first state declarations of rights and the First Amendment was hardly as libertarian as we have traditionally assumed. They did not intend to give free rein to criticism of the government that might be deemed seditious libel, although the concept of seditious libel was – and still is – the principal basis of muzzling political dissent. There is even reason to believe that the Bill of Rights was more the chance product of political expediency on all sides than of principled commitment to personal liberties.

At the Constitutional Convention of 1787, a motion to add a bill of rights to the document being drafted was unanimously rejected. When the proposed Constitution was submitted to the states, the two great public controversies over it were the magnitude of the sovereignty it required the states to surrender to the federal government and the absence of a bill of rights. "Yet it is astonishing to discover that the debate on a bill of rights, during the ratification controversy, was conducted at a level of abstraction so vague as to convey the impression that Americans of 1787–1788 had only the most nebulous conception of the meaning of the particular rights they sought to insure," Levy wrote. The subject, he went on, was "a grand topic for declamation," but no one seemed to know what it meant in any specific way. Scanty records of debates on the matter reveal almost nothing about popular or private sentiment on the subject, and contemporary newspapers, pamphlets, and broadsides reveal little more. Surely, Levy repeatedly pointed out, if there had been some broadly accepted view or philosophy that prevailed at the time, it would have been mentioned somewhere.

Eleven of the original states had constitutions of their own, and ten of them didn't mention freedom of speech. The one state that constitutionally protected it was Pennsylvania, and during the Revolution its authorities were perhaps the most vicious transgressors of that right in America. When Representative James Madison, "the Father of the Constitution," proposed to the First Congress the addition of a bill of rights to that document to satisfy popular demand, he called for protection against state violations of the rights of conscience, the press, and trial by jury; his proposal said nothing about speech.

A committee of the House of Representatives added freedom of speech to the proposal, and the House itself approved the amendment by the two-thirds majority required by the Constitution. The Senate apparently felt that the states had already been too circumscribed by the body of the Constitution and refused to extend the Bill of Rights beyond the authority of the federal government. In the end, the First Amendment stated, "Congress shall make no law respecting an establishment of religion, or prohibiting the free exercise thereof; or abridging the freedom of speech, or of the press; or the right of the people peaceably to assemble, and to petition the government for a redress of grievances." The states were left free to do much as they pleased. Congress seemed to have little interest in the matter altogether; the people had demanded a bill of rights, they had been given one, and the affair was settled.

"The congressional debate on the amendment," Levy wrote, "was unclear and apathetic; ambiguity, brevity, and imprecision in thought and expression characterize the comments of the few members who spoke. It is doubtful that the House understood the debate, cared deeply about its outcome, or shared a common understanding of the finished amendment." And the public appeared to understand even less about what had been done in its name. "In the glorious act of reverting from a state of nature to a civil government by framing a social compact, Americans tended simply to draw up a glittering catalogue of 'rights' that satisfied their urge for expression of first principles," Levy noted. "It was a terribly important and serious task, but it was executed in an incredibly haphazard fashion that verged on ineptness." While Levy's conclusions are doubtless correct historically, a more crucial fact is that the Bill of Rights – which was demanded by the great body of the people as protection against official tyranny, and supported by many of their most eminent leaders, including a number of the authors of the Constitution – was adopted. However haphazard or inept or political the process by which it was devised may have been, the document became an integral part of the supreme law of the land. From that moment on, the question has been: What does it mean and how is it to be enforced?

A few years later, a majority of the members of Congress demonstrated their disregard for free speech and a free press by approving the Sedition Act of 1798, which made it a criminal offense, punishable by up to two thousand dollars in fines and up to two years in prison, for anyone to utter or print "any false, scandalous and malicious" statements against the government or any of its officials in a manner that might defame them or lead to public contempt, hatred, or a bad reputation for public institutions or public officials. Of course, the act was an attempt by the Federalists, who controlled all three branches of the government, to destroy their Republican opponents, and to silence those who defended the excesses committed in the French Revolution. And, of course, the misuse of the law helped bring about the downfall of the Adams Administration and the election of Jefferson to the Presidency.

In Levy's view, another result of the Sedition Act was that it produced America's first serious debate on the issue of free speech. It was not until that stage that the progressive forces led by Jefferson actually repudiated the doctrine of seditious libel at last and held that citizens were free to criticize and condemn the national government and its managers without hindrance. But this libertarian attitude was wholly theoretical. It was not proposed in the form of legislation by any member of Congress during that period, it had no power under law, and it left the states free to punish anyone for attacks on the federal government. (In practice, it emerged years later, Jefferson had belied his glorious defense of free speech and a free press by covertly urging this last course — that opponents of *his* Administration be silenced by prosecutions under state sedition laws.)

When the Sedition Act expired, in 1801, Congress did not renew it, and the issue of its constitutionality did not reach the Supreme Court while the law was on the books. Between 1798 and 1801, however, several of the Court's Federalist justices individually upheld the act while sitting on circuit cases. Subsequently, the Court was asked to rule on the question of whether the act had been constitutional — to see if it constituted a precedent — but the Court refused to face the issue until 1964, when it finally stated, "Although the Sedition Act was never tested in this Court, the attack upon its validity has carried the day in the court of history."

Unfortunately, Dean Levy ended his study of the myth of free speech with the Jefferson Administration, and neither he nor other legal scholars have dealt adequately with an even more persistent, and pernicious, myth — that the Supreme Court has always been the "bulwark," the "bastion," the "palladium" of personal freedom in the United States. If that freedom means the right of the individual not to be arbitrarily and unnecessarily interfered with by government, then the Supreme Court has done very little to guard our freedom. When the Court has been most needed by the individual — at times of national hysteria that have produced repressive legislation and tyrannical acts by state and national governments — it has remained silent or has judicially endorsed the most undemocratic measures and practices. During the first century and a half of the nation's existence, the Court, like all other public institutions on every level in the United States, devoted most of its attention to establishing and preserving the sanctity of private property. The business of the nation was business, and the Court nearly always upheld the interests of the business power over the interests of the individual. The spirit of the Declaration of Independence, the Constitution, and the Bill of Rights was defined by the Court's reading of the letter of the law.

With passage of the Fourteenth Amendment, in 1868, some libertarians began to argue that its clause forbidding any state to "deprive any person of life, liberty, or property without due process of law" meant that the entire Bill of Rights was binding on the states. In other words, they contended, personal rights were no less important than property rights. For over half a century, a large majority of the Court refused to listen to such claims, even when they were made by its own members, including Justice Louis Brandeis, who charged his fellow-justices with holding that "the liberty guaranteed by the Fourteenth Amendment includes only liberty to acquire and to enjoy property." That charge, which Brandeis made frequently in his dissenting opinions during the nineteen-twenties, was demonstrably true. While the Court did not interfere with attempts by the federal government and state governments to rigidly control speech, it denied the power of the federal government and state governments to impose any controls whatever upon freedom of contract — such as the freedom of children to contract to work in coal mines, sweatshops, and mills for twelve to sixteen hours a day. In fact, it wasn't until 1941 that the Court upheld the right of government to impose limits on the use of child labor.

The Supreme Court did not directly address the issue of free speech under the First Amendment until 1919. During the First World War, Congress passed the Espionage Act and a new Sedition Act. In fiscal year 1919–20, the federal government indicted nearly two thousand people under these laws, and eight hundred and seventy-seven people were convicted under them. Not more than a handful of these people had posed any threat whatever to the security of the nation. At roughly the same time, many states enacted sedition laws of their own — often aimed at radicals who tried to organize labor unions and lead strikes — and no one knows how many thousands of people were prosecuted and imprisoned for violating those laws.

Only a few cases prosecuted under federal and state sedition laws reached the Supreme Court. The first of them was Schenck v. United States, which was decided in the spring of 1919, four months after the war ended. Charles Schenck, the secretary of the Socialist Party, was convicted in federal court of mailing some broadsides charging that the draft was despotic and unconstitutional and urging men of draft age: "assert your opposition to the draft." The only precedents the Court had before it were the English common law of seditious libel and a few state cases. Confronted by the first opportunity in the history of the Republic to uphold the individual's right to speak freely against the government, the Supreme Court unanimously upheld government's right to suppress such speech.

The Court's opinion was delivered by Justice Oliver Wendell Holmes, who barely nodded toward the First Amendment before going on to lay down his famous rule: "The question in every case is whether the words used are used in such circumstances and are of such a nature as to create a clear and present danger that they will bring about the substantive evils that Congress has a right to prevent." Holmes's clear-and-present-danger test — extensively used by the Supreme Court and thus lesser courts for a generation to measure the legal propriety or impropriety of speech — demonstrates the clear and present danger that the Court has often posed to individual freedom. On practically every ground, the test is obnoxious. As Professor Thomas I. Emerson, of the Yale Law School, who is the leading authority on the First Amendment, has pointed out, the test is "excessively vague;" it "furnishes little clarity in advance of a judicial decision;" its serious application would plunge judges "into consideration of a mass of historical, political, economic, psychological and social facts" which would require "both evaluation and prophecy of a sort no court is competent to give;" and, most important of all, it allows "the state to cut off expression as soon as it comes close to being effective."

By far the worst effect of the clear-and-present-danger test is that from the start it made speech more punishable than action. Under ordinary criminal law, the state has to prove that a person meant to commit a criminal act and then committed it – that is, both the intent *and* the act must be demonstrated. In the case of a prosecution for criminal speech, on the other hand, proof of either criminal intent *or* act is usually sufficient for a conviction. Although legal scholars have missed the point, this flaw can also be traced back to Holmes. In expounding on the clear-and-present-danger test a few months after he first stated it, he said, "I do not doubt for a moment that by the same reasoning that would justify punishing persuasion to murder, the United States constitutionally may punish speech that produces or is intended to produce a clear and imminent danger that it will bring about forthwith certain substantive evils that the United States constitutionally may seek to prevent." Holmes's use of "or" rather than "and" may have been inadvertent. But that seems unlikely in view of the fact that Brandeis, his closest associate on the Court, subsequently used exactly the same terminology, including the "or," in his exposition on the test.

The effect of this usage over the years has been to make the law covering criminal speech closely akin to the law covering criminal conspiracy, which is very different from ordinary criminal law. Under the law of conspiracy, for instance, the state has to prove only that a person agreed to commit a crime with one or more others. No crime need actually be committed, for, under most statutes, the only factor besides intent that the prosecution needs for a conviction is *any* overt act that might conceivably be connected to the prospective crime. If three men talk about how they would like to hold up a certain bank and later one of them walks past the bank they talked about, all three are guilty of criminal conspiracy and can be sent to prison for long terms; moreover, an act of any of the three is considered, legally, to be the act of all three. The law of conspiracy also allows prosecutors wide latitude procedurally and requires far less in the way of protection for defendants. In sum, a person who is charged with committing a criminal act is innocent until proved guilty, whereas a person who is charged with conspiring to commit a criminal act is innocent until proved partly guilty. By carelessly linking the law of speech to the law of conspiracy, Holmes made words easier to punish than, say, murder.

There are no figures available for the number of people who were sent to prison, or kept in prison, because of the clear-and-present-danger test. One of those who went to prison because of it was an obscure immigrant by the name of Jacob Abrams. Angered by the Allied invasion of Russia in 1918 – an attempt to stop the revolution there and bring Russia back into the war against Germany – Abrams slapped together some semi-literate leaflets calling for a general strike to protest the invasion and persuaded a confederate to fling them out of a window of a loft building in lower Manhattan. The Abrams case reached the Supreme Court a few months after the Schenck case, and Abrams' conviction – including a sentence of twenty years in prison – was upheld by a vote of seven to two, on the ground that his leaflets constituted a clear and present danger to the United States. Holmes, with Brandeis concurring, wrote a bitter dissent that upheld the clear-and-present-danger test but attacked this wanton application of it, since "nobody can suppose that the surreptitious publishing of a silly leaflet by an unknown man, without more, would present any immediate danger."

In the course of that dissent, Justice Holmes expounded another notion that was to become almost as misused, and ultimately pernicious, as the clear-and-present-danger test. This was the concept that democracy would survive and flourish most successfully if it had a "marketplace of ideas" in which robust discussions of public issues were constantly going on. The doctrine had an ancient lineage that stretched back through John Stuart Mill and John Locke to Socrates, but it had not been directly applied before as a legal principle. In time, Holmes said, open discussion would teach men "that the ultimate good desired is better reached by free trade in ideas – that the best test of truth is the power of the thought to get itself accepted in the competition of the market, and that truth is the only ground upon which their wishes safely can be carried out."

The marketplace-of-ideas doctrine has been a favorite recourse of members of the Supreme Court and of lesser courts ever since

Holmes enunciated it, and they have paid endless tribute to it. But though the doctrine has an appealing ring to it, like so much of what Holmes wrote, it is little more than high-minded rhetoric. No one believes in it, and no one lives by it. If the marketplace-of-ideas theory were to be put into practice in even the most superficial manner, it would mean, to begin with, that all our public schools would offer their students courses in such subjects as Socialism, Communism, Fascism, agnosticism, atheism, free love, peaceful overthrow of government, and the evils of war. And it would provide those who entertain unpopular views with a fair chance to express themselves publicly through television, radio, newspapers, and magazines. While the marketplace-of-ideas notion is, in itself, a healthy and constructive ideal, in practice it is largely a myth – and, again, it assures the people that they have what they lack and lulls them into a dangerous complacency. Perhaps more perniciously, the concept has been distorted by being judicially viewed in a utilitarian fashion – that is, as justifying courts in measuring the social worth of ideas. Under this approach, ideas that contribute to the vitality of society (arguments for and against racial equality, say) are acceptable and protected by the First Amendment but ideas that concern only the individual (such as pornography that is "without redeeming social value") are unacceptable and unprotected. In the end, then, the marketplace-of-ideas standard places the interests of society far above the rights of the individual.

In the early nineteen-twenties, Benjamin Gitlow, a Communist leader, was sentenced to from five to ten years in prison for violating a New York State law against "criminal anarchy." His offense was printing and distributing a pamphlet entitled *The Left Wing Manifesto,* which called for a general strike and the ultimate replacement of the existing government. In 1925, the Supreme Court upheld the right of the state to enforce its "criminal anarchy" statute against Gitlow on several grounds. First, the Court stated, the language in the manifesto amounted to "direct incitement." This conclusion was based on two sentences from the pamphlet, which the Court quoted: "The proletariat revolution and the Communist reconstruction of society — the struggle for these — is now indispensable. . . . The Communist International calls the proletariat of the world to the final struggle!" Second, the Court temporarily put aside the clear-and-present-danger test in favor of an older judicial measure known as the bad-tendency test, which had its roots deep in ancient common law and the rule of seditious libel. The Court explained, "That a state in the exercise of its police power may punish those who abuse this freedom [of speech and the press] by utterances inimical to the public welfare, tending to corrupt public morals, incite to crime, or disturb the public peace, is not open to question."

The infamous Court of Star Chamber could not have done better. Under this dictum, the state could punish its citizens for any criticism or dissent — in fact, for any expression that government found antagonistic to its own concept of its interests — and in effect the law of seditious libel was still on the books. To further justify its position, the Court cited the old judicial tradition that "every presumption is to be indulged in favor of the validity of the statute," and it could be declared unconstitutional only if it was found to be "arbitrary or unreasonable."

This judicial tradition, which is still very much alive, is both absurd and cowardly. It allows the judiciary to make the legislature superior to the courts and the executive, and thereby fatally weakens the delicate tripartite balance that is supposed to support our system of government. It allows the courts to sidestep fundamental issues that deeply affect the daily lives of the people. And it encourages irresponsibility in legislatures, which are always the first institutions to respond to popular hysteria by enacting repressive laws — often under the lawmakers' mistaken impression that the courts will correct their demagoguery. Judicial deference to legislatures is defended on the ground that since representative bodies are democratically elected, courts should not interfere unnecessarily with them. This rationale — called judicial self-restraint — misses a major point: the purpose of the courts is to provide a check, intentionally undemocratic, on legislative tyranny. As Hamilton wrote in *The Federalist,* the courts were designed to erect an "excellent barrier to the encroachments and oppressions of the representative body."

In any event, the Court, in the Gitlow decision, tossed off the remark, more or less in passing and without explanation, that freedom of speech and the press were now "fundamental personal rights" and could not be abridged by the states. In other words, part of the Bill of Rights had finally been made a basic right of *all* citizens. But the Court's dictum on this point was rendered utterly meaningless in the case at hand, because the Gitlow decision upheld a state's flagrant denial of the very right that was supposedly being guaranteed.

Despite the Court's initially timid and confused attempts to deal with the issue of freedom of speech, in the past half century it has gradually adopted a more generous attitude. Even so, it has never laid down any sensible guidelines in this area, and the theories it has used have been exceedingly narrow and often open to repressive use. It was not until the nineteen-thirties that a majority of the Court – under the stewardship of Chief Justice Charles Evans Hughes – finally questioned the dominance of property rights over personal rights.

The most important First Amendment case in that period was De Jonge v. Oregon, decided in 1937. In that case the Court unanimously upheld the right of free speech and assembly not just in theory but in practice more effectively than ever before. Dirk De Jonge, a member of the Communist Party, had been sentenced to prison for presiding over an open meeting held under the auspices of the Communist Party at which charges were made about police brutality during a longshoremen's strike. The Court's reversal of his conviction was the first sign of an emerging awareness among its members that free speech could create not only discord but also the means for allowing social change with some stability. Speaking for the Court, Chief Justice Hughes said, "The greater the importance of safeguarding the community from incitements to the overthrow of our institutions by force and violence, the more imperative is the need to preserve inviolate the constitutional rights of free speech, free press and free assembly in order to maintain the opportunity for free political discussion, to the end that government may be responsive to the will of the people and that changes, if desired, may be obtained by peaceful means. Therein lies the security of the Republic, the very foundation of constitutional government."

The Hughes influence generally prevailed on the Court until the end of the Second World War. In earlier American wars, freedom of speech had been one of the first casualties. During the Revolution, the states viciously suppressed the slightest criticism of that cause; during the Civil War, military government was allowed, in areas under Union domination, to stamp out dissent and imprison dissenters by the hundreds; and, of course, during the First World War the Espionage and Sedition Acts were widely used to silence radicals. Almost none of this kind of repression went on during the Second World War – partly because by then the First Amendment guarantees of free speech and a free press had been made more and more binding upon the states by the federal courts under expansion of the Gitlow dictum, and this change hindered states from harassing radicals or other unpopular critics through use of state laws. Perhaps more important, though, was the fact that the movement toward forcible repression of unpopular speech has always been aimed at the far left, and during the war that side could not be openly attacked as long as its most extreme embodiment – the Soviet Union – was America's ally. With the end of the war, the opening of the Cold War, and the advent of McCarthyism, the libertarian trend on the Court, as elsewhere in the country, abruptly ended. Once more, the Supreme Court buckled under the pressure of the popular hysteria that swept the nation, and upheld most of the repressive laws enacted to curb free speech and free association.

In the earliest of the anti-Communist cases to reach the Supreme Court – American Communications Association v. Douds, decided in 1950 – the issue was Congress's attempt to force Communists out of the labor-union movement. The law involved was the Taft-Hartley Act, Section 9 (h) of which provided that no union could enjoy the benefits of the National Labor Relations Act, including the right to organize workers or to bargain collectively, unless each officer filed an affidavit stating "that he is not a member of the Communist Party or affiliated with such party, and that he does not believe in and is not a member of or supports any organization that believes in or teaches the overthrow of the United States Government by force or by any illegal or unconstitutional methods." The oath was much the same as those in laws under which various British monarchs had their opponents hanged, disembowelled, castrated, drawn and quartered, and then beheaded. The Supreme Court upheld Section 9 (h), and reached back to a 1939 free-speech case to justify its decision on the basis of what has come to be known as the balancing test. By means of this test, the Court weighed the interests of society in preserving order against the importance of protecting individual rights guaranteed by the First Amendment.

Professor Emerson, along with many other legal scholars, has criticized the balancing test on a variety of grounds: it allows courts to come down with equal facility and justification on either side of any issue; it does almost nothing to discourage those who want to suppress speech; it requires courts that use it seriously to examine *all* the facts and far too broad a range of issues in *every* case before them; it permits legislative tyranny, since courts are extremely reluctant to knock down laws if there is the slightest rational defense for them; it is an ad-hoc test that depends entirely on the courts for interpretation and leaves the person who exercises the "right" of free speech in jeopardy if he or she miscalculates the effects of that speech; and, finally, it renders the First Amendment largely meaningless by changing its absolute prohibition against laws abridging free speech into a relative prohibition against *unreasonable* laws abridging free speech. Yet the balancing test has been the Court's principal method of judging First Amendment cases for the past quarter of a century. That means, of course, that it has also been the chief measure used by lower federal and all state courts, as well as by public officials, the police, and the public at large. All of them, it might be added, have floundered about helplessly in the judicial bog created by the Supreme Court.

Still, the Court has some achievements to its credit in defending free speech. Although the Court upheld applications of the Taft-Hartley, the Smith, and the McCarran Acts in the early nineteen-fifties — and thereby, in effect, upheld the sedition-law rulings handed down in the twenties — it later nullified its decisions in most of these cases on technical, procedural, and administrative grounds. Unfortunately for the victims of these laws, the judicial nullification of them took a good many years, during which a lot of people were financially and socially ruined, and sometimes unjustly imprisoned for long periods. And since the Court has, typically, refused to face the issues in almost all those cases directly by deciding them on forthright First Amendment grounds, they still stand as precedents for suppression of free speech in the future.

On the other hand, the Court has at least given broad protection to matters of belief; it has curbed the casual demagoguery of legislative investigating committees; it has knocked down most state loyalty oaths; it has upheld the right of peaceful assembly and demonstrations or protests, which made the immense civil-rights and anti-war movements of the nineteen-sixties possible (and probably kept them from turning to outright violence) ; it has greatly improved the libel and privacy laws; and it has begun to widen the rights of expression by government employees on every level. "These are no small accomplishments," Professor Emerson has written. "Taken as a whole, they definitely outweigh the failures."

On the most crucial ground — preserving the essential bases of individuality — that conclusion is surely wrong.

The Declaration of Independence, the Constitution, and the Bill of Rights had a single purpose: to create a society in which men could live securely with minimal interference by government. Every increase in the power of government diminishes the power of its citizens. To resist this encroachment and preserve their sovereign power in a democracy, they must be free to criticize, to admonish, to question, to berate, to attack, to harass, and to threaten their servant the government. Without the fullest freedom of speech, they cannot do any of these things openly and thus effectively. Moreover, the right to speak freely is the basis of all other democratic rights, for it makes possible and nourishes the opportunity to think. As every tyrant has always known, to silence speech is to stop thought. And, as Justice Benjamin Cardozo said about freedom of thought and speech, "it is the matrix, the indispensable condition, of nearly every other form of freedom." Only with thinking do men become individuals, and it is that individuality — the right of each man to be, and to fulfill, himself — that the authors of the Constitution sought ultimately to preserve and encourage.

From the time of John Locke, men who hoped to rid themselves of despotic government spoke longingly about the preservation of "life, liberty, and property" as the only legitimate concern of government. By the time Jefferson wrote the Declaration of Independence, the phrase had been changed in many political discourses and increasingly in popular usage to "life, liberty, and the pursuit of happiness." The alteration, which Jefferson incorporated in the Declaration, was a remarkable one. In no other country but America and in no other century but the eighteenth could happiness have been made a revolutionary goal. And yet the term was precisely right, for it was an intense expression of individualism — the epitome of the place and the time. Nothing is more individualistic than happiness, or the pursuit of it, and every human endeavor, from the accumulation of money to mystical contemplation, can be a personal means to that general end.

In effect, the Constitution changed the meaning back to life, liberty, and property, and ever since that document was adopted the Supreme Court has put *its* emphasis on property rather than individuality. Indeed, America, which professed to believe that it had finally solved the ancient problem of society versus the individual, has only made the problem worse. While the individual is more rhetorically honored than ever before, he is officially — most of all, judicially — ignored, scorned, and mistreated in a way that can happen solely when the well-being of the state, and not of its citizens, becomes the purpose of society.

By any measure, the Supreme Court is the most conservative branch of the government, and in many broad and narrow ways it is the most conservative public institution in the United States. That, too, was probably inevitable, because any President who was naming a new justice to the Court and any Senate that had to confirm or reject a nomination would be likely to look for one trait in the man who was being handed so much power for a lifetime — caution. All Presidents have succeeded in this search far beyond their hopes, and the Court, in general, has been so cautious that it has usually done no more than endorse the prevailing national mood as exemplified in acts of the legislature and executive bodies it is supposed to oversee. Only one Supreme Court — the Warren Court — can be said to have got out in front of the dominant public sentiment of the time, and even then the advances it made amounted to no more than the simple act of giving the people some of the rights that the nation had falsely assured them they had possessed all along. It was also probably inevitable that the deeply cautious men who were given this great power would favor the side that had so grandly bestowed its highest honor on them — the state. That most men who have served on the Court have been strongly predisposed toward the state rather than toward the individual is proved by the record of the Court. That record, to this day, is a judicial monument to statism.

All of the rules and tests used by the Supreme Court to measure the extent, or limits, of our basic freedom — the right to think and to speak as free men — have been essentially statist. The bad-tendency test, the clear-and-present-danger test, the incitement test, and the balancing test all weigh in on the side of the state, for the interests of the state can always be made to *seem* paramount to the interests of the unpopular or powerless individual. And if there is ever any doubt about which interest is weightier, the Court's traditional deference to legislative enactments on all levels resolves the question in favor of the state unless the laws in question are patently absurd.

Even the most democratically inspired statements of the Court — the marketplace-of-ideas concept, for instance, or Chief Justice Hughes' fine affirmation of the right of free speech and assembly among the most despised members of society in the De Jonge case — are basically statist. The contribution of free speech in the marketplace of ideas essentially affects the individual only incidentally. The goal of that marketplace is to improve and protect society, not to provide the means of individual self-fulfillment. And the Hughes defense of free speech in De Jonge as an instrument for bringing about social change peacefully and with stability preserved — a theory that seems to lie behind the attitude toward dissent on the part of the most enlightened people in power today — has everything to do with society and very little to do with the individual. One of the least important but most illustrative examples of the Court's egregious bias toward the state is its presumption that it has the right to determine what kind of writing or movies citizens may read or watch, or, as it recently ruled, that local legislators, judges, and juries have this right. What conceivable business is it of such people to tell any adult that whatever *they* consider to be pornographic or obscene lies beyond the reach of liberty?

Above all, though, the crushing liability that the state automatically imposes upon any individual who asserts individual rights — the loss of time, energy, money, peace of mind, privacy, and, in the end, one's essential individuality — overwhelmingly demonstrates the lack of concern for the individual that is inherent in our judicial system, from top to bottom. That system has clearly placed the presumption of right on the side of the state — and continues to betray the democratic ideal of protecting the individual against government.

It is astonishing to discover how little awareness of this fundamental problem there has always been on the Supreme Court. The closest it has ever come to recognizing the true nature and role of individual rights in our society was back in 1927, in an opinion delivered by Justice Brandeis, who concurred with the Court's decision upholding a California sedition law but dissented from the majority's restrictions on freedom of speech. He wrote, in part:

> Those who won our independence believed that the final end of the state was to make men free to develop their faculties; and that in its government the deliberative forces should prevail over the arbitrary. They valued liberty both as an end and as a means. They believed liberty to be the secret of happiness and courage to be the secret of liberty. They believed that freedom to think as you will and to speak as you think are means indispensable to the discovery and spread of political truth; that without free speech and assembly discussion would be futile; that with them, discussion affords ordinarily adequate protection against the dissemination of noxious doctrine; that the greatest menace to freedom is an inert people; that public discussion is a political duty; and that this should be a fundamental principle of the American government. They recognized the risks to which all human institutions are subject. But they knew that order cannot be secured merely through fear of punishment for its infraction; that it is hazardous to discourage thought, hope and imagination; that fear breeds repression; that repression breeds hate; that hate menaces stable government; that the path of safety lies in the opportunity to discuss freely supposed grievances and proposed remedies; and that the fitting remedy for evil counsels is good ones. Believing in the power of reason as applied through public discussion, they eschewed silence coerced by law — the argument of force in its worst form. Recognizing the occasional tyrannies of governing majorities, they amended the Constitution so that free speech and assembly should be guaranteed. . . . Those who won our independence by revolution were not cowards. They did not fear political change. They did not exalt order at the cost of liberty.

By restating the fundamental point — that society exists for the good of the individual — this declaration went a long way toward elevating the individual's position within society. At the same time, though, Brandeis barely hinted at what society's responsibility toward the individual was or should be. Since that time, this problem — the crux of democracy, it might be called — has almost never been considered seriously, let alone resolved. If, as Brandeis said, the Framers "believed that the final end of the state was to make men free to develop their faculties," and if we share this purpose today, then a further question must be addressed: What aspects of individuality does the state endanger most in its essential relations with its citizens? The answer may be found in the relationships created by differences in power. The difference in degree of power between the citizen and the state is so immense that it may finally be a difference in kind, and perhaps it can only be understood by analogy – that is, by reducing it to a more commonplace size. The relationships between child and parent, between student and teacher, between employee and employer are more measurable relations of power, and yet are very similar to the relationship between the individual and government. Whether the more powerful party in any of these personal associations is benevolent or despotic, the possibility of intrusion on the rights of the child, the student, or the employee is always – in kind, if not in degree – the same. The danger to individuality in all such associations, personal and impersonal, is threefold: the ever-present threat to one's sense of dignity, to one's feeling of being free, and to one's need for privacy. It is these three essential characteristics of individuality which permit and encourage one to strive for self-fulfillment – or, in Brandeis's words, to "develop" one's "faculties."

Government on all levels in the United States has almost always ignored these three basic roots of individuality. At best it has failed to nourish them and at worst it has poisoned them. To a large extent, the courts – most of all, the Supreme Court – are to blame, and if the individual is finally swallowed up by mass society, as seems so likely at the present time, it will be the Supreme Court that will have most to answer for before history's bar of justice. Except for the Hughes Court and the Warren Court, that institution has turned its majestic back on the individual.

Under Chief Justice Earl Warren, the Court defended and asserted individual rights as never before. In fact, its most effective, and thus most controversial, decisions were aimed at protecting some of the most vital and ordinary rights of the individual – the right of every black child to a decent and nonracist education; the right of every citizen, wherever he lives or whatever his status, to a vote of equal weight; the right of every suspect and defendant, rich or poor, to equal protection of the laws in any criminal prosecution. Above all, some crucial decisions of the Warren Court finally made almost all of the Bill of Rights binding on the states, and thereby gave every citizen the rights due him. Unfortunately, though, the Warren Court did not address itself with the same concern and boldness to the First Amendment cases that came before it. That problem was left to the future.

Overnight, the Supreme Court was transformed by President Nixon from an institution that had begun to face the plight of the individual back into an institution that would uphold the power of the state. Just at the time that the individual was most imperilled, he lost his greatest defender. There seems no chance that the Court, now or in the immediate future, will come back to the rescue of the individual in time to save him from the immense power of the technological, economic, and social forces that threatens to crush him.

In the decisions so far handed down by the Burger Court on First Amendment issues — chiefly those concerning the press, obscenity, and loyalty oaths — its members have demonstrated a strong predisposition toward the state. (The most outstanding exception to this tendency was a decision that did not involve the First Amendment — the ruling on abortion, which is as immediately and intensely personal as anything can be.) At present, there seems no chance that President Nixon's four appointees to the Court, all of whom are confirmed statists, will alter their views substantially. The retirement of Justice William O. Douglas, one of the boldest champions of the individual ever to sit on the Court, left only Justices William J. Brennan, Jr., Thurgood Marshall, and, with increasing frequency, Potter Stewart on the side of the individual. Even if Douglas's replacement, Justice John Paul Stevens, were to oppose the Nixon foursome, Justice Byron White would give it a five-to-four majority. Throughout his judicial career, White, who was President Kennedy's appointee to the Court, has embodied the pro-state bias that has characterized that tribunal during most of its existence, and he has joined the Nixon appointees to give them a firm majority in most cases. Of the justices on the majority side, White best reflects the general attitude of today's Court toward its role in society — to defend a state that is essentially benevolent. That view misses the point, of course, for even if a state is benevolent its interests are *always* opposed to those of the individual.

III

"People in civil-liberties cases are the battering rams of freedom," Burt Neuborne said after the James case had been going on for a couple of years. "Unfortunately, what happens to them is what happens to battering rams." Neva James probably felt the battering more acutely than her husband. "Whenever I read in the papers about a Supreme Court decision upholding someone's rights, I always think about the family and wonder what happened to them and how many years of their lives were messed up," she said. "Our experience has had a strange effect on me. It has both given me a more radical view of society and made me less willing to stand up to it."

To Charles James, his wife's reaction was perhaps the worst effect of the case. "Neva has come to feel that if one believes in freedom and exercises it once, that jeopardizes one's ever exercising it again," he said. "If that has happened to someone like Neva, who is a person of deep good will and strength, God knows what's happening to other Americans." As for James's own reaction to his case, he explained, "Like most people, I was brought up to believe in our system. The freedom I was taught and believed in — all that stuff we were told about Jefferson and Lincoln — were things that I thought the leaders of our country still cared about and believed in, too. Then I finally saw that they want the system to be believed in but not used. I used it, and look what happened!"

When Neuborne prepared an appeal from District Court Judge Burke's decision against James, to be submitted to the United States Court of Appeals for the Second Circuit, he began with the argument that the school board's lawyer, Treinin, had used and that Burke had accepted — that is, the case was *res judicata,* or judicially settled, and couldn't be raised again. Judicial rulings of the Second Circuit, Neuborne stated in his brief, required litigants who wanted to appeal from a state action to the federal court system to first exhaust state administrative remedies. James had obeyed that rule and now was being punished for it, because if Treinin and Burke were correct in their claim that the issue was *res judicata,* then a person who exhausted state administrative remedies would be barred from appealing to any federal court, and a person who did not exhaust state administrative remedies would also be barred from appealing to any federal court. In short, the federal court system would be quite superfluous.

With that out of the way, Neuborne moved on to the central issue of James's armband and his right to freedom of speech. As a constitutional lawyer, Neuborne was fully aware that the Supreme Court and all inferior courts increasingly relied on the balancing test in cases like the one at hand. Although he objected to the test on just about every ground — most of all on the ground that it was finally unfair and useless — tradition compelled him to rely on it, too, as his basic argument on James's behalf. Citing the recent case of Hanover v. Northrup, in which a seventh-and-eighth-grade woman teacher was dismissed for refusing to lead her class in reciting the Pledge of Allegiance because the current state of the nation made it impossible for her to say that it provided "liberty and justice for all," Neuborne went on to quote the District Court judge in that case, who ruled that her refusal was "a form of expression protected by the First Amendment," and that the school officials who fired her had failed to demonstrate that her act caused enough disruption of her class to justify *their* act.

As Neuborne explained later in private, the word "disruption" was the key to the James case, because it was the measure used by courts in such matters to apply the balancing test — that is, if there was no substantial disruption, the interests of the state were not put out of balance by the act of the individual. In his brief, Neuborne contended that the Hanover and James cases were "indistinguishable," except that some of Mrs. Hanover's students had followed her example, whereas none of James's students had followed his. That, of course, made his act less disruptive than one that had already been judicially upheld.

Moving on to another case — Pickering v. Board of Education, in which a public-school teacher was fired for writing a letter to a local newspaper attacking the school board's fiscal policies and its "totalitarianism" — Neuborne pointed out that the Supreme Court, in 1968, upheld Pickering's right to express himself in this manner, even though some of the statements in his letter were false, since he had not disrupted the school's operations. In fact, the Court said, publication of the letter had been "greeted . . . with massive apathy and total disbelief." Neuborne then observed that the Addison school board had informed James in writing that he was entirely free to express any views that he wanted to outside the school. That concession, Neuborne argued, made the Pickering and James cases nearly identical, for "James's armband contained no elements of coercion or intimidation, and in no way interfered with the orderly teaching of his 11th-grade English class, [so] the effect of his armband was no different than if he had written a letter to the school or local newspaper vigorously expressing his aversion to war."

Brown, the school-district principal, now stated in an affidavit that he feared at the time that "the armband would tend to be disruptive and would possibly encourage pupils to engage in disruptive demonstrations." Actually, most of the students who were asked about the armband's effect on them said they hadn't known what it stood for. Although this attitude made it clear that a black armband could not conceivably have created any kind of demonstration in a place as deeply conservative as Addison, Neuborne ignored that point in favor of another legal precedent — a far more effective tactic than any citation of reality. In the case of Tinker v. Des Moines Independent Community School District, he stated, a girl in junior high school wore a black armband to school to protest the war in Vietnam, and the school authorities justified her suspension, as Brown now tried to do, on their apprehension that there might be a disturbance if she was allowed to stay in school. In that case, Neuborne explained, the Supreme Court ruled that the First Amendment gave the girl the right to wear such a symbol, and that this right could not be abrogated because of some school officials' "undifferentiated fear." (Actually, their fear had been differentiated, for they had not objected when some other students, during the same period, wore Iron Crosses to demonstrate their support for the war.)

Again and again, Neuborne assured the court that there was unquestionably a strong need for order in public schools and that any teacher who endangered it should be severely dealt with. Having obediently tugged his forelock to the state, he made his main statement on this issue:

> The state does, of course, possess a substantial interest in assuring that teachers do not coerce or intimidate students. However, such an interest may be protected without depriving teachers of the ability to express themselves in a non-coercive and non-intimidating manner. Thus, were James alleged to have expressed his aversion to the killing in Vietnam in a coercive or intimidating manner, appellees would be perfectly justified in conducting a hearing and, if persuaded of the charges, imposing appropriate sanctions. However, no one has accused James of coercion or intimidation. No student has even suggested that he or she felt intimidated by James' armband. In the absence of such intimidation or coercion, the state lacks a legitimate interest in curbing James' expression.

Despite his concentration on this point, Neuborne felt that it was rather trivial in comparison with an issue that was more basic to the case – the function of education in a democracy. Lawyers tend to place the points that they believe will most influence the judge in the body of their briefs and to place what most influences *them* in footnotes. (This is such a widespread practice, in fact, that a perusal of the main texts of briefs on important constitutional cases will give the reader a fair idea of what most lawyers in the field think the law is, while a reading of the footnotes will show what they think it should be.) In Neuborne's brief, his main point appeared in a footnote on a statement made by the State Commissioner of Education, who, Neuborne said, seemed to assume in his ruling on James's act that "any expression of opinion by a teacher to a student on political issues would have an inherently coercive impact." Neuborne went on to say that "a false façade of neutrality would seem more subject to abuse than the honest expression of opinion in a non-coercive, non-intimidating manner," and he added, "After all, the function of the public schools is to educate citizens for active participation in a democracy. So long as it is non-coercive, a teacher's healthy exchange of ideas and opinions with students can only benefit the democratic process."

Of course, this point essentially reflected the marketplace-of-ideas approach. Since that concept was so widely praised by jurists in theory, Neuborne used the notion, but since it was so widely ignored by them in practice, he put it in the footnote. The point that he believed in far more deeply — that James had not merely been unnecessarily denied a basic right but had been ruthlessly deprived of his basic individuality by an uncaring state — appeared nowhere in Neuborne's brief. It did not because Neuborne realized that his job as a lawyer was to persuade a three-judge panel of a federal court to grant his client's plea for reinstatement in his job, and not to present a brief that defined and defended the true nature of individuality in society. Any argument of that sort, he feared, would simply be considered by most judges to be legally irrelevant.

Treinin's brief submitted ten points to justify James's dismissal. Four of them were devoted in one way or another to the contention that the case was *res judicata.* (Nothing that Neuborne or the courts had to say about the absurd nature of this claim was to have any effect on Treinin — or on the lawyer for the Commissioner of Education, who, in the capacity of *amicus curiae,* submitted a brief at every stage of the case, largely relying on the same claim.) The only point in Treinin's brief besides this one that the Court of Appeals was to consider was his contention that "the issue of free speech is not involved." To support this view, he started out by quoting a well-known statement by Oliver Wendell Holmes in a case involving a policeman who was fired for engaging in political activity: "Petitioner may have a constitutional right to talk politics but he has no constitutional right to be a policeman. There are few employments for hire in which the servant does not agree to suspend his constitutional right of free speech as well as of idleness by the implied terms of his contract. The servant cannot complain as he takes the employment on the terms which are offered to him."

While Treinin listed thirty-three cases in a "Table of Authorities" at the front of his brief, he neglected to date only one of them — the Holmes decision, which was handed down in 1892, when Holmes was a member of the Supreme Judicial Court of Massachusetts. Since that time, legal opinions on the subject had changed completely. Treinin also relied on a similar state case dealing with teachers' rights — this one a 1954 ruling of the New York Court of Appeals which stated, much the same as Holmes had, "Petitioner may work for the school system upon the reasonable terms laid down by the proper authorities. If he does not choose to work under such terms, he is at liberty to retain his beliefs and associations and go elsewhere." And he also cited another New York case, in which the state Appellate Division, in 1961, justified its claim that there was bound to be "some loss of academic freedom in all organized education" by referring to what happened to Socrates.

By the nineteen-sixties, federal courts had repudiated the old Holmes doctrine entirely. In 1967, for instance, the Supreme Court stated that "the theory that public employment which may be denied altogether may be subjected to any conditions, regardless of how unreasonable, has been uniformly rejected." And, a year later, the Court's decision in Pickering was widely interpreted as amounting to a declaration that teachers and other public employees cannot be deprived of their basic rights unless the state can show a compelling need for limiting them in order to accomplish other, more essential ends. But Treinin ignored Pickering altogether. In fact, the only contemporary case that he found relevant on this point was Goldwasser v. Brown. In that case, a teacher who was employed by the federal government to teach English to foreign military officers enrolled in a school at an American military installation was fired for spending classroom time lecturing his students on American foreign policy and race prejudice. The Court of Appeals for the District of Columbia upheld the dismissal in 1970, and the Supreme Court declined to intervene.

Treinin based his claim that freedom of speech was not an issue in the James case largely on the Goldwasser ruling. He began by quoting the Court of Appeals' observation in Goldwasser that "the free-speech interest of the teacher is to have his say on any and every thing about which he has feelings, provided there is no significant likelihood of his impairment of his efficiency." Although the statement seemed like an outright defense of an act such as James's, Treinin ignored that interpretation and went on to say that Goldwasser, like James, was not hired to teach, in the court's words, "current events, political science, sociology or international relations;" that both Goldwasser and James were English teachers; that in Goldwasser the court said, "Observations on Vietnam . . . would appear to have, at best, minimal relevance to the immediate classroom objectives;" and that, like James, Goldwasser was dismissed for what he did in, not outside, the classroom. "Thus," Treinin noted triumphantly, "we have a situation parallel to our case."

He did not mention that the Court of Appeals upheld Goldwasser's dismissal essentially because he sacrificed large amounts of classroom time to air his personal views and thereby failed to perform the duty for which he had been hired. To Treinin, the Goldwasser case was such a compelling precedent that he was prompted to ask how anyone could claim the Hanover case to be "of any persuasive force." While Mrs. Hanover's refusal to lead a recitation of the Pledge of Allegiance by her students seemed to be a far more divisive act against society than James's act of wearing a black armband, Treinin did not see it that way. In concluding his argument on the issue of freedom of speech, he wrote:

> Apart from disagreeing with the [Hanover] decision, it can be pointed out that in that case there is absent the background of explosive political division and conflict represented by [James's] position; there is absent the background of marches on Washington; protest throughout the land; division portrayed in newspaper headlines and television news reports — an entirely different context is presented. Mrs. Hanover is momentarily expressing a personal feeling. Mr. James throughout the day sought to publicize an emotionally charged political position.

There was absent from Treinin's description the fact that Mrs. Hanover refused to lead a recitation of the Pledge the same week that James was suspended the second time for wearing a black armband. There was also absent the fact that she refused because she did not believe in the Pledge's guarantee of "liberty and justice for all," in view of the way that America was still treating its black citizens not long after their dissatisfaction with life in America had resulted in terrifying riots in cities across the country.

The winter of 1971–72 was a long, hard one for the James family. At the beginning of it, James had a job on a crew that cleaned out a local store each morning before it opened. The crew worked from 5 A.M. until 9 A.M., and the pay was so low and the turnover so high that within a few weeks James became senior member and foreman. One morning just before Christmas, the manager of the store found a small pile of refuse that had been swept up in one aisle but not removed. He demanded that the sweeper who was responsible be fired. When James said there was no way of knowing who was responsible, he was ordered to pick out a member of the crew at random and fire him or her as an object lesson. Appalled by this arbitrary callousness, James replied, "O.K., I choose me. I'm fired. See you," and walked out.

At Christmastime, there was almost no money and very little food in the James house, and Mrs. James gave each of the children two dollars to buy presents for the others. "It was a bad time," she recalled. "Charles and I were so terribly low, and the children had nothing to look forward to during the holidays." The day before Christmas, there was a knock at the front door, and when she opened it she saw two men carrying several large plastic bags full of toys and candy. They were from the Arctic League, a local charity organization. "I'd always hated such charity — it seemed so demeaning to the poor," she said. "But I was never so glad to see anyone in my life. We were really grateful. Those gifts made our Christmas." A little later, Amy, the second-oldest daughter, came home and asked where all the gifts had come from. When she was told, she laughed and said that her two dollars had seemed so little that she had given up trying to find anything presentable for her sisters and had donated the money to the Arctic League.

That winter, James did whatever odd-job work he could find, and he also earned some extra money from a treasure trove he found when he removed a pile of trash behind the small barn on their property — some old bottles, just under the topsoil, that turned out to be of Civil War vintage and worth a few dollars apiece. Members of the Elmira Meeting of the Religious Society of Friends gave him antiques and secondhand furniture, and he sold those, too. Mrs. James took private orders for knitting and sewing, and with welfare aid the family got through the winter.

Toward the end of that period, Neva and Charles James finally came to realize that they could not continue to base their lives on the expectancy of a favorable decision on his case. "We once had the idea that it would be just a little while more before the case was settled and we were back on our feet, but it had gone on for so long that we knew we just couldn't wait any longer," Mrs. James explained. "We knew by then that a decision wouldn't change what had happened to us and our family."

Neuborne had submitted his appeal from the District Court ruling to the Court of Appeals for the Second Circuit, in Manhattan, early that winter, and the court set a date for a hearing on the case at the beginning of May, 1972. Mrs. James didn't want to go to it. "By then, I'd seen that we were living two lives, and I was determined to stop it," she said. Finally, though, she decided to go to the hearing — not so much for the event itself as to get the chance to see some of their old friends from the days, a few years before, when they had lived in New York City.

One of their friends in Manhattan was away at the time of their visit, and he lent them his apartment, stocked with steaks, the kinds of delicacies they hadn't been able to afford for years, and several bottles of their favorite Riesling. Some old friends dropped by soon after they arrived, and a party was arranged for the following night. "I got a feeling of being home again," Mrs. James said afterward. "It wasn't the city, it was the people who made me feel appreciated and needed, instead of like a case. For two and a half years, I had felt like the wife of a forty-odd-year-old father of four and English teacher who had been fired for wearing a black armband to school." Her sense of euphoria lasted through that day and into the next. The following morning, the Jameses took a subway to Foley Square. "We came up from underground into the thrill of New York, and I was just bubbling," Mrs. James said. "I was going to court, and for the first time it didn't matter to me how the case came out."

James felt much the same way, until they reached the courtroom where his case was to be heard, in the federal courthouse. Neuborne's assistant was on hand, but Neuborne wasn't. He had been tied up in Washington because of an urgent summons the afternoon before from Justice Marshall, who wanted to discuss a case pending before the Supreme Court, and was then on his way to New York by plane. The assistant explained to the Jameses that usually the three-judge panels of the Court of Appeals held hearings only during morning sessions, and that if Neuborne didn't arrive soon the case might be either postponed for several weeks, and probably end up with another panel of judges, or be assigned then and there to the assistant for argument.

"I was frightened – desperate, really," James said. "I knew that I couldn't emotionally stand another delay. I also knew that the panel we had drawn was one of the best we could hope for. And I knew that the assistant didn't have Neuborne's grasp of the case." The problem was quickly resolved, for when the three judges on the case were told about the delay and the reason for it they cheerfully agreed to wait for Neuborne and to reconvene after lunch.

James was greatly relieved, but then he was suddenly overcome by some of the deepest emotions he had felt since he first wore the armband. "At that point, I realized that I cared very much about my own vindication — not about Neva or the children or mankind but about *me*," he said. "Then, a couple of minutes later, I became strangely absorbed by abstract concerns — the whole mural of history and the hope for justice over the centuries seemed to unroll before me. How many people, I wondered, have waited just to have a fair hearing? I became aware at that moment that there is so much suffering, so much hope held by those who seek justice. Once you experience misfortune and lose control over your life, even in a very small way, you come to see how big a community you belong to. Then you realize that most of those who have seen misfortune haven't even tongues to speak of it, let alone the power to do anything about it. That I had been able to do something about it made me feel a little better. But I was still terribly agitated by it all. Finally, I had to get away from everyone, and I went out into the hall and looked out the window across Foley Square and on uptown. I kept asking myself, 'Is it necessary that men go through this forever without any change?' I don't know the answer. I don't understand why it is that we can build snowmobiles and go to the moon but we can't handle injustice."

Neuborne reached the courtroom at a little before one o'clock, and when the judges returned to the bench, at two o'clock, he rose, formally introduced himself, and delivered a brief statement on James's behalf — mainly devoted to the assertion that his act of wearing a black armband to school to protest the killing in Vietnam was a case of symbolic expression protected by the First Amendment and had caused no disruption in the school.

Then Treinin got up and spoke at length on the many points covered in his brief. The judges had asked Neuborne only a few questions, but they pressed Treinin again and again on his various claims — especially on his contention that James's armband had been a divisive and potentially disruptive symbol. At one point, Judge Irving R. Kaufman, then the senior member of the panel and now Chief Judge of the Second Circuit, asked Treinin whether he would have felt that James had been justifiably fired if the Quakers who prepared and wore black armbands had decided instead to wear black ties and James had done that. Without hesitation, Treinin answered, "Yes, Your Honor." The judges looked amused. Later, when Treinin raised his favorite spectre – of a violent confrontation when fifty faculty members turned up at a public school like Addison High with half of them wearing black armbands and half of them wearing red-white-and-blue sashes – the three judges looked even more amused. And when Treinin made his favorite legal argument – that the case was *res judicata* and could not properly be considered by the federal courts – Kaufman swivelled his chair around impatiently.

The Jameses watched and listened with awe. "The judges asked really hard questions, and made points that neither lawyer had even mentioned," Mrs. James said. "It was clear that they had really studied the case, and understood every facet of it. People had kept telling us that this was an important case, but I couldn't believe that it was important to anyone but us. Then, as I listened to the arguments, I realized that it *was* important to the judges, and that they were as concerned about the act of wearing a black armband as they would have been if a life were at stake."

After the hearing, Treinin rushed up to Neuborne in the corridor outside the courtroom and cried, "It's going to the Supreme Court! It's going to the Supreme Court!"

Realizing that he believed he had lost, Mrs. James turned to him and said, "Oh, come on, Mr. Treinin. You've won twice. We ought to have at least one!"

Treinin ignored her and exclaimed to Neuborne, "It'll be five to four! Five to four!"

When Treinin left, Mrs. James turned to Neuborne and asked, "Is there any chance that Charles will finally win?"

Neuborne looked at her wearily, nodded and shrugged at the same time, and answered, "We have to believe there's *some* justice."

The Jameses' delight with their visit to New York, the renewal of old friendships, and the apparent outcome of the hearing ebbed away as soon as they got home. "We were back in the other of our two lives," Mrs. James said. "Then we heard that Brown, the district principal, was telling people that even if the Court of Appeals ruled against the school the decision wouldn't be forthcoming for at least six months. That meant Charles wouldn't be reinstated in his job before Christmas. I just knew I couldn't stand it that long."

To everyone's surprise, the Court of Appeals delivered its decision in less than three weeks, on May 24th. The ruling was unanimous, and reversed the finding of the District Court, which was ordered to conduct "proceedings not inconsistent with this opinion." Neuborne telephoned James with news of the victory, and told him that he would be back at work in his old job when school opened in the fall and that he might also be paid his salary retroactively – some twenty-five thousand dollars in all. "We were living completely on welfare then – in fact, things had never been worse for us when word of the reversal came in," Mrs. James said. "We were absolutely ecstatic and danced a wild jig."

The Court of Appeals based its decision in the James case solely on the issue of freedom of speech. Judge Kaufman wrote the opinion, which began, "The First Amendment proscription against any law abridging freedom of expression, perhaps more than any other constitutional guarantee, frequently brings into sharp focus the inexorable tension between enduring concerns for individual freedom and the authority required to preserve the democracy so crucial to realizing that freedom. For several decades, the courts have struggled with principles and concepts necessary to strike a functional balance between protected speech and the government's legitimate interest in protecting our democracy."

In other words, the court's decision was to rest on the balancing test, which indicated that Judge Kaufman and his colleagues were not proposing to break any new ground in *their* struggles with principles and concepts. His formulation of the test revealed more about the problem than about the solution: "Any limitation on the exercise of constitutional rights can be justified only by a conclusion, based upon reasonable inferences flowing from concrete facts and not abstractions, that the interests of discipline or sound education are materially and substantially jeopardized, whether the danger stems initially from the conduct of students or teachers." Of course, different students and teachers, different school officials, different judges, and different jurors might interpret "reasonable," "interests of discipline," "sound education," "materially and substantially jeopardized," or "stems" in different ways.

The court's decision relied heavily, as Neuborne had predicted, on the matter of disruption or the lack of it. In the second paragraph of the opinion, Judge Kaufman approvingly noted that James's appeal "is quick to agree that . . . disruptive activities on the part of teachers or students which threaten the essential functions of our schools" should not be tolerated. Then, at seven places in the seventeen-page decision, the Judge pointed out that James's armband had created no disruption whatever. In short, since the state had not been abused in any manner, the individual was free. At several points in the opinion, Judge Kaufman also paid rhetorical obeisance to the hallowed tradition of a marketplace of ideas, and observed that since another teacher at Addison High School was permitted to post a "Peace with Honor" sign on his classroom bulletin board, the school's "actions under such circumstances would indicate that its regulation against political activity in the classroom may be no more than the fulcrum to censor only that expression with which it disagrees." On the question of Treinin's favorite point — that the case was *res judicata* — the opinion said, "We consider this to be wholly without merit." And Treinin's nearly total reliance on the Goldwasser case as a precedent was dismissed in a footnote as "clearly inapposite."

While the decision vindicated James, it so narrowly circumscribed the rights of teachers in general that it was ultimately another victory for the state over the individual. In the long run, Treinin and his clients, who believed they had lost, had actually won, for the ruling could later be used by the conservative — or statist — side they represented as a precedent for restricting personal rights. Among the main participants in the case, Neuborne alone viewed the decision as an extremely dangerous triumph for one man. "What the court really said was that if a citizen's self-expression has any appreciable effect, it falls outside the protection guaranteed by the First Amendment," he explained. "James's act was upheld only because it was futile."

A few days after the decision came down, Treinin appealed to the Chief Judge of the Court of Appeals for the Second Circuit, Henry J. Friendly, one of the nation's most respected conservative jurists, for an *en-banc* hearing before all nine members of that court to reconsider the ruling. Legally speaking, the request was pointless, for ordinarily such a hearing is granted only if a case is of great and urgent importance. But the move indicated that Treinin and Brown were prepared to go to almost any lengths to stop James from returning to work at Addison High School. As expected, the request was turned down, in July, whereupon Treinin vowed to take the issue of reinstatement and back pay to trial when the case was returned to the District Court. Of course, the Court of Appeals ruling that James had been illegally dismissed contained the implicit conclusion that he was entitled to get his job back. But since that conclusion had not been stated explicitly, his adversaries were able to skirt the obvious meaning of the judgment until a direct order was given them, and they refused to reinstate James voluntarily.

Neuborne faced a twofold problem: on the one hand, he wanted to make sure that he obtained such an order before the school year began, so that his client would get his job back in time; and, on the other hand, he didn't want to go before Judge Burke, who had ruled against James in District Court earlier. Fortunately, Burke went on vacation the first of August, and Neuborne's motion for reinstatement was heard a few days later, in the District Court in Buffalo, before Judge John T. Curtin. Treinin argued that if James was reinstated and then dismissed after another court appeal, this would disrupt the educational process. It was a curious defense for circumventing the law, and Judge Curtin rejected it.

He also rejected the claim that many issues of fact in the case had still not been settled, since, he observed in his ruling, Treinin "was unable to specify at oral argument what those issues are."

Accordingly, the Judge ordered James reinstated at once in his job for the 1972–73 school year, and warned, "The court will not entertain an application for a stay of this order." The school board obeyed, and James was given back his job, at a salary of nine thousand seven hundred and ninety dollars a year.

A couple of days later, rumors began going around that a mob was being organized to ride James out of Addison on a rail if he appeared at the school. A woman teacher there vowed that she would not remain on the faculty if James rejoined it, and a male teacher swore to "get" him. Mrs. James learned from some sympathetic teachers at the school of a plan to provoke a confrontation between James and the town, so that it could later be shown in court that he was a disruptive influence. Frightened by this prospect, she telephoned Neuborne, and he immediately called Brown to say that neither James nor he sought any trouble and that both of them felt that the disagreement could be settled and relations resumed amicably between the two sides. To help out, Neuborne offered to fly to Elmira and speak before the residents of Addison to explain the law and appeal for common sense and calm. Brown flatly rejected the offer, saying that Neuborne's appearance there would only inflame the opposition. The situation was serious, he went on, and he asked Neuborne to stay away from the town.

Afterward, Neuborne wondered if the threat to keep James out of the school was real. "I think they were trying to make it seem worse than it was to keep the board's side whipped up," he said. "There may have been half a dozen of the usual local loudmouths — Legionnaire types, mostly — but I'm sure the threat was mostly noise. People like that are the first to moan about the lack of law and order. They certainly want order — as long as it's *their* kind of order—but they don't give a damn about the law."

Proof of this attitude emerged a couple of days later, when Brown announced that James would supervise six study halls and a lunch period — in other words, he would not be given back his teaching job as the court had ordered. Neuborne warned Treinin that if this flatly illegal maneuver was carried out, he would ask Judge Curtin for a contempt-of-court citation and a stiff fine. At that, Brown agreed to give James some classes to teach. On Neuborne's urging, James went to talk to Brown about what courses might be assigned to him, and to his surprise Brown was friendly and offered to coöperate fully. According to James, he said that he would speak to some of the other English teachers and ask them if they had any electives that they might give to James. Only a couple of weeks remained for James to prepare any courses he might teach, but he heard nothing more from Brown.

On orientation day — the day before the school opened for that year — James arrived early and checked his mailbox to see if there was any word from Brown. There wasn't. Then James talked to all the members of the English department and asked if anything had been said to them about giving up electives. Nothing had been. A number of them told him that they would be delighted to give up a course or even two, so James went to discuss the matter with Brown.

As soon as he broached it, Brown asked what pressure he had exerted on these teachers. "You may think you're going to take over my school, but I'm still running it," Brown told him.

James denied that he had any desire to be anything but an English teacher. Finally, Brown told him that he could have two or three elective courses if anybody signed up for them, and three or four study halls, and that if this approach didn't work he would consider taking classes away from other teachers and giving them to James.

"Since he had been so full of pedagogic theory in my case," James said later, "I told him that it seemed unsound educational practice to start students off with one teacher and then switch them around later." Infuriated by the remark, Brown said that he could not understand a man who stayed on where he wasn't wanted, and that he wouldn't work there for another day if the school board didn't want him around. "Brown didn't seem to have the faintest idea that I wasn't working for him," James remarked. "I suppose it never occurred to him that I was working for the students."

That fall term James was given two elective courses – one in modern poetry, with ten students, and one in public speaking, with two students; of course, it is impossible to teach public speaking unless the class is large enough to serve as an audience.

At the end of September, Treinin submitted a petition for a writ of certiorari – that is, a request for a review of the case – to the Supreme Court. The petition was largely a rehash of the arguments he had made before the lower courts. The Supreme Court denied his petition on December 4th, and as usual in such cases gave no explanation for the denial. Treinin immediately petitioned the Court to reconsider its decision. This time, he relied almost entirely on the thoroughly discredited contention that the case was *res judicata.* Early in January, 1973, the Supreme Court turned down this plea, too.

Despite the intransigence and hostility demonstrated on all sides, Neuborne clung to the hope that if those involved were given enough time they might work out their anger, settle their differences decently, and let things return to normal. Above all, he hoped that they wouldn't have to go back to court. "It's still possible that Brown and the members of the school board will begin to ease off, and start being civilized," he explained. "If they keep James on and give him at least a fair chance, I'm sure that he'll give up his right to back pay, and everything will be smoothed over. What has bothered me from the start of this case is what bothers me in all civil-liberties cases: everybody becomes so absorbed by issues and principles that they forget what is happening to the individual. I've tried desperately to end this case at every stage, and not make a big thing out of it. We've won an important case, but I'd happily give that up if all this could be erased. The crucial point – what we've been battling over – is Charles James's inherent right to a decent and meaningful life. But the battle itself has almost destroyed that right. Charles James is Humpty-Dumpty on the wall. Five years from now, some law professor will cite the

James case as the great turning point in the fight for teachers' rights. But that won't do Charles any good. If he falls off that wall now, all the law in the world won't put his life back together again."

At Addison High School, James's life was a quiet, unrelenting torment. School officials refused to have any direct contact with him, and dealt with him through administrative memoranda on the most trivial subjects. James assumed that he was being harassed in this manner in the expectation that he would finally react in a sufficiently intemperate way to justify his dismissal. To avoid the slightest misstep, he got Neuborne's advice on how he should answer every memorandum, and the need for that kind of constant consultation on such insignificant matters further reduced James's drained self-confidence and further increased the distance between the two sides.

During this period, Mrs. James watched her husband with increasing anxiety. "Charles is very constrained," she told a visitor at the time. "He has to be extremely careful about everything he says and does – even the slightest inflection in tone or the smallest act. He always used to rely on his wit as an escape valve at times of trouble, but now he's even afraid to make jokes, because anything might get him into more trouble. Now he has no outlet and no one to talk to openly except me. Fortunately, I'm not subject to this isolation and harassment. We have enough money to live on again, and I'm at home and free to do what I want to do – work in my garden and sew and cook and look after the children. But Charles is terribly frustrated. For instance, the teachers at Addison are negotiating a new contract right now, and he was asked to help represent them. They think that because he won his case he knows how to do things. Charles has had to refuse to get involved in any way, and has remained strictly neutral. At the same time, he doesn't want to insult them by seeming to be uninterested, so he's had to listen patiently to them hour after hour without being able to say what he thinks. And the kids at school sense his frustration, so they go to him with *their* frustrations. The same is true of some of the teachers, who come to him privately to complain about the school administration. He can't say or do anything to help them, either. So in the end he has been given all these other people's troubles to add to his own."

The Jameses had only a few close friends left — most of them fellow-Quakers from the Elmira Meeting. In the spring of 1973, a couple of these people hinted that perhaps James should do what his enemies wanted — get out of the area and settle someplace else where he and his family could start again. But James refused to listen. For one thing, there was the farm that he and Neva had bought for a few thousand dollars and had fought to save and make into a place of their own, and he could not bring himself to dig up their only roots. But, far more important, he felt that his manhood was at stake. He had grown into middle age trying to live decently and thoughtfully, and, as Neuborne remarked, "he had suddenly found himself facing the schoolyard bully again." James knew that if he backed down and walked away from the fight now, he would sacrifice not just the bitter years he and his family had struggled through but the little self-respect he had left.

When it became clear, early in 1973, that the school board would not voluntarily give James the back pay due him, Neuborne decided that he might have to make an additional appeal to the District Court for an order instructing the board to make up for the lost income. At that point, there were three legal possibilities: first, a summary judgment by a District Court judge one way or the other on the merits of the issue; second, a trial before that judge; or, third, a trial before a federal jury. The decision on which course would be followed lay with the District Court, and once again the key to the case was the question of whether or not James's act of wearing a black armband to school had caused any disruption there.

"The facts in this case have gone undisputed for three and a half years," Neuborne said at the time, "and to change them now would seriously raise the question of whether the principals on the other side were telling the truth in the first place." Since the Court of Appeals had unanimously concluded that there was not "a scintilla of evidence" to suggest there had been any disruption, he added, the District Court would be obliged to weigh that conclusion heavily in its consideration of the case. Under federal rules, moreover, any decision by the District Court would be reviewable by the Court of Appeals, and at least one of the judges there who originally heard the case would have to be included in the review panel. These factors put the odds strongly in James's favor. What unbalanced them the other way, however, was the chance that a District Court judge would agree to a motion by Treinin for a jury trial. In that event, the jury might be allowed to decide what "disruption" meant on a factual basis, and might rule against James on any of a number of unpredictable grounds.

To protect James as fully as possible against this last eventuality, Neuborne flew out to Elmira and took depositions from Carl Pillard, James's immediate supervisor, and Brown. This procedure – known in legal circles as "discovery" – is designed to enable litigants to learn what their opponents have in mind (in this case, what Brown might mean by "disruption") and to pin them down to a specific, recorded story so that they cannot change their approach later on if things seem to be going badly for them in court. Neuborne suspected Brown and Pillard would now claim that the armband had caused some kind of "psychological disruption," and they did. After the depositions were completed, he was jubilant. "They just kept making charges, but they don't have any evidence at all," he said. "They haven't the beginnings of a case, so I'm going to ask the court for a summary judgment in James's favor."

Once again, though, Neuborne put off going back to court, in the hope that the school board might still settle the case out of court. Two days after the depositions were taken, however, the local superintendent of schools informed James by letter that his appointment at Addison High School would end on June 30, 1973, and would not be renewed. When Neuborne learned about this, he telephoned Treinin to ask that he be permitted to speak on James's behalf at the school board's hearing on the superintendent's recommendation, and Treinin persuaded the members of the board to agree – presumably because if they refused to even listen to Neuborne this might be held against them in District Court.

Neuborne appeared before the board at an open meeting held on the evening of May 7th. Speaking calmly and expressing sympathy for the board under such trying circumstances, he asked that the members consider giving James a fair chance to show his abilities as a teacher by allowing him to teach at Addison High on a normal schedule the following school year. "He's an experienced teacher, who has never before – ever – had it suggested that he's not an English teacher of the highest competence," Neuborne said. "I frankly have no desire to see this become a test case any more, or to run back into court. I hope you believe me when I say this is true – that what I want is I want this thing to go away, and I want everybody to be able to return to the kinds of lives that they can lead in a community like this, where Mr. James can be of value and an accepted member of the faculty. . . . Whatever can possibly be done to keep situations like this out of court should be done to keep it out of court. It's a rotten way to solve problems. It's inefficient and it polarizes people. It makes people say and do things that they don't really mean. And what I'm hoping that we can do tonight is arrive at a way in which Mr. James can be permitted to have his professional credentials tested in the same way that you would test any other person that comes into Addison, and that's to give him a full year's teaching and not a truncated, very abnormal teaching experience, at the end of which, on the basis of a rather short observation, judgment is passed on his competence as a teacher. Back in '69, he obviously acted out of the deepest ethical, moral, and religious scruples. Again, we can either agree or disagree with them, but – by this time and with what he's been through – I don't think anyone now can question the deepness of sincerity that drove him to do what he did back in 1969. His family has been through a tremendous ordeal, and I hope that we can now put it behind us and let him return and be the kind of teacher that I'm sure, and that based on his past record, he can be. I don't want to see him suffer any more for what was truly an act of principle, which harmed no one, and which, I would hope, would not continue to be carried against him."

The board then went into executive session, with both Brown and Treinin present and both James and Neuborne excluded.

Neuborne protested that the arrangement was "dreadfully unfair" and against an explicit order on such matters handed down the year before by the Supreme Court. The members of the board ignored him, and after deliberating in private for half an hour they emerged and Treinin announced that they had reconfirmed their earlier decision. The reason, he explained, was what happened when James was temporarily suspended for wearing the armband the first time and then was allowed to return to his job on the condition that he would not engage in any more political activity. "He came back," Treinin said, "didn't say a word to the board, and he broke his promise" by wearing the armband again a month later. As it happened, James had made no promise and, in fact, could not have made such a promise, since he claimed from the outset that his reasons for wearing the armband were wholly moral and religious and had nothing to do with politics. Treinin also charged that James had not even mentioned his religious convictions until many months after he was fired. That was also false.

Treinin then said to Neuborne, "So do you see, Burt, why perhaps this board, in all good conscience, looks with a rather jaundiced eye on any commitment that Mr. James might make?"

For the first time in his legal career, Neuborne lost his temper. Getting to his feet slowly, he said, in a voice shaking with anger, "I wasn't present in that meeting, and I don't know what allegations were made about Mr. James's principles or not. I do know this: He's probably the most principled man it's ever been my privilege to meet, and has suffered grievously for four years because of those principles. I think this board is committing an unconscionable act in continuing what is a personal vendetta by Mr. Brown against Mr. James."

"Oh, please!" Treinin cried.

Neuborne waved him aside and went on, "Let me say this now. I will not tolerate —"

"No, please, Burt —" Treinin begged.

"I have conducted this litigation up until this time under the assumption that we were dealing here with an abstract question of law in which there was no animus whatever —"

"There isn't! There isn't!"

Neuborne ignored him and went on, "I want to say now that on the basis of not being permitted into that executive session, not knowing what happened in there, and on the basis of Mr. Treinin's, essentially, character assassination of Mr. James —"

"Oh, no!" Treinin shouted.

"Good faith?" Neuborne asked, looking contemptuously at Treinin. "He said he vows his good faith!"

"I do! I do! I do!"

"I call that character assassination," Neuborne told him. Then, turning back to the members of the board, he said, "I now consider that the future litigation in this case just cannot be continued on the same terms and conditions that we continued in the past. I want to put the board on notice, and I want to put Mr. Brown on notice, that I no longer seek damages from this board in an institutional setting. I seek personal and individual damages from you, because I consider that you violated James's constitutional rights. And I will take every step within my power to see to it that those rights are protected. Good day, gentlemen."

Without the help of the American Civil Liberties Union and its state and local branches, James would never have been able to fight for his rights; the fee for private legal representation in his case, for instance, could have run upward of fifty thousand dollars. At the same time, though, the various offices of the Union are invariably short on staff and funds, and often clients have to wait for more important or pressing cases to be disposed of before theirs are attended to. Throughout the summer of 1973, Neuborne was completely tied up on such a case — an effort by four Air Force pilots and Representative Elizabeth Holtzman to persuade the federal courts to declare the American bombing of Cambodia illegal. As a result, it wasn't until mid-September that he got back to the James case. Neuborne filed a motion before the District Court in which he asked for a summary judgment ordering that James be reinstated once more in his job and given his salary for the two and a half years that he was illegally deprived of it.

At the beginning of October, Brown submitted an affidavit to the District Court stating that the Addison school board had no authority to grant James tenure. James hadn't asked for tenure and had, in fact, offered to waive tenure even if he seemed to be technically entitled to it once he was reinstated. Brown also claimed that to reinstate James at that point would disrupt the school — a concern that hadn't seemed to bother him when he suspended James and got him fired. Then Treinin submitted a brief opposing Neuborne's motion. In sum, it contended that a trial on the issue would show "that damages done to the students by 'inherent psychological disruption' may be greater than that inflicted by the physical disruption of a classroom riot." In rebuttal, Neuborne pointed out that there was no evidence of any kind of disruption, but Treinin insisted that there was. "The physical marks that may result [from such a riot] will soon heal," he wrote. "Not so with thoughts implanted in the mind of the student. Once instilled, without opposing ideas on the subject, it becomes the core for the thinking of the student on the issue presented, unopposed by differing points of view. . . . No greater disruption can be envisioned in the educational context than that students be exposed only to a single point of view on great political issues."

At the end of October, District Court Judge Burke, who had originally heard the case and summarily dismissed James's complaint, disqualified himself from participating in the case. When Chief Judge John O. Henderson took over, Neuborne assumed that he would quickly, and favorably, dispose of the matter, since back in August he had ruled, in a similar case, that a teacher who was illegally dismissed was entitled to full back pay. On November 17th, Judge Henderson held a hearing on Neuborne's motion and reserved judgment. The rest of November and then December and January passed without word. Appalled by what seemed to be judicial neglect of a citizen who had already suffered needlessly from the law's delay, Neuborne contemplated asking for an immediate judgment. He also considered filing an official, and public, complaint before the Court of Appeals about the District Court's intolerable and unnecessary delay and the hardship it imposed on his client. Before he could do either, however, he received word, on February 19, 1974, that Judge Henderson had died. Apparently, his illness had been the major cause of the delay.

Judge Henderson's death and Judge Burke's disqualification left only one judge in that court to handle the case – John T. Curtin, who had ordered James reinstated in his job back in August, 1972, following the Court of Appeals' decision. Neuborne waited a decent interval after learning about Henderson's death, and then, on March 14, 1974, wrote Judge Curtin a letter outlining the facts in the James case and asking for a speedy disposition. "Mr. James has been unable to secure a teaching job, and his family is, therefore, in serious financial straits," Neuborne wrote in conclusion. "While Mr. James' economic plight should in no way affect your judgment on the merits of his motions, I hope that it will prove relevant to a determination of the speed with which action may be taken in this case."

Judge Curtin invited the opposing lawyers to join him in his chambers to discuss the case on April 1st. The result of the meeting was that he agreed to hold a one-day trial, on May 14th, without a jury. He said that he would hear Treinin's arguments on the question of the "psychological disruption" that might have been caused by James's black armband and then would allow two expert witnesses to testify in support of this position. After that, the Judge went on, he would either render summary judgment or, if the defendants' arguments seemed to raise serious questions, he would allow Neuborne a chance to offer a rebuttal and to present two expert witnesses of his own on the other side. In any event, the Judge made clear, he would deliver his decision soon after the day's testimony.

In the corridor outside Judge Curtin's chambers, Neuborne got into a discussion of the case with Treinin and told him that under a recent Supreme Court ruling James was entitled to, and that he intended to, sue Brown and two other school officials as individuals for depriving him of his constitutional rights. Treinin seemed stunned, and asked Neuborne why he was behaving so vindictively. "Because I believe your clients have acted in bad faith in this whole matter from the beginning," Neuborne said.

On April 9th, Neuborne filed a motion to consolidate James's earlier claim for back pay with the new claim that the defendants had illegally and intentionally deprived him of his right of free speech under the First Amendment and of his right to due process of law, on several counts, under the Fourteenth Amendment. For this, Neuborne contended, James was entitled not only to his back pay but to "compensatory" damages of fifty thousand dollars and to "punitive" damages of twenty-five thousand dollars from each of the three defendants.

On May 13th, Treinin responded by asking the court to try the cases separately — the first one, for back pay, before Judge Curtin alone, and the second one, for compensatory and punitive damages, before a jury — so that the facts in one would not influence the jury about the facts in the other. Because of the new issue that Neuborne had brought up, Judge Curtin postponed the trial on the subject of back pay — set for May 14th — to an unspecified time. Eight days after that trial was to have taken place, Neuborne told the court that he accepted the defendants' proposal to separate the two trials but asked that the case involving back pay be resolved as soon as possible "to alleviate the serious financial distress under which the James family is now laboring." The other case, Neuborne said, could wait. A few days later, Judge Curtin asked both sides to submit their papers on the various issues to him by June 17th. Neuborne hoped that the Judge would hold the trial on back payment at once, and that a jury trial on the other issues would be held sometime in the summer.

In response to James's back-pay suit, Treinin claimed, as expected, that the black armband had caused "inherent psychological disruption" among students at Addison High School. During the trial, which was finally held in July, 1974, and lasted two and a half days, Treinin tried to demonstrate this point — not by presenting as witnesses the students who might have suffered from such disruptions or teachers who had observed these traumatic effects upon their charges but by putting two "expert witnesses" from the State Education Department on the stand. One of them was Anthony E. Terino, director of the Division of School Supervision and holder of an honorary Doctor of Letters degree from the College of Mount St. Vincent, in Riverdale, who testified at great length about the malignant effect on young minds that could be expected when only one side of a controversial issue was presented to them.

"Now, the wearing of anything that represents one side of an issue is in a certain sense, a form of indoctrination – you might call it a form of propaganda," he said at one point, and he later added, "If we allow indoctrination to take place, where do we stop? This is precisely what happened in Nazi Germany."

The other expert witness for the defense, Thomas D. Sheldon, who was deputy commissioner for elementary, secondary, and continuing education, concentrated on the same point. When asked what he thought about James's wearing an armband to school, he said, "I think it was very, very poor pedagogy."

On cross-examination, Neuborne quoted from the Court of Appeals' decision – "It does not appear from the record that any student believed the armband to be anything more than a benign symbolic expression of the teacher's personal views" – and asked Sheldon if he knew of any documentation or even investigation of the mysterious effects that were claimed for the armband.

"No, I do not," Sheldon answered.

Brown also testified about the pressing need for assuring that students be given a chance to hear all sides of controversial issues. Neuborne asked him how many teachers were on the faculty of Addison High School, and Brown said that there were a hundred.

"In the high school there were ninety-nine teachers not wearing an armband and one teacher wearing an armband on Moratorium Day, would that be accurate?" Neuborne asked.

"I assume so," Brown answered.

"And you thought you would aid the students of that school to see all points of view by having the one teacher take off his armband?"

"I don't understand your logic, Mr. Neuborne."

Brown stated that he could have seen some justification for James's wearing the armband if it had borne some relation to the subject he was teaching but that he could see no way to connect a black armband with poetry. Neuborne then asked Brown about a physics teacher at the school who had pinned a bumper sticker saying "PEACE WITH HONOR" to his classroom bulletin board. Brown replied that the quotation didn't seem to him to be "a political thing," and added, "However, I can envision where, within a physics class, this might be an appropriate topic for conversation and instruction, especially as it relates to the use of atomic-war materials."

Because of the James family's continuing privation, which was repeatedly cited in the court records of the case, Neuborne hoped that the Judge would act promptly to alleviate the Jameses' hardship, which, after all, had been created by an illegal act on the part of the state. And, because of the obvious flimsiness of the defendants' claims in the suit for back pay, Neuborne also expected the Judge to resolve the simple issue involved by deciding in James's favor at the end of the trial. However, it wasn't until more than four months later that the Judge, whose calendar had been unusually full, finally announced his decision – by way of a twenty-six-page opinion stating, in brief, that James's act had caused "neither actual disruption nor the slightest threat of it." Accordingly, Judge Curtin ordered that James be paid his school salary for the two and a half years that he had been unlawfully deprived of his job – a total of $26,804.50. But then the Judge subtracted the income James had received during this period – $5,840.25. That left him with an award of $20,964.25.

To make up for this loss, Neuborne asked that interest of $6,088.32 plus "reasonable" legal fees be added to the award. Treinin angrily opposed both, and when Judge Curtin granted the requests, Treinin appealed the entire decision on the case to the Court of Appeals for the Second Circuit. Although that court was exceedingly unlikely to reverse itself by upholding the defendants' claims about disruption, Neuborne warned James that Treinin might appeal an adverse Court of Appeals decision to the Supreme Court, however hopeless such a move would be, that in a trial of the suit for compensatory and punitive damages a conservative upstate jury might find against James, and that even if he won such a case Treinin would probably start the long train of appeals all over again – in short, that the case could go on for a couple of years more.

Oral arguments on Treinin's appeal from the District Court's judgments were to be held before the Court of Appeals in New York City on April 9, 1975. In late March, the two sides were summoned to that court to discuss the issues informally with a referee, under a new system that was set up to encourage out-of-court settlements in such cases as a means of relieving congested court calendars. The two sides got nowhere. At the end of the meeting, Treinin asked Neuborne what his client would settle the whole case for, and Neuborne hastily calculated that if no further court action was necessary an acceptable sum would be fifty-five thousand dollars. That was impossible, Treinin snapped, and stalked off. But then, four days before the oral arguments were to be held, he telephoned Neuborne and said that his clients had consented to pay James fifty-five thousand dollars as a final settlement for all his claims.

Neuborne passed the offer on to James, who was reluctant to accept it, because he believed that any settlement should include his reinstatement at Addison High School. Actually, he had no intention of going back to work there, but he felt that he should hold out for reinstatement both as a matter of principle and in order to set a precedent for teachers who might be similarly denied their rights in the future. However, his wife finally persuaded him that, principle or no principle, it was dishonest to hold out for something that he had no intention of accepting, and he told Neuborne to take the offer. James added that he would like to have fifty thousand dollars and that the A.C.L.U. could keep anything over that amount as legal fees. Neuborne then told Treinin that if he would add a thousand dollars to the offer, for printing costs incurred during the latest round of the case, the matter could be settled at once. The night before the oral arguments, Treinin agreed to this, so Neuborne drew up the final papers and informed the Court of Appeals that the case was being settled out of court.

Among the papers that Neuborne drafted was a statement to be signed by the defendants admitting that they had wrongfully deprived James of his constitutional rights and were paying the agreed-upon sum to make amends. Treinin indignantly rejected this proposal, and declared that his clients would never sign the statement. Again James was reluctant, as a matter of principle, to accept their offer unless they signed the statement. And again his wife urged him to settle the case on the proposed terms, so that they could put the affair behind them once and for all and start living for themselves rather than for one abstract principle after another. One thing they agreed on was that they would refuse any financial settlement if that would undermine a firm legal precedent, and Neuborne assured them that the precedent was now established. James had fought so long to vindicate a principle – his right to express his conscience – that he found it extremely difficult to settle for a sum of money. But he desperately needed the money, and when his wife became ill and was ordered into the hospital by her doctor for diagnostic tests, James finally gave in – as it happened, on Mother's Day – and told Neuborne to accept the offer.

By mid-May, the final papers were signed by all the principals, and on May 30th James received the first installment, a check for forty-six thousand dollars. By then, his wife was fully recovered. They paid off eight thousand dollars in debts and bought their twelve-year-old daughter a bicycle.

"I feel a kind of despair," Neva James said not long ago. "All this has made me finally accept something that I didn't want to believe: We can't trust our government anymore. We can't even trust it to obey its own rules. As far as the political process in this country goes, I have no confidence at all. At the same time, I have no illusions that we will be able to bring about change of any consequence. Maybe one student will see now, as a result of all this, that he has a right to stand up for what he believes in. But I don't have any hopes of changing people. All I have left is the hope that we can finally find a way to live simply and self-sufficiently, and stay out of it."

Charles James had a different reaction to what he had been through. "What's happening in this country today is that the government feels it can't allow people to be as important as the state," he said. "In a small way, I forced the state to recognize me, and to deal with me as an individual. That's the positive side of this case, because even though the state is blind and stupid and uncaring it still spent a lot of time and a lot of money trying to figure out what to do about a teacher who wore a black armband to school."

As for the question of whether it had been worth it to him, as a man, to stand up and fight for his rights, James had no doubts. "I didn't wear the armband to change anyone's mind," he explained. "I wore it only as a symbol of conscience. I didn't do it so I would lose my job, or to hurt my family, or to be a martyr. I did it because I had to live with myself. Politicians won't tell us the truth. Our local leaders won't tell us the truth. So a man who feels the truth has to tell it for himself. No man should take a simple statement of conscience away from another man. If I had walked out of Brown's office without my armband on, I would have been without identity or self-respect. And if I hadn't fought on I never would have felt free again."

Part Two

The Liberty of Every Man

I

Suspicion of outsiders is a peculiarly strong trait among people who live in mountains. In part, this suspicion may be traced back to the settlers of such places who sought, and handed down to their descendants, the kind of privacy that mountains naturally provide. Then, too, mountains are among the last places that the influence of civilization reaches, since commerce, which carries civilization in its baggage, invariably seeks the more accessible markets first. Before European civilization reached the region that is now called Kentucky, the land was so savagely fought over by Cherokee and Iroquois Indians that it became known among them as "the dark and bloody ground." The arrival of white men in the area did little to improve its reputation. In the Appalachian Mountains of Kentucky, history has transformed the inhabitants' inbred dislike of change and mistrust of outsiders into confirmed hatred and fear.

The historical event that began this process was the Civil War. As a Border State, Kentucky was legally, if not socially and economically, committed to slavery. In all, about a fifth of its population was made up of slaves, but in the mountains there were few blacks, there was the ingrained sense of independence that made an institution like slavery distasteful, and there was the old reluctance to have anything to do with the outside world. On the other hand, the mountain people regarded themselves as Southerners and resented the federal government's attempts to infringe on what they regarded as their sovereign rights. As with the other Border States, Kentucky's allegiance was desperately sought by the Union and the Confederacy, and although Kentucky did not secede from the Union, many of its citizens did. The cleavage that the war created among neighbors and friends and within families has still not been mended. "If a brother killed a brother during the bloody conflict, they were probably from Kentucky," a historian of the state has said.

During the Civil War, bands of mountaineers lay in wait along the Cumberland Gap — the main route south across the mountains — to "bushwhack" Northerners on their way south to join the Confederacy. At the same time, other bands of mountaineers raided Union camps and infantry units on the march, with such destructive effect that the Union commander in the area finally decreed that four Southern sympathizers would be shot for every Union soldier killed by raiders. When peace came at Appomattox, the mountain people suffered more severely than anyone else in the South. There was little food, and the money system collapsed. Pro-Confederate and pro-Union raiders consisting of local citizens turned into outlaws and went on fighting each other, stealing cattle and crops, burning and pillaging, and raping and murdering. Local government broke down completely, and the law belonged to whoever commanded the largest number of armed men.

After the war ended, the rapidly expanding industrial apparatus in the North and the railroad network spreading throughout the country created an immense need for fuel, and at the time the only practical fuel for industrial use was coal. Northern coalfields soon proved inadequate, and wages there were far higher than wages in the South, so the coalfields running through West Virginia and Kentucky were opened up in the latter part of the nineteenth century. The coal industry had to have some degree of social order to function — courts to define and enforce mining rights, towns to house miners and their families, and law-enforcement officers to maintain, or impose, peace. The industry got what it wanted, and before long despotism replaced anarchy and brought to the mountains worse turmoil, bloodshed, and despair than the war had.

Coal miners have generally led the struggle for trade-union recognition in the Western world, and have generally been among the last to appreciate the benefits. Few of them have suffered more for their efforts than the miners of the Appalachian Mountains. They fought for a decent share of the enormous wealth they produced, and coal-company owners fought back savagely, with a private army of "gun thugs," often led by Pinkerton agents backed by local and state police and, if needed, by federal troops. The miners' attempts to organize, beginning in earnest in the eighteen-nineties, led to battles that sound like a list on a Civil War memorial — the Matewan Massacre, Paint Creek, the Coal Creek Rebellion, the Battle of Evarts — and the armed warfare went on until the Second World War. Most coal towns were ramshackle, filthy places that were owned by the coal companies. Miners' rents, insurance payments, and bills at company-owned stores were deducted from their earnings, and on payday they often got no cash; to keep them at work in the mines, some coal companies paid them in scrip, which was worthless outside local company stores. Anyone who joined a union was immediately fired and evicted from his house or shack, and anyone who came into such towns to organize workers in trade unions was beaten or murdered.

It wasn't until passage of the National Labor Relations Act, in 1935, that coal miners were allowed to organize for collective bargaining, and even that modest victory didn't last for long. In the late forties, the coal business — suddenly beset by competition from cheaper and cleaner fuels like oil and natural gas and by the expectation that nuclear power would soon replace all other forms of industrial energy — collapsed. The only way to save even part of it was through mechanization, and the larger coal companies, which alone could afford the cost, quickly turned to mechanized mining. Many of them gave up, too, and sold out to independent operators, who kept the smaller mines open — but only on a non-union, take-it-or-leave-it basis. For the miners, it was either work for low wages again, go on welfare, or move to a Northern industrial city and look for some other kind of work.

In 1965, Harry Caudill, author of *Night Comes to the Cumberlands,* wrote:

> Thus, hordes of industrial workmen were left stranded in the mining communities. They were men who had been educated for the mines; their communities were poorly built and were without decent schools, hospitals, or roads. In the last decade the jerry-built communities have turned into people-sties. The land is scarred with crumbling shacks, tipples, commissaries, and culm heaps. The demoralized people, long dependent on public assistance for their bread, have littered the roadside and streams with countless automobile hulks and trash dumps. The creeks and rivers are reeking sewers.

Over the years that followed, the coal region of Appalachia sank even further into poverty and squalor. In the late nineteen-sixties, Pike County, Kentucky, the easternmost part of the state, had an adult-illiteracy rate of nearly one-fourth, and almost half of its families were officially designated as poor — a rate that put Pike County in the bottom three per cent of the nation in terms of family income. At the same time, Pike County produced more coal than any other county in the United States. One result of that production was that Pikeville, the county seat, with a population of less than five thousand, had more than sixty millionaires. While upward of a hundred million tons of coal are taken out of Kentucky mines each year — there are said to be thirty-three billion tons of coal under Kentucky — coal-mine owners there pay an annual license fee of only a hundred dollars per mine. Until a couple of years ago, local and state authorities made few attempts to impose a tax of even a few cents per ton of coal to repair some of the devastation left behind by the coal companies.

The greatest devastation of all has been left behind by strip miners, who began tearing off the surface of the mountains early in the nineteen-sixties. Essentially, strip mining amounts to contour plowing around mountainsides with bulldozers in order to uncover the edges of the coal deposits, which run in great horizontal seams through the hills, and then the coal is scooped up or dug out by other surface machines. During recent years, more than half the mining done in the area has been strip mining. In 1966, the Kentucky legislature passed a law to control strip mining. As it turned out, the law contained a few loopholes—"just big enough," one Kentucky conservationist has said, "to drive a coal train through." In the year following passage of the law, strip miners in Kentucky were licensed to strip twice the acreage stripped the year before the law was enacted.

The legal basis for strip mining is a document known as a broad-form mineral deed, which allows its possessor to dig from the earth any mineral deposits within a stipulated area and at the same time relieves him of any obligation to repair the damage done to the surface land in the course of such mining. Broad-form deeds were extensively used during the coal boom of the late nineteenth century, when unwary farmers sold the mineral rights to millions of acres of land for fifty cents an acre. The financial losses they suffered were, of course, immense, but at least the damage done to their land was comparatively modest, since coal mines were then entirely underground except for the entry pits and surrounding buildings. A couple of decades ago, however, courts began to allow the deeds to be used for strip mining—mainly in Kentucky, which is the only state that still recognizes them as legal. Anyone with a broad-form deed and enough capital to rent a bulldozer, a digger or auger, and a truck can move onto the property of a landowner whose ancestors leased it away, and strip the place of crops, timber, buildings, and all.

Strip mining has defaced much of the wild beauty of the mountains in Kentucky. Trees, boulders, and topsoil are ripped out and sent crashing down the mountainsides; heavy rains bring landslides that block roads and crush houses; rapid and irreparable erosion transforms the heavily wooded hills into barren rock; and in some areas the steady flow of acidic water from the coal kills all vegetation, fish, and wildlife as it seeps and pours down into the valleys.

The effect on the mountain people was described not long ago by one of them, a retired miner living in a small frame house set in a valley, or "hollow," below a strip-mining operation. "We can't get nothing done," he said. "The coal companies have most of the local lawyers on retainer. The lawyers say that the water and mud running on your property is God's work. We can't lie down and sleep at ease anymore. Every time it rains we get nervous—afraid of flood or rock or mud slides. I had a slide down by my house three months ago. A whole slide of earth filled the creek and almost covered the highway—some hundred and fifty feet to two hundred feet in length. We kept after them until they fixed it up a little. But they have stripped parts of the mountain down to bare rock. Now, how is that going to hold water coming down from a strip mine?"

Given the history of the Kentucky mountains, their inhabitants' attitude toward outsiders is hardly surprising. And yet, given local poverty and ignorance, which turned the region into what has sometimes been called a welfare reservation, the need for outside help has been compelling. In the mid-nineteen-sixties, President Johnson declared war on poverty, and the federal government opened its first front in Appalachia. A couple of years earlier, a group of students from Berea College, in Kentucky, began spending their weekends working for the poor in the hills and hollows—chiefly by painting and cleaning up dilapidated one-room schoolhouses and building some new schools to replace those beyond repair. The students called themselves Appalachian Volunteers, or A.V.s, and soon came to the attention of the Office of Economic Opportunity, which the President and Congress had set up to direct the anti-poverty program. By then, the A.V.s were sufficiently organized and operational to qualify for, and receive, O.E.O.'s first grant in the region.

Gradually, part-time college students were replaced by full-time employees in the three Appalachian states that were in the worst shape—Kentucky, West Virginia, and Virginia—and by 1967 there were sixty full-time Volunteers in the field, more than half of them in Kentucky, and the federal government was giving the outfit around a million dollars a year. Field workers were paid up to ten thousand dollars a year and provided with cars and small expense accounts, and "internes," or local trainees, got four thousand dollars a year. At the same time, the government sent scores of young men and women who had enlisted in the Peace Corps and in Volunteers in Service to America, or VISTA, the domestic equivalent of the Peace Corps, for training and work under direction of the A.V.s.

To a large extent, the anti-poverty effort was aimed at helping poor mountain people — almost all of them white — to go about getting what the law entitled them to: welfare assistance, Social Security benefits, Medicaid, Medicare, veterans' support, food stamps, and free-lunch programs in public schools. In addition, the A.V.s encouraged local citizens to set up coöperative stores, community centers, and production-and-sales facilities for local handicrafts. An O.E.O. official who worked with both the A.V.s and other anti-poverty groups in the mountains described the Appalachian Volunteers' project as "the most significant program in the area," and added, "There isn't much else going on. The local establishment is in total control of the community-action programs. No one else is willing to organize the poor to take on the power structure besides the A.V. crowd." In the past, he went on, poverty in the mountains had seemed an intractable problem, because the poorest of the poor lived hidden away in remote, almost inaccessible places and were seldom seen outside them. "The Volunteers went into the hollows and found them, talked to them, listened to them," he said.

The results were modest. The mountain people were even more suspicious of the newcomers than they had been of earlier intruders. Most of the Volunteers were recent college graduates or college students from the North, and some of them wore long hair and bizarre clothes. Local suspicion was further aroused by the participation of the federal government. Apart from some locally favored New Deal programs, in the past "the Feds" had meant war and conscription or, worse, Internal Revenue Service agents who went through the mountains smashing up stills and arresting moonshiners. Now local politicians began using this suspicion to block the federal program, which threatened their control and power. The more successful the program was, the more they opposed it, especially when the Volunteers pointedly ignored them and began working directly with the people. Until then, all federal funds for welfare programs had been funnelled through local authorities — sometimes loosely known as the courthouse gang — but suddenly they discovered that they were to have no say about policy and no access to the money that the A.V.s were to spend in the mountains.

The greatest threat emerged during the contest over strip mining. Local citizens who opposed strip mining got together and formed the Appalachian Group to Save the Land and People. In the spring of 1967, the A.V.s, who were given a fairly free rein by O.E.O., decided to join the fight against strip mining. "Our field men were getting a tremendous amount of community concern about it in every one of the ten counties where we were working," an A.V. official said. To a large extent, the A.V.s' move was designed to head off the growing resort to terrorism among local strip-mining opponents, some of whom formed small bands of men who dynamited strip-mining equipment left on site during the night and sniped at bulldozers and trucks by day. But local businessmen and politicians saw nothing constructive about the newly formed alliance against strip mining, and demanded that their representatives in Congress drive the war on poverty out of the mountains.

In June of 1967, the Puritan Coal Company was strip-mining a steep slope of land on Island Creek, not far from Pikeville. As the bulldozer ground on, back and forth and down the hill, a farmer named Jink Ray, whose property extended up into the area to be stripped, watched in mounting trepidation and anger. Rocks and rubble rolled down the hill closer and closer to his house, where he had lived for forty-six years, and he knew that in time rain would wash down more debris and uproot a stand of trees that were almost ready to be cut for timber, and that sooner or later erosion would undermine his house. Finally, on June 29th, the bulldozer reached his property line. Ray — a bespectacled, mild-mannered man — stepped in front of the bulldozer. The operator of the machine stopped and shouted at him. Ray stood fast. The operator raced the bulldozer's engine and lurched forward a couple of feet. Ray closed his eyes and stayed where he was – throughout that day. The strippers left, but the next morning they were back. Ray was waiting for them, this time accompanied by a handful of his neighbors. A man from Puritan showed Ray a broad-form deed, but he refused to accept its validity. The bulldozer operator was ordered to proceed, and as he did Ray and his friends stood before the huge machine. It stopped.

Within a few days, a couple of dozen of Ray's neighbors had set up a local chapter of the Appalachian Group to Save the Land and People, and they took turns blocking the bulldozer with their bodies. Word of the confrontation soon reached newspapers and television stations in the area, and reporters and cameramen flocked to the scene to cover the story, which immediately got widespread attention. A couple of weeks after Ray first stepped in front of the bulldozer, he was handed a court order to desist. Again he refused, and the contest went on for over a month.

To avoid a confrontation that might lead to bloodshed, Governor Edward Breathitt temporarily suspended Puritan's permit, and finally he reached a decision that astonished everyone: the slope above Jink Ray's property was too steep to be safely stripped, and the Puritan Coal Company's permit to work in Pike County was revoked. Afterward, the St. Louis *Post-Dispatch* reported:

> Coal interests were furious, and have not recovered from the blow. They recognize a distinct threat to their livelihood. No one is yet sure of the extent of the impact of the Jink Ray episode. It has aroused the interest of city groups, such as the League of Women Voters, in the strip-mining controversy. It has made politicians painfully aware of the need for some kind of change, and this is an election year in Kentucky. Certainly it has spurred organization of additional landowner groups by the Appalachian Group to Save the Land and Peple. A.V. and VISTA workers have dared the wrath of local officials in a number of counties by talking up the potential of landowner organizations.

Jink Ray's most active supporter was a young member of the A.V.s by the name of Joseph Mulloy, who had just reached the conclusion that the land and the people of Appalachia would be saved only if strip mining in the area was stopped at once and for good. Mulloy had grown up in Louisville and had attended the University of Kentucky, where he got involved with the original A.V.s. When O.E.O. took over, he quit college and enlisted in the war on poverty as a full-time field man with the A.V.s. "We wasted our time for a couple of years setting up community centers, repairing schoolhouses, providing fun and games for the youngsters, and summer programs — all of which are incidental to the main concern," Mulloy said shortly after the bulldozer was ordered off Ray's land. "A life-and-death struggle is going on over strip mining here that can spell doom to the future of this area. The only way to end it is to organize people, to get them together to voice their demands." Mulloy, a round-faced, soft-spoken young man with curly hair and glasses, visited the site of the Ray-Puritan standoff daily — to take a turn standing or sitting in front of the bulldozer. He also helped Ray's neighbors organize the chapter of the Appalachian Group, and he and Ray were often seen talking together intently. Before long, it was locally accepted that Mulloy was Jink Ray's chief tactician.

Late that July, just before the Governor acted to settle the controversy, Mulloy was at home one evening with his wife, who was a full-time VISTA, when he was unexpectedly visited by a couple of local citizens. One was Perry Justice, who was a Pikeville mortician and the sheriff of Pike County, and the other was Robert Holcomb, who was head of the Pikeville Chamber of Commerce and of the Independent Coal Operators Association, which represented coal-mining interests in fourteen states and had its headquarters in Pikeville. "They asked me a lot of questions about the A.V.s and what we were trying to do," Mulloy said afterward. "And I acknowledged that we were very concerned about strip mining. They both told me that they agreed with me that it was a bad thing. They stayed only about fifteen minutes and didn't really give me much of an opportunity to answer their questions." On their way out, the sheriff told Mulloy a story about a man who had got in trouble in a nearby town and was blown up by a bomb in his car.

Probably the most energetic and effective A.V. interne in Kentucky was Edith Easterling, an imposing woman in her forties with a long, sharp nose and dark hair pulled back in a ponytail. Mrs. Easterling, who worked under Mulloy, had long been active in the community where she lived — the Marrowbone Creek area, some twenty miles south of Pikeville. By the time the Volunteers arrived in Kentucky on a full-time basis, her four children were nearly grown up, and her husband was retired after working for thirty-five years in the mines. For mountain people, the Easterlings were fairly well off. He had a pension of a hundred and fifty dollars a month from the United Mine Workers, together with Social Security benefits, and they had paid off the mortgage on their house — a neat yellow bungalow that was one of the few decent places on the narrow, rutted road up Poorbottom Hollow, which was otherwise lined with collapsed sheds, dilapidated shacks, and rusty hulks of derelict cars. With the four thousand dollars a year that Mrs. Easterling earned from the A.V.s, she was able to be far more independent, and outspoken, than most other people in the mountains dared to be.

"At the time the A.V.s came to the mountains, I was cooking lunches at the local school for extra money," she said later. "I was always very interested in education, and I collect books and paper and pencils whenever I can and take them to the schools. It's important, I think, because you got people out here in the mountains who have third-grade educations and Ph.D. minds. Anyway, the A.V.s heard about me and came over to see me in the spring of 1966. I was trying to get a water system put in for the Marrowbone Creek area, and they agreed to help. Maybe because I got tied up with these people, who were looked at as agitators by local officials, I didn't get rehired by the school as cook the next autumn. So the A.V.s offered me a job, and I took it that fall and went to work with Joe Mulloy. I was mostly a community worker in recreation, and I set up the Marrowbone Folk School in a building that the people here put up on my land. We had recreation for the kids. We bought games for them to play evenings at the Folk School, where they come and sit around the stove during the winter. It's the only place for them to go. We try to have a Christmas party for them, so that each kid gets some kind of a Christmas gift. Many of them don't get anything at home – not even a decent meal. Anyway, we had some music by local talent and community meetings once a week to discuss problems. We also put out a little newspaper, the Marrowbone *News*. People really enjoyed that newspaper. We were making progress before the war on poverty in the mountains was shut down after what happened here.

"One of the great things was that people were speaking out for themselves for the first time – say, on welfare problems or before a county judge on one matter or another. It was a type of way to get people to see to their own rights. In this hollow here, more than sixty per cent of the people are on welfare or some sort of aid. They're afraid to speak out, because they're afraid they'll lose the little bit they got. And they probably would. Still and all, people aren't quite so afraid to organize themselves together like they used to be. There's a big organization fighting black-lung disease now, and it has been really successful. We're forcing mine owners to put in ventilating systems now. There's been some improvements as well in the welfare system that are important. Before, they wouldn't even answer the phone at the welfare office. We threatened to get some of them fired for that, and it scared them plenty. Now they answer the phone, and we can really negotiate.

"But some people didn't like what we were doing at all. We've been persecuted pretty bad. They call on the phone and threaten to kill us, and someone shot the windows out at the Folk School. At least, though, people here learned something from it all. They learned what their government is really like. Take the anti-poverty program. Why, the crumbs that fell off the rich people's table were so small nobody could hardly see them. If the government sets out to spend some money to help the poor, there'll be ten men standing between Washington and the poor man doing everything in the world – scheming, cheating, maybe killing – to get that money into their own hands. They say to us, 'You don't know how to do it because you haven't got any education, so we'll do it for you.' Then they take the money, and we're right where we were. Of course, the anti-poverty programs weren't intended to do anything except give people money for political purposes. When somebody tried to make the programs really work, they didn't like that and had to get rid of him."

Around the time that Mulloy was visited by Justice and Holcomb, Mrs. Easterling was called on by a man she knew named Thomas Ratliff. Although Ratliff was a lawyer, he hadn't practiced much law. Instead, he had gone into the coal business not long after getting out of law school. Once the large coal companies gave up most of their business in the area, Ratliff leased or bought some coal "docks" — the loading platforms from which coal is poured into open railroad cars — to serve the smaller mine operators who took over much of the industry in Kentucky. Before long, he was a millionaire, and then he went into politics. In 1963, he was elected Commonwealth Attorney for the thirty-fifth judicial district of Kentucky, which included Pikeville and the surrounding area, and in 1967 he was running for lieutenant governor on the Republican ticket.

Mrs. Easterling, a lifelong Republican, had been chairman of the Republican Party in the Marrowbone district in 1963. "I worked really hard to get the Republicans into office that year," she said. "I worked especially hard for Thomas Ratliff, and helped elect him. Then the new bunch was the worst crowd we'd ever had in there. That's one of the most disheartening things there is — to tell people how it's going to change things if this person or that person gets elected, and then it doesn't change, except maybe for the worse. Seeing the dirty work that goes on, you wonder what there is to fight for."

When Ratliff called on Mrs. Easterling, she suspected that he wanted to find out what she knew about Mulloy's part in the affair at Jink Ray's, because she worked for Mulloy and was actively supporting Ray. But it turned out that Ratliff was more interested in another anti-poverty worker — a man named Alan McSurely, who had been hired by the A.V.s the previous spring and then fired, after a month on the job, because of his radical views about what had to be done to straighten out American society in general. McSurely stayed on in Kentucky, and went to work for the Southern Conference Educational Fund, or SCEF, which was based in

Louisville, as an organizer of the poor in the mountains. He and his wife lived just outside Pikeville, and were good friends of both the Mulloys' and Mrs. Easterling's. SCEF had been set up in 1938 to combat racial and economic inequality in the South, and, like every organization with such aims, it had repeatedly been denounced as a Communist front. During the Republican gubernatorial primary campaign in Kentucky in the spring of 1967, Louie Nunn charged his opponent, Marlow Cook, with having "coddled" SCEF from his post as county judge and political boss of the Louisville area. Nunn vowed to run organizations like SCEF out of Kentucky if he was elected, and he won the primary.

Now Ratliff, Nunn's running mate in the forthcoming gubernatorial election, mentioned the McSurelys to Mrs. Easterling. They were both Communists, he told her, and she should keep away from them. She flatly rejected the advice. "I couldn't see why Thomas was so set against the McSurelys," she said afterward. "They weren't doing anything at that point that I could see should nettle him — none of the picketing with Jink Ray, or black-lung work, or fighting the strip miners. But he said I was one of his crowd and should listen to him. I told him no I wasn't — not after what his crowd had done as soon as they got into office. Then he asked me what McSurely was doing, and I told him he was writing a book on how much better it would be for the unemployed and the working poor if they were organized. Thomas heard me out, and then he said, 'Edith, I don't think he's ever going to write that book.' "

Late in the afternoon on Friday, August 11, 1967, the McSurelys drove over to the Mulloys' house, which was also near Pikeville, for a visit. The four played a lazy game of basketball, and then sat in the shade and drank iced tea and talked about life in the mountains. The week before, the McSurelys had been evicted from a large house they had lived in since coming to Kentucky the previous April, and had moved into a run-down five-room cottage, which they had had to paint and repair. Their small savings were gone, and Mrs. McSurely — a short, dark-haired, attractive woman of thirty-one with a soft North Carolina drawl — was five months pregnant and anxious about her future. Right then, she was especially anxious about the next few hours, since she and her husband had no money and no food in the cottage. Mrs. Mulloy said that they were welcome to take whatever they liked from her garden, and Mrs. McSurely said that she had a yen for summer squash, so her husband — a tall man, also thirty-one, with a floppy forelock of brown hair and a habit of smiling when he spoke — picked some squash. Then the couple got into their old Ford and drove home. It was a mile from Pikeville, in an area officially designated as Pleasant Valley but usually known as Harold's Branch, after the narrow stream by that name running along one side of the road down the hollow.

Mrs. McSurely went into the kitchen to cook the squash, while her husband sat down at a makeshift desk made out of an old door on top of some cartons in the spare bedroom to work on a "white paper" for a forthcoming staff meeting at SCEF. "We were trying to discover how we could develop a workable technique for organizing the black-white coalition that everybody was talking about," McSurely has explained. "This was to be the basis for what SCEF could do throughout the South." At the time, McSurely himself was more interested in another kind of coalition — one between workers and the unemployed poor — which he had become convinced was the only solution to poverty and injustice in general. Moreover, there was no opportunity for a meaningful black-white alliance in Pike County, even if one could be forged, since only one per cent of the people there were black.

The unfinished "white paper" lying beside McSurely's typewriter was entitled "This Was the War That Was," and it began, "The United States Government's official War on Poverty, sometimes called the War on the Poor, will die a strategic death sometime in the fall of 1967, after some exciting but disastrous skirmishes throughout the land. Its short, unhappy life holds many lessons for those of us who were taken in by it." McSurely went on to describe "our illusions" — namely, "our naïve illusion, our tragic, pathetic, and stupid illusion that the United States Government could seriously endorse, finance, or in any serious manner support the organizing of the exploited poor in our land — the men and women and children who provided the manpower to give the country the accumulated money it uses to try to rule the world." The paper continued:

> [President] Kennedy knew that he was never going to get the segregationist vote. He had stopped worrying about it, and was concentrating on building up his support among the poor, the Negroes in the big cities, and the working class. Remember that at the time there was still some romantic flavor to the young college people trying to register Negroes in Mississippi and Alabama, and it appealed to folks in the big city, black and white. With this big-city support, plus enough of the suburban liberals . . . he would have a much wider margin in 1964. So when the Special Task Force on Poverty put together its ideas, these were the political realities in 1961–2.

Arguing that "most of the programs they threw into the pot were leftovers from the New Deal," McSurely described the programs and then wrote, "After the assassination, President Johnson had to complete some of JFK's programs. One of the first which he sent to Congress in early 1964 was the Economic Opportunity Act. LBJ's weakest point in his 'Democratic consensus' was his liberal flank. And he knew that the Poverty War and the Civil Rights Act were *the* liberal causes of that year." After describing what the poverty war had failed to accomplish, and why, McSurely wrote:

> The poverty in our cities, the poverty in our South, the poverty in the mountains, the poverty of the migrant worker are caused by the corporate system which produced and now must maintain this poverty. The fortunes that were amassed in this country out of the shortened lives of black slaves, colonized miners in Appalachia, tenant and migrant farmers in the South and far West, and Indian landholders are the same fortunes that have made it possible for the corporate liberals to set up their handout programs, to try to prevent these exploited peoples from regaining their heritage. And these fortunes are what has enabled the United States oil

> empire to stretch its greedy fingers around the world, and to make additional capital to cool out any of the audacious few who have learned legal ways to demand their rights. . . . And the fortunes that were amassed from the skins of the exploited workers here and around the world are the same fortunes that have promoted the technological advances which for the first time make it possible for large populations of people to be out of work, to be "drones" on society, and not to starve (except for a few).

That was as far as McSurely had got, and now he wrote in ink at the end of the last page, "But why were we duped?" Then he sat back and yawned. He stared at the paper for a few minutes, trying to think of what he wanted to say next. Finally, though, he gave up, and turned to a box that he hadn't unpacked yet and began rummaging through it. He ran across his high-school annual and saw a photograph of himself on the basketball team, and began thinking about his youth and all that had happened to him since.

Out in the kitchen, Margaret McSurely went about her cooking chores gloomily. "I was really down that day," she recalled. "I don't know why – maybe it was because I was becoming more and more convinced that Al and I were wasting our time in Kentucky. I knew the people didn't want us there, and wouldn't listen. And I was afraid, too. They kill you in those mountains for less than Al was doing. And I was beginning to be afraid for my unborn child most of all."

By dusk, she had nearly finished preparing dinner and was about to summon her husband when she noticed that their dog, a half-grown German shepherd called Major, was behaving strangely. He was sniffing around the room, his ears flat and his tail between his legs. Then Mrs. McSurely happened to glance out the window and saw several cars pull up sharply on the roadside in front of the house and a dozen men, some in police uniforms and some in ordinary clothes, jump out with drawn guns. "I figured they were after an escaped prisoner," she said. "But then they came toward the house."

Through the window of the spare bedroom McSurely saw a couple of men run around to the back of the house and heard the clumping of footsteps on the front porch. He got up to see what was going on, and just as he reached the front door it burst open and half a dozen men rushed through, half falling down and waving their guns wildly. One of them was Sheriff Justice. "Where is Alan McSurely?" he shouted.

"I'm right here," McSurely answered from the back of the crowd that had rushed past him.

Two of the sheriff's deputies ran to his side, pinned his arms behind him, and pushed him to the center of the living room. Then the sheriff took out a search warrant and read it to him in a loud voice: "You are commanded to search, in the day or night time, the house, outbuildings, cabins, now occupied, used, maintained, controlled, owned or managed by Alan McSurely, which property is located in Pike County, Kentucky, which premises are located in Pleasant Valley. . . . And if you find in or upon said premises seditious matter . . . you will seize and take possession of it, and deliver it, together with the body of said Alan McSurely together with this writ, to me at my office as speedily as possible." The warrant, which was dated that day, was signed "Bill Pauley, Judge, Pike Quarterly Court."

McSurely had heard enough during his few months in the mountains about lynch mobs and prisoners being shot "while trying to escape" to be very frightened. Despite the Keystone Cops entrance of the raiders, they looked alarmingly serious. He recognized the sheriff and a magistrate from Marrowbone Creek named Foster Bentley, and then he saw, to his surprise, Commonwealth Attorney Ratliff. Since Ratliff was the highest-ranking official in the group, McSurely asked him what the charge was.

"Sedition," Ratliff replied.

Dumbfounded, McSurely asked, "Sedition against what?"

"Against the United States of America, the Commonwealth of Kentucky, and Pike County," Ratliff answered sternly. Then he smiled.

Mrs. McSurely went to her husband's side, and Ratliff ordered the two of them to sit on the sofa. One of his men shoved McSurely onto it before he could obey, but Mrs. McSurely, who was obviously pregnant, was treated politely. "When the sheriff read the warrant, I knew it was all a legal farce," she said later. "But I was certain that it was a very dangerous situation. I didn't know if they were going to kill Al or not. He was trembling with cold — from fear, I believe. So I got a sweater for him to put on, which I figured he'd need in jail — if he ever got to jail."

McSurely's fear mounted by the moment. "I was really scared," he recalled. "Guys were pushing me around all the time, and one of them said to me, 'Hold your head up. I want to see how you'll look when you hang.' It was like a party to them but a lynch party to me. They acted as if we were very dangerous people, and a couple of them kept calling me a Communist and a dirty Red. Of course, they didn't know what a Communist was or what the word 'sedition' meant. I wasn't angry at that point. My basic feeling was one of fear and self-protection, and I was just trying to keep cool. All I wanted to do then was stay alive."

Ratliff summoned four more men, who had been left outside to guard the house, and ordered those assembled in the small, stuffy living room — twelve besides him and the McSurelys — to search the entire house for "seditious materials." The men dispersed, and then Ratliff pulled a chair up to a bookcase in the living room and began examining the books, one by one. There were a large number of works about Communism, including a couple of dozen by Marx, Engels, and Lenin, together with *Quotations from Chairman Mao Tse-tung;* there were many other leftist books on a variety of social, economic, and political subjects; and there were works by Camus, Brecht, Dostoevski, William Cullen Bryant, and A. J. Liebling. When Ratliff came upon a Bible, he turned to the McSurelys in surprise and asked, "What's *this* doing here?" Neither of them answered, and he put it aside.

From time to time, one of Ratliff's men came into the room to show him something that seemed particularly incriminating, such as a paper by McSurely entitled "Manifesto for Radical America;" a folder containing a dozen or so lapel pins inscribed "S.N.C.C. for Black Power;" some handbills headed "Government of the Black, by the Black, for the Black;" another paper by McSurely called "A New Political Union;" the unfinished copy of "That Was the War That Was;" several descriptions of how blacks and the poor might be welded together into an effective political organization; innumerable books, papers, and articles attacking America's role in Vietnam; some letters and records dealing with SCEF's organizational setup and programs; scores of leaflets and documents put out by various left-wing outfits that McSurely had been connected with; several folders containing the names, addresses, and telephone numbers of dozens of radicals around the country; and hundreds of letters to and from many of them.

After half an hour or so passed, Mrs. McSurely relaxed enough to begin thinking about ways to get help. Finally, she asked Ratliff if she might use the bathroom, and he nodded and told one of the men to accompany her there and stand guard outside. She got up and walked slowly into the main bedroom and then suddenly picked up the telephone and began dialling. The guard tried to stop her, but Ratliff heard the commotion and told the man to leave her alone. With that, she called a local lawyer by the name of Dan Jack Combs, whom she and her husband had met when they came to Pikeville and had got to know slightly in the intervening months. Combs, one of the two lawyers in eastern Kentucky who were sufficiently liberal to handle labor disputes, had a fairly sizable criminal-law practice, too, and was known as one of the most competent attorneys in that part of the state. Mrs. McSurely quickly told him what had happened and asked if he would represent them, and Combs promised that he would go over to the jail at once to be present when her husband was brought in.

After that, Mrs. McSurely dialled the Louisville number of Carl and Anne Braden, the directors of SCEF. Mrs. Braden answered, and when she heard what was going on she gasped. As it happened, her husband was the only person in Kentucky ever to be arrested and convicted under the same sedition statute, more than a decade before. She said that she would immediately get in touch with a couple of leading Movement lawyers, William Kunstler and Morton Stavis, who had shortly before set up a legal-aid center in New York for just such cases. Mrs. Braden also said that she would alert various Movement people throughout the country and ask them to telephone and wire the Pike County authorities in protest — a standard tactic that had been developed during the civil-rights struggle in the South to protect prisoners who might be beaten or murdered if no one knew that they were in the hands of the police.

When the guard escorted Mrs. McSurely back to the living room, he told Ratliff, "God, Thomas, she knows Dan Jack. That's who she was talking to on the phone." Ratliff's face fell — presumably, the McSurelys concluded, because he had expected them to get an outside lawyer who knew neither the local authorities nor the way things were done there. Then, too, Ratliff and Combs had known each other since the early fifties, and Ratliff, as a lawyer who had briefly worked the other side of the street from Combs, knew that he was probably the best man in that part of the state to help the McSurelys.

The news prompted Ratliff to expedite the search, and he ordered his men to seize every scrap of paper in the house. As he examined the materials the men brought into the living room, Ratliff saw that Mrs. McSurely was also employed by SCEF and that she had earlier worked in Mississippi and Georgia for the Student Nonviolent Coordinating Committee, or S.N.C.C., which had shortly before begun talking about something called "black power." Finally, he decided to arrest her, too, and wrote out a warrant and handed it to Sheriff Justice, who officially took her into custody. With that, McSurely relaxed a bit, certain now that what had so often happened in similar circumstances in the South — the murder of helpless prisoners — wasn't going to happen here, because he was sure that they wouldn't harm a woman. He also felt that she would be safer in jail than alone out in the hollow, because he knew that once word went around that he was locked up, the kind of local men who always had trouble in mind might come out to the cottage to "have some fun" with her.

At the end of the search, the raiders piled up their haul on the living-room floor. The seized materials took up nearly the entire room, and included five hundred and sixty-four books, twenty-six posters, and twenty-two boxes of pamphlets, booklets, documents, letters, personal papers, and a suitcase full of clothing that an excited deputy had flung onto the load. (Two hundred and ninety of the books were copies of *False Witness,* by Harvey Matusow, a professional anti-Communist witness in the witch-hunting days of the early nineteen-fifties, who had written the book to show how and why he had repeatedly lied in court and before legislative committees. The copies of the book had been given to McSurely by an official of the Mine, Mill, and Smelter Workers Union, which had helped subsidize the book, but McSurely, like the donor, didn't know what to do with them – other than to use the cartons they were packed in to support the door he used as a desk top.)

Most of the other boxes contained the kind of miscellaneous stuff that ends up together when one packs hurriedly, as the McSurelys had when they moved. A typical collection, listed in an official inventory afterward, was "National magazines, printing equipment [such] as ink, blotter, and two cans of Dri-Fast Ink, a Workbook on Maryland-National Capital Park and Planning commission, 150 4″ x 8″ envelopes, one bookend, ashtrays, civil-rights literature, a brochure on Metropolitan Washington, an annual report of the Council of Governments." Elsewhere in the pile on the living-room floor were some of McSurely's old college exam papers, several of his recent federal income-tax returns, a packet of Mrs. McSurely's love letters from the days before she met McSurely, and a personal diary that she had kept during an emotionally tumultuous period of her life a few years before. The collection was so large that Ratliff finally had to commandeer a pickup truck owned by a couple who lived across the road. Nothing had ever surprised them more, they later said, than Ratliff's announcement that their new neighbors were Communists who were plotting to overthrow the government of Pike County.

The raid and search at the McSurelys' took two and a half hours. At a little before eleven o'clock that night, they were ordered into the rear seat of the sheriff's car. Then the parade of the raiders' cars, together with the pickup truck, made its way to the county jail, a three-story gray stone cube immediately behind the courthouse in the center of Pikeville. Combs, it turned out, wasn't there. He had arrived at the jail shortly after Mrs. McSurely's telephone call to him, but after waiting for an hour he told the jailer that he would be back first thing in the morning, and warned him that there would be serious trouble if the McSurelys were harmed in any way. Ratliff and the sheriff led the prisoners into a small office, where they were divested of their personal belongings. After Ratliff took down their names, address, birthplaces, and ages, they were booked and the charge against them was read aloud. Ratliff showed them the sedition law, Kentucky Revised Statute 432.040, which stated:

> Any person who by word or writing advocates, suggests or teaches the duty, necessity, propriety or expediency of criminal syndicalism or sedition, or who prints, publishes, edits, issues or knowingly circulates, sells, distributes, publicly displays or has in his possession for the purpose of publication or circulation any written or printed matter in any form advocating, suggesting or teaching criminal syndicalism or sedition, or who organizes or helps to organize, or becomes a member of or voluntarily assembles with any society or assemblage of persons that teaches, advocates or suggests the doctrine of criminal syndicalism or sedition shall be confined in the penitentiary for not more than twenty-one years, or fined not more than ten thousand dollars, or both.

"Then they took me upstairs to jail," McSurely recalled. "It was cold and damp. Prisoners had broken all the windows in the place over the years, and the wind and rain blew in. The jailer took me into a big dormitory room with about twenty bunks. There were maybe fifteen guys lying there when I was taken in. I was really scared again. I didn't know what they might do to me. They all woke up — a couple of drunks, some guys in for fighting, a moonshiner, and a rapist. I went over and lay down on an empty bunk. I figured I'd just go to sleep, so that if they killed me I'd be dead when I woke up. That's the kind of crazy thought one has when scared, and I was really scared. One of the prisoners asked a deputy outside the cell what I was in for. 'Oh, he's a Communist,' the deputy told him. Then another guy asked me what I was in for. I said, 'Sedition.' They asked me what that was. I said, 'It means teaching people to overthrow the government.' I said it very slowly and clearly, in the hope that they would get a focus for their thoughts and remember only that, and forget what they'd like to do to me. They said 'Oh.' Then I said I wanted to get some sleep and lay back down. I heard them talking about me. One said he'd heard about me and that I was some kind of a writer. I was so scared I fell asleep, as I do when I'm very upset. But the next morning everything was all right, and in time I got very friendly with some of them."

Mrs. McSurely was put in a smaller cell with two other women — one of whom had been arrested for using profanity in public and the other for trying to kill a woman her husband was carrying on with. "They asked me what I was in jail for," Mrs. McSurely said later. "I told them, 'Sedition.' They thought I said 'Soliciting.' When I explained that 'sedition' meant overthrowing the government they both said that was what should be done. I got to know those two women and some others who came through the jail while I was there pretty well. It was clear that there was no justice for the poor. In most cases, they were fined by the magistrate, the same as people who were well off. But the difference was that people with some money could afford to pay their fines, whereas these women couldn't and had to stay in jail until their time was up."

That night, Mrs. McSurely asked the jailer for an extra blanket and a quart of milk, but was turned down. By this time, she was no longer concerned about her own safety, apart from the danger that she might contract a disease from the filthy conditions in the jail. But she was worried about what might happen to her husband at the hands of the jailers or the other prisoners. "It was during this time that I developed a very close relationship with the baby inside me," she said. "They had come and taken just about everything from me. I didn't know if I'd ever see Al again. But I knew they couldn't take the little boy — I was sure it was a boy — growing inside me. He was my new life, my second chance, and I got a deep mystical feeling about him that was to sustain me."

Unknown to the McSurelys at the time, the raiding party went out on another foray shortly after they were locked up — this time to the Mulloys' house. Ratliff seemed far less interested in Mulloy, despite his active role in the strip-mining controversy, and merely spent a few minutes searching his place after arresting him for sedition. The raiding party confiscated only a handful of documents dealing with the work of the Appalachian Volunteers, along with some books that seemed incriminating, among them *Poems of Chairman Mao,* which Mulloy had bought at Mildred's Newsstand in Pikeville, and Joseph Heller's *Catch-22*.

Alan McSurely was born in Dayton, Ohio, in 1936, and moved to Arlington, Virginia, in the early nineteen-forties, when his father took a job in Washington as a reporter for *Aviation Week*. The elder McSurely died while Alan was a senior in high school, and his mother went to work to support him and his two sisters. She was determined that all three children would go to college, and Alan was sent off to the University of North Carolina, at Chapel Hill. After four years there – with a year off while he worked in Arlington as a mailman and got married – McSurely took a job teaching a course in "human relations" at an electronics training school in Washington. "I taught guys who were going to be repairmen how to get along with bosses and guys who were going to be bosses how to get along with repairmen," he said. By then, he had two children and an increased sense of responsibility, so he began studying nights for a master's degree in psychology at George Washington University. About that time – 1960 – the McSurely family moved into a trailer outside Alexandria, Virginia. "No marriage can decently survive life in a trailer," he said recently, "and that was the beginning of the end of mine."

As his marriage disintegrated, McSurely went to work as a counsellor at a juvenile court in Fairfax County, Virginia, and also finished the course work for his M.A. He had a case load of about fifty youngsters, several of them black children from a village called Gum Springs, near Mount Vernon. All of the residents of Gum Springs were black, and most of them were descendants of George Washington's slaves.

"I had a group of six kids, and we met once a week for group counselling," McSurely recalled. "As far as I could make out, I had no effect on them, but they had a tremendous effect on me. Week by week, I got to see what their lives were like and how our society had blighted them. Then I got to know Saunders B. Moon, who was the black principal of the all-black school in Gum Springs. He wanted to get his best kids into desegregated schools, but the school board was afraid that the idea would spread, and threatened to fire him if he didn't stop. I desperately wanted to do something about the place, and said, 'Let's organize.' That was my first attempt. We got together the county workers who might be interested — social workers, public-health nurses, and so on — and tried to organize them. We failed completely. Then we tried working through the P.T.A. to set up programs for improving schools, housing, medical care, and community recreation. We advertised what we were doing, and had a little more success. Then Saunders said to me, 'If we only had a newspaper, we could get the word out to the people.' We put a little paper together, and that helped a lot. Then came the great black-and-white-together March on Washington, in the summer of 1963. Then John Kennedy was killed. And then on Christmas morning Saunders dropped dead. I was all alone, but I decided to stick it out. Another fellow and I put out the little newspaper once a week for a couple of years. We sold it in churches and stores, on the streets, anywhere we could, and finally it caught on. That was when the county officials started opposing us every time we tried to do something. They wouldn't even let us use the school for public meetings. I had got my first taste of what it's like coming up against a county government that feels its power threatened."

Late in the fall of 1964, a man from the United Planning Organization in Washington — an agency set up to implement the anti-poverty law enacted by Congress earlier that year — visited Gum Springs to see what was being done to help the poor there. He was impressed by what he saw and by McSurely, and offered him a job setting up similar local programs in the suburbs of the capital. By then, McSurely had broken up with his wife, and he needed money to support his two children, so when U.P.O. offered him a salary of ten thousand dollars a year, which was four thousand dollars more than he was making, he accepted. A few months after joining U.P.O., he became director of all its anti-poverty programs in suburban Washington.

"I knew from the beginning that the best we could do was to teach some people, as rapidly as possible, how to organize and what to understand about the problems they faced before the local powers came in and took control," McSurely said later. "I knew it was impossible to actually do much of anything for the poor besides give them a start toward helping themselves politically. I had no illusions that they would be helped directly by the process, but merely hoped that they would learn how the system works, so they could use it themselves to establish a power base and then exert some leverage to get money for their people and seats on committees. I tried to get them moving before the local courthouse gang saw that there was money and power in the poverty fight and took it over. It was clear that nothing else could be done, because there were two basic problems we couldn't do anything about. One was that racism was rife in the suburbs, and the other was that the Johnson Administration lacked any real commitment to the program. It was politically motivated and politically run. It was also the biggest boondoggle of the decade."

McSurely's second wife, Margaret, was born in 1936 in Ashland, Kentucky, and was taken at the age of three months to Winston-Salem, North Carolina, where her father was to serve as pastor of the First Baptist Church for a quarter of a century. She attended Wake Forest College for a little over a year, and then dropped out of school after marrying a fellow-student who was a senior. They had two children in the first four years of marriage, and her husband taught at a girls' college in Virginia until he decided that he wanted to be a doctor. "Before then, I didn't have enough confidence to strike out on my own," Margaret has said. "I saw myself merely as someone who could take care of a man who might do something in the world. But when my husband went to medical school, I had to get a job to help support the family, and I soon learned that I could make it in the big world on my own."

After a series of small jobs as a clerk, a typist, and a receptionist, she wound up, in the early nineteen-sixties, working in Washington for Drew Pearson, the columnist. At first, she answered his fan mail, but in time she became his personal assistant, in charge of writing his letters and typing up the diary he kept. "I found it fascinating to learn who had said what to him in private," she recalled not long ago. She also found Pearson, who was then approaching seventy, a fascinating man, and within a few months she became his mistress. Shortly before she took up with Pearson, she and her husband separated, and they were later divorced.

In 1964, Margaret began to get interested in what was going on in Mississippi politics – chiefly in the emergence of the black Mississippi Freedom Democratic Party, which claimed to be the true representatives of the Mississippians who could be expected to vote for the Democratic Party in the greatest numbers. S.N.C.C. sent Pearson its press releases regularly, and Margaret found the stories in them dramatic and appealing – especially stories about the Freedom Democratic Party's best-known member, Mrs. Fannie Lou Hamer. "I read the S.N.C.C. releases very carefully, and tried to get Drew to write something about what was going on in Mississippi, but he wouldn't listen," Margaret said. "Then he took me to the Democratic National Convention, which was held in Atlantic City that summer, and I met Mrs. Hamer and some of the others from the Freedom Democratic Party. I was deeply moved by their stories and their dedication. Then I began to look at my own life – suburbanite, absentee mother, Pearson's girl friend – and I didn't like myself very much. I began working with the Freedom Party delegation while I was at the Convention. My allegiance and my whole life changed very suddenly. I also went to work for S.N.C.C. at the Convention.

"One evening, an old black man came up to me in the S.N.C.C. office and asked if I had enough to eat. I realized then, for the first time, that food was really a problem for these people – just getting enough to eat so they could keep going – while I was living in a fancy hotel and eating and drinking whatever I pleased. Until that time, I had never talked to black people, except for my parents' maid, and I became deeply ashamed. I tried again to get Drew to write about the Mississippi Freedom Democrats. But instead of calling Mrs. Hamer he called a member of the credentials committee at the Convention, who told him that the Freedom people did not represent the state and would not be seated as its proper delegates, and that's what Pearson wrote in his column. I quit. He was very upset, and said he didn't want to lose me. He was getting old, and I was his one tie with younger people. Also, I had attacked him not personally but politically. He wasn't used to that from people like me. The liberals usually fawned all over him, but here he was, being called a right-winger by one of them. He didn't understand what had happened to me. After I met the blacks from Mississippi, I felt my life should go to the people. I decided then that I would live with the oppressed and die with them."

Early that fall, Margaret left her children with her ex-husband, and went to work for S.N.C.C. in Batesville, Mississippi. "I worked with kids mainly, teaching them how to type so they could get jobs," she explained. "I learned a lot about their lives, and I can never forget it. The problems of the people there are horrible — little children covered with sores, no food, no clothes, no medicine, shacks falling down over their heads." During the time she was in Batesville, Pearson wrote several letters urging her to come back to him, and when she refused he hired a private plane and flew down to Mississippi to talk to her. He offered to make her a reporter on his staff if she would return, but Margaret told him that it was too late. Not long afterward, she returned to Washington to work for S.N.C.C. there, and when Pearson learned that she was in town he asked her to come to his house for a talk.

"I went and he showed me a document saying that I had driven a carload of racially mixed people, some of them Communists, from Mississippi to Washington," she said. "He told me that it was all going to be printed in the papers but that he would help me, and asked me again to come back to him. I told him I didn't want to have anything more to do with him."

Subsequently, S.N.C.C. transferred Margaret to its office in Atlanta. "I was there for a year, and the experience was bitterly frustrating," she said. "We never seemed to win. Also, I had concluded by then that black people should run their programs for themselves, since white people, however well-meaning they were, always ended up by taking over. During this period, I began to see the real problems of capitalism and what it does to the poor. For the first time, I was able to read Marx without being afraid to face what I read. It all made a lot of sense to me. Anyway, I quit and went back to Washington. I was very tired and pent up — full of rage about what America was doing to the poor and the black. Sometimes my rage fantasies got too much for me, and I considered getting out of this country for a year or so. Instead, I went back to a psychiatrist I had gone to when my marriage was coming apart, and then I took a job with U.P.O. Before long, that seemed as futile as everything else. I was assigned to plan summer programs for black kids in Washington slums. That was unsatisfying, too, because I learned that they periodically threatened to riot only so that more of them would be put on our payroll."

From time to time, Margaret worked with McSurely on her projects at U.P.O., and before long they fell in love and began living together. He had also concluded by this stage that it was a mistake for whites and blacks to work together on civil-rights and anti-poverty programs, and, again like her, he had concluded that the only solution to the problems besetting American society was Marxism. Neither of them saw much to be gained by officially becoming Communists, since the Communist Party of the United States struck them as being hopelessly old-fashioned and stultified, and they decided to experiment and devise their own approach as they went along. In the early winter of 1967, the couple took a long trip across the country, looking for a place where they might settle down to live and work.

"Finally, we chose to move to the Southern mountains and work with poor whites," Margaret said. "We thought that the poor people were going to make the revolution."

On April 1, 1967, the McSurelys — they planned to marry as soon as his divorce came through, so she took his name — moved to Pikeville. He had taken a job with the A.V.s under the impression that he would be the group's director of training, and was to be paid a salary of ten thousand dollars a year. She went to work for SCEF as a researcher on the coal industry and its effects on the mountain people, at a salary of seventy-five dollars a month. They found a large old frame house for a rental of fifty dollars a month, and on April 2nd they moved in. While Mrs. McSurely was unpacking, McSurely went off to town to get the gas and electricity turned on.

During his absence, a visitor arrived at the house — a young man by the name of Gary Bickel, who had recently joined the A.V.s as a temporary consultant on setting up agricultural coöperatives. Bickel struck Mrs. McSurely as being in "a greatly agitated state," and she gathered that he felt some kind of intense competition with McSurely. She talked to him for a few minutes, and then he left, saying he would come back in a couple of days to speak to her husband. The following Saturday morning, Bickel reappeared at the house, and this time McSurely was in. He asked the young man in for coffee and a chat, and before long he learned that Bickel was indeed engaged in some sort of competition with him — principally over some suggestions for various programs that McSurely had sent on to the A.V.s before joining them. Bickel had read the papers, and now he said that he disagreed with McSurely on some fundamental points.

"He seemed especially interested in my views on the democratic process — letting the people decide and so on," McSurely has recalled. "He had been to a poor people's meeting and had seen them develop their own bylaws, and thought it was a wonderful process. The bylaws were written by one of the 'people,' all right — an old Socialist union organizer from the thirties. Bickel talked about the 'folks' and the 'poor people' as if they were children. It made me sick and mad."

As Bickel got up to go, he mentioned that he had heard a lot of comments about a paper McSurely had written called "A New Political Union," and said that he would like to read it. McSurely gave him a copy of it, and Bickel left.

Later that day, the McSurelys drove to Nashville so that Mrs. McSurely could attend a three-day meeting being held there jointly by SCEF, S.N.C.C., and the Southern Students Organizing Committee (S.S.O.C.). The affair, which was held at the headquarters of the General Board of Evangelism of the Methodist Church, was attended by some eighty officers and members of the three groups, including several clergymen. The participants were kept under constant, and fairly obvious, surveillance by the Nashville police, who may have been rather surprised at the tameness of the meetings and discussions, which always opened and closed with a prayer. All of the meetings were open to the public except a conference at which Stokely Carmichael, one of the emerging leaders of black militants in S.N.C.C., was present.

Carmichael had shortly before begun speaking of "black power," and although few people seemed to know what it was supposed to mean, it seemed to frighten just about everybody. Now Carmichael explained what *he* meant by the slogan — that from now on black people should run their own affairs. Blacks should work with blacks, and whites should work with whites, he said, and while members in both groups who agreed on fundamental policies and tactics should coöperate, from this point on black men and women should determine and work for their own goals, while the white people who had been working with them should go out and organize poor whites.

"It was very hard for some of the people there to take," Mrs. McSurely said later. "One white man who had spent more than twenty years teaching in a black school in the South asked Stokely if this meant that he had to give up his work now. Very gently and with great sympathy for the man's bewilderment and pain, Stokely said yes, that was what had to be done. He knew how difficult what he was asking was for many of the people there, and he was very calm and sensible. Most of the rank and file of the groups present already had reached the same conclusion — as Al and I had — but Stokely was trying to get the old-timers among the directors of our movement to agree. Anyway, there was none of the brimstone nonsense — that black power meant violence and race war — as so many white politicians were saying at the time."

Before the meeting, leaflets were handed out around Nashville announcing that Carmichael was going to speak on "S.N.C.C. — Black Power for Communism" and that the public was welcome. Although the leaflet was obviously fraudulent — it was supposedly written and distributed by SCEF, which was described in it as a Communist-front group allied with S.N.C.C. — newspaper and television news reports about it stirred up tension in the city. That evening, Carmichael spoke at a public rally held at Tennessee State University, a black school in Nashville, without creating any disturbance, and the next afternoon he spoke at Vanderbilt University. A couple of hours later, when a drunken black soldier was thrown out of a bar, some black students who had often had trouble with the owner of the place picketed it. In time, the police came and tried to disperse them, some rocks and bottles were thrown, the police charged, and some of the participants were arrested. Over the next two days, there was sporadic sniping and arson. Although the National Guard was called out, the affair was a modest kind of riot for that period, with only seventeen people injured and thirty thousand dollars in property damage.

The McSurelys left town shortly after the meeting at which Carmichael explained black power, and drove directly to Knoxville for a staff meeting of the A.V.s. When they arrived, McSurely was met by a friend he had known for years who had worked with him in Gum Springs and was now a field man with the A.V.s, too. "Al, you're in real trouble," the man told him. "Gary Bickel has been Red-baiting you over that paper you gave him, and you're about to get fired."

Bickel, it emerged, had photocopied "A New Political Union" and sent it around to officers and members of the A.V.s, accompanied by a note saying that McSurely was both a Leninist and a Trotskyite and that for the good of the A.V.s he should be fired at once. Most members of the staff, McSurely was stunned to learn, appeared to agree with Bickel; in fact, the outfit's director, a man named Milton Ogle, was said to have been so perturbed by the paper that he had been unable to sleep after reading it. McSurely had written "A New Political Union" back in January, and had sent copies of it to various people he knew around the country, including the friend in the A.V.s who had just warned him.

Near the beginning of the paper, McSurely predicted that the 1968 Presidential candidates would be Robert Kennedy and Ronald Reagan. Such a contest, he observed, would be "an intramural football game, arranged by the owners of both teams, to see which team gets to play around with the lives of 96% of American citizens for four years" — a game, he added, that was "sick" and had led more and more people "to see the need for gaining national power." Then McSurely wrote, "Taking national power is necessary. Now is the time to begin a new national political union." After discussing whether those who agreed with this view should continue working "within the electoral system" or "without it" in small, well-disciplined cadres of the sort advocated by Lenin, McSurely recommended that this decision be postponed, together with an answer to the question whether the new union should have "strong central leadership and authority" or should "follow the ephemeral whims of the democratic process."

Having rhetorically answered the postponed question, McSurely went on to clarify what he proposed: "democratic contractualism, which consists of groups coming to a written agreement on programs and strategies through an educational and democratic process — and then carrying out this contractual agreement through a strong, centrally-controlled organization." Democratic contractualism called for an effort to get young people to vote ("Strategically, we must continue to demonstrate the glaring faults in our 'democratic' system for future non-electoral strategies"); for transfer of the steel, aluminum, oil, coal, automobile, airplane, train, ship, and highway construction industries to a "worker government" ("These sources of goods and services represent the strongest economic and educational influence on this nation's working class. Therefore, they should be controlled and developed by the working class"); for an end to racism ("National relocation programs and regional re-education programs [would be set up for] discriminatees and discriminators. Any person who claims he has been discriminated against and who wants to move himself and/or his family will be provided free moving and job counseling at his destination. Any person who violates anti-discrimination statutes will be enrolled in mass re-education programs, with emphasis on self-examination and group interaction"); and for a national convention to be held by democratic contractualists that summer to draw up a program for governing the country ("Once a *written* program is accepted and adopted by the National Committee, it serves as the guide for all party organizing and campaigning. . . . No compromises will be allowed. The national newspaper and committee will have to take a very hard stand on this rule. This is what we call democratic contractualism").

Although some people were inclined to call it puerile nonsense, the social discord of the period led others to recoil in terror at any suggestion that something more than reform was necessary to straighten out the country. To some of those who knew McSurely, his proposal seemed to be a fantasy that suggested far less about society's need than about his own need for authority. "Al is the kind of man who has to have a strict theory of existence to keep himself together," one acquaintance of his said. "His outlook is bound to scare some people, but it's all pretty harmless."

For his own part, McSurely was hurt and bewildered by the general reaction to what he had written, and later said about his critics, "Instead of reading the ideas, they began to project onto the paper their own fantasies about violence and political theories."

In the end, it was difficult to take either side very seriously. "If the A.V.s had been sensible, they would have simply told McSurely to shut up and do his work if he wanted to stay on the payroll," a man who observed the affair said later. "And if McSurely had really hoped to accomplish anything, he would have quietly gone about organizing a few stalwarts to work among the poor in the mountains. All that inflammatory rhetoric left over from the thirties was bound to bring him down, and anybody except a man hellbent on self-destruction would have seen it. Afterward, he claimed that he had been misunderstood. Sure he was misunderstood. What he failed to see was that you can't wave a pistol around, and then complain when you're shot down that it wasn't loaded."

In mid-April, a week after the issue was raised, McSurely was summoned to a staff meeting at the A.V.s' headquarters in Bristol, Tennessee — a six-hour debate on whether or not he should remain on the payroll. The decision was put off. At a large meeting of various anti-poverty groups held in the mountains two weeks later, McSurely delivered a report on various aspects of the A.V.s' training program, and afterward he felt that the report had been well received, that most of the anger had drained out of the opposition, and that he would be made training director after all. Five days later, Ogle summoned McSurely to the Bristol headquarters and fired him.

In a description of the episode written later by the A.V.s' former information officer, the dismissal was attributed to an unexpected quarter:

> About the worst you can say of Al McSurely's personal style is that it includes a dash of arrogance and a certain dogmatic conviction about his political views. That's not much of a criticism these days, but it was too much for some of the A.V.s; they were gradualists, reformers, uncertain politically, hopeful that somehow people were going to get together and make the system respond; and Al came on a little like a revolutionary. . . . But the A.V. staff was not as stirred by Al McSurely's thinking as was one of the organization's principal advisers, Harvard psychiatrist Robert Coles, who had written admiringly of the Volunteers . . . and had become one of the organization's big guns because of his close connections with a number of foundations. In 1967 the leaders of the A.V.s were plunging headlong into the foundation-wooing business, and the friendship of Robert Coles was regarded as crucial. His reaction to Al McSurely was ferocious; in a letter to the director of the A.V.s, Coles said that McSurely was "doctrinaire, arrogant, dogmatic, and brutally ideological . . ." The letter ended with Coles's resignation as an A.V. consultant. There was an immediate reaction from the A.V. leadership: McSurely was fired, and Coles was piped aboard again.

Although McSurely was angered by the dismissal, in time he came to view the event with some detachment. "Coles was spokesman for Robert Kennedy through Sargent Shriver, the director of the O.E.O., and in terms of looking after the government's interests he was right in getting me fired," McSurely said. "I guess he read my paper and saw that the A.V. structure was weak and that I would have undue influence. Coles didn't want me to be training VISTAS and the Peace Corpsmen who got training in the mountains before going abroad. But I would have liked to meet Coles, just to see a man who could make such a strong judgment about a person without ever having met or talked to him."

As for Dr. Coles, he recently explained his role in the affair by saying, "I made the judgment not about McSurely but about what he had written. The last thing the working people of Appalachia needed in the nineteen-sixties, or need today, is overblown Marxist rhetoric. I had spent years working with Appalachian families and felt that the kind of ideological language that McSurely was using would confuse the people of the region. The language certainly confused me."

Other critics of McSurely pointed out that it was hardly ethical for him to take money from the government and then use the money to try to overthrow the government; that after twenty years of anti-Communist fear in America it was not entirely reasonable to go around shouting words and phrases of such unmistakably Marxist lineage as McSurely's unless one wanted trouble; that the anti-poverty program was being conducted in an exceedingly hostile environment, in which politics were of primary importance; and, finally, that the likeliest result of McSurely's demagogic approach would be to overthrow not the system but any sensible attempts to make it responsive to the people's needs.

As sound as these criticisms may have been, in the end McSurely's opponents on the government's side were far more wrongheaded and self-destructive than he was. For one thing, McSurely had said and done nothing that was in any way illegal, and he was, like any citizen, entitled to the right of free speech. For another thing, his approach to the social problems of the nation was so unrealistic that it was bound to be utterly ineffectual, and it thereby conformed to the limits placed on such behavior by the Supreme Court — that is, if words and acts aren't likely to incite imminent lawless action, they are entirely within the protection of the Constitution. But, most important of all, the attack on McSurely provided exactly the sort of weapon that the true enemies of the war on poverty — businessmen who wanted cheap labor and right-wing politicians who served them — needed to crush it once and for all.

A few weeks after being fired, McSurely went on the SCEF payroll at a salary of seventy-five dollars a month, and continued doing much the same kind of work he had done with the A.V.s. He also went to work, on an irregular basis and at even less money, for the National Conference for New Politics, a disorganized movement on the left that was to founder and collapse within a few months, and for Vietnam Summer, which was one of the earlier attempts to mobilize anti-war sentiment across the country. In mid-July, McSurely's divorce became final, so he and Margaret went off to the next county and got married. By then, she was four months pregnant. She was also becoming more and more unhappy about living in the mountains, largely because she felt that her husband wasn't accomplishing much of anything and that she was accomplishing nothing at all besides keeping house for the two of them.

But McSurely was determined to go on fighting. "Whatever happens, Margaret and I are going to stay here," he announced.

Not long after McSurely was fired, Mulloy asked him if he could borrow his large house for a week; a group of thirty-two VISTA and Peace Corps trainees was arriving soon for a week-long session, he explained, and there was no other available place in the area that was large enough to accommodate it. Despite what had happened, the McSurelys agreed, and moved into the Mulloys' house while the Mulloys took over theirs. To make sure that the owner of the large house would not object to the arrangement, McSurely and his wife drew up a set of strict rules for the temporary occupants and took it to their landlord, a man named James Madison Compton. Once they showed him the rules and explained that the training session would be much like a religious retreat for laymen, he consented to the plan. And then Mrs. Easterling stopped by to tell Compton that the trainees and some local teenagers who had been recruited to participate in the week-long session would spend a good part of their time working at her Folk School, on Marrowbone Creek, and to assure him that she would make sure they took good care of his house and property.

The McSurelys had got along well with Compton and his family. He had helped Mrs. McSurely lay out and dig a vegetable garden; she ordinarily baked an extra loaf of bread every other day for him; and one of his sons cut the McSurelys' lawn and tended the yard. Now Mulloy attempted to make Compton even more comfortable about the VISTA and Peace Corps trainees' use of his house by agreeing to buy all groceries for their stay from a nearby general store owned by his son, James Marion Compton. Then Mulloy and Mrs. Easterling invited a number of local officials – including Commonwealth Attorney Ratliff, Chamber of Commerce President Holcomb, and Magistrate Bentley – to drop in during the training session to see what was going on. All of them accepted the invitation, but none of them showed up.

Five weeks later, on July 20th, the elder Compton told the McSurelys that they would have to move. He was apologetic, assured them that they had been good tenants, and explained that his daughter needed the house for her family – as it happened, in ten days' time. The only place the McSurelys could find that they could afford on their monthly income of less than two hundred dollars was the ramshackle cottage on Harold's Branch. They asked for a few days' extension of their stay in the large house so they could paint and repair the cottage, and Compton readily agreed. On their last day there, August 4th, the elder Compton stopped in to tell them how sorry he was to see them leave, and to wish them luck.

Exactly a week later, on August 11th, a group of men met in a room at the Pike County Courthouse. Among them were Pike Quarterly Court Judge Pauley, Commonwealth Attorney Ratliff, Pike County Sheriff Justice, Pike County Attorney Marrs Allen May, five of the county's eight magistrates, Chamber of Commerce President Holcomb, and the two Comptons. After a lengthy discussion, the lawyers in the group drafted the kind of affidavit that is required before a search warrant can be issued. The affidavit stated:

> The affiant, James [Marion] Compton, a reputable citizen of Pike County, Kentucky, who has first been sworn, says that he

> . . . has reasonable grounds to suspect and believe and that he does suspect and believe that seditious printed matter and printing press or other machinery to print and circulate seditious matter is being kept on the premises of Alan McSurely. . . . That the grounds for his belief or information are as follows: (1) That he knows the following facts: On August 4, 1967, he was informed by James Madison Compton, a reputable citizen of Pike County, Kentucky, that on said August 4, 1967, at approximately 12:00 noon, that the said James Madison Compton did observe certain seditious materials, being pamphlets, films, pictures and articles or equipment used in the teaching of sedition and printing and circulating seditious matter at or on the above described premises.

On the morning after the raid, Ratliff told reporters that Compton had evicted the McSurelys after seeing their collection of books and "a parade of strange-looking visitors at their house" – apparently the VISTA and Peace Corps trainees. Ratliff went on to say that during the raid on the McSurelys he had found a "Communistic library out of this world," which included instructions for using weapons and fighting guerrilla warfare, and he added, "We are going to do everything we can to get them out of Pike County. We don't approve of using federal money for the purposes they have been using it." Since the McSurelys hadn't had the use of federal money for several months, Ratliff seemed to be referring to the anti-poverty workers in general. "We had reports that these two people were here and that they were Communists," he went on. "This apparently is one of their training grounds. . . . They have been getting real close to our young people. They have what they call the Marrowbone Folk School out in the country, which, I understand, is an indoctrination school. They have helped get boys into the Neighborhood Youth Corps, and they have taken some young people to civil-rights meetings in Chicago and other places." Ratliff said that the McSurelys not only had connections with the A.V.s and VISTA but were working with radicals throughout the United States. "We found names and addresses of people all over the country and various white papers on how best to indoctrinate the mountain people, how they intended to take power in this country, how to exploit the strip-mine issue. . . . Every piece of evidence we have points to just one objective — to stir up dissension and create turmoil among our poor."

Ratliff also told the reporters that he would make the material he had seized available to congressional investigators and would demand that the federal government withdraw all anti-poverty funds and all anti-poverty workers from Appalachia at once. A reporter questioned Sheriff Justice about the books he and his men had confiscated and asked for a sample title out of the "Communistic library." Justice answered, *"Catch-22."* Robert Holcomb, the head of the local Chamber of Commerce and of the Independent Coal Operators Association, was asked by a reporter what role the latter organization had played in the raids, and Holcomb replied, "You might say we spearheaded the investigation."

For breakfast that morning, each of the inmates in the Pikeville jail was served a cold fried egg, half a slice of bologna, gravy, two pieces of plain white bread, a spoonful of applesauce, and coffee. Not long afterward, the McSurelys and Mulloy were taken to the courthouse for a bail hearing. Dan Jack Combs was there to represent them, and he asked Judge Pauley, who was presiding, to reduce their bail — five thousand dollars apiece for McSurely and Mulloy and two thousand dollars for Mrs. McSurely — but Pauley refused. Later that day, Mulloy was bailed out and released. But the McSurelys couldn't raise their bond money immediately, because the local bondsman refused to touch their case, and then they realized that they were probably safer in jail anyway. The raid the night before had shown them how helpless they were out at Harold's Branch, and had reminded them of all the stories they'd heard since arriving in the mountains about beatings and lynchings of people who got out of line. And Combs had warned them that within hours everyone in Pikeville would have heard about Ratliff's charges and that there was certain to be "some high feeling" against them.

By nightfall, the feeling in the community was high indeed. "When this thing broke, there was mass hysteria here, and a wild kind of paranoia took hold," Combs has said. "A few days after the hearing, I got up one morning and there was a cross burning on my front lawn. Then people started calling on the telephone and threatening me and my family. One man told my wife, 'You better tell Dan Jack to pack his bags when we run these Communists out of town. He is one of them. No one else would defend them. We'll shoot him if he doesn't get out.' I tried to tell people like that that I could represent a rapist or a robber without being a rapist or a robber, and, in fact, that I had even represented Republicans. But I got nowhere. Then the crazy attacks even began infecting me, so I asked Margaret if she and Al were Communists. She said, 'No, they're too conservative.' That helped some, but not a whole lot. A schoolteacher told the class my daughter was in that Dan Jack Combs should be run out of town. Plenty of other people felt that way, and worse. I learned that a contract had been given out on me – to beat me badly but not kill me. I walked looking back over my shoulder for a week or so. But I didn't think I had to be careful even in court. I was leaving there one morning when a fellow came up behind me. He had a knife and was just about to stab me when someone stopped him. Most of all, though, I was scared for the McSurelys. The community was so hysterical anything could have happened."

James Millstone, a top reporter for the St. Louis *Post-Dispatch,* went to Pikeville to cover the story, and talked to several local residents about their fears of a Communist takeover of Pike County. A man who worked in a hardware store told him, "Rumors have been around here that there's two of 'em a-livin' up there on Island Creek. I've heard they go out of a night. If they're what we heard they are, we want 'em out." Millstone pressed the man to explain what these people were supposed to be doing, but all he would say was "They go out of a night."

Then a fresh rumor swept through the community – that the McSurelys had already organized a contingent of Red Guards, on the Chinese model, and that it was mobilizing to rescue them. "Word went out there was going to be a riot, that people from up North was going to come down and bust the jail open and get the McSurelys out," a local woman recalled. "Everybody started getting guns. Somebody even borrowed a shotgun from Dan Jack."

Mrs. McSurely was frightened and dispirited. Most of all, she feared the effects that her experience might have on her unborn child, and asked to see the doctor who had been taking care of her. He visited her and after an examination said that neither she nor the baby would be harmed if she had to stay in jail for a couple of weeks. He was very kind to her and was deeply upset about the behavior of the townspeople. When he left the jail, he was accosted on the street by a man who insulted him for giving medical care to "that Communist slut." The doctor paused long enough to threaten the man with a horsewhipping if he said another word, and then strode on.

Mrs. McSurely was also depressed by her surroundings. The cell she was in was small, with dark-gray, stained walls, and contained four bunks that had wooden slabs for springs and thin, filthy mattresses. There were no sheets, and each woman had a single worn blanket. The cell had four windows, three of them entirely without panes and one with a few slivers of glass remaining here and there in its frame. Rain and the cold night air from the mountains blew in, leaving the cell clammy and its occupants shivering. A bare bulb, which had to be screwed in and out to turn it on and off, hung from the middle of the ceiling. In the adjoining bathroom there was no light, no glass in the window, no hot water in the basin, and no water at all in the shower. The food served the prisoners was scarcely enough to support an adult: a typical lunch consisted of half a cup of lukewarm red beans, watery mashed potatoes, and a slice of tomato, and a typical dinner consisted of more red beans, cold macaroni, half a canned peach, and a couple of soggy cookies.

Most depressing of all to Mrs. McSurely, though, were her thoughts about the future. She was confident that she and her husband would get out of jail before long and that the sedition charge would ultimately be thrown out, but she was also confident that McSurely would insist on staying in the mountains. And from the time of the raid on their house she had been convinced that if they remained in the mountains they wouldn't accomplish much and sooner or later they would probably be killed. To comfort herself, she borrowed some paper and a pencil from a sympathetic jailer and wrote down a few verses from the Gospels that she remembered from her childhood:

> And he lifted up his eyes on his disciples, and said, "Blessed are ye poor: for yours is the kingdom of God.
>
> "Blessed are ye that hunger now: for ye shall be filled. Blessed are ye that weep now: for ye shall laugh.
>
> "Blessed are ye, when men shall hate you, and when they shall separate you from their company, and shall reproach you, and cast out your name as evil, for the Son of Man's sake.
>
> "Rejoice ye in that day, and leap for joy: for, behold, your reward is great in heaven: for in the like manner did their fathers unto the prophets."

McSurely, on the other hand, was not wholly displeased to be in jail. At the age of thirty-one, he was a decade older than the thousands of idealistic young people who had been locked up around the country for protesting against racism and the war in Vietnam. His main concern at the time was his wife's pregnancy, and he smuggled a letter to her urging that she get in touch with the Bradens and see if they could at least raise her bond money. Once out of jail, he added, she could move back to the cottage if that seemed safe, or she could ask Combs to find her somewhere to live for the time being. He also suggested that she might send some telegrams to people in the Movement asking for money and public support. But these matters were secondary, and, in confirmation of her worst fears, he wrote, "It seems to me that our major problem on getting out is re-establishing ourselves in the Pikeville community. I think we need to . . . explain that our cause is their cause."

Before long, McSurely got a message from his wife. "I really feel hung up," she wrote. "I am worried and don't have your good spirits all the time. I need you. The baby moves around a lot. I think [staying here] looks bad, like I don't care about it. But I don't know where I would go if I got out without you."

He wrote back to her, "When we get out I will hold you for 3 days straight, and we will frolic and gambol with each other, knowing full well that our freedom is in here — that in our topsy-turvy society the only free ones are those who have engaged it and lost — for the time being." Then he wrote a poem:

Trying to lock ideas in jail
Is like trying to stop
Time by breaking the hands off a clock.
While our bodies are confined,
Our ideas fly through the
Thick wire screens to the people.
Trying to stop people from reading, writing, and speaking
Is like trying to stop someone from getting older.
When will they ever learn?

Immediately after the bail hearing, Combs filed a habeas-corpus motion, and on the following Monday, two days later, a hearing on the motion was convened by Judge James Stephenson, of the Pike Circuit Court. Combs argued that under state law an arresting magistrate had to set bond or transfer the authority to set bond to a county judge, and that neither step had been taken in this case; that the arrest warrants did not, as required under law, specify the amount of bond to be set; that the bonds imposed by Judge Pauley were excessive; and that the defense's request at the bail hearing for an immediate hearing to determine whether the case merited being sent to trial had been unjustly denied. For all these reasons, Combs stated, the defendants were being illegally detained and should be released at once. Judge Stephenson denied the motion.

Frequently during the hearing, the Judge, who had coal-mine interests, consulted the Commonwealth Attorney on points of law, and when Ratliff told him, in open court, that the jailer had overheard McSurely say over the telephone to a friend who called him from Washington that he "liked being in jail," the Judge said he was infuriated that the hearing was being held at all. Actually, McSurely had told his friend that he and his wife were "proud to be political prisoners, along with our brothers and sisters" who had been jailed for protesting against racism – many of them in the riots that blazed through the country's black slums that summer.

Judge Stephenson became even angrier when Ratliff told him that Mrs. McSurely's parents, who had arrived in Pikeville the day before to help their daughter, had told another judge that they had tried to post her bond but that she had refused to accept it. Combs immediately asked for a recess to discuss the matter with Mrs. McSurely's parents, the Reverend and Mrs. Ralph Herring, who then told him that they hadn't been near a judge but that Mr. Herring had mentioned to a fellow Baptist minister in town, whom they consulted, that they would raise the bail money somehow if their daughter was in any danger. When court reconvened, Combs tried to call Mrs. Herring to the stand, but Judge Stephenson refused to allow her to testify. If what Ratliff said was true, he sternly told Combs, then the habeas-corpus hearing was a "farce," which he would not countenance; if it wasn't true, he went on, then Ratliff would "take it back."

In the corridor outside the courtroom afterward, Combs angrily told reporters that Ratliff could "claim a victory in his political ambitions and also a gain for his strip-mine friends." Ratliff, when told what Combs had said about him, expressed shock at the "unjustified and grossly untrue" charge, and then he went on a local radio program to inform the voters that he had been compelled to take time off from his political campaign in order to investigate the sedition case but that he would press on with that work even if it cost him the election. "When I began to investigate these charges, I knew that the McSurelys and the Bradens and their kind would try to harm my candidacy for lieutenant governor," he said. "These are the smear tactics always used by their kind against anyone who opposes them."

The O.E.O. made a study of the affair, and in a confidential report to Sargent Shriver it was stated that the arrests of the McSurelys and Mulloy were "the result of a campaign on the part of some local officials, particularly Commonwealth Attorney Thomas Ratliff, to drive the A.V.s out of Pike County," and, in addition, that Ratliff "thinks it is a good campaign issue." According to an F.B.I. agent quoted in the report, Ratliff might lose the sedition case in federal court, but his primary objective of "ridding Pike County of the anti-poverty workers" would be accomplished. A little later, the St. Louis *Post-Dispatch* noted that Ratliff, "a decided underdog in the state-wide November election, is expected to profit handsomely from his association with the case," and added, "Some observers think he is in a good position to upset his Democratic opponent."

At the start of the sedition case, Combs assumed that it would be a straightforward criminal matter in which he would test the legal procedures, the witnesses, and the evidence presented by the prosecutor. While Combs was a capable lawyer, with a successful practice and fairly broad experience in criminal cases, he was not an expert on constitutional law. But Mrs. Braden, who had been involved in many constitutional lawsuits, knew where to find such an expert to help the McSurelys. The civil-rights movement of the late nineteen-fifties and the early nineteen-sixties created a small but increasingly skillful group of lawyers who began restudying the Constitution and devising new legal means of obtaining justice for their clients. In the mid-sixties, some of these lawyers moved on to assist the anti-war movement, and used many of the techniques and tactics they had devised during the civil-rights struggle. In 1966, one of the leading lawyers in this group, William Kunstler, went into partnership with Arthur Kinoy, a professor at Rutgers Law School, Benjamin Smith, a New Orleans civil-rights lawyer, and Morton Stavis, a Newark, New Jersey, lawyer in private practice, to set up what ultimately became the Center for Constitutional Rights, in New York City, as a kind of law firm for radical reformers who were persecuted, and often prosecuted, by government on one level or another. The Center, which was supported by private donations, charged no fees to its clients.

Now Mrs. Braden got in touch with Kunstler, and that weekend he flew out to Lexington, Kentucky, to take the first step in what was to be a bitter legal contest that would go on for more than eight years. It was obvious to Kunstler from the outset that the proper approach to the sedition case at that stage was to be found in a suit that SCEF had been involved in a few years before. In

1963, the Louisiana Joint Legislative Committee on Un-American Activities dispatched its agents to conduct a raid on SCEF's offices in New Orleans. They carted away everything in the place and arrested SCEF's executive director, Dr. James A. Dombrowski, on a charge of violating the Louisiana Subversive Activities and Communist Control Law. Dombrowski sued various officials of the State of Louisiana for violating his constitutional rights, and the issue went to the Supreme Court, which agreed that the state law was unconstitutional. In the decision, handed down in 1965, the Court stated that freedom of expression is "of transcendent value to all society" and that whenever official acts have a "chilling effect upon the exercise of First Amendment rights" and threaten immediate and irreparable harm to an individual, the injured party can go directly to the federal courts for a quick ruling on the matter, and thereby avoid the prolonged delay and additional hardship that state court proceedings often entail.

The Supreme Court's purpose in Dombrowski was to stop state prosecutors in the South from harassing civil-rights workers by prosecuting them under clearly unconstitutional state laws, which were certain to be ultimately overturned by federal courts. By tying up civil-rights activists in state and federal courts for months or years, segregationists hoped to sap their time, money, and energies to such a degree that they would finally give up and go home. The Dombrowski case was particularly important in Kentucky, for in the mid-nineteen-fifties Carl Braden, co-director of SCEF, was convicted of sedition against the state after a house that he had sold to a black family in a suburb of Lexington was blown up; unable to raise his forty-thousand-dollar bail while appealing the verdict, Braden spent eight months in prison. The Kentucky Supreme Court reversed his conviction after the United States Supreme Court ruled in Pennsylvania v. Nelson, in 1956, that state sedition laws were preëmpted by a congressional act passed in the nineteen-forties that gave the federal government the job of guaranteeing the states' republican form of government. It was precisely to stop the kind of harassment Braden had suffered that Dombrowski had been formulated.

Although the First Amendment's guarantees of freedom of

speech, press, assembly, and religion referred to in Dombrowski seemed to apply less pertinently to the McSurely case than did the Fourth Amendment's guarantee of freedom from "unreasonable searches and seizures," the Dombrowski decision — above all, the "chilling effect" it spoke of — was clearly relevant. Accordingly, on August 16th, five days after the raid and arrest, Kunstler filed a motion before the United States District Court for the Eastern District of Kentucky, in Lexington, asking that a three-judge panel be convened, as the Dombrowski rule specifically provided for, to consider the issue of whether Kentucky's sedition law was constitutional. He also asked for a temporary restraining order to prevent further prosecution of the McSurelys by the state on the sedition charge until the issue was settled, and for an order impounding the materials confiscated from their house.

District Court Judge Bernard Moynahan, Jr., rejected the last two requests but granted the request for a three-judge panel to hear the case, and sent notice of his decision on to the Sixth Circuit Court of Appeals, across the Ohio River in Cincinnati. On August 28th, Circuit Court Judge Bert Combs, a former Democratic governor of Kentucky (and no relation of Lawyer Combs, as Dan Jack was often called locally), named himself, Moynahan, and District Court Judge James Gordon to serve as members of the special panel. Two days after that, Judge Combs ordered that a hearing on the case be held on the afternoon of September 1st.

During the two weeks' time between the request for a federal-court hearing and the hearing, a number of other developments took place. The O.E.O., fearing that it would be politically contaminated by association with McSurely, announced that he had never been connected with it except for serving as a "consultant" to the A.V.s for "a short time;" this left out the fact that he had worked for an O.E.O.-funded organization for the past three years in Washington. Then Shriver and Governor Breathitt, a Democrat, issued a joint statement announcing that all federal funding of the A.V.s in Kentucky was to be cut off as of September 1st;

Breathitt publicly commended the move as being "in the best interest of the needy people of Kentucky."

On August 18th, a preliminary hearing on the McSurely case was conducted in Pike Quarterly Court to determine whether there was enough evidence supporting the sedition charge to send the case to a grand jury. Judge Pauley presided, and allowed two witnesses to testify. One of them was Sheriff Justice, who described the books by Communists and about Communism that he had seen at the McSurelys' place. (He was something less than an expert witness on the subject of Communist writings, since at the time he had on display in his funeral parlor several copies of *False Witness,* by Harvey Matusow, which had been taken from the McSurelys' and which Justice failed to realize described rigged hearings against supposed Communists.) And the other was the younger Compton, who stated that on one of his visits to the McSurelys' he had seen a photograph showing black people and white people together. (The picture was a framed enlargement of a photograph that had appeared in the New York *Times;* it showed Robert F. Kennedy in Mississippi, smiling at a couple of Negro sharecroppers, who were regarding him with the utmost suspicion.) Compton also testified that he had seen a picture of Nikita Khrushchev. (The picture was of Che Guevara.) Then Judge Pauley called a recess to enable him to peruse the materials seized in the raid. He reconvened the court an hour later, and announced that there was ample evidence to justify turning the matter over to a grand jury.

During this period, Mrs. McSurely became increasingly concerned about a matter that she hadn't given much thought to at first — some love letters that Drew Pearson had written her, which she had half hidden at the back of a shelf in her bedroom closet and which had been confiscated by the raiders. She assumed that Ratliff, and probably all the other local officials involved, had read the letters — a thought that made her angry and sick with embarrassment every time it occurred to her — and she was beginning to fear that the letters might be used in some fashion to harm Pearson. She sent word to him about what had happened through a couple of friends in Washington who already knew about her affair with the columnist. Pearson, who had based many of his "Washington Merry-Go-Round" columns on purloined letters, probably knew better than anyone else in the country what could be done with such documents, and he was frantic. But he refused to help, at least directly. Finally, after a week in jail, the two were bailed out by SCEF, through the Bradens, who had raised security for the bonds by putting up a SCEF office building in Louisville. Then, shortly after being released, Mrs. McSurely wrote Pearson an angry note — on the back of a SCEF press release announcing that a three-judge federal panel had been set up to hear the case:

> DEAR D.P.
>
> Thanks anyway about the bail. It's O.K. But if you had any sense you would do everything you could to get this case into the federal courts immediately and out of the hands of Pike Co. officials who stole everything and will use it. The 3-judge fed. panel must be convened before the grand jury hearing.
>
> MARGARET

The grand-jury hearing was scheduled for September 5th, a week and a half from the time she wrote Pearson. Pearson had wide influence in Democratic Party circles, but whether he used it in this matter is unknown. Under the law, personal letters cannot be published without their author's permission, except by official bodies such as grand juries, courts, and legislative committees that obtain legal possession of them. If the Pearson letters, along with the rest of the McSurelys' papers, were impounded by a federal-court order overruling Moynahan, Pearson would at least have time to work out some other means of getting the letters back or seeing that they were destroyed before they were made public. If they were, he knew that he could be hurt badly, because as a persistent critic of irregular official conduct on the part of public servants he would certainly be subject to criticism for his own irregular conduct as a private citizen. Conceivably, he might even be ruined by publication of the letters, and there were many people in the country who would have liked to see him ruined.

A few days after Pearson got Mrs. McSurely's note, Judge Combs set the federal hearing for September 1st — four days before the grand jury was to hear evidence on the state sedition charges. All this is not to say that Judge Combs was influenced, directly or indirectly, by Pearson or his friends. There were other reasons for the Judge to act expeditiously. While he could not be openly active in politics as long as he was on the federal bench, he was one of the most powerful Democrats in Kentucky and had wide influence that could be exerted in ways that would not involve him. At the time, the state Democratic Party was in trouble, and although it expected to lose the governor's chair to the Republicans, it still had a good chance to hold on to the lieutenant governorship against Ratliff, whose part in the sedition case was not helping his Democratic opponent. Judge Combs had another good reason for helping his party: he was not finished with politics and was soon to run for governor again. And, finally, the sole purpose of the Dombrowski rule was to provide quick federal-court remedies for citizens who were unjustly harmed by state actions against them.

Robert Matthews, Attorney General of Kentucky, promised that his office would support Pike County officials in their efforts to stamp out sedition, but he publicly warned that the Supreme Court had set up "some stumbling blocks which might cause pitfalls." Matthews was responsible for defending the state in cases involving it before federal courts, but on September 1st he merely appeared at the three-judge hearing and said nothing. It was Ratliff's case — not to mention Ratliff's political campaign — and he told the court that while Kunstler's brief may have been correct in asserting that the federal government had, as the Supreme Court had ruled in 1956, jurisdiction over subversion against it, the states were not thereby prohibited from defending themselves against local attempts to overthrow them. In conclusion, Ratliff assured the court that there had been no conspiracy on the part of local officials to run the plaintiffs — as the McSurelys and Mulloy were in the federal suit — out of Pike County.

When Kunstler's turn came, he contended that the case was identical to Dombrowski, and that the Kentucky sedition law was clearly unconstitutional, since it violated the free-speech, free-press, and free-assembly guarantees of the First Amendment, and that in its "overbreadth" and "vagueness" it violated the due-process clause of the Fourteenth Amendment. Kunstler then asked the court to enjoin Ratliff from continuing the sedition prosecution until the panel handed down its ruling. At that, Ratliff quickly assured the court that he would take no further action on the case until the panel came to a decision on the issue at hand. Judge Combs, who presided as chief judge of the panel, accepted the promise and did not issue an official injunction against further proceedings in the state case. To give both sides time to prepare briefs and responses, he set September 14th for pleadings before the panel.

Afterward, Ratliff told reporters that he had nothing against the McSurelys, and added, "We in Pike County, although we may not agree with their philosophy of life, certainly don't want to deny these people their freedom of speech."

Four days later, Circuit Court Judge Stephenson convened the fall-term Pike County grand jury for a hearing on the sedition case, with Lawyer Combs, Ratliff, and Assistant Commonwealth Attorney Herman Dotson present. When the hearing got under way, Ratliff rose and told the Judge, "As you know, there have been proceedings in the federal court on this matter, and I merely wish to advise the court that I agreed not to proceed in this matter as Commonwealth Attorney for this district. Now, I don't presume to impose my views or agreement on this court. I merely advise you of what has been done. No injunction has been issued against this grand jury, this court, or anything else, but I just wanted to advise Your Honor that I agreed as Commonwealth Attorney not to proceed in this matter. We still have the evidence, and the federal authorities do not have it, and we intend to keep it until — "

Combs jumped to his feet and angrily protested that Ratliff had promised the federal court that he wouldn't proceed in the sedition case.

Judge Stephenson waved aside the objection, saying, "Mr. Ratliff has stated that he does not intend to proceed. I would expect, then, that the Assistant Commonwealth Attorney would be before the grand jury."

Ratliff said that he meant to abide by his promise to the federal court, and added, "But, now, this grand jury I do not control."

Judge Stephenson nodded, and asserted that he had no control over it, either. "This grand jury is under no restraint," he said. "I can't tell them what they are going to consider and what they are not going to consider. . . . If the grand jury desires to investigate this matter, if the grand jury desires to hear this evidence, I will see that someone is made available to present this evidence to them." Turning to the grand jurors, he went on, "Now, of course, during your deliberations the Commonwealth Attorney or his assistant will be present to offer you assistance in interrogating the witnesses and advising you on any legal questions that may arise. . . . Should you desire to – and I take it you will – to look into this charge of sedition."

Ratliff repeated that he couldn't be involved, and his assistant, Dotson, said that he felt bound by Ratliff's promise to the federal court, too, so Judge Stephenson promised to appoint an outside lawyer to present the facts to the grand jury.

Combs again objected that the federal-court order was being ignored, and Ratliff snapped, "There is no order."

Judge Stephenson agreed, and said to Combs, "I have indulged you far enough." Then the Judge said to the grand jurors, "Now, the grand jury is free to look into these matters referred to if they want to, and I take it they want to."

Six days later, the grand jury returned indictments against the McSurelys, Mulloy, and, unexpectedly, the Bradens for "advocating criminal syndicalism or sedition." Accompanying the indictments was a report stating the grand jury's conclusions:

> 1. That a well organized and well financed effort is being made to promote and spread the communistic theory of the violent and forceful overthrow of the government of Pike County.
>
> 2. That communist organizers have been sent to Pike County by radical organizations which have paid them, supported them, furnished them with printed propaganda materials, controlled them and directed their work.
>
> 3. That some employees of the Appalachian Volunteers (A.V.)

and other federally financed anti-poverty programs have collaborated and cooperated with known communist organizers to help them organize and promote the violent overthrow of the constitutional government of Pike County. The officials of the A.V. knew or should have known that these communist organizers were actively working among the A.V. in Pike County. These organizers were brought to Pike County on the payroll of the A.V. and were fired because of their communist activities.

4. That local officials of the A.V. have cooperated with known communist organizers by allowing them to conduct training sessions among Vista workers, Peace Corps trainees, A.V. workers, and local citizens in which sessions these organizers were allowed to state their views.

5. That local officials of the A.V. have permitted known communists to take part in the writing of editorials in A.V. sponsored community newspapers and in directing schools sponsored and supported by A.V.

6. That A.V. have permitted known communists to infiltrate, influence and take part in community protests and projects when said A.V. knew full well that the purpose of these organizers was to exploit the local people and their cause so as to promote violence against the local government and the local courts.

7. That communist organizers have attempted, without success thus far, to promote their beliefs among our school children by infiltrating our local schools with teachers who believed in the violent overthrow of the local government.

8. That communist organizers are attempting and planning to infiltrate local churches and labor unions in order to cause dissension and to promote their purposes.

9. That communist organizers are attempting to form Community Unions with the eventual purpose of organizing armed groups to be known as "Red Guards" and through which the actual forceful overthrow of the local government would be accomplished.

Toward the end of the report, the grand jury recommended that the federal government's contract with the A.V.s be cancelled throughout the South and that if the state sedition law was found to be unconstitutional, then the state legislature should enact new laws to "control such activities." The report concluded, "This grand jury is made up of twelve citizens of Pike County. We are farmers, housewives, small businessmen and coal miners. We are members of both political parties. It is regrettable that certain persons have used certain newspapers and other news media to question the motives of this Grand Jury, our Courts, our citizens and our public officials who have made and investigated these charges. We found no evidence that these charges were made or prompted because of strip mining or for political purposes."

Not long afterward, Ratliff told a reporter, "I am not a nut on this thing. Frankly, I laughed about these things when I first heard them. Then I got into this material [of the McSurelys'] and I became convinced. After reading two thousand letters and umpteen pamphlets and articles, I believe that these people not only mean business but are doing business in this county." While this statement appeared to be a flat admission on Ratliff's part that he had conducted the raid on the McSurelys, confiscated their possessions, and put them in jail without believing in the legal justification for his acts, he seemed serious about the conclusions he later reached.

McSurely, for one, has come to believe in Ratliff's sincerity – on this point, at least. "Most of the things he accused us of were true," McSurely said later. "Ratliff had a more comprehensive view of us than we had of ourselves. He had read all that stuff we handed out, but we hadn't actually read most of it. We had never sat down and decided what it was that we were trying to do. Ratliff sat down and read all our stuff, and said, 'My God, these people are really serious. They mean it. They're going to start a revolution.' That was certainly the logical result of what we were trying to do. But we have never supported, or worked for, violent overthrow of the government. We merely hoped to bring down the government in Pike County by voting it out of office at the polls and replacing it with a people's government. Although we don't believe in the present system, we believe in what it is falsely claimed to be based on – the Declaration of Independence, the Constitution, and the Bill of Rights."

The grand-jury report produced another wave of public hysteria in the mountains of eastern Kentucky. Large portions of the report were printed in newspapers throughout the area, and were broadcast on radio and television stations. It soon became clear that the grand jury's conclusions would affect more than the McSurelys' future. "Whether ridiculed or taken seriously, the grand jury's action, following three months of unrest in the backwoods hills and hollows over the ticklish issue of strip mining, carried implications extending far beyond the mountain barrier," the *Post-Dispatch* observed in mid-September. "It brought the nation's anti-poverty program to another crossroads, testing once again whether Americans really want to allow the poor to assert themselves; it injected a strident new campaign issue into the state gubernatorial election and it raised the intensity of the strip-mining controversy."

Another effect of the report was that the public fear it generated further stirred up official hysteria. Twenty-four hours after it was released, the Bradens were driving from Louisville to Pikeville to be arraigned on the sedition charges, but their car had a flat tire and they couldn't get to a telephone. The Judge waited awhile, and then angrily issued bench warrants for their arrest. When they arrived at the courthouse and got out of their car, a couple of deputies recognized them, put them under arrest, and led them into court. The Bradens refused to post bond and asked to be released on their own recognizance. The Judge clapped them in jail.

Lawyer Combs demanded that Judge Combs reconvene the three-judge panel and find Ratliff in contempt for violating the agreement reached with the federal panel. There was little likelihood that the request would be granted. Not only had Ratliff kept his word, whatever he did in violation of the spirit of his promise, but there was little reason for the Judge to make him a political martyr who could then claim that he was a victim of a partisan cabal to ruin his election chances.

Three days after the grand jury handed up the indictments, the federal panel heard further arguments on the sedition issue, and this time Ratliff specifically demonstrated what he hoped to prove in a state trial – namely, that Mrs. McSurely and the Bradens had attended the April meeting in Nashville at which Stokely Carmichael had spoken and after which there had been a riot; that Mrs. McSurely formerly worked for S.N.C.C.; that the McSurelys were distributing material put out by Vietnam Summer advocating a Vietcong victory in Vietnam; and that they were preaching Communist philosophy to the people of Pike County. During cross-examination of Mrs. McSurely, he took great delight in eliciting from her that she knew H. Rap Brown, which apparently impressed no one else, and then he took great pains, with no success, to prove that the Bradens were "card-carrying" Communists.

Afterward, Professor Robert Sedler, of the University of Kentucky Law School, who served as *amicus curiae* for the Kentucky Civil Liberties Union throughout the case, observed that Ratliff's strategy was obviously to brand the Bradens as Communists and then to link the McSurelys with the Bradens and Mulloy with the McSurelys. By these means, Ratliff would be able, in any local trial of the case, to make it appear that all attacks on local and state officials, coal-mine owners and operators, and businessmen who supported them were part of a Communist plot. "It is almost impossible to believe that the jury would not have returned a verdict of guilty," Sedler said. "This would indelibly have branded the anti-poverty workers as 'Communists' in the minds of the people in the area. Assuming that the conviction would later have been reversed, it could be said that this was on a technicality. In other words, if the case were allowed to come to trial, the government officials would have the political victory irrespective of the final result."

Judge Combs proved to be more than equal to Ratliff's legal and political strategy. At the end of the hearing, to the astonishment of the litigants and their lawyers, the Judge announced the court's findings: the sedition law was "so vague and of such sweeping application" that it was obviously unconstitutional; the Dombrowski rule was applicable; and since the plaintiffs had already suffered irreparable harm, it was "ordered and directed that the Commonwealth of Kentucky, and all courts of the Commonwealth, the defendants herein [Ratliff, the state attorney general, the sheriff, and the jailer], and any and all persons acting in concert and accord with them be and they are hereby enjoined from taking any further action or proceeding in any manner against these plaintiffs under the statute in issue herein." Then Judge Combs ordered that the Bradens, who had been made a party to the suit, be released from jail at once and that all five plaintiffs be freed from state bond, placed under bond to the federal court until any appeal might be settled, and freed on their own recognizance. Finally, he denied the motion to find Ratliff in contempt, and ordered him to serve as custodian of the materials seized in the raids, which were to be held "in safekeeping until final disposition of this case."

(It was fortunate for the McSurelys that their case came up when it did, for in 1971, in Younger v. Harris, the Supreme Court sharply limited the Dombrowski rule. The result was to restrict citizens' access to federal courts in situations like the McSurelys' by compelling such defendants to go through state-court procedures first in many cases. Had this decision been on the books when the McSurelys were arrested, they would probably have had to go to trial in a Kentucky court, would undoubtedly have been convicted and sentenced to prison, and, like Braden, might have had such high bail imposed by a state court pending appeal that they could have remained in prison for months or even years. Moreover, in the end the Supreme Court might have refused to review their convictions.)

Judge Combs was not finished with Ratliff. A few weeks later, just before the statewide election, the federal panel handed down its formal opinion, written by the presiding judge. After describing the passage of the Kentucky sedition law in 1920, during the national hysteria that followed the Bolshevik Revolution, Judge Combs observed, "It was good politics to be against Communism." He went on to recount the events that had brought the current sedition case before the federal court, and then wrote:

> The statute in question is clearly unconstitutional under even the most flexible yardstick. It is too broad and too vague. It contravenes the First Amendment to the Constitution of the United States because it unduly prohibits freedom of speech, freedom of

> the press, and the right of assembly. It fails to distinguish between the advocacy of ideas and the advocacy of action. It makes it a criminal offense merely to possess, with intent to circulate, literature on the subject of sedition. It imposes the penalty of imprisonment for advocating an unpopular political belief. It would turn the courts into a forum for argument of political theories, with imprisonment the penalty for the loser. It contains no requirement of criminal intent. The unwary and the ignorant could be enmeshed in the dragnet as easily as the covert plotter.
>
> One of the definitions of sedition in the 1920 Act is "the advocacy or suggestion by word, act, deed, or writing . . . of the change or modification of the government of the United States or of the Commonwealth of Kentucky, or of the Constitution or laws of either of them . . . by means other than by lawful means. . . ." A person could thus be indicted for suggesting a change in the state or federal Constitution "by means other than by lawful means." What is lawful would of necessity have to be decided by the presiding judge. This is a plain violation of the Sixth Amendment to the federal Constitution, which guarantees the right of the accused "to be informed of the nature and cause of the accusation." Under the Sixth Amendment, a person cannot be charged merely with violating the law; the charge must be more specific. . . .
>
> It is difficult to believe that capable lawyers could seriously contend that this statute is constitutional. . . . In addition, the conclusion is inescapable that the criminal prosecutions were instituted, at least in part, in order to stop plaintiffs' organizing activities in Pike County. That effort has been successful. Not only has there been the "chilling effect" on freedom of speech referred to in Dombrowski, there has been in fact a freezing effect.

The Republican candidate for governor of Kentucky was elected that November, but Ratliff lost his race by a large margin, with even the voters of Pike County rejecting him.

Although it would be difficult to find a court opinion that seemed to dispose of a case with greater finality than Judge Combs' opinion did, the McSurely case was far from over. In fact, it had scarcely begun, because so far neither the lawyers nor the courts had addressed the main issue — the Fourth Amendment's prohibition "against unreasonable searches and seizures." To make full use of the Dombrowski rule, Kunstler had concentrated on the unconstitutionality of the sedition law, which clearly violated the rule's prohibitions against official incursions upon the First Amendment's rights of expression and assembly, and up to that point he had paid only cursory attention to possible violations of the "unreasonable searches and seizures" clause of the Fourth Amendment. Actually, this clause lay at the heart of the case and at the heart of what Justice Louis Brandeis called "the right to be let alone — the most comprehensive of rights and the right most valued by civilized men."

Despite the Fourth Amendment's sanction and despite the federal court's overturning of the Kentucky sedition law, the McSurelys were no closer to getting their things back than they had been immediately after the raid. As a matter of fact, they were further away than ever, because the focus of the case suddenly and unexpectedly shifted to a new question: Were they legally entitled to have exclusive possession of their property if it was returned to them?

"We never dreamed this question would come up," Mrs. McSurely said recently. "And when it did, we couldn't believe what was happening to us."

On August 11, 1967 — by coincidence, the day of the raid on the McSurelys — the United States Senate approved Resolution 150 of the Ninetieth Congress authorizing the Senate Committee on Government Operations "to make a full and complete study and investigation of riots [which engulfed scores of American cities that summer], violent disturbances of the peace, vandalism, civil and criminal disorders, the commission of crimes in connection therewith, the immediate and longstanding causes." The following day, the committee's chairman, John L. McClellan, Democrat of Arkansas, chose the Permanent Subcommittee on Investigations, of which he was also chairman, to conduct the investigations authorized by the resolution.

Over the years, Drew Pearson and his colleague Jack Anderson had repeatedly attacked Senator McClellan on the ground of conflict of interest. The day before Resolution 150 was approved by the Senate, the Pearson-Anderson syndicated column, "Washington Merry-Go-Round," dealt with McClellan's efforts to get a bill through Congress imposing an eighteen-month moratorium on all copyright-infringement lawsuits against cable television, or C.A.T.V. At the time, performers and writers whose work was being pirated by C.A.T.V. had begun to threaten damage suits, so, according to the column, C.A.T.V. lawyers drafted a bill for a moratorium, and it was introduced by Senator McClellan, who was also chairman of the Judiciary Subcommittee on Patents, Trademarks, and Copyrights. "I will oppose anything I think will destroy C.A.T.V.," McClellan stated on the floor of the Senate.

The "Washington Merry-Go-Round" reported, "He has neglected to mention to his colleagues, however, that he holds valuable stock in one of the C.A.T.V. giants – Midwest Video, which has outlets in Mississippi, Missouri, New Mexico, South Dakota, and Texas." The same column also went into McClellan's efforts to protect the banking business, and said, "Probably nothing can get McClellan out of his Senate chair faster . . . than a challenge to the banks. He has bitterly opposed the chartering of new national banks, which would give the old-line banks some competition." After listing some examples of the Senator's attempts to block new charters, the column went on, "In all his fire-and-brimstone attacks on new charters, McClellan never mentioned that he was a stockholder in both the West Memphis Bank and the First National Bank of Little Rock, the two old-line banks fighting the charters. Indeed, McClellan is listed as one of the top 20 stockholders in First National."

Still another passage in the column described an attempt, some years earlier, by an oil-company lobbyist to bribe Senator Francis Case, Republican of South Dakota, by handing him a brown-paper bag containing twenty-five hundred dollars in cash just before election time. When Case denounced the man before the Senate, Albert Gore, chairman of the Subcommittee on Privileges and Elections, rose and vowed to investigate the episode. But Lyndon

Johnson, then Majority Leader and long a friend of the oil industry, spent ten days persuading him to turn the investigation over to McClellan. Gore finally gave in, McClellan conducted some desultory hearings, and the oil people were absolved of all wrongdoing. "What the public never knew was that McClellan's law firm in Little Rock then represented Standard Oil of New Jersey, Seaboard Oil, Tidewater Associated Oil, and Carter Oil," the column concluded.

Apart from the problem of conflicting interests, it would have been difficult to find a more unsuitable senator than John McClellan to investigate the riots that swept the country that summer. Most of the riots were in the North, and McClellan was a Southerner; almost all of them were in sizable cities, and McClellan came from Sheridan, Arkansas; almost all of them involved blacks, and McClellan had an unblemished record of racism; almost all of the riots demonstrated an overwhelming need for an objective and searching study of the nation's fundamental social and economic inequities, and McClellan was obsessed by the bootstrap theory of life and the professed belief that most of the nation's ills were the work of left-wing subversives. But McClellan was a powerful senator, and since he wanted the assignment of investigating the series of national calamities, he got it.

Liberals and moderates in both parties were appalled by the choice. "There is no charity in the man," one Democrat said in private. And a Republican dismissed him as "a ruthlessly self-interested bigot." Still, few senators dared oppose his appointment openly, for he was too powerful, and vindictive, to take on as an enemy. But even his severest critics held out some hope that he would approach the worst domestic crisis to confront the nation since the Civil War with a little common sense. These hopes were shattered by his announcement of one of the first hearings to be held by his subcommittee — on the small and comparatively insignificant "riot" that had taken place in Nashville the previous April. The announcement made it clear that McClellan's aim was to confirm his own earlier pronouncements — that the terrible discord tearing at the nation was the work of Communists and their dupes. If he could convince the public on this point, he would, of course, go a long way toward breaking down the civil-rights and anti-poverty movements with one stroke.

Soon after Judge Combs ordered the McSurelys' possessions impounded, an investigator from McClellan's subcommittee telephoned Ratliff in Kentucky and asked if he still had custody of them. He replied that he did, and on October 8th a subcommittee investigator by the name of John Brick flew to Kentucky and registered in Pikeville at the Landmark Motel, which was owned by Ratliff. That evening, Ratliff and Thaddeus Scott, a detective on his staff, visited Brick in his room. A little later, Ratliff and Scott left, and not long afterward Scott came back alone and delivered a bundle of manila folders to Brick. The folders contained photocopies of some of the McSurelys' documents seized in the raid, and Brick spent a couple of hours examining them. The next morning, Scott drove to the Landmark again, and he and Brick went to the Pike County Courthouse, where Brick was shown into a locked room that contained all of the McSurelys' confiscated possessions. He spent an hour perusing the originals of the papers he was most interested in, and then he left and walked down the street to the post office, where the federal government maintained its local office. Brick inspected the official files on the federal suit, including the decision of the three-judge panel, the order to Ratliff to hold the seized materials "in safekeeping," and an inventory of what was contained in them.

Brick returned to Washington briefly and then came back to Pikeville. On October 12th, he spent four hours going through the McSurelys' papers once more, and afterward he flew to Washington with copies of two hundred and thirty-four documents of the McSurelys'. Over the next three days, he conferred several times with McClellan, who, according to Brick's later testimony in court, was particularly interested in a love letter from Pearson to Margaret that began "Dearest Cucumber." According to a source within McClellan's office, the Senator also spent a good deal of time reading, and chuckling over, her diary.

During this period, the time for an appeal from the federal panel's ruling on the sedition case lapsed, and Lawyer Combs informed Ratliff that he would move for an order instructing Ratliff to return the McSurelys' papers to them. Afterward, Ratliff denied that he had been informed of Combs' intention or that he had notified Brick of it. Within a matter of hours, however, Brick, on McClellan's personal instructions, drew up some subpoenas – one for Ratliff and one each for the McSurelys. On the evening of October 16th, Brick flew back to Kentucky to serve Senate subpoenas for the McSurelys' papers. At a little after eight o'clock the next morning, Brick climbed the steps to the McSurelys' house at Harold's Branch.

"There was a knock on the door, and when I opened it a little man was standing there holding a sheaf of papers," Mrs. McSurely recalled. "He asked if this was where Alan and Margaret McSurely lived, and I said, 'Yes, it is.' Then he introduced himself and told me that he had some subpoenas for us from the United States Senate. His hand with the papers was shaking so I thought he was cold, and invited him in for a cup of coffee. I just couldn't believe it about the subpoenas. I had figured we'd win the sedition case all right, even though it might take a couple of years, but I never expected to be subpoenaed by the Senate. Anyway, he came inside, and I introduced him to Al. Then he gave us the subpoenas. I said, 'Let's go into the kitchen. It's warmer in there.' The man was so nervous he wouldn't sit down or take the cup of coffee I poured for him, and once he nearly fell on the floor, it was so slanty. He kept saying, 'I'm just doing my job,' and 'The Senate doesn't want you, it just wants your papers.' He said they were for the subcommittee hearings on the Nashville riot. It was all so fantastic I couldn't believe it was happening. Why would the Senate want our silly papers? I kept wondering.

"Then suddenly something clicked in my mind about the name Brick. I remembered that when I was so upset during the time my first marriage was breaking up and I was having an affair with Pearson I went to a psychiatrist who had a secretary named Mrs. Brick. It wasn't a common name, so I asked if it might be his wife. He got even more nervous, and said that it was. I asked him how she and their daughters she had talked to me about were, and he said they were fine. Now things were even more fantastic. After about fifteen minutes, Brick left. Once he was gone, I started to worry about Mrs. Brick, because I knew she typed up the doctor's notes on his sessions, and I was sure there had been a lot of stuff taken down about Pearson and me. When I thought of that, I got on the phone immediately and called the psychiatrist and told him what had happened. He said he was certain that Mrs. Brick would never divulge anything she had learned in her work, even to her husband, but he promised to destroy my file just the same."

Stunned as the McSurelys were by the delivery of the subpoenas, they were dumbfounded by their contents, which ordered them to "produce all books, records, correspondence, documents, and other papers which are in the possession and control of Alan McSurely or Margaret McSurely or their agents and which relate to or pertain to" the Southern Conference Educational Fund, the Student Nonviolent Coordinating Committee, the Southern Students Organizing Committee, the Appalachian Volunteers, the Volunteers in Service to America, the United Planning Organization, the Action Coordinating Committee to End Segregation in the Suburbs, Jobs or Income Now, the National Conference for New Politics, Students for a Democratic Society, Vietnam Summer, the Mississippi Freedom Democratic Party, the Communist Party, the Progressive Labor Party, and all "Marxist-Leninist organizations."

Of course, the McSurelys were unaware of Brick's earlier visits to Pikeville and his examination of their papers. Although Mrs. McSurely had told her husband long before about her affair with Pearson, McSurely didn't know about the existence of the love letters or about her diary. "I was too embarrassed by having my soul bared before all those sick men who must have read them to even talk about it with Al," she said later. "I didn't dream that the Pearson stuff, while personally embarrassing, would turn out to be a matter of life and death. What worried me most was that the names and addresses of our friends in the Movement all over the country were in those papers, and so were many of their letters to us. These innocent people had written us about their work and their personal struggles and their views about society. All of them were subject to reprisal in one way or another."

McSurely, for his part, was more upset by the attempt to take away their personal papers — as he put it, "by the ruling class showing how low it would stoop to try and stop us." He telephoned Lawyer Combs, who immediately filed a motion for the return of the papers. Then the couple sat down to discuss what they should do about the Senate subpoenas. "Our friends were at stake," McSurely said. "Our personal lives were at stake. Our work, our privacy were at stake. We decided that we had to fight."

II

"Whenever you shall find a painter, male or female, I pray you to suggest a scene and a subject for the pencil," former President John Adams wrote in 1817, in a letter to a friend who had asked him about the origins of the American Revolution. "The scene is the Council Chamber in the old Town House in Boston. The date is in the month of February, 1761. . . . In this chamber, round a great fire, were seated five Judges, with Lieutenant-Governor Hutchinson at their head, as Chief Justice, all arrayed in their new, fresh, rich robes of scarlet English broadcloth; in their large cambric bands, and immense judicial wigs. In this chamber were seated at a long table all the barristers at law of Boston, and of the neighboring county of Middlesex, in gowns, bands, and tie wigs." One of the lawyers at the table was Adams himself, who was then twenty-five years old and had just been admitted to the bar of the Massachusetts Bay Colony. He made notes of the events that took place in the Council Chamber before the Superior Court of Judicature – events which, he wrote more than half a century later, "began the Revolution in the principles, views, opinions, and feelings of the American people."

Having set the scene, Adams went on to describe the subject that concerned the men gathered in the Council Chamber. To begin with, he wrote, the British had captured Montreal the year before, and thereby eliminated any serious French threat to the British colonies to the south. Once this security was established, the British immediately set out to subject these colonies "to the unlimited authority of Parliament," including the authority to tax the Americans enough to pay the cost of keeping them in subjection while they were exploited by British mercantile interests. Adams went on, "With this view and intention they sent orders and instructions to the collector of the customs in Boston, Mr. Charles Paxton, to apply to the civil authority for writs of assistance, to enable the custom-house officers, tidewaiters, landwaiters, and all, to command all sheriffs and constables, &c., to attend and aid them in breaking open houses, stores, shops, cellars, ships, bales, trunks, chests, casks, packages of all sorts, to search for goods, wares, and merchandises, which had been imported against the prohibitions or without paying the taxes imposed by certain acts of Parliament, called the acts of trade."

Writs of assistance empowered their possessors to break into anyone's property and search it for any smuggled goods, and to compel any Crown officer or subject to help search for and seize such evidence. These writs did not contain the names of suspects or descriptions of what evidence against them was to be looked for. Apart from the writs' authorization to the holders to enlist anyone's assistance in carrying out their orders, they were the same as what are called "general warrants," and the two terms came to be used interchangeably. In England, officials began employing writs of assistance and general warrants in earnest during the sixteenth century, and they were widely used in the bloody days of the Court of Star Chamber, when anyone who opposed, or even appeared to think of opposing, the Crown could be arrested, tortured, and convicted of treason, on the basis of forcibly confiscated evidence, for the slightest display of disloyalty to the sovereign. The Star Chamber lineage of such writs and warrants gradually led to widespread public disfavor, and by the middle of the eighteenth century their use in England was restricted to occasional cases of seditious libel — that is, almost any criticism of any part, member, or action of the government.

Most of the Acts of Trade were passed in the seventeenth century, and they contained authority to control colonial trade and colonial taxes, along with bits and pieces of royal prerogative that ministers in London pasted together to justify granting writs of assistance as a means of enforcing the trade statutes. "I never turned over the leaves of these statutes, or any section of them, without pronouncing a hearty curse upon them," Adams wrote, and added, "All these rigorous statutes were now to be carried into rigorous execution by the still more rigorous instruments of arbitrary power, '*writs of assistance.*' "

One of the most rigorous of the statutes was the Molasses Act, which imposed a heavy tax on the importation of sugar and molasses from non-British ports in an effort to stop the busy and profitable trade between American colonists and merchants in the French and Spanish islands of the West Indies. New England, for example, sent horses, cattle, lumber, casks, and salted cod to the West Indies, and brought back in exchange molasses, which was distilled into rum and then exchanged in America for everything from tobacco to slaves. The Molasses Act, a potentially oppressive instrument, had seldom been enforced and was easily circumvented by American colonists, who simply got false English receipts in Jamaica, a British possession, for molasses that had actually come from French and Spanish islands, and for many years everyone winked at the deception. But in 1760 the Prime Minister, William Pitt the Elder, suddenly ordered the Molasses Act strictly enforced, and the order went out to British customs collectors in the colonies to use all means, including writs of assistance, to find and confiscate contraband molasses.

In October, 1760, George II died, and by a statute of Queen Anne all writs of assistance expired six months after the death of the sovereign. Paxton, who had been using such writs in the ordinary conduct of his office for several years, applied for a new set of writs from the Superior Court of Judicature, which was sitting in Boston. By this time, merchants and lawyers there had become aware of the grim results that enforcement of the Molasses Act would bring to commerce in the colonies. Manufacturers and farmers would have no market for their wares and produce except British markets at British prices; colonial shippers, who could not hope to make a profit under the new taxes, would have to let their vessels rot at the wharves; the five thousand seamen they employed would have to find other work or starve; and no one would benefit but the British.

Under English law, enforcement of the Molasses Act and the other Acts of Trade lay with the colonial Court of Admiralty, which was independent of the Bay Colony and subject only to the orders of the king. The judge who headed that court was answerable solely to him, and was to decide any question of tax evasion on information provided by royal officers, with no jury present; he received his income from money gained by the sale of forfeited goods, which he alone could order. And the royal governor, appointed by the king and not responsible to the colony, was to receive a third of all forfeitures of the condemned contraband.

Once these facts became known to the merchants of Boston, sixty-three of them demanded a hearing before the Superior Court on the question of new writs. Unfortunately for their cause, Chief Justice Stephen Sewall, who sympathized with them, died shortly before the court convened in Boston in February, 1761. The newly appointed governor, Sir Francis Bernard, who had been shifted to Massachusetts after loyally serving the king as governor of New Jersey, appointed as chief justice his lieutenant governor, Thomas Hutchinson, another devoted servant of the Crown, who was also a member of the local governing council and a probate judge, and who was permitted to keep these posts while serving as chief justice. "Every observing and thinking man knew that this appointment was made for the direct purpose of deciding this question in favor of the crown," Adams wrote. "An alarm was spread far and wide."

One of the most alarmed subjects in the Bay Colony was James Otis, Jr., who was advocate general of the Admiralty Court there. For one thing, his father, who was Speaker of the Massachusetts House of Representatives, had been promised the first vacancy on the Superior Court by the two governors who preceded Bernard. For another, the younger Otis was deeply influenced by Montesquieu — particularly by his warning against investing executive, legislative, and judicial powers in one man. And, finally, Otis was convinced that Great Britain meant to crush the colonies through taxation. He immediately resigned as advocate general — a position that Adams described as "a sure road to the highest favors of government in America" — and accepted the appeals of the merchants of Salem and Boston "to defend them against the terrible menacing monster, the writ of assistance." They put up a very large legal fee, but Otis declined it, saying, "In such a cause I despise all fees."

"There were no stenographers in those days," Adams noted fifty-seven years later. "Speeches were not printed; and all that was not remembered . . . was lost in air." But Adams had his minutes of the court hearing and his memories, and five and a half decades later they still filled him with wonder as he recalled Otis's attack on the writs of assistance and the Acts of Trade, which, Adams wrote, "imposed taxes, and enormous taxes, burdensome taxes, oppressive, ruinous, intolerable taxes." As Adams listened to Otis's five-hour "declamation, invective, philippic, call it which you will, against the tyranny of taxation without representation," he became increasingly spellbound and increasingly fearful. "A contest appeared to me to be opened, to which I could foresee no end, and which would render my life a burden, and property, industry, and every thing insecure," he wrote in his autobiography. "There was no alternative left but to take the side which appeared to be just, to march intrepidly forward in the right path, to trust in Providence for the protection of truth and right, and to die with a good conscience and a decent grace, if that trial should become indispensable."

According to Adams' reconstruction of the day's events, Otis rose and addressed the court, saying, "May it please your Honors, I was desired by one of the Court to look into the books, and consider the question now before [you] concerning writs of assistance. I have accordingly considered it, and now appear, not only in obedience to your order, but likewise in behalf of the inhabitants of this town, who have presented another petition, and out of regard to the liberties of the subject. And I take this opportunity to declare that . . . I will to my dying day oppose with all the powers and faculties God has given me all such instruments of slavery on the one hand and villainy on the other, as this writ of assistance is. It appears to me the worst instrument of arbitrary power, the most destructive of English liberty and the fundamental principles of law that ever was found in an English lawbook. . . .

"In the first place, may it please your Honors, I will admit that writs of one kind may be legal; that is, special writs, directed to special officers, and to search certain houses and so on specially set forth in the writ. . . . Your Honors will find in the old books concerning the office of a Justice of the Peace precedents of general warrants to search suspected houses. But in more modern books you will find only special warrants to search such and such houses specially named, in which the complainant has before sworn that he suspects his goods are concealed. And you will find it adjudged that special warrants only are legal. In the same manner I rely on it that the writ prayed for in this petition, being general, is illegal. It is a power that places the liberty of every man in the hands of every petty officer. . . . In the first place, the writ is universal, being directed 'to all and singular Justices, Sheriffs, Constables, and all other officers and subjects,' so that, in short, it is directed to every subject in the King's dominions.

"Every one with this writ may be a tyrant; if this commission be legal, a tyrant in a legal manner also may control, imprison, or murder any one within the realm. In the next place, it is perpetual; there is no return. A man [with this writ] is accountable to no person for his doings. Every man may reign secure in his petty tyranny, and spread terror and desolation around him. In the third place, a person with this writ, in the daytime, may enter all houses, shops, and so on at will, and command all to assist him. Fourthly, by this writ not only deputies and so on but even their menial servants are allowed to lord it over us. Now, one of the most essential branches of English liberty is the freedom of one's house. A man's house is his castle, and whilst he is quiet he is as well guarded as a prince in his castle. This writ, if it should be declared legal, would totally annihilate this privilege. Customhouse officers may enter our houses when they please; we are commanded to permit their entry. Their menial servants may enter, may break locks, bars, and every thing in their way; and whether they break through malice or revenge, no man, no court can inquire. Bare suspicion without oath is sufficient.

"This wanton exercise of this power is not a chimerical suggestion of a heated brain. . . . Mr. Pew had one of these writs, and when Mr. Ware succeeded him, he endorsed this writ over to Mr. Ware; so that these writs are negotiable from one officer to another; and so your Honors have no opportunity of judging the persons to whom this vast power is delegated. Another instance is this: Mr. Justice Walley had called this same Mr. Ware before him, by a constable, to answer for a breach of Sabbath-day acts, or that of profane swearing. As soon as he had finished, Mr. Ware asked him if he had done. He replied, 'Yes.' 'Well, then,' said Mr. Ware, 'I will show you a little of my power. I command you to permit me to search your house for uncustomed goods,' and went on to search his house from the garret to the cellar, and then served the constable in the same manner. But to show another absurdity in this writ: if it should be established, I insist upon it, every person . . . has this power as well as custom-house officers. The words [in the writ] are 'It shall be lawful for any person or persons authorized,' and so forth. What a scene does this open! Every man, prompted by revenge, ill humor, or wantonness, to inspect the inside of his neighbor's house, may get a writ of assistance. Others will ask it from self-defense. One arbitrary exertion will provoke another, until society be involved in tumult and in blood. . . .

"Thus reason and the [British] constitution are both against this writ. Let us see what authority there is for it. Not more than one instance can be found of it in all our law-books, and that was in the zenith of arbitrary power, namely, in the reign of Charles II, when Star Chamber powers were pushed to extremity by some ignorant clerk of the Exchequer. But had this writ been in any book whatever, it would have been illegal. All precedents are under the control of the principles of law. . . . No acts of Parliament can establish such a writ; though it should be made in the very words of this petition, it would be void. An act against the constitution is void."

Adams apologized for his version of the speech, saying that in comparison with Otis's words his own were as "the gleam of a glowworm to the meridian blaze of the sun." To convey a better idea of the impression Otis had made on the assemblage in the Council Chamber that day, Adams wrote, "Otis was a flame of fire! — with a promptitude of classical allusions, a depth of research, a rapid summary of historical events and dates, a profusion of legal authorities, a prophetic glance of his eye into futurity, and a torrent of impetuous eloquence, he hurried away every thing before him. . . . Every man of a crowded audience appeared to me to go away, as I did, ready to take arms against writs of assistance. Then and there was the first scene of the first act of opposition to the arbitrary claims of Great Britain. Then and there the child Independence was born. In fifteen years, namely in 1776, he grew up to manhood, and declared himself free."

A couple of years after Otis, "the great incendiary" of New England, ignited colonial resistance to British rule, two heated disputes over the use of general warrants broke out in England. This time, the issue was freedom of the press. In April, 1763, Lord Halifax, the Secretary of State, moved to suppress an anonymously written and secretly published anti-government periodical called the *North Briton* by reaching back, as his colleagues in charge of colonial affairs had in dealing with America, to the days of the Star Chamber. For this case, Halifax relied on the traditional use of general warrants to prosecute seditious libels against the government. He issued a general warrant whose only stipulations were that anyone involved in the writing, printing, or circulation of the most recent, and most derogatory, copy of the *North Briton* — No. 45 — was to be arrested, and his papers were to be seized. Crown officers arrested forty-nine people, chief among them the suspected author of No. 45, a member of Parliament by the name of John Wilkes.

"I scarcely ever met a better companion," Edward Gibbon, the historian, wrote of Wilkes. "He has inexhaustible spirits, infinite wit and humor, and a great deal of knowledge. A thorough profligate in principle as in practice, his life [is] stained with every vice and his conversation full of blasphemy and bawdry. These morals he glorifies in, for shame is a weakness he has long surmounted."

Apparently, Wilkes had been waiting for an opportunity to challenge the government, for he clearly enjoyed the affair hugely. Calling the general warrant used against him "a ridiculous warrant against the whole English nation," Wilkes refused to accompany the officers until they procured a sedan chair for his comfort. They did, and carried him off to Halifax's house, down the street, where the Secretary of State tried to get him to confess. Wilkes stood fast, and was carted off to the Tower of London, while, on orders of the Crown, his house was broken into and all his personal papers were confiscated. On this occasion, Wilkes was confined in modest quarters in the Tower, but was allowed to have his manservant minister to his needs. (He soon became such a celebrity – in all likelihood, his goal from the start – that when he was again imprisoned, he was given a luxurious suite, and partook of sumptuous foods and wines sent to him by admirers, the company of roistering male friends, and the favors of many women who visited him.)

To sustain the publicity he needed, Wilkes had to continue his case – on grounds chosen not by the government but by himself. He immediately sued the officer who had ransacked his house, and charged him with trespassing upon his private property. He argued that the search was illegal, because it was based on a general warrant, which was illegal under the unwritten British constitution. It was a novel argument, for general warrants had been used in seditious-libel cases by Secretaries of State in almost every reign since the overthrow of Charles I, more than a century before, and no one had ever contested their legality. Even so, Wilkes's argument prevailed, and a jury awarded him damages of a thousand pounds, or around twenty-four thousand dollars at present rates. (Six years later, he collected damages of four times that amount in a suit against Lord Halifax for false imprisonment in the *North Briton* case.)

After winning the trespass suit, Wilkes was harassed and prosecuted by the Crown on a variety of legal pretexts, and each time he won reëlection to the House of Commons the government's supporters there voted his election void. George III, who regarded Wilkes's expulsion from Parliament as "a measure whereon my crown almost depends," foolishly persisted in his efforts to get rid of his enemy to such an obvious extent that finally William Pitt the Elder remarked that "the King's ministers . . . had made [Wilkes] a person of the greatest consequence in the Kingdom." Benjamin Franklin was in England during one of Wilkes's campaigns for reëlection, and noted, "I went last week to Winchester and observed that for fifteen miles out of town there was not a door or window shutter next the road unmarked [with No. 45]; and this continued here and there quite to Winchester, which is sixty-four miles." The public cry "Wilkes and Number Forty-five forever!" was heard everywhere – even George III's small children would burst into his sitting room and shout it at him – and when Crown officers later arrested Wilkes for another offense great crowds rescued him and carried him through the streets of London in triumph. Although there is little evidence that many of these ordinary citizens appreciated the issues underlying the case – "the crowd always want to draw themselves from abstract principles to personal attachments," Edmund Burke remarked at the time – the clamorous public support for Wilkes ultimately secured some measure of freedom of the press and largely destroyed general warrants as a political weapon in Britain.

On legal grounds, though, a similar English case during the same period was to have more fundamental and lasting effects on the subject of general warrants. Six months before Wilkes's first arrest, Lord Halifax issued a warrant for the arrest of John Entick, described in contemporary records as a "clerk," who was thought to be involved in publishing an anti-government periodical called the *Monitor, or British Freeholder*. This time, the warrant was more specific, because it at least named Entick, but it was also general, because it ordered the seizure of his books, papers, and documents. Crown officers spent four hours ransacking Entick's house, and then took him and every scrap of paper they could find off to Halifax's office. But when Halifax and his men examined the confiscated papers, they found no evidence against Entick, and he was released.

He did nothing about his mistreatment by the government at the time, but after Wilkes won his suit Entick sued the officers who had searched his place, also on a charge of trespass, and won damages of three hundred pounds. Apparently fearing the consequences of another legal victory by its opponents, the government filed an "exception" to the verdict, a form of appeal, and the case – Entick v. Carrington – came before the Court of Common Pleas in the autumn of 1765 for final disposition. The court was presided over by Lord Chief Justice Pratt, later the first Earl of Camden and Lord Chancellor of England, who was widely known as "the incorruptible judge," a description that indicated the extent of corruption in England then. Camden, as he is known to history, had been Attorney General during the contention over writs of assistance in America, and although he took no public position on that matter, he was said to have privately advised against the use of such writs, on the ground that they were probably illegal. As Lord Chief Justice, he had also presided over the Entick and Wilkes trials, and had ruled on both occasions that general warrants were indeed unlawful.

In Entick v. Carrington, counsel for the Crown defended general warrants with several arguments: that they had been used by Secretaries of State ever since Cromwell's time; that they resembled ordinary warrants issued to recover stolen goods; that no one subjected to them had complained before; that no court had ever judged them illegal; and that they were essential if public clamors were to be quieted and the state protected.

Entick had retained Wilkes's lawyer, a barrister named Glynn, and in answering the claim that such warrants had long been used Glynn told the court, "If they have, it is high time to put an end to them, for if they are held to be legal, the liberty of this country is at an end." He went on, "It is the publishing of a libel which is the crime, and not the having it locked up in a private drawer in a man's study. But if having it in one's custody was the crime, no power can lawfully break into a man's house and study to search for evidence against him. This would be worse than the Spanish

Inquisition, for ransacking a man's secret drawers and boxes, to come at evidence against him, is like racking his body to come at his secret thoughts. The warrant is to seize all the plaintiff's books and papers without exception, and carry them before Lord Halifax. What? Has a Secretary of State a right to see all a man's private letters of correspondence, family concerns, trade and business? This would be monstrous indeed! And if it were lawful, no man could endure to live in this country."

Moving on to the Crown's contention that a general warrant used to uncover seditious libel was little different from a search warrant for stolen goods, Glynn said of the latter, "It is never granted but upon the strongest evidence that a felony has been committed, and that the goods are secreted in such a house. And it is to seize such goods as were stolen, not all the goods in the house. But if stolen goods are not found there, all who entered with the warrant are trespassers. However frequently these warrants have been granted since the Revolution, that will not make them lawful, for if they were unreasonable or unlawful when first granted, no usage or continuance can make them good." Moreover, he added, the custom relied on by the government was comparatively brief. "They go no farther back than eighty years," he said, "and most amazing it is they have never before this time been opposed." Then, in conclusion, he urged the court "to demolish this monster of oppression, and to tear into rags this remnant of Star Chamber tyranny."

In a unanimous decision, the judges of the Court of Common Pleas found in Entick's favor. Lord Camden delivered the opinion, in which he agreed with every point Glynn had made, and went on to say that when such warrants were employed against a man "his house is rifled, his most valuable secrets are taken out of his possession before the power for which he is charged is found to be criminal by any competent jurisdiction and before he is convicted either of writing, publishing, or being concerned in the paper." Such power, Camden declared, "is not supported by one single citation from any law book extant," and no judge on the Court of King's Bench, the principal court of criminal jurisdiction, had ever assumed such power, apart from Lord Chief Justice

Scroggs. (Known to later generations as "the worst chief justice in British history," Scroggs revived this Star Chamber practice, among others, during a murderous official purge of Catholics in the latter part of the seventeenth century.)

To the claim that no one had opposed the use of general warrants before, Camden replied, "I answer, there has been a submission of guilt and poverty to power and the terror of punishment. But it would be strange doctrine to assert that all the people of this land are bound to acknowledge that to be universal law, which a few criminal booksellers have been afraid to dispute." Getting down to the specific use of such a warrant, he continued, "It is executed against the party, before he is heard or even summoned; and the information, as well as the informer, is unknown. It is executed by messengers with or without a constable . . . in the presence or the absence of the party [served] as the messengers shall think fit, and without a witness to testify what passes at the time of the transaction, so that when the papers are gone, as the only witnesses are the trespassers, the party injured is left without proof. If this injury falls upon an innocent person, he is as destitute of remedy as the guilty. . . .

"The great end for which men entered into society was to secure their property," Camden wrote. "That right is preserved sacred and incommunicable in all instances, where it has not been taken away or abridged by some public law for the good of the whole. . . . Papers are the owner's goods and chattels: they are his dearest property, and are so far from enduring a seizure that they will hardly bear an inspection. And though the eye cannot by the laws of England be guilty of a trespass, yet where private papers are removed and carried away, the secret nature of those goods will be an aggravation of the trespass, and demand more considerable damages in that respect. Where is the written law that gives any magistrate such a power? I can safely answer, there is none. And, therefore, it is too much for us, without such authority, to pronounce a practice legal which would be subversive of all the comforts of society." In conclusion, Lord Camden declared the warrant used against Entick "illegal and void."

A few months later, the House of Commons decreed that the

seizure of papers in any case of seditious libel was unlawful, and then it passed a resolution stating that general warrants were universally illegal, except in cases specifically designated by act of Parliament. In America, the Wilkes and Entick cases, Camden's opinion, and Parliament's decrees were as closely followed as transmission of news across the Atlantic permitted. The results of these events in England were widely discussed and applauded in the colonies, and, a quarter of a century later, they became the foundation for one of the pillars of American liberty.

The Fourth Amendment to the United States Constitution declares, "The right of the people to be secure in their persons, houses, papers, and effects, against unreasonable searches and seizures, shall not be violated, and no Warrants shall issue, but upon probable cause, supported by Oath or affirmation, and particularly describing the place to be searched, and the persons or things to be seized." The amendment was adopted in 1791, along with the rest of the Bill of Rights, and three-quarters of a century later Judge Thomas Cooley observed in his work *Constitutional Limitations,* which was the most influential legal treatise of the time, that the citizen's "immunity in his home against the prying eyes of the government" and protection against "arbitrary control of the person" are the two basic foundations of personal liberty.

Today, most Americans – or, at least, most middle-class white Americans – probably assume that this right against arbitrary intrusion by government upon their persons and property is secure. That assumption is baseless. Over the years since the Fourth Amendment was adopted, it has been flouted millions of times. Every day, hundreds of local, state, and federal officers illegally search people and illegally break into and ransack their homes and places of business, and there is almost nothing the victims can do about it. The reason for both the official lawlessness and the public's helplessness before it may be found in the peculiar nature of the law being violated. "The Bill of Rights in general and the Fourth Amendment in particular are profoundly anti-government documents," Anthony Amsterdam, the nation's leading constitutional scholar, observed recently. To a large extent, it is probably this characteristic that has led to their being so widely unenforced. While anti-government sentiment was a necessary cause and an inevitable result of the Revolution, once that sentiment was embodied in written sanctions against *all* government, as it was in the Bill of Rights, the new government was expected to interpret, implement, and enforce these sanctions against itself. That was too much to expect, even from a restricted system like ours — with its separation of powers and its various other checks and balances — because all governments in all places at all times try to increase their power, at the expense of the individual. In short, government is *always* the enemy of the individual.

The greatest and most dangerous power against the individual possessed by every state is its police power, and the use of that power determines whether the state tends toward freedom or slavery. According to Professor Amsterdam, there are "few issues more important to a society than the amount of power that it permits its police to use without effective control by law." Although the United States has restricted police power more than many nations, most of this control lies in rather general formulations contained in federal or state constitutions. Legislatures have been exceedingly reluctant to initiate any regulations over police procedures or conduct, and the only specific restrictions on such matters have come from the courts or from legislatures' passing weak laws to head off stronger court restrictions, or passing strong laws to repeal court rulings. "Handcuffing" the police in any manner, even with the shackles of the Constitution, is so politically risky that the courts have had to take over what should be a legislative responsibility in order to impose *some* control over the police. In general, though, the only limits upon them are those they impose on themselves — more often than not as a way of assuring the people that they are living under a government that is strictly controlled by the rule of law.

A 1967 report of the President's Commission on Law Enforcement and Administration of Justice pointed out that every day policemen make hundreds of thousands of decisions that "can affect in some way someone's dignity, or self-respect, or sense of privacy, or constitutional rights," and that this is done virtually without controls of any sort. And Kenneth Culp Davis, an authority on police practices, has observed, "The system is atrociously unsound [when] an individual policeman has unguided discretionary power to weigh social values in an individual case and make a final decision as to governmental policy for that case, despite a statute to the contrary, without review by any other authority, without recording the facts he finds, without stating reasons, and without relating one case to another."

Professor Yale Kamisar, of the University of Michigan Law School and a leading authority on the Fourth Amendment, said recently, "The idea that the police have been 'handcuffed' by the courts is laughable, because in many fundamental areas no one has touched them. The real problem is there's so much criminal business that the police have to decide which suspects to arrest — for most citizens, the most fundamental area of all. So we end up with selective arrest — a matter that is entirely decided by the police. This amounts to total discretion, which often winds up being used against blacks, radicals, 'troublemakers,' and anyone who doesn't show the proper respect. Nothing at all has been done about this by the courts, and there is no review of such decisions by the police anywhere. The reason for the neglect, I think, is that the media have convinced the public that there are too many curbs on the police, when actually there are almost none. Every time the Supreme Court tries to do something about controlling police abuses, local newspapers and TV stations send their crime reporters out to get the reaction of the police. These reporters are completely on the cops' side, because that's their beat and because they keep seeing brutal criminals being let off on 'technicalities.' The technicalities, as it happens, are part of the Constitution. Anyway, these reporters almost never go to talk to civil libertarians or law professors to get the other side, so in the end the public is terribly prejudiced in favor of the police, and is ready to let them do whatever they please."

Of course, judicial review may be available — if one has the money, the willingness to take on an entire police department, several years to spend in court contests (should the case be considered proper for review), and unflagging determination to assert one's rights. But in general the police have greater freedom to conduct themselves as they please than any other government officials. If the public were to demand that law-enforcement officers be given greater freedom than they already have — as seems to be the public mood these days — there would be little aside from self-restraint on the part of the police to stop the Republic from gradually being transformed into a police state. Since the executive branch is by its nature rather inclined toward authoritarian control over disturbing elements in society and also contains such influential and control-minded groups as the Federal Bureau of Investigation, the Central Intelligence Agency, and the military, it is unlikely that any move toward greater control over the police will come from that direction. Nor is an effort toward this end apt to come from the legislative branch, for, as Amsterdam has observed, "even if our growing crime rate and its attendant mounting hysteria should level off, there will remain more than enough crime and fear of it in American society to keep our legislators from the politically suicidal undertaking of police control."

The only official check upon the police that exists, then, is to be found in the courts' imposition of rules upon them. This function was served, with astonishing devotion to the purpose of the Bill of Rights, by the Warren Court for fifteen years. In general, though, the Supreme Court has come down on the side of government in its contests with individual citizens over their inalienable rights, and has often weakened and even perverted the clearest commands of the Constitution. This process has been demonstrated again and again in cases involving the Fourth Amendment, which has been described as "one of the most litigated provisions of the Bill of Rights." The Court has dealt with this litigation so inconsistently and so confusingly that no one can say today with any certainty what the amendment means.

According to Amsterdam, the Court's approach in such cases has been "splendid in its flexibility, awful in its unintelligibility, unadministrability, unenforceability, and general ooziness." And, according to Jacob W. Landynski, a specialist in the field, "Few decisions of the United States Supreme Court have generated as much powerful controversy over the past few decades as those dealing with issues raised under the Fourth Amendment. . . . The issues bring into sharp focus the classic dilemma of order vs. liberty in the democratic state. The Court has come under heavy fire from opposing directions. According to some critics, it has often proved heedless of the community interest in eradicating crime and has gone too far in the direction of protecting individual liberty. In the view of others, the Court has sometimes been too accommodating to the claims of law enforcement and insufficiently vigilant in safeguarding the principles on which the Fourth Amendment is based."

Both sides have missed the point, for even the most liberal decisions of the Court on the Fourth Amendment have been essentially conservative. While the Court has sometimes ruled that a given search and seizure of given material from a given person under given circumstances was unreasonable and thus unconstitutional, it was a hundred and seventy years after the amendment was adopted before the Court finally made it somewhat more difficult for prosecutors in general to use illegally seized evidence against suspects — an essential restriction if the Fourth Amendment is to mean anything at all. But even that modest protection of the people's right to be secure against government intrusion and persecution appears likely to be modified or abolished altogether by the Court's current majority before long. Above all, though, the Supreme Court, past and present, has done almost nothing to prevent those transgressions from being committed in the first place or to punish the police who commit them. If Amsterdam is correct in saying that "the regulation of police behavior is what the Fourth Amendment is all about," then the Court has never even faced the basic issue. Since one Supreme Court decision, however sweeping, never stops official abuses of citizens' rights — indeed, it usually takes repeated decisions over a long period of time to persuade lower courts and law-enforcement officials that such abuses *are* abuses — the Court's failure to address the issue of misbehavior on the part of the police makes any judicial remedy far more difficult and unlikely. By avoiding the problem, the Supreme Court has made it worse — perhaps even insoluble.

The first significant Fourth Amendment case to come before the Supreme Court was Boyd v. United States, which was decided in 1886. Under a federal law enacted in 1874, domestic importers of foreign merchandise who were accused of evading customs duties could be compelled to produce, upon order of the government, any "business book, invoice, or paper;" refusal to obey such an order was tantamount to a confession that the government's accusations were true, and could result in forfeiture of the goods involved. In the Boyd affair, a New York City case, the government confiscated thirty-five crates of imported plate glass for nonpayment of duties, and when the owners sued for return of the glass the government demanded their invoice from a previous shipment of the same kind of glass to demonstrate its value. The owners handed over the invoice under protest, contending that the order was unconstitutional, because it forced them to testify against themselves and thereby violated the Fifth Amendment's guarantee: "No person . . . shall be compelled in any criminal case to be a witness against himself."

Since the law authorizing the government to issue such an order and to impose forfeiture was a civil rather than a criminal statute, the case seemed unrelated to the Fifth Amendment. And since the order to produce a specific invoice bore no obvious resemblance to the kinds of physical and general searches that the Framers feared, the case seemed unrelated to the Fourth Amendment. But the Supreme Court ruled that the order was a search, that the penalty of forfeiture made the offense "criminal," and that the government's seizure of private papers to be used as evidence against a person amounted to compulsory self-incrimination under the Fifth Amendment and made the seizure itself unreasonable under the Fourth Amendment. The Court reversed a lower court's ruling in favor of the government, saying, "We think that the notice to produce the invoice in this case, the order by virtue of which it was issued, and the law which authorized the order were unconstitutional and void, and that the inspection by the district attorney of said invoice, when produced in obedience to said notice, and its admission in evidence by the court were erroneous and unconstitutional."

Justice Joseph P. Bradley, who delivered the Court's opinion, declared that the law at issue was worse than the "obnoxious" writs of assistance denounced by Otis. In a famous piece of Court dictum, Bradley explained, "It may be that [the statute] is the obnoxious thing in its mildest and least repulsive form; but illegitimate and unconstitutional practices get their first footing in that way, namely, by silent approaches and slight deviations from legal modes of procedure. This can only be obviated by adhering to the rule that constitutional provisions for the security of person and property should be liberally construed. A close and literal construction deprives them of half their efficacy, and leads to gradual depreciation of the right, as if it consisted more in sound than in substance."

The Boyd opinion has been praised as "a landmark of constitutional interpretation" and "the boldest pronouncement on the subject ever to come from our highest tribunal." According to Landynski, "Seldom has a Supreme Court decision been so variously esteemed by responsible commentators. The Supreme Court itself, in later years, even when departing from the letter, and occasionally the spirit, of the Boyd case, never failed to refer to it reverently." The esteem and reverence are astounding, for the Boyd opinion is nearly all sound and very little substance. While its premise (that arbitrary government invasions of personal privacy violate individual rights) and its conclusion (that the product of those invasions cannot be used against the victims) seem unassailable, the path between premise and conclusion was littered with misread precedent, mistaken facts, and misunderstood constitutional doctrine. While most of the points that were wrong are minuscule, the law is a sum of tiny parts. And it is often such seemingly minuscule matters that determine how later courts decide crucial constitutional issues.

The precedent was Lord Camden's opinion in Entick v. Carrington, which, Justice Bradley said, "every American statesman, during our revolutionary and formative period as a nation, was undoubtedly familiar with . . . as the true and ultimate expression of constitutional law." Bradley depended heavily on Camden's claim that search warrants for private papers originated in Star Chamber proceedings and had never been approved by judges outside that tribunal, and on Camden's assertion that the seizure of such papers and their use to convict someone amounted to compulsory self-incrimination. In Entick, however, the papers involved were political in nature and were seized by way of a general warrant, whereas in Boyd a specific business invoice was sought by way of a specific statute approved by Congress, which has the authority, under the Constitution, to regulate commerce. Camden had set out to demonstrate the illegality of general warrants in order to prove that the seizure of Entick's papers amounted to a trespass. That was Entick's claim, and that was Camden's finding. In his opinion, Camden raised the issue of the papers' self-incriminatory nature more or less by analogy, not as a key element in what made a search and seizure illegal.

Now Bradley sought to prove through Entick that it was the sanctity of the papers itself that made their seizure unreasonable and thus unconstitutional. But private papers are given no special status in the Bill of Rights or in the body of the Constitution. Since there was no precedent for his conclusion apart from Entick, which was not applicable, Bradley reached out to the Fifth Amendment as a means of interpreting the Fourth Amendment. "They throw great light on each other," he said. "For the 'unreasonable searches and seizures' condemned in the Fourth Amendment are almost always made for the purpose of compelling a man to give evidence against himself, which in criminal cases is condemned in the Fifth Amendment; and compelling a man 'in a criminal case to be a witness against himself,' which is condemned in the Fifth Amendment, throws light on the question as to what is an 'unreasonable search and seizure' within the meaning of the Fourth Amendment."

It was a novel, confusing, and unnecessary argument, and it has since been rejected by the Supreme Court. Bradley could have more simply and properly reached his final decision — as two other justices on the Court at the time reached it — by finding that the compulsory production of the invoice in Boyd constituted a fundamental violation of the Fifth Amendment's guarantee against involuntary self-incrimination, and letting it go at that. By carelessly distorting history and twisting logic, Bradley forced a case that essentially didn't concern the Fourth Amendment into the scope of the amendment's sanctions, and thereby introduced the confusion that has distorted constitutional interpretation of this issue ever since.

Although Supreme Court opinions often display admirable rhetoric and deplorable logic, neither has anything to do with the real function of the Court: to make decisions on matters of fundamental law. If the decision in Boyd were to be disregarded because of its faulty reasoning, many of the Court's other decisions would also have to be ignored, because the opinions that usually accompany them are often marred by the same flaw. While it is true that the law is what the Supreme Court says it is, it is also true that the Court's conclusions have always been drawn out of the combined brilliance, prejudices, blindness, sloppy thinking, imprecise writing, and ideals of individual justices — in short, that we live under a government of men, not laws. Still, when the Court speaks it states the meaning of the law for the rest of us. And in Boyd the Court stated that the Fourth Amendment meant that the compulsory production of the invoice "and its admission in evidence by the court were erroneous and unconstitutional proceedings." In other words, the use of unconstitutionally acquired evidence is itself unconstitutional. This statement is crucial to the long legal fight over what the Fourth Amendment means, and yet it has been ignored or misread by Court after Court.

In Weeks v. United States, decided twenty-eight years later, in 1914, a United States marshal, accompanied by local police in Kansas City, Missouri, broke into the home of a man who was suspected of trafficking in lottery tickets and searched the place without a warrant. According to Weeks's complaint against this intrusion, they seized "all of his books, letters, money, papers, notes, evidences of indebtedness, stock certificates, insurance policies, deeds, abstracts, and other muniments of title, bonds, candies, clothes, and other property." He sued to get back his possessions, and a federal District Court ordered that whatever was irrelevant to the case be returned, but allowed the federal prosecutor to retain any pertinent evidence. When this was introduced at the trial, Weeks repeatedly objected, his objections were repeatedly overruled, and he was convicted and sentenced to prison.

In his appeal to the Supreme Court, he claimed that his rights under the Fourth and Fifth Amendments, as interpreted in Boyd, had been violated. The Court upheld his claim on the ground of the Fourth Amendment alone, and reversed the conviction. "If letters and private documents can thus be seized and held and used in evidence against a citizen accused of an offense, the protection of the Fourth Amendment declaring his right to be secure against such searches and seizures is of no value, and, so far as those thus placed are concerned, might as well be stricken from the Constitution," Justice William Rufus Day said for a unanimous Court. "The efforts of the courts and their officials to bring the guilty to punishment, praiseworthy as they are, are not to be aided by the sacrifice of those great principles established by years of endeavor and suffering which have resulted in their embodiment in the fundamental law of the land."

Once again the Court's reasoning in reaching this conclusion was unclear. While Day seemed to be saying that both the unreasonable seizure and the use of evidence discovered by means of it in a prosecution violated "those great principles" embodied in "the fundamental law of the land" and were unconstitutional, he did not say this directly. Instead, he said that the warrantless seizure of papers in the case at bar was "in direct violation of the constitutional rights of the defendant;" that the lower court's refusal to return the papers was "a denial of the constitutional rights of the accused;" and that by admitting the papers as evidence during the trial "prejudicial error was committed." On this last and most important point, he didn't specifically say whether this prejudicial error violated the Constitution or was unlawful on other grounds. Of course, if it is unconstitutional not to give such evidence back to its owner, it would appear to be equally unconstitutional to use that evidence in court, for the use is the purpose behind the refusal. In short, the body of the opinion strongly suggested that this prejudicial error amounted to a violation of the Fourth Amendment itself, but, again, Justice Day did not say so directly. In his conclusion he said that it was not up to the Court to determine what recourse the victim of this particular search and seizure might have against state and local officials. Since none of the Bill of Rights was then binding on the states, the decision applied only to the federal government.

Just as law-enforcement officials are supposed to keep up with the inventive capacity of criminals for breaking the law, so the courts are supposed to keep up with law-enforcement officials' comparable ingenuity in circumventing the law. Nothing in Weeks specifically prohibited the federal government from using evidence illegally obtained by state officials, so federal officers soon began avoiding the Court's sanction against *their* use of evidence *they* had found through unreasonable searches and seizures by persuading local policemen to unreasonably search and seize evidence and hand it on to them — in keeping with what came to be known judicially as "the silver-platter doctrine." This method was used countless times after 1914 to evade the Weeks decision, until the Court finally got around to banning the practice forty-six years later.

Such delays — whatever their effects on thousands of citizens whose basic rights have been denied them — not only are typical of the Supreme Court but are justified by it on the basis of "judicial self-restraint." Although the Court was set up by the Framers to decide what laws are fitting and what laws are not, the Court has always resisted making constitutional rulings on basic grounds unless it feels that it is compelled to. When the point of compulsion is reached and how it is determined are mysteries. But the effects of postponement are disagreeably clear: by condoning delay as a matter of judicial principle, the Court has ignored the individual rights it was designed to secure. Along the way, it has also made its own task immeasurably more difficult, for if it accepts brazenly unethical and unjust police practices by not rejecting them outright at the first opportunity, it encourages their use and inevitably creates anger on the part of the police and the public when it finally says, many years too late, that some long-accepted practice is illegal. And the indignant public reaction when the Court gets around to giving the people the rights they should have had all along under the Constitution then discourages the Court from taking other long-overdue stands on other constitutional issues.

The Supreme Court moved with uncommon speed — within a mere six years — to control another shortcut that became popular among federal prosecutors soon after the Weeks decision was handed down: finding evidence illegally and then using it as the basis for subpoenas to get hold of the same evidence legally. In Silverthorne Lumber Co. v. United States, federal agents arrested the Silverthornes, father and son, at their homes in upstate New York, while a United States Attorney, a United States marshal, and other federal officers broke into the lumber company and confiscated all the books, records, and papers they found there without a warrant. The Silverthornes sued for the return of their property, and a federal District Court ordered the United States Attorney to obey the demand. He did — after he had photographed the documents he wanted to use as evidence and had obtained subpoenas for the originals. The Silverthornes refused to obey the subpoenas, and the court, while deploring the methods used by the government to get the documents, upheld its right to have them, and sent the younger Silverthorne to jail for contempt of court.

In 1920, the Supreme Court found the lower court in error on its contempt citation and the government in violation of the Fourth Amendment. "The proposition could not be presented more nakedly," Justice Holmes said for the Court. "It is that although of course [the] seizure was an outrage which the government now regrets, it may study the papers before it returns them, copy them, and then may use the knowledge that it has gained to call upon the owners in a more regular form to produce them; that the protection of the Constitution covers the physical possession but not any advantages that the government can gain over the object of its pursuit by doing the forbidden act. . . . In our opinion such is not the law. It reduces the Fourth Amendment to a form of words. The essence of a provision forbidding the acquisition of evidence in a certain way is that not merely evidence so acquired shall not be used before the court, but that it shall not be used at all" — unless, he added, it was also found by means that were entirely independent of the illegal act.

Holmes's reference to "a provision forbidding the acquisition of evidence in a certain way" can only refer to the Fourth Amendment's sanction against "unreasonable searches and seizures," so the "essence" of this provision — "that not merely evidence so acquired shall not be used before the court, but that it shall not be used at all" — must be intrinsic to the Fourth Amendment. Once again the Court failed to state definitively, although it clearly seemed to mean, that the use of unreasonably seized evidence in any manner is unconstitutional.

In Olmstead v. United States, decided in 1928, the issue of wiretapping reached the Supreme Court for the first time. Despite a Washington State law against wiretapping, over a five-month period during the Prohibition era federal agents there listened to and recorded an enormous number of business and personal conversations over various telephones used by a group of bootleggers, who were then prosecuted and convicted on the basis of evidence gained by means of the taps. They appealed to the Supreme Court, and argued that the use of such evidence during their trial violated their rights under the Fourth and Fifth Amendments, as interpreted in Boyd, Weeks, and Silverthorne.

In 1928, the Court upheld the convictions by a five-to-four vote, and ruled that the wiretapping at issue had not violated the Fourth Amendment, because it did not constitute a search and seizure. Since the telephone wires had been tapped outside the defendants' homes and places of business, there was no illegal entry and thus no search, Chief Justice William Howard Taft explained. And since the Fourth Amendment guaranteed the security of "the person, the house, his papers or his effects" — or "things," he said — there was no seizure, for only spoken words had been seized.

Olmstead remained on the books for thirty-nine years, and during that period electronic surveillance became so highly developed and so widespread that by the time the decision was overruled, in

1967, it was too late to destroy the monster that Taft had unleashed. (The Federal Communications Act of 1934 was thought to forbid wiretapping, but law-enforcement officials, emboldened by Taft's statement that the Fourth Amendment did not apply to wiretapping, found loopholes in the law, and the practice flourished. It wasn't until 1967 that the Court found both bugging, which hadn't been covered by the 1934 law, and wiretapping to be violations of the Fourth Amendment. That same year, however, the Court also ruled that bugging and tapping were permissible under extremely circumscribed conditions, and the following year Congress used this tiny opening to enact an extremely broad and viciously repressive law that, among other things, allowed the government to wiretap and bug just about anyone. This law, the Omnibus Crime Control and Safe Streets Act of 1968, was passed in the wake of the assassinations of Dr. Martin Luther King, Jr., and Senator Robert F. Kennedy, after scores of riots blazed through the nation's black slums, and just before the Presidential election of Richard Nixon, who had made crime his main campaign issue. At the time, Congress was so intimidated by the public's fear of crime that it cravenly followed the demagogic leadership of the crime bill's chief sponsor, Senator McClellan.)

Chief Justice Taft's unexpected defense of the basic principle behind exclusion was probably inadvertent, because throughout his career on the bench he had repeatedly demonstrated his obsessive loathing of anything that was even faintly "progressive." But at a crucial point in Olmstead he said, "The striking outcome of the Weeks case and those which followed it was the sweeping declaration that the Fourth Amendment, although not referring to or limiting the use of evidence in courts, really forbade its introduction if obtained by government officers through a violation of the Amendment. Theretofore many had supposed that under the ordinary common-law rules, if the tendered evidence was pertinent, the method of obtaining it was unimportant. . . . But in the Weeks case, and those which followed, this Court decided with great emphasis, and established as the law for the federal courts, that the protection of the Fourth Amendment would be much impaired unless it was held that not only was the official violator of the rights under the Amendment subject to action at the suit of the injured defendant, but also that the evidence thereby obtained could not be received." The Weeks decision, he added, "announced an exception to the common-law rule by excluding all evidence" obtained through unreasonable seizures.

While it has been contended that by "exception" Taft meant to say that exclusion was a mere rule, like the common-law rule it replaced, and was not intrinsic to the Fourth Amendment, another statement in his opinion refutes that interpretation: "Nor can we, without the sanction of congressional enactment, subscribe to the suggestion that the courts have a discretion to exclude evidence, the admission of which is not unconstitutional, because unethically secured." If this nearly incoherent sentence means anything, it means that it was up to Congress to forbid the use of unethically secured evidence, and the Court was restricted to forbidding the use of unconstitutionally acquired evidence. Since the Court had forbidden the use of unreasonably seized evidence in Weeks and later cases, and since Taft supported those decisions in Olmstead, his statement is an affirmation of the principle set down in Boyd, Weeks, and Silverthorne — that exclusion is fundamental to the Constitution rather than merely a procedural rule of evidence. Whether or not that was what Taft meant to say, that was what he said.

For the sake of clarity, it could be said that in constitutional matters the difference between a rule and a principle is that a rule is a judicially imposed mode of legal procedure, which can be altered if it is found impractical, and a principle is an essential and immutable, though sometimes only implicit, feature of the Constitution without whose application a given sanction in that document would lack meaning and effect. In other words, the difference between rules and principles is much the same as the difference between means and ends. A rule is a judicial means of implementing a constitutional mandate, and a principle is an integral part of that mandate.

Even though the Supreme Court seems to have said, and to have said in a variety of ways, in its earliest and most important Fourth Amendment opinions that exclusion of unreasonably seized evidence is fundamental to enforcement of that amendment and is thus a constitutional principle, there is still deep, and often acrimonious, disagreement among legal scholars and Supreme Court justices about whether exclusion is a principle or a rule. Unaccountably, all of them have ignored the precedents that so strongly support one side in the dispute — Boyd, Weeks, Silverthorne, and Olmstead, among others — and they devote their attention instead to such questions as whether exclusion unduly hampers prosecution of criminals, whether it is an effective deterrent against misbehavior on the part of the police, whether some other method might not be more suitable to uphold the Fourth Amendment's injunctions, whether it is necessary to preserve judicial integrity and the public's respect for fairness under the law, and, finally, whether the Fourth Amendment itself is a desirable, or even feasible, means of serving the public interest.

The conflicting views on the subject of exclusion among scholars and judges are bewildering. According to Professor Landynski, the "exclusionary rule" (as it is invariably called today) "infused life into the hitherto lifeless body of the Fourth Amendment" and is "the most creative single act of the Supreme Court in this area of constitutional law." According to Professor Amsterdam, the rule is not "an explicit command of the Constitution" but was "fashioned by judges," and though exclusion of relevant evidence "is an evil in itself" because it often frees the guilty, "it is a necessary evil because the supposed alternatives to it are pie in the sky." According to Justice William J. Brennan, Jr., in a recent dissent from a Court decision that greatly weakened the use of the rule, "The Court seriously errs in describing the exclusionary rule as merely 'a judicial-created remedy designed to safeguard Fourth Amendment rights generally through its deterrent effect. . . .' Rather, the exclusionary rule is 'part and parcel of the Fourth Amendment's limitation upon [governmental] encroachment of individual privacy.' " According to Chief Justice Warren E. Burger, the Court's recent reversal of a man's conviction for a brutal murder on the basis of the rule "illustrates graphically the monstrous price we pay for the exclusionary rule in which we seem to have imprisoned ourselves;" and, in another case, he called upon Congress to prohibit the exclusion of evidence "from any criminal proceeding because of violation of the Fourth Amendment."

Over the past few decades, the issue of exclusion has created increasing confusion and discord among law-enforcement officials, lawyers, and judges. On the one hand, there are those who believe that it is the only means of safeguarding the individual against unwarranted invasions of privacy. On the other hand, there are those who believe that the only means of safeguarding society lie in the right of the state to invade that privacy in the name of crime control, and, if it is necessary to fulfill that purpose, to get rid of the Fourth Amendment altogether. At the present time, a majority of the Supreme Court's members seem determined to abolish exclusion by finding that it is merely a rule and that it doesn't work.

"All in all," Professor Thomas I. Emerson, another leading constitutional scholar, has observed, "the future of the Fourth Amendment remains in some doubt."

When Madison submitted the provisions making up most of the Bill of Rights — "the great rights," he called them — to the First Congress, meeting in New York City, he intended them to be made binding on state governments as well as on the national government. His colleagues in the House generally agreed with him, and adopted the amendments with that understanding. But a majority of the Senate's members — who were then chosen by state legislatures and were far more conservative than members of the House — insisted that the Bill of Rights apply only to the national government, whose potential for despotism they feared the most. Madison, for his part, feared the people themselves and their immediate representatives — state legislators — far more.

"The prescriptions in favor of liberty ought to be levelled against that quarter where the greatest danger lies, namely, that which possesses the highest prerogative of power," he said. "But this is not found in either the executive or legislative departments of government, but in the body of the people, operating by the majority against the minority." Of course, that majority most easily controls local legislatures. Accordingly, Madison wanted the states to be as restricted in their powers over the individual as the national government was, chiefly by way of the courts. When he introduced the amendments that were to make up the Bill of Rights, he said, "If they are incorporated into the Constitution, independent tribunals of justice will consider themselves in a peculiar manner the guardian of those rights; they will be an impenetrable bulwark against every assumption of power in the legislative or executive; they will be naturally led to resist every encroachment upon rights expressly stipulated for in the Constitution by the declaration of rights."

Although there are no clear historical records to explain why this declaration of rights was not written into the Constitution when it was drafted, in the summer of 1787, it appears that the Framers took most of the guarantees later formulated in the Bill of Rights for granted. They were viewed as natural and inalienable rights that the states would be bound to respect, and if any state wanted to deny its citizens such rights, it was pointed out, "parchment barriers" would not stop it. In any event, it is clear that most of Madison's political colleagues – that is, a majority of the larger and more representative body of Congress, the House – shared his views, and that these were rejected by only a few men in the Senate who basically spoke for the propertied interests that controlled state legislatures. It is likely that most of the men of the time who held positions of influence throughout the new nation viewed the rights of the individual chiefly as one right – to control private property as its owner saw fit. That was why such men had fought the Revolution, and that was why they reluctantly accepted the Constitution and the Bill of Rights, as a means of establishing and limiting a federal government. To a large extent, they ran the states, and they meant to go on running them, and would accept federal interference only when it was necessary to maintain peace among them, to protect them from foreign invasion, and to facilitate commerce.

This form of personal freedom seems to have been what many other Americans also wanted, and it was largely what the federal system was designed to provide. Government at every level in the United States was directed toward assisting the people to protect and enlarge their property, for that government was dominated by men who had no other aim themselves. Of course, there were also many other people in the United States during this time of expansion and plunder who did not view possession of property as the paramount good. They were the political descendants of men like Madison. And the words they spoke and wrote led to the first major break in this national pattern – the Civil War, which was essentially a contest over whether people were property, too.

After the war, the Southern states went on depriving the freed slaves of liberty, and to right this continuing wrong the nation, in 1868, adopted the Fourteenth Amendment: "No State shall make or enforce any law which shall abridge the privileges or immunities of citizens of the United States; nor shall any State deprive any person of life, liberty, or property, without due process of law; nor deny to any person within its jurisdiction the equal protection of the laws." While the amendment was essentially a civil-rights document, some lawyers argued at the time, and other lawyers argue today, that it was also designed to apply the entire Bill of Rights to the states through its due-process clause. But the Supreme Court disagreed with that view from the outset, and still does. A quarter of a century after adoption of the amendment, three justices held that it "incorporated" the Bill of Rights into the Constitution and made all its provisions applicable to the states. But their view did not prevail, and although as many as four of the nine justices have taken this position, it has never commanded a majority. As mentioned earlier, it wasn't until 1925 that the Court found *any* part of the Bill of Rights binding on the states; in that year it declared that freedom of speech and freedom of the press "are among the fundamental personal rights and liberties protected by the due-process clause of the Fourteenth Amendment from impairment by the states." But resistance on the Court to the idea of imposing the entire Bill of Rights on the states – known as the "incorporation doctrine" – was too strong, and not until the time of the Warren Court were almost all of its criminal-justice guarantees finally made binding — one by one, in case after case — on the states.

To a large degree, it was this process that raised such howls of protest on the far right. Most of the critics of the Warren Court seemed to be the philosophical, and often the propertied, descendants of Madison's opponents. Like those forebears, today's conservatives fear federal power — in this case, the power of the Supreme Court — when it limits their power to control the states. They do not fear the police, for they own the police, who serve them and protect their most cherished personal right — the sanctity of private property. Despite all the bitter attacks on the Warren Court, it did nothing more than finally give the people the rights that they and the Framers assumed were perpetually theirs. As a result of this long and unjust delay, the present generation of Americans is the first generation to enjoy the freedom — on paper, at least — that the Declaration of Independence, the Constitution, and the Bill of Rights so boldly declared to the world to be the right of all men.

Since nine out of ten people who come up against the law in this country come up against state law, the potential for tyrannical oppression, and its reality, lies with the states now nearly as much as it did in Madison's day, despite the application of the Bill of Rights to them. "Far too many cases come from the states to the Supreme Court presenting dismal pictures of official lawlessness, of illegal searches and seizures, illegal detentions attended by prolonged interrogation and coerced admissions of guilt, of the denial of counsel, and downright brutality," Justice Brennan said in a lecture during the days when the Warren Court struggled, with very modest success, to limit these practices. "Judicial self-restraint which defers too much to the sovereign powers of the states and reserves judicial intervention for only the most revolting cases will not serve to enhance Madison's priceless gift of 'the great rights of mankind secured under this Constitution.' "

The perils of judicial self-restraint and deference to state powers are nowhere clearer than in the Supreme Court's handling of the exclusionary issue in Fourth Amendment cases. Although today most lawyers trace the exclusionary rule back to the Weeks case, actually Weeks established it as a principle, and it wasn't until thirty-five years later, in 1949, that the Court backed off from that decision and declared that the principle was merely a rule. In short, the end had been reduced to a means. That reduction was made without observable study of the precedents in Boyd, Weeks, Silverthorne, and Olmstead, and without overruling any of the findings in those cases, which so strongly suggested that exclusion was a constitutional mandate.

The case was Wolf v. Colorado, and the Court's opinion was delivered by Justice Felix Frankfurter, one of the sternest advocates of judicial self-restraint and deference to state power ever to sit on the highest bench. The basic question posed by Wolf – a case involving prosecution of a physician for conspiracy to perform abortions – was whether the Fourth Amendment should be applied to the states under the incorporation doctrine. When the Supreme Court has decided that a provision in the Bill of Rights must finally be binding on the states, it usually follows one of the guidelines it has set up over the years: either the guarantee is among "those fundamental principles of liberty and justice which lie at the base of all our civil and political institutions," or it is "so rooted in the traditions and conscience of our people as to be ranked as fundamental," or it is "of the very essence of a scheme of ordered liberty."

Frankfurter preferred the last guideline, for to him order was as essential as liberty to the survival of the Republic. "The security of one's privacy against arbitrary intrusion by the police – which is at the core of the Fourth Amendment – is basic to a free society," he said for the Court in Wolf. "It is therefore implicit in 'the concept of ordered liberty' and as such [is] enforceable against the states through the due-process clause." This statement appeared to be a strong defense of the liberty of the individual, but Justice Frankfurter immediately transformed it into a defense of the primacy of order in the state by declaring that the exclusion of unreasonably seized evidence "was not derived from the explicit requirements of the Fourth Amendment" but "was a matter of judicial implication," and was not binding on the states, which were free to choose this method or any other "deterrent remedy" in their efforts to discourage the police from arbitrarily intruding upon citizens' privacy. In sum, Frankfurter ordered that the Fourth Amendment was now binding on the states but then ruled that the only means of making that order enforceable was not binding on the states. Accordingly, he upheld the conviction.

In one of three dissenting opinions in Wolf, Justice Frank Murphy said, "It is disheartening to find so much that is right in an opinion which seems to me so fundamentally wrong." What he found right was that the Fourth Amendment was to be binding on the states from then on, and what he found wrong was that, having gone that far, the Court could "yet be unwilling to make the step which can give some meaning to the pronouncements it utters." Continuing, he said, "Alternatives are deceptive. . . . For there is but one alternative to the rule of exclusion. That is no sanction at all." As for Frankfurter's "bland citation" of "other remedies," Murphy went on, "Little need be said concerning the possibilities of criminal prosecution. . . . Self-scrutiny is a lofty ideal, but its exaltation reaches new heights if we expect a district attorney to prosecute himself or his associates for well-meaning violations of the search and seizure clause during a raid the district attorney or his associates have ordered."

Another supposed alternative, Murphy said, was a trespass suit for damages — "a venerable means of securing reparation for unauthorized invasion of the home." But this was "an illusory remedy," he added, because in a trespass suit the measure of damages is the extent of injury to the property invaded — a few dollars, at most, if the police are at all careful. Equally illusory would be a suit for punitive damages, because some states permit none under any circumstances. In those that do, the plaintiff has to prove malice on the part of the officer, and if that point is proved, then often physical damage must be shown before punitive damages will be awarded. Once they are, the good intentions of the officer will be considered in mitigation, whereas the bad reputation of the plaintiff will be considered as an aggravation. "And even if the plaintiff hurdles all these obstacles, and gains a substantial verdict," Murphy went on, "the individual officer's finances may well make the judgment useless — for the municipality, of course, is not liable without its consent. Is it surprising that there is so little in the books concerning trespass actions for violation of the search and seizure clause? . . . The conclusion is inescapable that but one remedy exists to deter violations of the search and seizure clause. That is the rule which excludes illegally obtained evidence. Only by exclusion can we impress upon the zealous prosecutor that violation of the Constitution will do him no good."

In addition to these drawbacks, juries almost always take the word of a policeman over the word of someone who appears unsavory or at least suspicious. And anyone who challenges the police through a lawsuit must be prepared for official persecution — in the form of false arrest, surveillance, and more illegal searches — later on. And, finally, it is difficult to find a lawyer who will take such a case, which is bound to be, as Amsterdam has said, an "investigative and litigative nightmare." But even the dissenters in Wolf made exclusion seem a utilitarian means, not an end. And all of them ignored the main point — the purpose of exclusion was to stop government from breaking its own laws.

In stating that privacy was fundamental to the Constitution but that illegal invasions of privacy could be used to prosecute a victim in a state court, Frankfurter virtually assured that privacy would be less secure than ever. And his finding that exclusion was not constitutionally required because it is nowhere mentioned in the document was exceedingly odd in view of the fact that privacy, which he called the Fourth Amendment's purpose, is nowhere mentioned there, either. There are many constitutional principles — such as the presumption of innocence and proof beyond a reasonable doubt — that are not set down explicitly in the Constitution, and yet they are considered fundamental to our legal system. "Frankfurter's statement that exclusion was the result of 'judicial implication' and was thus not intrinsic to the Fourth Amendment is just plain silly," Professor Kamisar said recently.

"Almost everything the Court has said about what the Constitution means has been the result of judicial implication. The authors of the Constitution purposely made it not too explicit, so that later generations could translate its implications to meet the needs of their time." Finally, Frankfurter's conclusion in Wolf is even more mysterious given his famous statement in an opinion he delivered half a dozen years earlier: "The history of liberty has largely been the history of observance of procedural safeguards." Professor Amsterdam, who once served as Frankfurter's clerk, has added to this reminder, "And the history of the destruction of liberty . . . has largely been the history of the relaxation of those safeguards in the face of plausible-sounding governmental claims of a need to deal with widely frightening and emotion-freighted threats to the good order of society."

Justice Frankfurter was the epitome of the conservative justice, and his views on the Fourth Amendment are the best expression put forth by one side in the long struggle between the justices who have favored the needs of the state and the justices who have favored the rights of the individual. Frankfurter was probably as intelligent as any man who has served on the Supreme Court, he was a student of the historical foundations of this nation, he was a believer in finding and applying the intent of the Framers, and he was a confirmed statist. Whenever he was faced with a choice between the state and its citizens, he almost always came down on the side of the state. Above all, Frankfurter was a tidy man, and for him order invariably took precedence over liberty, for liberty is, of course, an untidy and even boisterous affair. On philosophical grounds, justices like Frankfurter have usually rationalized their stand on the conviction that the Framers guaranteed the states *their* rights, and that any serious infringement of those rights would destroy the basic framework of our society — federalism.

That premise is open to question. While it is true that the Framers wanted a strong central government to hold the states together, it is also true that they feared government on any level because of its ungovernable tendency to usurp the rights of the individual. Again and again, American history has demonstrated the dangers inherent in a strong central government and in strong state governments. Over a century ago, the Southern states' proclaimed right to suppress freedom forced the national government to assert its rights, and the confrontation ended up in the Civil War. The continuing suppression of black people, South and North, over the next century was largely state suppression, and this ended up, a few years ago, in the worst outbursts of rebellion this nation had experienced since the Civil War. These, too, were the price of states' rights, and so were all the examples of police brutality and prosecutorial shortcuts cited by Justice Brennan. More important, though, the federalist claim that, historically, the Bill of Rights was intended to be applied only to the federal government and not to the states ignores two vital facts. Again, that decision was a political act by a handful of senators who were then not elected by the people but were appointed by and spoke for the states. And, further, the Bill of Rights was written and adopted because the people demanded it as their price for accepting the Constitution. They did not demand that such rights be given to them only when they ran afoul of the federal government but demanded protection against all official tyranny.

On logical grounds, too, the Frankfurter argument that the Bill of Rights could not be applied to the states, except selectively — "The issue is closed," he said in Wolf — collapses under examination. In the early nineteen-sixties, Justice Brennan said, "The Bill of Rights is the primary source of expressed information as to what is meant by constitutional liberty. The safeguards enshrined in it are deeply etched in the foundations of America's freedoms. . . . Each is a protection with centuries of history behind it, often dearly bought with the blood and lives of people determined to prevent oppression by their rulers." Given the undeniable truth of this statement, the Supreme Court's fumbling about with guidelines to find out whether one or another of these protections is "fundamental" or part of "ordered liberty" is an absurd exercise. While Frankfurter contended that if one provision in the Bill of Rights is not fundamental, then all the provisions in it are not fundamental, it could as properly be argued that if one provision in the Bill of Rights is fundamental, then so are all the others. In fact, history has supported the second view more persuasively than the first, since today only one criminal-law provision in the Bill of Rights — the right to indictment by a grand jury in a "capital or otherwise infamous crime" — has not been made binding on the states by the Supreme Court. In the end, the Court's piecemeal application of this protection and that protection, undertaken so grudgingly and so belatedly, stands as another judicial monument to statism.

Exactly two hundred years after James Otis pleaded for the rights of Americans against government invasions of their security and privacy, the Supreme Court finally granted that right to every citizen. In the spring of 1957, the Cleveland Police Department received a tip that a suspect in a bombing incident was hiding out in a local house, which was also said to contain some gambling equipment. The police went to the house, without a warrant, and demanded admission. The tenant, a woman named Dollree Mapp, telephoned a lawyer and on his advice refused to let the police in until they showed her a valid warrant. They kept the house under surveillance for three hours, and then, with the help of reinforcements, smashed in the rear door and entered. Miss Mapp demanded to see a warrant, and when an officer held out a piece of paper she grabbed it and thrust it inside the front of her dress. The officers overpowered her and retrieved the paper — apparently not a warrant, for no such document was ever introduced as evidence in the case. The police then searched the house, and found neither the suspected bomber nor any gambling paraphernalia. But they found four pamphlets, a couple of photographs, and a scrawled drawing — all of which seemed to them to be obscene.

The materials seemed obscene to the city prosecutor and to a jury, too, and Miss Mapp was convicted of possessing obscene matter and sentenced to prison. The Supreme Court of Ohio heard an appeal on the case and ruled that while the conviction was primarily based on the use of evidence "unlawfully seized during an unlawful search" and thus offended the ordinary sense of justice, the evidence was still admissible in court because the police hadn't used brutal or "offensive" physical force to obtain it. In 1961, the United States Supreme Court overturned Wolf and reversed Miss Mapp's conviction, saying, "We hold that all evidence obtained by searches and seizures in violation of the Constitution is, by that same authority, inadmissible in a state court." In other words, the exclusionary rule was now binding on the states as well as on the federal government.

It has been said that when the Supreme Court is divided on a major issue the Chief Justice often assigns the least convinced member of the majority to write its opinion – presumably on the theory that he will be best able to convey the common denominator that underlies the majority's views. In Mapp, Justice Tom C. Clark got the job of writing the Court's opinion. It was an unfortunate choice, for Clark transformed a landmark decision into a muddled heap of confusion and error that created more bitter contention over the issue of exclusion than ever – mainly because he so confusingly elaborated on and qualified the Court's overall finding that his opinion became a favorite weapon of those who hoped to destroy the Fourth Amendment.

While he appropriately began the opinion with a long-overdue examination of the crucial passages in Boyd (which held that the government could not, under the Fourth and Fifth Amendments, compel a person to produce papers that might incriminate him), he failed to examine them in any meaningful way, and ended up by doing little more than to cite quotations from their rhetorical flights. Moving on to Weeks (which laid down the exclusionary rule prohibiting the use of unreasonably seized evidence against a defendant in federal courts), he chose the crucial passage, but this time he misinterpreted it by saying "the Court in that case clearly stated that use of the seized evidence involved 'a denial of the constitutional rights of the accused.' " As noted earlier, this quotation from Weeks applied not to the use of such evidence in court but to the lower courts' refusal to honor the defendant's demand that the unlawfully seized evidence be returned to him; the denial referred to in Weeks pertained not to the use of unreasonably searched and seized evidence but to the unreasonable search and seizure itself as an outright violation of the Fourth Amendment.

Then Clark went on to say that "in the Weeks case, this Court 'for the first time' held that 'in a federal prosecution the Fourth Amendment barred the use of evidence secured through an illegal search and seizure.' " But the quotation here was not from Weeks; it was from Frankfurter's opinion in Wolf, in which he specifically said that the exclusionary rule was "a matter of judicial implication" and was not intrinsic to the Fourth Amendment; that was clearly opposite to the majority view in Mapp, where Frankfurter was one of the three dissenters. Clark also compared exclusion under the Fourth Amendment to exclusion under the Fifth Amendment, and observed that if the right to privacy was, as the Court had long agreed, "basic to a free society," then the inadmissibility of evidence obtained by way of unconstitutional searches and seizures was as binding on the states as was the Fifth Amendment's sanction against the use of involuntary self-incrimination. "The Court has not hesitated to enforce as strictly against the states as it does against the federal government . . . the right not to be convicted by use of a coerced confession," he said.

Just about everything that could be wrong with this argument was wrong. To begin with, the Fifth Amendment explicitly states, "No person shall . . . be compelled in any criminal case to be a witness against himself," but the Fourth Amendment contains no such specific prohibitions. If it did, there wouldn't be any dispute over the nature of the exclusionary rule. And, for another thing, the Court had not only hesitated to apply the Fifth Amendment to the states but had ceaselessly dodged that issue for a quarter of a century, and, in fact, it did not make the injunction against involuntary self-incrimination binding on the states until three years *after* Clark spoke in Mapp. Then, too, Clark's persistently opaque writing in the opinion — for instance, "The right to privacy, when conceded operatively enforceable against the states, was not susceptible of destruction by avulsion of the sanction upon which its protection and enjoyment had always been deemed dependent under the Boyd, Weeks, and Silverthorne cases" — makes it difficult to take the opinion very seriously.

Above all, though, Clark's insistence that exclusion *was* intrinsic to the Fourth Amendment was undermined by his own key statement on the issue, that exclusion is a "command which this Court has held to be a clear, specific, and constitutionally required — even if judicially implied — deterrent safeguard without insistence upon which the Fourth Amendment would have been reduced to 'a form of words.' " By stating that exclusion was "judicially implied," he gave crucial support to critics who could now insist, and have insisted ever since Mapp was handed down, that exclusion is what they like to call a "judge-made remedy," and that it can be dispensed with by subsequent Court rulings or by order of Congress. And by stating that exclusion is a "deterrent safeguard" he gave further crucial support to the same critics, who could go on arguing, as they long had been and still are, that however worthy such deterrence might be it is incidental rather than fundamental to the Constitution.

In sum, while Clark stated that Mapp was designed "to close the only courtroom door remaining open to evidence secured by official lawlessness" in violation of Fourth Amendment rights, his opinion actually opened the door further and allowed room for other justices to disagree by applying their own biases and rationalizations — a process that has harshly but correctly been called "judicial perjury."

Although the authors of the Fourth Amendment demanded that warrants be specific enough to avoid the evils of writs of assistance and general warrants, over the past half century or so the Supreme Court has devoted most of the attention that it has paid to the subject to formulating ways in which the police can conduct searches with no warrants at all. "From a historical standpoint," Professor Telford Taylor, of the Columbia Law School, has observed, the Court has "stood the Fourth Amendment on its head." In doing so, the Court has ignored both the intent of the Framers and the letter of the law. What makes this additional failure by the Court so important is a "staggering fact" pointed out by Professor Leonard W. Levy: "An overwhelming majority of police searches, at least ninety per cent of those that come to the attention of courts, are warrantless." (For example, between 1929 and 1961, only two search warrants were issued by the Minneapolis Police Department, while tens of thousands of suspects were searched.)

As Levy goes on to describe the exceptions to the warrant requirement in the Fourth Amendment that have been approved by the Supreme Court, the police can search a person or a place without getting prior approval from a magistrate (the usual procedure to show that due process of law has been fully observed) if the search follows a lawful arrest or is carried out "under emergency conditions." When the police make arrests, they are empowered to search suspects and their immediate surroundings in order to protect themselves from attack with concealed weapons and to prevent evidence from being destroyed. If evidence may be lost unless the police act swiftly, they also do not have to have a warrant to make a search. Further, when they are, as the Court has put it, in "hot pursuit" of a suspect, they need no warrant, and when a suspect is in or near a vehicle that can be driven off with evidence of a crime, that, too, can be searched without a warrant. And the police can stop and frisk anybody on the street as long as they have "articulable suspicion" – not probable cause – to believe that a crime has been or is about to be committed. In a recent Burger Court decision, anyone who is stopped for a traffic violation, however minor, can be searched, together with the car, and any evidence of any kind of crime that is discovered can be used in court.

The chief restriction upon searches and seizures is that they usually must be made at the time of an arrest, and an arrest – a seizure of the person under the Fourth Amendment – cannot be carried out unless there is "probable cause" to believe that the suspect has committed, is committing, or is about to commit a crime. But this restriction is fairly easy to get around, for all the police have to do, in many cases, is wait until the suspect goes to a place where they believe there is evidence of his criminal behavior before arresting him and then search the immediate surroundings.

To a great degree, the Supreme Court has gradually undermined the strictures of the Fourth Amendment by repeatedly ruling that what clearly seem to be illegal searches are in fact not searches at all. According to Burt Neuborne, formerly Charles James's A.C.L.U. lawyer and now a professor of constitutional law at New York University, "There is a corrosive effect on the Fourth

Amendment in general precisely because exclusion makes the amendment an important right for the individual to assert against the government. The result is that the government — in this instance, the Supreme Court — feels pressed to construe the word 'searches' in the Fourth as narrowly as possible in order to maintain the authorities' right to search and seize more or less as they want to. Taft showed the Court how to do this in Olmstead by holding that wiretapping — obviously a search and seizure, as the Court finally admitted after forty years — was not a search or seizure at all. Nowadays, the question is posed again and again: 'What is a search and seizure?' And the government more and more often answers that searches aren't really searches, so that the exclusionary rule can't be used. Of course, this kind of judicial conduct immensely increases the already immense number of warrantless searches being made."

If the fact that ninety per cent of all searches that come to the attention of the courts are undertaken without warrants is as staggering as Levy feels, so is the fact that, as he points out, ninety per cent of all these arrests that precede such searches never lead to trials. No more than ten per cent of all criminal cases in this country go to trial. The rest are settled by means of guilty pleas or dismissal, and in none of these cases does the exclusionary rule come into use at all, since it is entirely confined to the admission of illegally obtained evidence in court. The most unjust of such cases are those in which the victims are innocent, are released, and can do little about what has happened to them.

Often, too, Levy points out, the police search a person or a place illegally in order to harass people they suspect of being criminals or people they simply don't like. In such cases, the search, even if it is preceded by an arrest to make it appear legal, rarely ends up being considered by any court. Searches of this kind are used, Levy says, for a "punitive end," and again the exclusionary rule never comes into play. Another common police tactic is the use of perjured testimony in court to justify what was actually an illegal search — as, for instance, when a policeman stops a suspect on the street, searches him merely because he looks suspicious, finds evidence of a crime, and then claims in court that the defendant happened to drop the evidence on the sidewalk just as he was passing, which provided probable cause to believe that a crime had been committed and the legal right to arrest the suspect and confiscate the evidence. In the end, Levy concludes, "by any reckoning the exclusionary rule applies to a trivial fraction of all prosecutions."

Despite the limited use of exclusion, it is under heavy and mounting attack. The most prominent of its critics is Chief Justice Burger, who bitterly assailed the rule in a recent case that had nothing to do with the issue. In 1965, half a dozen agents from the Federal Bureau of Narcotics entered the apartment of a man named Webster Bivens and, although they had neither a warrant nor probable cause to believe that he had committed a crime, arrested and manacled him in front of his wife and children, searched his apartment for narcotics, and after finding no evidence of any wrongdoing took him to a federal courthouse, where they forced him to undress and submit to what is known as a "strip search" — that is, a search of the rectum (or, in the case of a woman, a search of the rectum and the vagina). Again they found nothing, and finally they let Bivens go. As it happened, he was an ex-convict; as it also happened, he was innocent.

What Bivens went through is what hundreds, perhaps thousands, of other people go through at the hands of federal and state law-enforcement officers in this country every day. But Bivens decided to fight back, and he sued the agents, charging them with causing him mental anguish, and demanded fifteen thousand dollars in damages from each of them in recompense. A federal District Court dismissed the complaint, saying that if the search was lawful the suit had no basis, and that if the search was unlawful the agents were not liable, because they had acted not for the government, which cannot legally authorize unlawful acts, but for themselves, and the Fourth Amendment's protections do not cover private citizens' invasions of each other's privacy. A Court of Appeals upheld this finding. But the Supreme Court overturned the decision in 1971, and held, by a six-to-three vote, that although there is no federal law making federal officers liable for damages they cause through violations of the Fourth Amendment, the amendment itself implicitly allows damage suits against them when they flout it. If Congress were to implement this decision by way of a law specifying how individuals could collect substantial damages, the ruling could have a great effect, but as it stands now it merely means that an injured person has the same chance of collecting damages in federal courts as he has in state courts — little or none.

Chief Justice Burger, in a lengthy dissent from the Bivens decision, which had nothing to do with the question of excluding evidence, quoted a statement by Benjamin Cardozo that has long been cited by opponents of exclusion — "The criminal is to go free because the constable has blundered" — and then moved on to a 1954 Supreme Court decision that "catalogued the doctrine's defects":

> Rejection of the evidence does nothing to punish the wrongdoing official, while it may, and likely will, release the wrongdoing defendant. It deprives society of its remedy against one lawbreaker because he has been pursued by another. It protects one against whom incriminating evidence is discovered, but does nothing to protect innocent persons who are the victims of illegal but fruitless searches.

Although Burger emphatically stated that he did not question the need for some kind of "remedy to give meaning and teeth to the constitutional guarantees against unlawful conduct by government officials," he called the hope that the police would be deterred from unlawful searches and seizures by way of exclusion "hardly more than a wistful dream," and added, "Some clear demonstration of the benefits and effectiveness of the exclusionary rule is required to justify it in view of the high price it extracts from society — the release of countless guilty criminals." He could find no justification. First of all, he said, the rule applied no sanction against the offending policeman but struck instead at the prosecutor, who ordinarily has nothing to do with police behavior. Nor, Burger went on, could judicial exclusion of illegally obtained evidence have much effect on police officers, because they "do not have the time, inclination, or training to read and grasp the nuances of the appellate opinions that ultimately define the standards of conduct they are to follow," and because the ordinary delay — often several years — between the time a policeman commits an unlawful act and the time an appellate court announces that it was unlawful reduces "the presumed educational effect" to the point where "it would be surprising if he ever becomes aware of the final result." And since many illegal searches, like the one in Bivens, do not result in prosecution, the rule fails when it is most needed. In passing, the Chief Justice stated, "Suppressing unchallenged truth has set guilty criminals free but demonstrably has neither deterred deliberate violations of the Fourth Amendment nor decreased those errors in judgment that will inevitably occur given the pressures inherent in police work having to do with serious crimes."

Commenting on Burger's attack on exclusion, Professor Levy said recently, "If the rule does not in fact deter the police and is a failure, hard-liners on law and order, like Burger, would let sleeping dogmas lie. The rule deters not the police but the conviction of the guilty. That is the real reason that the rule is under heavy fire." That might seem like a fairly sound reason, but, Levy went on, there is no alternative to the rule, and until one is found it must be retained if only for its "great symbolic value."

Professor Amsterdam, on the other hand, felt that critics like Burger approached the subject of "deterrence" with a misconceived premise. "It suggests that the police have a God-given inclination to commit unconstitutional searches and seizures unless they are 'deterred' from that behavior," he said in the course of a recent lecture. "Once the assumption is indulged, it is easy enough to criticize the rule excluding unconstitutionally obtained evidence on the ground that it 'does not apply any direct sanction to the individual officer whose illegal conduct results in the exclusion,' and so cannot 'deter' him. But no one, to my knowledge, has ever urged that the exclusionary rule is supportable on this principle of 'deterrence.' It is not supposed to 'deter' in the fashion of the law of larceny, for example, by threatening punishment to him who steals a television set — a theory of deterrence, by the way, whose lack of empirical justification makes the exclusionary rule look as solid by comparison as the law of gravity." In Amsterdam's view, the "deterrent" effect of the rule was to be found in the "restraints" it imposed, even if largely ineffective, because they at least gave some meaning to the Fourth Amendment.

This point has probably been made most cogently by another scholar, Dallin Oaks, who wrote a few years ago:

> If constitutional rights are to be anything more than pious pronouncements, then some measurable consequence must be attached to their violation. It would be intolerable if the guarantee against unreasonable search and seizure could be violated without practical consequence. It is likewise imperative to have a practical procedure by which courts can review alleged violations of constitutional rights and articulate the meaning of those rights. The advantage of the exclusionary rule — entirely apart from any direct deterrent effect — is that it provides an occasion for judicial review, and it gives credibility to the constitutional guarantees. By demonstrating that society will attach serious consequences to the violation of constitutional rights, the exclusionary rule invokes and magnifies the moral and educative force of the law.

As worthy as all these arguments are, they miss a major point implicit in the arguments put forth by critics of exclusion. That point was made startlingly explicit by Chief Justice Burger in his Bivens dissent. If it is true, as he contends, that the police cannot grasp the meaning of appellate-court decisions, then they cannot enforce the law. And if it is true, as he also contends, that they cannot be educated to see the meaning and purpose of the law, then more control, not less, should be imposed over them.

In 1970, federal agents searched a machine-tool plant owned by a man named John P. Calandra under a warrant authorizing a search of the premises for evidence of illegal gambling equipment.

They found no sign of that, but came upon a record of what seemed to be a loan-sharking operation. The following year, a grand jury that was investigating this subject in the area summoned Calandra and questioned him, on the basis of the evidence seized by the federal agents at his plant, about his involvement in the loan-shark business. He refused to testify, on the ground that since the evidence seized had not been particularly described, or described at all, in the search warrant, the exclusionary rule prohibited the use of such evidence before a grand jury. A federal District Court upheld Calandra, and so did the Court of Appeals for the Sixth Circuit.

In January, 1974, the Supreme Court handed down its ruling on the Calandra case. In a six-vote majority decision — the four Nixon appointees plus White and Stewart — the Court accepted the Justice Department's argument that the exclusionary rule should *not* be binding on grand juries. The Court's opinion, which was written by Justice Lewis F. Powell, was anything but "strict construction," for it implicitly overruled Silverthorne and ignored the purpose of Mapp in order to justify the majority's bias; in fact, the opinion misconstrued almost every fundamental finding of the Court on the issue of the exclusionary rule. Powell declared that the exclusionary rule's "prime purpose is to deter future unlawful police conduct and thereby effectuate the guarantee of the Fourth Amendment against unreasonable search and seizures," that "the rule is a judicially created remedy designed to safeguard Fourth Amendment rights generally through its deterrent effect, rather than a personal constitutional right of the party aggrieved," and that such a rule could be judicially modified. At a critical point, Powell relied, in an entirely misleading fashion, on Clark's opinion in Mapp by claiming that forbidding the use of unlawfully seized evidence before grand juries would not "significantly" deter the police from indulging in unlawful searches and would "delay and disrupt grand jury proceedings," and would "unduly interfere with the effective and expeditious discharge of the grand jury's duties."

Of course, there is no appreciable difference in effect whether evidence sought illegally is for use in court or for use before a grand jury. And, of course, delay is an inevitable result of scrupulous fairness under the law. The Bill of Rights, it might be added, was not written to make life easier for policemen and prosecutors.

Justice Brennan, who wrote the minority opinion for himself and Justices Douglas and Marshall, found the Court's decision a "grievous error" and "a startling misconception, unless it is a purposeful rejection of the historical objective and purpose of the rule." He explained that deterrence was, at best, "a hoped-for effect of the exclusionary rule, not its ultimate objective," and added, "Indeed, there is no evidence that the possible deterrent effect of the rule was given any attention by the judges chiefly responsible for its formulation. Their concern as guardians of the Bill of Rights was to fashion an enforcement tool to give content and meaning to the Fourth Amendment's guarantees." He continued, "I am left with the uneasy feeling that today's decision may signal that a majority of my colleagues have positioned themselves to . . . abandon altogether the exclusionary rule in search and seizure cases. . . . Unless we are to shut our eyes to the evidence that crosses our desks every day, we must concede that official lawlessness has not abated and that no empirical data distinguishes trials from grand jury proceedings. I thus fear that when next we confront a case of a conviction rested on illegally seized evidence, today's decision will be invoked to sustain the conclusion in that case also that 'it is unrealistic to assume' that application of the rule at trial would 'significantly further' the goal of deterrence." Once that happened, he warned, the Fourth Amendment would be a "chimera."

The concept of "judicial integrity" – that is, public confidence in the courts – is often cited in defense of the exclusionary rule. But its critics, including Chief Justice Burger, have argued that when clearly guilty defendants are released by judges because clear proof of guilt is excluded during their trials, public respect for the courts is scarcely heightened. In Calandra, Brennan cited one statement after another made by the Supreme Court over the years about the imperative need for preserving the people's regard for their institutions of justice. Powell dismissed Brennan's point in a brief final footnote. "There is no basis for this alarum," he said.

"Illegal conduct is hardly sanctioned, nor are the foundations of the Republic imperiled by declining to make an unprecedented extension of the exclusionary rule to grand jury proceedings where the rule's objectives would not be effectively served and where other important and historic values would be unduly prejudiced."

This kind of pro-state bias has apparently never been shaken by the most famous statement on the subject of the people's trust in their government's decency – in Justice Brandeis's dissent in the Olmstead case against allowing evidence obtained by illegal wiretapping to be used in court:

> To prove its case, the government was obliged to lay bare the crimes committed by its officers on its behalf. A federal court should not permit such a prosecution to continue. . . . When these unlawful acts were committed, they were crimes of the officers individually. The government was innocent, in legal contemplation, for no federal official is authorized to commit a crime on its behalf. When the government, having full knowledge, sought, through the Department of Justice, to avail itself of the fruits of these acts in order to accomplish its own ends, it assumed moral responsibility for the officers' crimes. . . . And if this Court should permit the government, by means of its officers' crimes, to effect its purpose of punishing the defendants, there would seem to be present all the elements of a ratification. If so, the government itself would become a lawbreaker. . . . Decency, security, and liberty alike demand that government officials shall be subjected to the same rules of conduct that are commands to the citizen. In a government of laws, existence of the government will be imperilled if it fails to observe the law scrupulously. Our government is the potent, the omnipresent teacher. For good or for ill, it teaches the whole people by its example. Crime is contagious. If the government becomes a lawbreaker, it breeds contempt for law; it invites every man to become a law unto himself; it invites anarchy. To declare that in the administration of the criminal law the end justifies the means – to declare that the government may commit crimes in order to secure the conviction of a private criminal – would bring terrible retribution.

Although the Constitution does not contain the word "privacy," it is generally accepted today, on the Supreme Court and off, that the basic purpose of the Fourth Amendment is to secure individual privacy against arbitrary intrusions by government – in Otis's words, against the "power that places the liberty of every man in the hands of every petty officer." In other areas, the Court has taken some remarkably long strides, considering its generally statist character, to protect individual freedom. Among these are its decisions over the past decade ruling that individual privacy is unconstitutionally violated by state laws against the use of contraceptives by married couples, by state laws limiting the freedom to read whatever one wants to read within the confines of one's home, and by state laws against a woman's freedom to control her own body by aborting an unwanted fetus. On the other hand, some of the Court's latest decisions on the issue of privacy – most notably, that the states can enact and enforce laws making what state legislators deem to be "unnatural" sexual acts between adults punishable by imprisonment – suggest that the Court has begun to reject its own earlier declarations that the "penumbra" of the Bill of Rights protects each citizen's essential privacy. After all, what is more private, aside from one's innermost thoughts, than one's bedroom? Most important, though, the Supreme Court's persisting failure to protect us against capricious and unjust acts of the police could ultimately destroy personal liberty in America.

The pressures of our "mass society," the reach that modern surveillance techniques can extend into the most intimate corners of our lives, the increasing demand for legal and illegal shortcuts that would enlarge the freedom of the police to do what they want in the name of "crime control," the mounting danger that at a time of economic or political crisis a demagogue might rise and be followed, and, above all, the immense and overweening power of government on every level – all these require that the police power in this nation be strictly limited if the individual is to be free. As matters stand, Amsterdam has pointed out, our privacy and liberty are today "enjoyable only at the sufferance of expanding, militaristically organized bodies of professional police," who cannot be held in check unless "an independent judiciary plays a direct, strong role in their regulation."

While the Framers accepted the need for a strong central government, they also feared what it might do to individual liberty. One of their most specific fears was of military power, which they had suffered from so painfully under British rule, and in the Constitution they diffused that power by making the President the commander-in-chief of the armed forces and then giving Congress the authority to provide for the common defense, to declare war, to make rules for the land and naval forces, to raise and support armies, and to appropriate funds (for no more than two years at a time) to pay for military expenses. These were fairly stringent safeguards against military usurpation of civilian government, but they did not fully satisfy the people, who were unwilling to ratify the Constitution without further protections. A bill of rights was promised them, and in the Second and Third Amendments additional barricades against the military were set up — guarantees that there would be a decentralized militia, that the people had the right to keep and bear arms, and that troops could not be quartered in any private house in peacetime without the owner's consent.

Fear of the military was amply justified by history, but there was no comparable fear of today's supplement to military force — the police — because there were no police in any organized sense. Most communities had no more protection than paid day and night watchmen or public-spirited citizens who took turns patrolling the streets at night. In New York, where Congress was sitting when it approved the Bill of Rights, there were only night watchmen until 1845, when the first police force was organized. Of course, the Framers couldn't guard the new Republic against something that didn't exist. But the Supreme Court could — simply by strictly enforcing the Bill of Rights. Given the reluctance of legislatures to impose any but the mildest limits upon the nation's police, there is no other source of control over them besides judicial power, judicial right, and judicial duty.

The Supreme Court's failure to control the police could not be illustrated more fully than by its timidity and vacillation over the issue of excluding from court all evidence acquired through illegal searches and seizures. The exceedingly modest nature of exclusion and the exceedingly limited use of it would lead one to expect that the Supreme Court would try to expand, not contract, it, since courts have no other effective means of enforcing the Fourth Amendment's right to privacy. In Mapp, Justice Clark quoted Cardozo's statement that often "the criminal is to go free because the constable has blundered," and then added, "The criminal goes free, if he must, but it is the law that sets him free." The point is the only notable one made in Mapp, and it goes to the heart of the issue, for under our legal system guilty men must often escape punishment so that the innocent may, too.

To rid our lawbooks of the exclusionary rule would be to wipe out the Fourth Amendment and the protection, however meagre, that it gives to our shrinking privacy. The right to be secure in one's person and possessions cannot be assured as the law now stands, because the police can invade both at will without much fear of punishment. The only security a citizen has is that the fruits of the invasion cannot be used to prosecute him. That is something, at least, for while the police are not deterred by exclusion from illegally rummaging in one's private papers and possessions, they can be prevented from disclosing, publicly in open court, what they rummaged through.

The dangers of the policeman's freedom to destroy our freedom may not seem very great to most of us, and it isn't — at least, not today. But it is rashly indulgent not to raise barriers, as the Framers tried to, against future tyranny, especially when all the tools are ready at hand. "When I myself look back into that variegated political landscape which no observer can avoid suffusing with the color of his own concerns, the hues that gleam most keenly to my eye are the hues of an intense sense of danger of oppression of the individual," Amsterdam said recently. "I find that sense of danger all the more striking because so many of us in this country today have lost it. It is largely left to 'those accused of crime' and to the dwellers of the ghettos and the barrios of this land to view the policeman as 'an occupying soldier in a bitterly hostile country.' . . . But the authors of the Bill of Rights had known oppressive government. I believe they meant to erect every safeguard against it. I believe they meant to guarantee to their survivors the right to live as free from every interference of government agents as our condition would permit."

To statists like Chief Justice Burger, who believe that the state is benign and must be given greater and greater powers to protect itself against its more rebellious and destructive citizens, it is order and security, not individuality and liberty, that count most. But their belief and trust in government as a force for good is as dangerous as it is misguided, for, Justice Brandeis warned, "Experience should teach us to be most on our guard to protect liberty when the government's purposes are beneficent. Men born to freedom are naturally alert to repel invasion of their liberty by evil-minded rulers. The greatest dangers to liberty lurk in insidious encroachment by men of zeal, well-meaning but without understanding."

In *Privacy and Freedom,* Professor Alan F. Westin, of Columbia University, considers the "process of surveillance by authorities to enforce the rules and taboos of the society" to be universal. The only differences among various kinds of societies in this regard is one of degree. In totalitarian states, he explains, "autonomous units are denied privacy, traditional confidential relationships are destroyed, surveillance systems and informers are widely installed, and thorough dossiers are compiled on millions of citizens" – that is, all individuality is destroyed. And he goes on to say that while "American individualism – with its stress on unique personality in religion, politics, and law – provides a major force for privacy in the United States," there are still strong pressures against privacy here, too. Among them are middle-class morality, xenophobia, religious and racial prejudice, isolationism, puritanism, and the often overwhelming force of the demands for conformity.

Social pressures against personal freedom are destructive enough, but when added to them is the relentless and often malevolent use of state power – by the police to break into and ransack the homes of citizens or to stop and search people on the streets at will, by such government offices as the F.B.I. and the

C.I.A. to listen in on their most intimate communications and follow all their moves — the prospects of freedom look bleak. And the prospects are far bleaker when the state, even a democratic state such as ours, has leaders who instinctively favor order over liberty, legislators who ignore the people's most pressing needs, and judges who so often protect the interests of the state over the rights of its citizens.

Once again, Justice Brandeis made the point better than anyone else:

> The makers of our Constitution undertook to secure conditions favorable to the pursuit of happiness. They recognized the significance of man's spiritual nature, of his feelings and of his intellect. They knew that only a part of the pain, pleasure, and satisfactions of life are to be found in material things. They sought to protect Americans in their beliefs, their thoughts, their emotions, and their sensations. They conferred, as against the government, the right to be let alone — the most comprehensive of rights and the right most valued by civilized men. To protect that right, every unjustifiable intrusion by the government upon the privacy of the individual, whatever the means employed, must be deemed a violation of the Fourth Amendment.

It has been nearly half a century since Brandeis made this statement, and in that time the dangers he saw have been immensely magnified. But the gravest danger of all posed by official violations of our right to privacy is still the threat to freedom of thought. The freedom to think lies at the heart of all freedom, and as privacy shrinks so must thought. Once we fear that the expression of our thoughts — our spoken and written words — can be seized at any moment, even illegally, by local police or federal agents, we are bound to become more cautious about what we say or write. And if this fear persists and grows, our willingness to express anything but the most orthodox thoughts will diminish to such a degree that finally the spirit of thought will be lost to us altogether. That will mean the end of freedom, for without thought there is no individuality, and without individuality there is no democracy.

III

When John Brick, the staff investigator from the Senate Permanent Subcommittee on Investigations, served Alan and Margaret McSurely with subpoenas in mid-October of 1967, he told them that the Senate wanted only their papers, not them in person. Since there was no date on the subpoenas for any appearance before the subcommittee, the McSurelys soon concluded that Senator McClellan's intention was to let Commonwealth Attorney Ratliff boost his race for the lieutenant governorship of Kentucky by personally presenting the documents at one of the subcommittee's first hearings, on the riot that had taken place in Nashville during the previous spring. That hearing was to begin on November 1st, only a few days before the Kentucky election, and the publicity that Ratliff was expected to receive as a crusader against Communists and other radicals might be decisive for his political race.

"Everyone was frantically trying to accomplish his own ends," McSurely said afterward. "There was Pearson in Washington trying desperately to keep our sedition case out of the local courts in Kentucky, so that his love letters to Margaret wouldn't be spread out for all to see, and then hoping desperately, though he never approached her about this, that we wouldn't let McClellan have our papers. The law says that once you testify on any subject, you have to tell everything you know about it, so if Margaret had gone before the subcommittee and answered any questions about any letters, she would have had to answer questions about the Pearson letters, which could have been dragged in under some pretext, and that would have given McClellan a chance to put them in the public record. Ratliff was trying desperately to get publicity just before the election as the scourge of Communists in Kentucky. McClellan was trying desperately to get Pearson and us. And we were trying desperately to hold ourselves together and fight back."

On October 17th, the day the subpoenas were served, the McSurelys' local lawyer filed two motions in the federal District Court, in Lexington, one asking it to temporarily restrain Ratliff from turning the materials over to the Senate, and the other asking that the McSurelys' possessions be returned to them at once. On October 30th, the District Court denied both motions and later gave the McSurelys twenty-four hours to make an emergency appeal to the Supreme Court. They did, and charged that the subpoenas "constitute an unreasonable search and seizure" and "are in language as broad as the traditional writs of assistance." On November 10th, Supreme Court Justice Stewart, who was responsible for the Sixth Judicial Circuit, which includes Kentucky, ruled that the documents should remain in custody until a three-judge panel of the District Court in Lexington could consider the McSurelys' objections to the subpoenas.

On December 5th, a hearing was held before the panel. A lawyer from the Department of Justice who represented McClellan and the subcommittee ignored the Fourth Amendment altogether and told the court that "this Senate committee has bent over backward in trying to be as scrupulous as it can be about the rights of these plaintiffs" and "has never attempted to be in any way surreptitious." His main argument was based on an affidavit from Senator McClellan saying that the subpoenas were justified on the basis of what had been uncovered during his hearings on the Nashville riot. The McSurelys' lawyer then asked how it was possible to justify subpoenas issued on October 16th by way of hearings that began on November 1st.

Eight days after the three-judge panel met, it overruled the McSurelys' objections without explanation, and ordered Ratliff to turn the documents over to the subcommittee. This time, the court gave the McSurelys five days for another appeal to the Supreme Court. Once again they filed an appeal there, and on January 29, 1968, some six weeks later, the Court granted them a stay, pending its study of the issue, and asked both sides for briefs on it. Then, after studying the matter, the Court dismissed the McSurelys' appeal on March 18th, on the ground that the Court lacked jurisdiction, which properly lay with the Sixth Circuit Court of Appeals, and gave them thirty days in which to appeal their case to that court. They did, and finally, on July 29th, the Sixth Circuit Court ruled that the District Court had erred in not giving the McSurelys' papers back to them, and ordered this done, but added, "without prejudice to the right of the Senate committee to proceed with the enforcement of the subpoenas against Mr. and Mrs. McSurely." On October 23rd, the District Court ordered Ratliff to return the confiscated materials to them at 2 P.M. on November 8th.

Promptly at the designated hour, Pike County officials returned the McSurelys' possessions to them at the courthouse in Pikeville. As they were loading their things in their Volkswagen bus (which they bought when their old Ford gave out), Brick came up to give them the photocopies he had obtained of certain documents, as required by the Court of Appeals' order. He handed McSurely an inventory of the copies, and began returning them one by one.

"Brick had a silly little grin on his face as he talked," McSurely recounted. "As he handed me love letters of my wife's that he had taken and spread around the Senate, he would giggle and say, 'Now, here's a letter from Drew Pearson to Margaret which says, "Dearest Cucumber," ' and he would say, 'Mark that off.' And then he would hand me another one and he would say, 'Here's another letter from Drew. What do you think of this one?' Then he would giggle again. Margaret was so embarrassed that she walked off to get away from it. She had told me about her affair with Pearson, but I hadn't known about the letters or her diary until after we got the subpoenas. It made me sick and mad as hell to think of those vicious old men up in Washington pawing over my wife's personal life like that. Anyway, when Brick finally finished handing me all that stuff with his little grin and I had signed the inventory, I walked away."

Brick called out to him, "Now we are going to get these documents back. If you don't give them to us, you are going to be in contempt of Senator McClellan and his committee."

McSurely turned and said to him, "I am full of contempt for Senator McClellan and his committee."

Immediately afterward, a deputy United States marshal served the McSurelys with a new set of subpoenas prepared by the subcommittee. These were much the same as the original ones, except that now the McSurelys were "hereby commanded to appear and attend before the Senate Permanent Subcommittee on Investigations" at a hearing on January 14, 1969, and to bring with them nearly everything that the earlier subpoenas had demanded.

Over the fifteen months that the McSurelys had been embroiled in various court battles—first in local courts after the raid on their house and their arrest, then over the confiscation of their possessions, and finally over the subpoenas—they had tried to maintain some kind of ordinary life. The attempt had not succeeded. McSurely went on trying to organize coal miners to fight black-lung disease, to get local people to start more community efforts to help themselves, and to find leaders among the poor who could persuade them to demand their rights in everything from free school lunches for their children to militant protests against strip-mining the mountains of Kentucky. But the protracted court actions took up much of his time and thought, and made any attempt to live normally almost impossible.

During that period, Mrs. McSurely was deeply depressed about their life in the mountains, and was anxious to leave. "I was tired of being a lightning rod for freedom," she said later. When the raid and arrests took place, she was five months pregnant, and the couple's son, Victor Alan McSurely, was born in December, 1967. "I knew we weren't doing any good there," Mrs. McSurely went on. "The people didn't want our help. Al was rushing all over the mountains but not accomplishing much of anything, and all I was doing was taking care of him and Victor. I didn't tell him then, but I was terribly scared. After our arrest, I feared every night that we would be killed. I was sure someone would try to get us."

Half a mile outside Pikeville on the highway going east, a small road curves up through the narrow valley, or hollow, where the McSurelys lived. Set back in the corner formed by the two roads was the small hospital that Victor had been born in. On the side of the hospital facing – and about a hundred feet from – the branch road was a large window in the obstetrics-ward lounge, where Mrs. McSurely stayed after the baby was born, because the charge for a bed there was three dollars a day less than in the ward. "I used to lie in my bed right next to that big window and think that a sniper would fire through it and kill me," she said. "It may seem absurd to outsiders, but cowards down there really do kill women and children – and for next to nothing."

One evening a year after the baby was born, Mrs. McSurely put him to bed, had some dinner alone while she waited for her husband to come home, and then wandered nervously about their small house – a one-story five-room, white-clapboard cottage that was about a dozen feet off the same branch road leading past the hospital, half a mile down the hollow. McSurely had been away since early that morning, off in a neighboring county to talk to some people about setting up a coöperative food store there, and then had gone on to Dickenson County, Virginia, just across the state line, to see a man who had telephoned him with information that he thought might help in the miners' fight against black-lung disease.

"Al came back at about eleven o'clock that night," Mrs. McSurely recalled. "He was bone-tired, and he had a bite to eat, took a bath, and went to bed. I cleaned up, and after checking Victor, who was in a crib in our bedroom, I turned in, too. It must have been about half past midnight. I had a hard time getting to sleep, and was just beginning to feel it come on when I heard a car coming down the road toward the house going real fast. Then it slowed, and I heard a thump, and then there was a terrible blast. It sucked out all the air, and everything – glass mostly – flew everywhere. Victor started screaming. The first thing that crossed my mind was 'Well, they finally did it.' I was sure Al was dead. The room was full of the smell of sulphur, so I knew it was dynamite. There was dirt in my mouth. I ran and picked up Victor, and then I saw Al running around the room looking for his pants. We got out of there and ran across the road to a neighbor's house. It was terribly cold, nearly zero, and very still that night. When Al and the neighbor went back to look at the damage from the blast — a hole torn in the side of the house, just under our bedroom window — they discovered a gas pipe had been ruptured by the explosion. The whole hollow could have blown up if the gas had collected there for long, so they got a wrench and turned off the gas. The neighbors said they'd heard a car drive up the hollow and stop and stay there for half an hour or so, then come back fast, and then there was the explosion. We never learned who the men in that car were, because I don't think the police and the F.B.I. really tried to find out. Whoever it was must have waited for Al to get home and for us to go to bed and turn out the lights and go to sleep. I guess they meant to kill us in our beds, so we wouldn't have a chance. If the bomb had gone through the window, as they obviously intended, they would have succeeded."

The McSurelys couldn't decide which law-enforcement agency to call, but finally chose the state police, and half an hour later a trooper arrived at the scene. After examining the bomb damage, he said to them, "The next time this happens, you should call the Pikeville police, so they can block off the road."

Realizing then that there almost certainly would be a next time, the McSurelys quickly packed a few clothes and personal belongings in their Volkswagen bus, wrapped Victor in a blanket, and set off, at four o'clock in the morning, for Lexington. "That was it for us and Pike County," McSurely said. "A couple of days later, I bought a gun, and Margaret and I drove down to the house just long enough to pick up the rest of our stuff and get out for good."

A week afterward, the McSurelys moved into the basement of his mother's small house in Alexandria, Virginia, just outside Washington, and began mapping out a strategy for their fight against the Senate subpoenas and their command that the couple appear before McClellan's subcommittee three weeks later. "We were both very frightened," Mrs. McSurely said. "We knew the power McClellan wielded was enormous, and we knew that we didn't matter to him at all. We were just helpless citizens who happened to suit his political needs at the moment. And we knew that we faced a year in prison for contempt of Congress if we refused to honor the subpoenas. But we also knew that we had to. We weren't fighting just for blacks in the South or the poor in Appalachia any longer. Now we were fighting for ourselves — and for everybody else."

The history of congressional investigations is in large part the history of American politics," Telford Taylor wrote in *Grand Inquest,* a legal and historical account of such inquiries over the years. Taylor's book appeared in 1955, shortly after the conclusion of Senator Joseph R. McCarthy's attack on liberals in the guise of a congressional investigation into Communist influence in high places in the United States government — part of what Taylor called the "cold civil war" between the right and left wings in this country. By the end of 1954, McCarthy's demagoguery had run its course, and he had destroyed himself. That year, the Republicans lost control of Congress, and McCarthy died not long afterward. But his spirit survived — indeed, flourished — in his successor as chairman of the Permanent Subcommittee on Investigations, John McClellan, who used this inquisitorial forum of McCarthy's to carry on the domestic cold war, in a less flamboyant but a more lasting and effective fashion, for nearly two decades. As McClellan seems to view American society, little that is wrong with it cannot be attributed to Communist subversion or to his other favorite scourge — criminals and those who are "soft" on them.

The first hearing on the riots held by the Permanent Subcommittee on Investigations concerned a gunfight between police and some snipers at Texas Southern University, a predominantly black college in Houston. The lead-off witness from Houston was its mayor, who told the members of the subcommittee, "It is impossible for me to discuss a big-city riot in Houston, because Houston has not had one." That point interested Senator McClellan less than the information that Stokely Carmichael, the militant field director of the Student Nonviolent Coordinating Committee, had spoken in Houston not long before the disturbance there, and that many anti-poverty workers in the area were either members or officially designated as "friends" of S.N.C.C. McClellan kept trying to establish a connection between Carmichael and black discord in Houston, but the officials of that city who testified kept assuring him that Carmichael had had no influence on the community, and one of them said, "He did a very intellectual speech that night."

However, when the second set of hearings was held, on another black "riot" in the South – this one in April, 1967, near the campus of Fisk University, also a predominantly black school, in Nashville, Tennessee – city officials assured McClellan that Carmichael had indeed had a great influence on the community. He had gone to Nashville a few days before the disorder there to speak at Tennessee State University, at Fisk, and at Vanderbilt University, and also to attend a small civil-rights conference being held in the city at the time by members of the Southern Students Organizing Committee (S.S.O.C.), the Southern Conference Educational Fund (SCEF), and S.N.C.C. Several officials who testified pointed out that the riot in question had broken out there a few hours after he spoke at Vanderbilt. The clash – between Fisk students and the police – had resulted in few serious injuries and little property damage.

Even so, McClellan was intensely interested in the incident. And he was particularly curious about what he called a "secret meeting" held by SCEF and attended by Carmichael the day before the fracas. A colloquy between Chairman McClellan and Captain John Sorace, who oversaw the Nashville Police Department's intelligence division, followed:

McCLELLAN: Do you have any information as to what occurred in any secret meetings?

SORACE: We have no direct information on the SCEF meeting. There was a flyer put out alleging that Carmichael was to speak about Communism and black power. The SCEF people have denied issuing such a flyer.

MCCLELLAN: Did you see the flyer?

SORACE: Yes.

MCCLELLAN: Do you have it with you?

SORACE: We don't have it with us; no, sir.

MCCLELLAN: Do you have it in your files?

SORACE: We do.

MCCLELLAN: I would like you to send it to us or get a copy of it to us for the record.

SORACE: We will.

MCCLELLAN: Attach a letter when you transmit it, saying "This is the flyer" about which you testified. I wish you had it with you.

A little later, McClellan asked Sorace and two of his subordinates whether they knew what had been said at the meeting, and they explained that although they had managed to infiltrate the groups attending the conference, no undercover agent had been present at the SCEF meeting, so they had no information on what took place there. The official minutes of the meeting read:

> Mr. Stokely Carmichael, in Nashville to speak at Vanderbilt, met with the [SCEF] board in a closed session Friday morning. He explained his position on the need for black power in politics and economics: In the last twenty years, the gap between the income of blacks and whites has doubled. Laws have been enacted which create an image of improvement, but coalition groups have not had enough power to implement them. Unless blacks have power, any coalescence with whites works to the advantage of the whites. For power, blacks must organize. Integration, if it occurs, will be a byproduct rather than the end sought. Following Mr. Carmichael's talk was a lively question-and-answer period.

At the beginning and the end of the session, prayers were offered by three ministers who attended the conference, which was held in the Methodist Board of Evangelism Building.

Sorace sent McClellan the flyer, which had been handed out on the streets of Nashville before the SCEF meeting and which purportedly had been issued by SCEF in conjunction with S.S.O.C. and the Nashville Committee for Alternatives to War in Vietnam. The flyer said, in part:

> The Southern Conference Educational Fund, Inc. (SCEF) is actively engaged in anti-Vietnam and peace activities, and is headed by Carl Braden, who was accused in a state trial in Louisville, Kentucky, in 1954 of being head of the Communist Party of Kentucky and who later went to prison for refusal to answer questions concerning this before the Un-American Activities Committee. N.C.A.W.V., S.S.O.C. and the S.N.C.C. are highly gratified to be a part of this SCEF Conference, noting that these organizations have received valuable assistance from SCEF, both materially and spiritually. . . . It is regretted that a majority of the SCEF directtors' and staff meetings will not be open to the general public and to the news media; however, one of the meetings will be addressed by invited guest Stokely Carmichael, controversial S.N.C.C. Chairman, and this address will be open to the public and the news. Carmichael will address the SCEF Conference on the theme "S.N.C.C. – Black Power for Communism."

The organizations involved denied issuing the flyer, and it is difficult to imagine how anyone could believe they had issued it – undoubtedly the reason Sorace hadn't bothered to bring a copy of it to the hearing. But McClellan ordered it put into the record, and afterward he repeatedly cited its reference to the title of Carmichael's speech and to Braden's alleged, and still unproved, membership in the Communist Party.

Another subject that McClellan was interested in during the hearings on Nashville, and that he brought up again and again, was the presence of Alan and Margaret McSurely at the SCEF conference and at the private session addressed by Carmichael. During the first round of the subcommittee's hearings on the Nashville riot – early in November of 1967 – no mention had been made of the SCEF "secret meeting" or of the McSurelys. On November 10th, the Supreme Court ordered the District Court to hold a hearing on their request for the return of their papers and the move to quash the subpoenas, and the District Court set December 5th for the hearing. With that, McClellan suddenly ordered another round of hearings on the Nashville disturbance – held on November 21st – and this was the occasion on which he questioned Sorace about the "secret meeting" and the McSurelys.

At the time, the couple and their lawyers knew nothing about this event, either, and it wasn't until the December 5th hearing before the District Court that they got some idea of what seemed to have been happening. At that hearing, Brick was forced to divulge – by way of a "stipulation" as to the facts in the case – that he had secretly examined and obtained copies of the McSurelys' papers and had taken them back to McClellan in Washington. Also at that hearing, the Justice Department lawyers representing the subcommittee submitted an affidavit from McClellan stating that he had received information from Ratliff (without mentioning how that information had been received) and from the hearings on the Nashville riot (without mentioning any dates) indicating that the McSurelys had been connected with eight organizations which were "involved to some extent in causing the riots."

At no time during the subcommittee's long hearings was any evidence introduced to link five of these eight organizations with the riots supposedly being investigated. At no time during the hearings did McClellan attempt to question any of the thirty-odd other participants at the so-called "secret meeting." And at no time, then or later, was there any evidence that this meeting and the McSurelys were in any way connected with the Nashville riot.

Shortly after the December 5th hearing, the McSurelys' lawyers began to develop a theory about their opponents' behavior. "It looked as if the second round of hearings on Nashville had been convened mainly to get Sorace's testimony on the record, in order to make it appear that McClellan had independent evidence about the McSurelys, apart from the covert use of their papers, on which to base the subpoenas for their stuff," one of the lawyers explained. "In other words, we felt that the second hearings were set up to furnish a cover for the actual basis for the subpoenas – Brick's illegal copying and seizure of the McSurelys' papers – and to conceal McClellan's role in this dirty business, which we had known nothing about until the stipulation in court on December 5th. As far as we can make out now, concealing McClellan's role was to be the government's goal for the next five years."

Early in January, the McSurelys' appearance before the subcommittee was postponed — without explanation but presumably because just about everybody in the capital was getting ready for the inauguration of Richard Nixon on January 20th — and the McSurelys moved back to Kentucky, this time to Lexington, where they went on working for SCEF. The subcommittee hearing was then scheduled for mid-February, but it was again postponed without explanation, and was finally fixed for March 4th. Shortly before that date, the McSurelys returned to the basement of his mother's house.

Kunstler handled the case at the subcommittee hearing, and in preparing the McSurelys for what they might expect he warned them that if they simply appeared before the subcommittee and refused to turn over the subpoenaed documents Senator McClellan would probably try to bar them from offering any detailed explanation of their reasons in order to keep the unseemly acts that he and his staff had engaged in off the official record. According to Kunstler, McClellan would try to limit that record to the subcommittee's authorization by the Senate to investigate the riots of 1967, the Chairman's explicit request for information pertaining to those riots from the McSurelys, and their refusal to comply with the subpoenas. In other words, Kunstler explained, McClellan would probably allow only enough evidence to be entered in the record to justify a contempt-of-Congress citation, which carries a penalty of up to a thousand-dollar fine and a year in prison, but not enough evidence to justify the McSurelys' resistance to the subpoenas. If that was McClellan's strategy, Kunstler went on, the McSurelys should have a counter-strategy to get the story of what had happened to them — that is, their essential reason for refusing to honor the subpoenas — into the record in some way, so that a trial jury might find the circumstances sufficiently extenuating to acquit them, and so that if the two were convicted they would have a sound basis for an appeal.

In the end, he recommended an unusual tactic — a civil suit for damages against the members of the subcommittee and its senior legal aides for violating the McSurelys' constitutional rights. The purpose of such a suit, he said, would be threefold: to obtain compensation for the McSurelys as a means of making up in some way for what they had been put through, to discourage politicians like McClellan from treating other citizens as he had treated them, and to get the crucial story of the case on the record in an official and detailed form. On the last point, Kunstler explained that even if McClellan allowed the McSurelys to tell their story at the hearing, they might become so carried away by their outrage at what had happened, and was still happening, to them that they would neglect to make the fine legal points that might be essential to their defense in the event of a trial and an appeal.

The McSurelys approved of this tactic, so Kunstler and Nancy Stearns, also of the Center staff, drew up a civil "complaint" against McClellan and the other members of the subcommittee (Democratic Senators Henry M. Jackson, Sam J. Ervin, Jr., Edmund S. Muskie, and Abraham Ribicoff, and Republican Senators Robert P. Griffin, Karl E. Mundt, Charles A. Percy, and Jacob K. Javits), together with the general and chief counsels of the subcommittee (Jerome S. Adlerman and Donald F. O'Donnell). The complaint recounted the McSurelys' experiences from the time they moved to Kentucky in April, 1967, to the present, and charged that the subpoenas were the result of a conspiracy between members and aides of the subcommittee on the one hand and Kentucky officials on the other that was aimed at "intimidating, deterring, and stigmatizing" the plaintiffs and "preventing them from pursuing their political, poverty, peace, and/or civil-rights activities."

This conspiracy, the complaint went on, had deprived the plaintiffs of their constitutional rights under the First Amendment by denying them "the fundamental guarantees of freedom of speech, press, assembly, association, thought and belief, [and] the right of citizens to petition their government for redress of grievances," and under the Fourth Amendment by denying them "the right of citizens to be secure in their houses, persons, and papers from unreasonable searches and seizures." The McSurelys were joined in the suit by SCEF, S.N.C.C., S.S.O.C., and Students for a Democratic Society, and the complaint asked for compensatory damages of fifty thousand dollars for each of the McSurelys and fifty thousand dollars for each of their co-plaintiffs – or a total of three hundred thousand dollars.

As a further tactical maneuver, Kunstler decided not to file the complaint with the federal District Court for the District of Columbia until the morning of the hearing, in order to delay official notice of the lawsuit to McClellan and thereby cut down the time he would have in which to devise a counter-counter-strategy to keep the McSurelys' story off the subcommittee's record – in all likelihood, Kunstler assumed, by ruling at the hearing that he had been informed of the lawsuit and that it was a private lawsuit and was not pertinent to the issue before the subcommittee.

Another tactic that the McSurelys and Kunstler worked out was the creation of as much publicity as they could manage, in order to expose McClellan's misuse of his political power and thus limit the lengths to which he might go if he were operating in relative secrecy. The three discussed, and at times disagreed on, how they should create and employ such publicity. One matter they agreed on was that the McSurelys should get together as many friends and friends of friends as they could persuade to attend the hearing and to alert some sympathetic reporters. One matter they disagreed on was Kunstler's suggestion that they might also arrive at the hearing room with a large locked box – or "treasure chest," he called it – which they would ostentatiously place on the witness table. Then, when McClellan asked if the box contained the subpoenaed documents, McSurely was to fumble with the lock for a few minutes to create interest on the part of the press, and finally open the box, take out dozens of copies of the civil complaint, and submit them to members of the subcommittee, the audience, and the press.

"Kunstler is a great lawyer, and we agreed with his basic strategy all the way," McSurely remarked afterward. "But we thought the Abbie Hoffman tactic was the worst possible one for us to take. During that period, the press was painting the New Left as a pack of Yippies and crazies, and the last thing we wanted was to be made to look like a couple of nuts, too. We had just spent two years trying, with our own lives at stake, to be an example that would help persuade the working class that their natural allies were radical students and blacks. The Yippie movement had turned white workers bitterly against students, so we didn't want to do anything far out to give McClellan and his friends the chance to tag us as Yippies and increase working-class antagonism. Also, we were very angry — our house had been dynamited just a few weeks before and we'd come close to being killed — and we felt that the whole subcommittee thing was so ludicrous and outrageous that we shouldn't have to defend ourselves at all. We hadn't done anything wrong. It was those murderers in Kentucky and those thieves in the Senate who had done wrong. Finally, Margaret and I decided that if we were going to resist we should do so in a straightforward and legal manner, and take the worst that McClellan had to offer."

Angered by the recollection, McSurely paused for a moment and then went on, "We were very conscious of the historical background of what the far right had done in the past and was now trying to do to us. In the fifties, men like Joe McCarthy were very quick to grasp the uses that television could be put to as a way to persuade the general public that Communists and Socialists were some kind of slimy snakes writhing through the nation's vitals. They allowed themselves to be put entirely on the defensive by pleading the Fifth Amendment or trying to make their political position look more moderate than it actually was. I felt that this had been a terrible mistake. These men were hounded out of their jobs and often sent to prison, and the public applauded. I think that when they were dragged before congressional committees they should have stood up and said, 'Sure, we want to overthrow the system — if men like you run it. Send us to jail for our opinions, if that's your aim. Here's what our opinions are, and, whatever you do to us, we'll go on fighting you in the name of the people.' That would have made the issues clearer to the public, but the dissenters and rebels acted as if they had something to hide, and became more suspicious in the public mind than ever. We were determined not to make that mistake."

The McSurelys finally persuaded their lawyer to take a strictly legalistic approach to their case, and Kunstler finally persuaded them to generate all the publicity they could accept as suitable to that approach. To this end, they got together a couple of hundred friends, friends of friends, relatives, and sympathetic supporters who agreed to attend the subcommittee hearing, and then McSurely telephoned several reporters to alert them to the event. The day before the hearing, however, Senator McClellan convened a meeting of the subcommittee's parent body, the Committee on Government Operations, of which he was also chairman, told its members that the witnesses who were scheduled to appear at a subcommittee hearing the following day were planning to hold a riot at it; in the end, Senator Jackson moved that the hearing be held in executive session; and then Senator Ribicoff seconded the motion, which was unanimously approved. This tactic was by no means new. In *Grand Inquest,* Taylor wrote, "Senator McCarthy has devised and exploited a new type of hearing which is neither secret nor public. It is secret in the sense that the press and the general public are excluded, but public in the sense that . . . at the end of the hearing the chairman, or members of the committee or its staff, give the press their version of what has occurred . . . to make sensational headlines having no basis in fact."

When word of the plan to hold the hearing in executive session reached Kunstler, the night before, he called the McSurelys, and they met with him to revise their strategy. They decided not to inform their prospective audience that it would be excluded the next morning but to use the secret nature of the hearing as a further reason for not complying with the subpoenas. Kunstler reminded them that they could shout at McClellan all they wanted to about their friends' being shut out of the hearing, as long as they also got the specific legal reasons for their resistance to the subpoenas into the official record. Without that, he added, they would have little hope of staying out of prison.

As soon as the doors to the United States Courthouse were opened on the morning of March 4th, the McSurelys and Kunstler hurried in and filed the civil suit. Then they walked to Capitol Hill and the New Senate Office Building, where they found a crowd of close to two hundred people waiting for them in the broad, marble-floored corridor outside the hearing room of the Government Operations Committee. Several Capitol policemen, thirty of whom were on hand to control the crowd, were blocking the door to the committee chamber, and would admit only the McSurelys and Kunstler. When several members of the crowd loudly objected to their exclusion, the officer in charge warned them that any resistance on their part to Chairman McClellan's orders would be met with their immediate arrest. Kunstler asked the McSurelys' supporters to stand by, and McSurely announced to them that he and his wife would hold a press conference following the hearing.

Once inside the hearing room, Kunstler informally asked McClellan to admit the people waiting outside, but the Senator brusquely retorted that he had no say over the matter, since the full committee had unanimously approved holding an executive session and it was too late to round up its members to reconsider their vote. The senators who were present – Ervin, Mundt, and Griffin – took their seats on either side of the Chairman, and the proceedings began. After citing the authority conferred by the Senate on the subcommittee to conduct an investigation of the riots, McClellan declared that one of the subcommittee's primary purposes had been "to determine whether the outbreaks of violence were spontaneous or if they were instigated and precipitated by the calculated design of agitators."

The Nashville "riot," he went on, had been investigated by the subcommittee, by the Senate Judiciary Committee, and by both sides in a civil lawsuit growing out of the riot, and in the course of all these inquiries it was "disclosed that officials, employees, and members of the Student Nonviolent Coordinating Committee were deeply involved in the precipitation and instigation of the riot," which had directly followed some "inflammatory speeches by Stokely Carmichael." Continuing, McClellan noted that SCEF had held a "secret meeting" shortly before the riot, and pointed out that among those who attended were Carl and Anne Braden, co-directors of SCEF, who had "been identified as members of the Communist Party by the testimony of an F.B.I. informant in Kentucky courts and before congressional committees," and the McSurelys. "Carmichael made a speech at the meeting, from which the public and the press were barred," McClellan added – apparently seeing no irony in the fact that if private meetings were inherently suspicious, so was this executive session. "Evidence in the record shows that a press release disseminated before the meeting gave the title of Carmichael's speech as: 'S.N.C.C. – Black Power for Communism.' "

When McClellan finished his statement, Kunstler formally moved that the hearing be opened to the public, explained that the McSurelys had just filed a civil suit against the members of the subcommittee, and asked that the suit be made a part of the hearing record. "Since the complaint contains very specific contentions of unconstitutional, illegal, and unlawful action on the part of this committee in connection with the authorities of Pike County, it is our feeling that the executive session hides from the public the situation that is delineated in that complaint and that the public should be admitted to this hearing," he said. Continuing, he pointed out that the McSurelys would waive any protection they might have in an executive session, and again urged that the facts in the complaint, which were by then a matter of record in various federal courts, be included in the subcommittee transcript.

McClellan asked his colleagues if any of them supported the motion. While none of them could have known much about the circumstances that led up to the subpoenas, none of them showed any interest in the constitutional issues involved or in the rights of the witnesses, and none of them even asked for time to glance through the explanation in the complaint. Instead, they remained silent, and McClellan announced, "The committee unanimously rejects the request of the counsel." In quick succession and in the same manner, the committee also unanimously rejected Kunstler's motion that the hearing be postponed until the civil suit was settled and his motion that the subpoenas be quashed, on the ground that they were based on an unconstitutional search and seizure.

Afterward, McClellan asked the McSurelys, in turn, if they were prepared to surrender the subpoenaed documents. "We are not going to take any position on whether we will bring the records and documents until this hearing is opened," McSurely answered. "The issue before this committee today is whether the public has a right to hear what is going on in this committee."

McSurely repeatedly tried to make a speech he had prepared – about how the strife in Appalachia, such as guerrilla warfare against strip mining, was the result of despair and disorganization among the people there, not of any subversive agitation; about how such rural "riots" had no connection with urban disorders, except that both were the inevitable result of the same kind of despair and disorganization; about how the slum riots were the last thing that men like Carmichael wanted, since such anarchic outbursts provided the police with the excuse they needed to arrest or kill blacks, including black leaders who were frequently out in the streets at the time trying to persuade the rioters to go home; and, finally, about how it was the economic, social, and racial oppression created by men like McClellan that perpetuated the injustices which led to such riots.

McClellan cut McSurely off before he got past the first few words of his speech, and said, "I take it that you challenge the right of the Senate of the United States and its committees to hold executive hearings?"

McSurely said that was correct, and later he added, "I think the whole country would understand better the causes of the urban disorders, because I think some of the causes are right in this room."

"Are you going to be respectful or not?" McClellan shouted. Finally, after several attempts, he forced each of the McSurelys to state that they would not comply with the subpoenas. And he warned them that they faced contempt-of-Congress citations, gave them three more days in which to produce their papers, and adjourned the hearing.

Immediately afterward, McClellan carried out the next act in the scenario that Taylor described in *Grand Inquest,* by telling Daniel Schorr in an interview for CBS News that the McSurelys were part of a worldwide Communist conspiracy. Schorr attended the McSurelys' press conference, told them what McClellan had said, and asked if they had any response to the charge. McSurely replied that indeed they were engaged in a conspiracy – to unite the unemployed, the working poor, and blacks into a coalition that could demand, and get, their rights as citizens of the United States.

When the McSurelys did not produce the documents within the prescribed time, McClellan presented the matter to the members of the subcommittee, and on March 24th they unanimously voted to cite the couple for contempt of Congress. On April 30th, the members of the parent committee also unanimously voted to cite the two for contempt. The following day, McClellan presented to the Senate a report on the issue, in which he charged, again, that S.N.C.C. was "deeply involved in the precipitation and instigation of the riot" in Nashville; that Carmichael made several inflammatory speeches there "in the two days just before the riot;" that SCEF was headed by the Bradens, who "have been identified as members of the Communist Party;" that the McSurelys worked for SCEF; that the day before the Nashville outburst SCEF held a "secret meeting . . . from which the public and the press was barred;" that Carmichael spoke at the meeting; and that "a press release disseminated before the meeting gave the title of Carmichael's speech as 'S.N.C.C. – Black Power for Communism.' "

Continuing, the report stated that the subcommittee had "received information" that some documents in possession of Kentucky officials "would be pertinent to the investigation" and that the "subcommittee's staff received copies of some of the documents and other material," which led to the subpoenas for the originals. Assuring the Senate that he had provided "protection of all civil and constitutional rights of the witnesses," McClellan charged that their "contemptuous" behavior left him no recourse but to seek a citation against them. Along with the report, he submitted a Senate resolution instructing the United States Attorney for the District of Columbia to prosecute the McSurelys for contempt of Congress. On May 5th, the resolution came up for a vote. No one objected, and within a matter of minutes the resolution was approved by the Senate.

The McSurelys were unaware of the subcommittee and committee votes against them, and learned about the contempt resolution only after the Senate passed it. During the couple of months preceding it, they were living in Lexington in comparative safety. They had found a pleasant apartment with a garden, and had renewed acquaintance with old friends and acquired some new ones. McSurely was writing a pamphlet for SCEF on black-lung disease among coal miners, and he worked on that project while his wife took care of the apartment and their son, set up a women's discussion group, and occasionally did some research for SCEF. The Bradens and other members of SCEF – who had supported them and continued to support them in their fight with the Senate – hoped that the McSurelys wouldn't become discouraged and leave the Movement but would go back to the mountains and continue their organizing work.

"They said you should never let yourself be run out of a place," Mrs. McSurely recalled. "But I refused to go back, because I was sure we'd be killed there unless we were armed and ready to kill, too. I was just tired of living in terror. Al drove down into the mountains from time to time to do research on black lung, and every time he left I wondered if I'd ever see him alive again."

She paused, looked off reflectively for a time, and finally went on, "Still, I felt bad. I kept thinking about the people in Appalachia and how desperately they needed help, any help at all. Living in the mountains taught me one thing I'll never forget – what it's really like to be poor. In the mountains, if you're a poor person you are without hope. You get up at four or five in the morning and start a tiny coal fire to get warm. Even in the summer it's cold in the mountains early in the morning, and you freeze day and night all winter long. You look at your fire and wonder if your coal will last until you get a few dollars from welfare aid, or an odd job if you're lucky, so you can buy a few pounds of the poorest grade of coal. And you're living on top of a mountain of coal. You never know if you're going to get anything to eat next week, so you eat everything you can when you get the chance, just like a starving dog. Mostly, breakfast is flour-and-water biscuits and gravy made out of bacon fat and more flour and water. You probably won't get any midday meal, and supper will be a slice of bacon and some boiled potatoes and, if it's summertime, some kind of greens. You probably don't have any plates or cups or knives or forks but eat with your fingers out of the cooking pot and drink water out of a tin can. Rent for your little shack is ten dollars a month, and sometimes you can't pay even that. And if you or your children get sick, get some serious illness, you know that's probably going to be the end."

Throughout the spring and early summer of 1969, the McSurelys discussed whether they should stay on in Lexington, move back to the mountains, or leave Kentucky. Mrs. McSurely was adamantly against living in any place like Pikeville, not merely because of the danger but because she had concluded that the adverse publicity created by the raid, their indictment for sedition, the Senate subpoenas, and the bombing of their house had made any hope that they could now be effective in the mountains futile. She contended that the best course to pursue would be to join a trade-union movement in a large city, where they would be among friends and would have some chance of carrying out their organizing work successfully.

But McSurely was unhappy about leaving the mountains altogether. "I felt, and still feel, that it was the best place for us to carry on our work," he said recently. "And I didn't like being run out of a place any more than the Bradens did. I guess my pride was hurt."

In the end, the decisive factor was the couple's shared conclusion that the most important thing in their lives right then was the contempt-of-Congress case, and that if they were to assist in their defense, the best course for them was to return to the Washington area, so they would be on hand to help their lawyers. In mid-July, the McSurelys moved back into the basement of his mother's house. He went to work at a children's summer-recreation center, and a few weeks later he found a job teaching eighth-grade mathematics at a public school in nearby Prince Georges County, Maryland. "We got a nice apartment not far from the school, and we tried to settle down," Mrs. McSurely said. "But the frustration and fear were beginning to set in on us again, because we didn't know whether we would be indicted or not. If we were and went to trial, we figured that, win or lose, Al would be fired as soon as the school board found out about it."

Under the separation-of-powers doctrine, the executive branch of the government prosecutes anyone whom either body of Congress cites for contempt, because a refusal to prosecute could destroy Congress's subpoena powers and render it incapable of obtaining information necessary to the legislative process. The separation-of-powers doctrine also requires, of course, that Congress not usurp the judicial or executive function. But when a subcommittee rubber-stamps a chairman's personal demand for a contempt citation, a committee rubber-stamps the subcommittee's approval, the Senate or House rubber-stamps the committee's approval, and the executive branch automatically prosecutes the person cited, then one member of Congress is effectively able to breach the separation-of-powers doctrine by dictating what the executive must do.

It is customary in contempt-of-Congress cases for the prosecutor appointed by the Department of Justice to operate independently of the department — that is, to consider himself a lawyer whose client is Congress — but, as it happened, Senator McClellan had so much influence with the department that his personal interest in the McSurely case was bound to be seen in a very special light. He was chairman of the Senate subcommittee that controls the budgets of various twigs on the executive branch, including the Department of Justice. In addition, he was ranking Democrat on the Senate Judiciary Committee, which controls nominations for federal judgeships and high posts in the department, and together these constitute the most important patronage that any Administration possesses. Moreover, as a leading member of the conservative coalition between Southern Democrats and Northern Republicans on the far right, McClellan was a natural ally of the Nixon Administration, which had been in office a little over three months when the Senate turned the McSurely case over to the Department of Justice. And as a domestic cold warrior and law-and-order politician, McClellan was expected to be an avid supporter of the Administration and, most of all, of the Justice Department and Attorney General John N. Mitchell. In return, the Administration was expected to keep McClellan happy by pushing for the kind of harsh anti-crime and anti-civil-liberties legislation that he often sponsored in the Senate.

Ordinarily, the Justice Department chooses lawyers from its United States Attorneys offices to serve as special prosecutors in contempt-of-Congress cases, but for the McSurelys' case Attorney General Mitchell picked David Bress, a Democrat who had been the U.S. Attorney for the District of Columbia in the Johnson Administration. A successful lawyer in private practice before working for the government, Bress was nominated, in 1968, on the recommendation of Supreme Court Justice Abe Fortas, to serve on the federal bench. President Johnson submitted Bress's name, in a package of five federal-court nominees, and President-elect Nixon promised to support the nominations, but shortly after he assumed office he ordered them withdrawn. After being publicly criticized for this, Nixon promised to reconsider the nominees on an individual basis, and it was rumored that Bress, who still had friends in high government places after Fortas resigned and Johnson left the White House – most notably Senator McClellan – would be renominated by the new President.

In any event, Bress turned out to be an exceedingly zealous prosecutor. When he presented the government's charges against the McSurelys before a federal grand jury, the only evidence he offered was Senator McClellan's report of the events in the case. The grand jurors heard no witnesses, and Bress – unknown to the McSurelys or their lawyers at the time – presented a strange version of the facts in the case. He told the grand jury that the McSurelys were from Tennessee (not Kentucky), that he thought they had been involved in litigation in Nashville following the riot there (they hadn't), and that the subcommittee had learned about the documents it had subpoenaed by way of a civil suit involving charges of police brutality during the Nashville disorder (not through Brick's secret examination and use of the McSurelys' papers, after he had also examined a federal-court ruling that declared the state sedition law under which the seizure was made to be unconstitutional, and that ordered the McSurelys' possessions held in "safekeeping" until their case was finally settled). And when one of the grand jurors asked Bress what reasons the McSurelys had given for refusing to honor the subpoenas, he ignored their explanations in the civil complaint and answered that the question raised a matter of law, not fact, and was up to a judge, not a grand jury, to resolve (a reply that stood against all legal precedent and tradition in grand-jury proceedings).

On August 20, 1969, the grand jury indicted each of the McSurelys on two charges of contempt of Congress – one charge for refusing to comply with the subpoenas at the subcommittee hearing and the other charge for not turning in their papers three days later, as McClellan had ordered. On September 5th, the McSurelys were arraigned on these charges before the federal District Court for the District of Columbia.

One of the most unjust features of the American system of criminal justice is the gross disparity between the government's resources and an ordinary defendant's resources. Unless a defendant in a case that is at all complicated is very rich or has the kind of broad public support that generates contributions (as in the case of Daniel Ellsberg, whose defense in the Pentagon Papers case cost more than a million dollars, most of it paid by public subscription), one must rely on legal charity. At best, this system provides low-cost or free counsel from organizations like the Center for Constitutional Rights, the American Civil Liberties Union, the Lawyers Guild, or private practitioners who specialize in constitutional law. At worst, this system provides court-appointed hacks of the kind who have been described as "walking violations of the Sixth Amendment's right to counsel." The comparatively few competent civil-liberties lawyers in this country who are willing to donate their time and skills to such generally unpopular causes as the defense of political radicals are overwhelmed with work. Not only are they forced to choose among thousands of clients who deserve proper representation but often they are forced to sacrifice the interests of one client to the more compelling interests of another because of the pressure of time and the shortage of manpower and money.

Throughout most of 1969, Kunstler and the small staff at the Center were largely preoccupied with the splashiest radical case of the decade — the Nixon Administration's prosecution of the group that became known as the Chicago Seven, who were charged with conspiracy to incite a riot at the Democratic National Convention the year before — and preparations for the McSurelys' defense had to be delayed. Nothing was done on their behalf to let uninformed senators know about the details of their case before the subcommittee and committee votes for a contempt citation or the Senate vote on the contempt resolution. Nor was any legal move made to counter the government's taking the case to a grand jury. In fact, it wasn't until nearly a month after the McSurelys were indicted that their defense got under way. By that time, at the end of September, the Chicago Seven trial was about to begin, and Kunstler had to devote all of his time — again at no fee — to that, so his partner at the Center, Morton Stavis, who had worked on the McSurely case off and on since it began in Kentucky, took over.

Stavis's strategy from the beginning was to try to develop an unchallengeable basis from which he could show the illegality of the subpoenas *before* any trial took place, and thereby knock out the indictments. For that reason, his first move in defending the McSurelys in the criminal case was to proceed with their civil suit against the members and aides of the subcommittee — by serving a notice in September that he intended to take depositions from the aides involved in the seizure and use of the McSurelys' papers. "By this means, I figured I would either get the story from Brick and the others, which would provide us with a defense, or if they refused I would have a legal foundation for knocking out the indictments on that ground," he explained. "In the mid-fifties, I represented a left-wing radical who refused to appear before the House Un-American Activities Committee and was cited for contempt. I served subpoenas on the members of HUAC demanding access to the committee's files to prove my charge that HUAC's subpoenas were unlawful because they were politically motivated. A federal judge upheld me, so HUAC, rather than open up its files, quietly dropped the case. I hoped we might have the same luck in the McSurely case, although I expected difficulty on other grounds."

One of those grounds was Article I, Section 6 of the Constitution, which gives members of Congress a form of immunity against private lawsuits by declaring that "for any speech or debate in either house, they shall not be questioned in any other place." Federal courts have generally interpreted the "immunity clause" to mean that members of Congress are not liable for anything they say in an official capacity, and after the McSurelys filed their civil suit the defendants' lawyers (a team provided free of charge from the Justice Department's Civil Division) cited the immunity clause as their principal defense. However, Stavis felt that if he presented a compelling case to show that the defendants in the civil suit had indeed acted unofficially — insofar as they had abetted Senator McClellan's personal and political designs in issuing the subpoenas and had not had a proper legislative purpose — he might persuade a federal court to allow him to question the subcommittee aides in order to prove this point. Stavis hoped to then use whatever he learned from such an interrogation to demonstrate in the criminal case that the subpoenas were solely based on the copies that Brick had provided — illegally, in Stavis's opinion — of the McSurelys' documents. (The government had admitted earlier that Brick got copies of the papers and took them back to the subcommittee, but claimed that the subpoenas had been partly based on other evidence.)

This sort of tangled legal maneuvering was necessary, Stavis explained, because of the criminal law's fundamental unfairness in permitting almost no "discovery" — that is, any opportunity for defendants to find out what kind of case the prosecution has, so that a proper defense can be prepared. In civil cases, on the other hand, the law allows virtually unlimited discovery, so Stavis planned to use the McSurelys' civil suit to build a foundation for their defense in the criminal case. Of course, the Justice Department lawyers — and undoubtedly Bress — realized what he was up to, and shortly after he submitted his notice to take depositions from the subcommittee aides the department submitted a motion asking that the civil suit be put off until the criminal case was resolved. When this issue was argued before the District Court in Washington in November, the presiding judge granted the government's motion and on December 18th ordered that all proceedings in the civil suit be held off until thirty days after the criminal case, including any appellate review, was completed. Stavis immediately appealed that decision to the Court of Appeals for the District of Columbia Circuit.

Meanwhile, the criminal case went ahead — slowly and with mounting bitterness on both sides. Among the numerous papers that Stavis filed with the District Court were a motion for a pretrial hearing (a common legal procedure in civil cases, though not in criminal cases, by which Stavis hoped to get a chance for discovery in the criminal case); a motion to inspect the minutes of the grand-jury session that led to the McSurelys' indictments (also a common procedure, which was not prompted by any suspicion on Stavis's part about Bress's presentation before that body) ; and a motion to dismiss the indictments on grounds ranging from the failure of the subcommittee to pay for the McSurelys' travel expenses to and from the hearing, in violation of a Senate rule, to the claim that the subpoenas violated the McSurelys' rights under the Fourth Amendment.

While Stavis conceded in his brief that congressional committees have the authority to order witnesses to appear before them and testify on matters that will assist Congress in framing legislation, as well as to demand that such witnesses bring with them documents on which they are to be examined, he argued that the subcommittee subpoenas clearly violated the Fourth Amendment and, in fact, that they constituted a "fishing expedition," since they ordered the McSurelys to turn over "all books, records, correspondence, and documents pertaining to eight organizations, without identifying a single specific paper." Starting on the first part of a two-part constitutional argument, Stavis pointed out that subpoenas were subject to the same constitutional safeguards as search warrants were. In that light, he added, the contempt prosecution of the McSurelys was clearly at odds with the Supreme Court's decision, in 1965, in the case of Stanford v. Texas, which was the most recent of the Court's many condemnations, over the years, of the use of general warrants. "The constitutional requirement that warrants must particularly describe the 'things to be seized' is to be accorded the most scrupulous exactitude when the 'things' are books and the basis for their seizure is the ideas which they contain," the Court stated in Stanford, and quoted an earlier Court decision:

> The requirement that warrants shall particularly describe the things to be seized makes general searches under them impossible and prevents the seizure of one thing under a warrant describing another. As to what is to be taken, nothing is left to the discretion of the officer executing the warrant.

The opinion in Stanford went on:

> We need not decide in the present case whether the description of the things to be seized would have been too generalized to pass constitutional muster had the things been weapons, narcotics, or "cases of whiskey." The point is that it was not any contraband of that kind which was ordered to be seized, but [was] literary material — "books, records, pamphlets, cards, receipts, lists, memoranda, pictures, recordings and other written instruments concerning the Communist Party of Texas." The indiscriminate sweep of that language is constitutionally intolerable. To hold otherwise

would be false to the terms of the Fourth Amendment, false to its meaning, and false to its history.

In an opposing brief, Bress dismissed Stavis's arguments as being either insubstantial or irrelevant, stated that the Fourth Amendment did not apply to the McSurely case, and ignored Stanford altogether.

Late in November, 1969, the issues Stavis raised were debated at a hearing before the judge who was assigned to the criminal-contempt case — John Lewis Smith, Jr., whom President Johnson had appointed to the District Court bench after being advised that Smith was an intelligent and rather kindly man whose presence would help balance such stern hardliners on that court as Judge John Sirica. Stavis and the McSurelys had been heartened when Judge Smith got the case, but at the hearing on their motions they were quickly disappointed, for he rejected each motion in turn, except their request to examine the grand-jury minutes, and reserved judgment on that until he had read them in private.

Stavis repeatedly pleaded that at a pre-trial hearing the court might look at the indisputable facts of what had happened — the illegal raid, the use of illegally seized documents to draw up illegal subpoenas — and find that a trial was unjustified. "It is time, Your Honor, that official lawlessness be stopped," Stavis said. "It is precisely for that reason that we have made these motions. Because I know what the government's answer is. The government's answer is: 'Wait until the trial. It will all come out in the wash at the trial. If you succeed, why, so be it.' What we are saying, Your Honor, this morning, and what these motions are about, is that this [case] has been such a history of lawlessness that the court has a right to look at this indictment on its face and look at the stipulated facts and if these defendants are entitled to protection now they ought to have it." Since the indictments ignored what had happened to the McSurelys in Kentucky and in their fight through the federal courts to have the Senate subpoenas quashed, Stavis hoped that the Judge's examination of the history of the case would convince him that there was an obvious and crucial difference between what the government claimed had occurred and what had actually occurred. In that event, the case would be thrown out at once. But Judge Smith was not interested.

Stavis then moved on to the second part of his constitutional argument – based on the landmark Silverthorne case of 1920, in which Justice Holmes redefined the exclusionary rule by saying of the Fourth Amendment, "The essence of a provision forbidding the acquisition of evidence in a certain way is that not merely evidence so acquired shall not be used before the court, but that it shall not be used at all." From the outset of the McSurely case, Stavis had hoped to tie it in with the Silverthorne doctrine as his basic strategy in persuading the federal court to quash the subpoenas and thereby avoid any trial. Now he pointed out to Judge Smith that the McSurely case was fundamentally like the Silverthorne case, for if the subcommittee subpoenas were tainted by being based on illegally seized evidence they, like the Silverthorne subpoenas, were invalid. And, of course, no contempt charge could be founded on a refusal to comply with an invalid, or unlawful, order. The only way it could be shown that the subcommittee subpoenas were tainted, he added, was by his questioning subcommittee staff members to discover the true basis for the subpoenas – whether they were, as Bress contended in official papers, based on evidence other than that seized in the Kentucky raid on the McSurelys, or whether the subpoenas were, as Stavis suspected, wholly based on what was found during that raid.

Bress, he went on, "says that if we intend to challenge [the validity of the subpoenas] we have to produce that evidence at the trial. Well, how? The evidence is in his hands. He represents the committee. He represents the staff of the committee. They know the extent to which they relied upon this illegally seized material. . . . I am entitled before the trial – *before* the trial – to find out material which is in the government's hands, and present that to the court at the trial. That is all that we are talking about now. It is a narrow question of discovery [based] on Silverthorne." Judge Smith wasn't interested in this argument, either, and replied that it was not his practice to hold pre-trial hearings in criminal cases. Stavis urged that the trial be postponed until his appeal in the civil suit, including his right to some form of discovery, was resolved, but the Judge said, "If that is in the form of a motion, it is denied." Stavis then asked for a ruling on his move to question the aides before a trial date was set, and Judge Smith rejected that, too, and set the trial for January 19, 1970.

Three weeks later, Judge Smith formally denied the motion for a pre-trial hearing, and at that point Stavis warned the McSurelys that they were in worse trouble than he had anticipated. Bress's strategy, he explained, clearly was to limit the issues to be tried — namely, to whether the subcommittee had been duly authorized to investigate a subject, whether the subpoenas were pertinent to that investigation and properly served, and whether the McSurelys had willfully refused to comply with the subpoenas. Moreover, he said, it appeared that Judge Smith was prepared to go along with Bress's approach. If the trial was conducted under the limits being proposed by Bress, Stavis told the McSurelys, they would have little, or perhaps no, chance to tell the jury what had happened to them before they refused to obey the subpoenas — in short, their reasons for refusing — and the jury would have no grounds for acquitting them.

Despite Senator McClellan's great power, the McSurelys clung to the hope — before, during, and for months after the hearing — that he would lose interest in them or would finally drop the matter if they made it clear that they meant to stand up and publicly expose what he and his staff had done. But when the Senate endorsed his demand for a contempt citation and the executive branch and then the judicial branch took his side — maliciously and conspiratorially, it appeared to them — they came to feel that the entire United States government was arrayed against them. And, as they and many others saw it, that government was rapidly moving toward open tyranny. All in all, it was a perilous time for anyone who even modestly opposed the Administration. And it was a terrifying time for people like the McSurelys, who had been singled out as fomenters of discord by a powerful senator and had become what seemed like two small targets for a shattering amount of firepower.

"Right after we were indicted, we thought we had a chance of winning the case, and strengthening the Constitution by such a victory," Mrs. McSurely said. "We thought we had to work in any way we could to strengthen freedom, and for the time being that meant working within the system. But then, when we got blocked again and again by the courts, we became more and more frustrated and less and less sure of our course. Everything they say can't happen here had happened here to us. Government people are so sanctimonious, as if they can do no wrong and always act out of the purest motives. That just isn't true, we learned over and over. Practically every person in the government who was involved in our case, except for a few judges, was viciously unfair. And that included Justice Department officials in the Johnson Administration who fought us every step of the way during 1967 and 1968 when we tried to get our papers back. Then, when it finally came time for us to have our day in court, Judge Smith was unfair to us, too. As he rejected our early motions and began to rule in a way that would narrow the trial to the point where the jurors wouldn't be able to figure out what had actually happened to us and why we had refused to obey the subpoenas, we began to wonder if we had any hope of escaping prison."

Drew Pearson died on September 1, 1969, a few days after the McSurelys were indicted. They concluded that his death relieved them of any further need to protect him from disclosure about his affair with Margaret, but at the same time they decided to continue on the course they had followed from the start—silence about everything contained in their private papers. One evening in late December, three weeks before the trial was due to start, the couple sat down to go over every detail in their case to prepare for anything that might help in their defense. They opened a bottle of Chianti, McSurely got out a legal pad and a pen, and they began, at his suggestion, with the story of the liaison with Pearson. The McSurelys had never discussed it in any detail — because she didn't want to talk about such an intimate, and now embarrassing, episode in her life, and he didn't want to know about it at all — and the conversation was painful for both of them. After she described how the affair began when she was working for Pearson as his personal assistant in the early nineteen-sixties, how she broke it off after she became involved in the civil-rights cause and he refused to write sympathetically about some of its more radical aspects, and how he had tried to get her back, Mrs. McSurely recalled the day that Brick served them with the first set of subpoenas, when she discovered that his wife was secretary to the psychiatrist who had treated her during the time she was going with Pearson.

"As Al and I talked, it suddenly dawned on both of us at the same moment that maybe McClellan was really after Pearson and not us at all, and was using us only to get those letters from Pearson to me into the record, so that he could ruin the man who was his greatest enemy in the press," Mrs. McSurely said. "We were stunned by the idea. And we were even more stunned when we began to wonder if the whole thing, including the raid on us in Kentucky, had been staged by McClellan so that he could get hold of those letters."

McSurely immediately telephoned Stavis at home and arranged to meet a couple of days later in New York with him and Nancy Stearns, of the Center, who was also working on the case. At the meeting, McSurely described the conspiracy theory, and he later said of the lawyers' reactions, "It just blew their minds." Stearns, it was true, was startled by the possible linkage between Margaret's therapist and McClellan's pursuit of her. But Stavis was more impressed by a new opportunity the theory provided — to claim on another ground that McClellan had not had any legislative purpose in mind when he issued the subpoenas but had used his office to carry on a personal vendetta. If the McSurelys were now willing to talk publicly about Margaret's relationship with Pearson, Stavis saw, he might be able to use that episode to justify his contention that the subpoenas had no legislative purpose. Most important of all, this might enable the defense to get on the record, and lay out before the jury during the trial, the tale of what the Kentucky and federal governments had done to the McSurelys, and thereby show, probably more effectively than by any other means, why they had resisted the subpoenas. Before Stavis could pursue this line, though, he had to make sure the McSurelys appreciated the effect that revealing this part of their story — juicy news by most journalistic standards — might have on Mrs. McSurely, and he pressed her for assurance that she understood what would happen if she told in open court about her liaison with Pearson.

"Mort kept going over and over the question of whether I was willing to divulge something that would ruin my reputation," she later said. "But I felt that my reputation had already been ruined when those sick men in Kentucky and in the Senate of the United States pored over my personal letters and my diary and then prosecuted me for resisting their invasions of my privacy. I thought that telling about this would show what kind of vicious people run this country and how much worse they are than a woman who had an affair with her boss."

Once Stavis was convinced that his clients appreciated the risk they were taking, he made the Pearson correspondence a part of his primary strategy for the trial.

By the time the trial was due to begin, Judge Smith had granted the McSurelys only one of their motions — to examine the grand-jury minutes. Early in January, 1970, they went to the District Court, and the Judge's clerk gave them the transcript of the grand-jury hearings, which, he said, they could read and copy but not duplicate. When they discovered Bress's misstatements of the facts in their case, the two were stunned, and McSurely carefully copied in longhand all the major errors. Afterward, in a state of high excitement, they telephoned Stavis and Stearns. Stavis wasn't as impressed as they expected, mainly because he knew that prosecutors have broad, and often unfair, leeway in presenting cases before grand juries; because he knew that to get the indictments dismissed on the ground of the prosecution's misrepresentations he would have to prove that there had been an intent to mislead the grand jurors, which would be a difficult and perhaps impossible task; and because he knew that if Judge Smith had not thrown out the case after reading the minutes in private he was not going to throw it out now.

But Stearns was, as she said, "staggered" by the new development. "I thought the grand-jury minutes were dynamite," she went on. "One of the principal guidelines laid down by the Supreme Court to determine whether official acts conform with the mandates in the Bill of Rights is the requirement of 'fundamental fairness' by the government when it prosecutes its citizens. If anything in the McSurely case was fundamentally unfair, it was the use of such crucially false facts before a grand jury, whatever Bress's intent."

Her indignation was so great that Stavis asked her to draw up a motion to dismiss the indictments because of the prosecutor's misstatements to the grand jury. About that time, Stavis made another move. Frustrated in his efforts to get pre-trial information about any contact between the subcommittee and the Kentucky authorities, he served subpoenas on Senator McClellan, Brick, and the clerk of the subcommittee, ordering them to produce at the trial all records of any such contacts. When the subpoenas were served, Bress immediately filed a motion to quash them. It was to be months before this issue was resolved.

Before Stearns had a chance to complete her grand-jury motion, Stavis called on her to help prepare for a key hearing, to be held a few days later, before the Court of Appeals on the issue of whether the McSurelys' criminal case or their civil suit took precedence. A three-judge panel heard both sides on this question, and directed that the two cases be stayed until the court handed down its answer. With that, the criminal-contempt trial, which was scheduled to open three days later, was indefinitely postponed.

Shortly before this, a niece of Stavis's heard about a teaching vacancy at the Walden School, in New York, and McSurely applied for and got the job. Early in February, 1970, the McSurelys moved into a small apartment in the Bronx, where they were to live for the next two years. They disliked New York, but living there gave them a chance to confer more frequently with Stavis and Stearns on the crucial steps yet to be taken in the case.

Finally, on March 26th, the Court of Appeals delivered its decision on the issue of which of the McSurely cases was to be litigated first. The court's opinion was written by Chief Judge David Bazelon, one of the most enlightened and capable jurists on the federal bench, who ruled that the McSurelys had waited too long, without making the legal moves open to them to expedite the civil case or delay the criminal case, to complain now about the way matters were proceeding. Despite this rebuke, Bazelon found that the District Court's order postponing all civil-suit actions until the criminal case was finally settled was unnecessarily severe, since it might prevent the McSurelys from getting information from witnesses who would be likely to forget what had happened after such a long time or who might be unavailable to testify when the civil suit was tried. For these reasons, he reversed the District Court's order delaying all proceedings in the civil suit, permitted the criminal case to go ahead first, and left it up to the District Court — in effect, to Judge Smith — to determine what means of discovery the McSurelys should have.

The last part of the ruling gave Stavis the opening he had been looking for, and he drafted a motion asking the District Court for permission to take depositions from McClellan and members of the subcommittee staff and to examine subcommittee files as a means of discovering whether the subpoenas were based on the independent evidence that Bress had claimed. Bress — faced with Stavis's determination to get out the facts and faced with the problem of keeping McClellan off the stand after a trial subpoena had been served on him — finally responded with an astonishing reversal of his stand on the issue. He replied, "The government concedes — and is willing so to stipulate — that but for the opportunity to examine the documents which was afforded to the subcommittee staff as a result of the seizure by agents of the Commonwealth of Kentucky, the subcommittee would not have known of the existence of said documents and hence would not have issued a subpoena for their production." This concession, Bress concluded, made the testimony Stavis was asking for unnecessary. In other words, the government admitted that it had been lying all along, and now claimed immunity from any examination of its earlier acts on the ground that it was finally telling the truth. Stavis — having at last extracted the legal nugget that he had been seeking since he began his discovery efforts — filed a reply in the form of a "supplemental motion to dismiss indictment," saying, "The position now stated by the government makes it clear that there is nothing left to try in this case," since the original seizure of the McSurelys' papers had already been found unlawful by a federal court. Bress retorted that the seizure had never been found to be a violation of the Fourth Amendment by any court. Rather, the District Court in Kentucky had ruled only that the sedition law under which the papers were seized, not the seizure itself, was unconstitutional on grounds other than those covered in the Fourth Amendment. Stavis replied that the District Court had not ruled on the Fourth Amendment in the case only because that issue hadn't been raised there. And when Bress contended that the Sixth Circuit Court of Appeals, which ordered the McSurelys' papers returned to them by Kentucky officials, had not found any violation of the Fourth Amendment, either, Stavis countered by pointing out that the Court of Appeals had explicitly refused to address any of the Fourth Amendment questions the McSurelys had raised at the time, because it decided the issue on narrower grounds, as federal courts usually do in order to avoid confronting a constitutional issue head on. Bress also argued that the District Court's finding that the Kentucky sedition statute was unconstitutional did not make it retroactively unconstitutional, so the state officials who seized the McSurelys' possessions under the provisions of that law had acted in good faith. To this, Stavis replied that their good faith had been seriously questioned by the District Court, which had said in its opinion on the state law, "It is difficult to believe that capable lawyers could seriously contend that this statute is constitutional. . . . In addition, the conclusion is inescapable that the criminal prosecutions [of the McSurelys] were instituted, at least in part, in order to stop [their] organizing activities in Pike County." Bress also argued that even if the seizure was illegal under the Fourth Amendment, the exclusionary rule did not apply to legislative investigations but was designed solely to prevent the government from using illegally acquired evidence against defendants in criminal trials; the testimony of a witness before a congressional committee was not evidence, he said, nor was a congressional hearing a trial. Stavis professed astonishment at the notion that the Constitution did not apply to Congress, since the Supreme Court had repeatedly said that it did. Bress conceded that the Fourth Amendment was binding on Congress but argued that the exclusionary rule was merely a rule of evidence and not an integral part of the amendment. With that, the old battle over the rule was joined. Its outcome was finally to decide the McSurelys' fate.

To begin with, Stavis cited a long series of Supreme Court decisions — culminating in the 1961 landmark decision in Mapp v. Ohio, which applied the rule to state as well as federal prosecutions — to demonstrate that the rule was, as the Court asserted in Mapp, "an essential part" of the Fourth Amendment. Above all, he went on, the Silverthorne doctrine — stating that illegally acquired evidence shall not only be inadmissible in court but "shall not be used at all" — controlled the case at bar. Bress contended that Holmes's statement in the Silverthorne case did not apply to "non-evidentiary purposes unrelated to a trial of the victim of the seizure but, rather, established only that an unlawful seizure cannot be used as an indirect method of obtaining evidence against the victim." This seemed a curious reading of Holmes's words "shall not be used at all," but Bress stuck to the position throughout the case — in all likelihood, Stavis concluded, because the Department of Justice had instructed him to, as part of the Nixon Administration's over-all attack on the exclusionary rule in particular and the Fourth Amendment in general. In conclusion, Bress argued that even if the original seizure of the McSurelys' papers was unlawful, the information obtained by the subcommittee by way of it was "acquired through the wrongful act of a stranger," not of anyone on the subcommittee. This seemed an equally curious claim, for the decision in another landmark case — Elkins v. United States, which the Supreme Court decided in

1960 – explicitly prohibited federal agents from using in court evidence that had been illegally seized and passed on to them by state officials. Stavis pointed this out, and Bress lamely replied that Elkins wasn't relevant.

On May 5th, Judge Smith presided over a hearing at which these various arguments were repeated. At the end, he denied Stavis's motion to take depositions and to examine the subcommittee's files, and granted Bress's motion to quash the subpoenas served on the clerk of the subcommittee, Brick, and McClellan. Then the Judge set June 22nd for the trial date. Ten days before it finally began, he formally denied Stavis's supplemental motion to dismiss the indictments and gave as his reasons all of Bress's arguments.

The defense had only one move left before the trial opened – the Stearns motion to dismiss the indictments because of the government's false statements to the grand jury. "The due-process clause of the Fifth Amendment to the Constitution guarantees to the defendants that all criminal proceedings against them shall be conducted with due regard for fundamental fairness," Stearns wrote. Moreover, she went on, a long line of precedents "clearly establish that willful misrepresentation by the prosecution of facts material to the case violates this guarantee of fundamental fairness." To demonstrate that Bress had grossly distorted the facts he laid before the grand jury in order to create an impression that the McSurelys were involved in the Nashville riot McClellan was purportedly investigating, Stearns quoted Bress's words from the grand-jury minutes:

> In 1967, Mr. McSurely and Mrs. McSurely were charged in Tennessee with violation of the state sedition statute, an attempt to overthrow the government. The federal court enjoined the prosecution of that suit. In connection with that event, there was later a suit brought by a number of people – I think the McSurelys were one, I'm not sure – against certain officials in Nashville, Tennessee, because of the manner in which the law-enforcement officials participated following the riot.

"In fact, the McSurelys were indicted for sedition in Kentucky, not in Tennessee," Stearns noted. "They had no connection whatever with the legal action initiated in Tennessee following and in response to the police conduct of the Nashville riots." When a grand juror asked Bress how members of the subcommittee knew that the McSurelys' papers were relevant to their inquiry, he answered, "The committee knew enough by the fact that the records had already been produced in the court in Tennessee that they were subject matter and relevant to the inquiry." In response to this, Stearns said, "At no time were the McSurelys' documents even discussed, much less produced, in the court in Tennessee." And, Stearns went on, Bress knew that the McSurelys had filed a civil suit against the members and some aides of the subcommittee, that the couple had both stated at the hearing that their reasons for resisting the subpoenas were described in the civil complaint, and that their lawyer had repeatedly tried to get the complaint entered in the official record. Bress also told the grand jurors, Stearns observed, that the McSurelys' reasons for not complying with the subpoenas "as a matter of law are not valid legal reasons." After citing several precedents to demonstrate that "it is improper for the prosecutor to instruct the grand jury on the law," Stearns concluded with the statement that this procedural violation in itself was sufficient reason for dismissing the indictments.

McSurely read the motion, and then sent Stearns and Stavis a memorandum suggesting that they withhold the motion until the last moment – not for the impact on the Judge, who clearly wasn't going to throw out the case on that or any other ground, but for the effect that Bress's distortions at such a key stage might have on the press. In line with this strategy, the McSurelys also prepared a press release and invited several reporters, together with a hundred or so friends and supporters, to attend the trial. Stavis accepted the suggestion, but he had little hope that it would have much effect.

At nine o'clock on the morning of June 22nd, Stavis submitted the grand-jury motion at the United States Courthouse, on the corner of Third Street and Constitution Avenue, in Washington, and then he, Stearns, and the McSurelys went to Courtroom No. 19, on the sixth floor, where the trial in the combined cases of United States v. Alan McSurely (Criminal Action No. 1376–69) and United States v. Margaret McSurely (Criminal Action No. 1377–69) was to commence at nine-thirty. On hand in the courtroom were about fifty of the McSurelys' supporters and three reporters. Before the trial began, McSurely told the reporters that he would hold a press conference outside the court building at the lunch break. Then Judge Smith entered the courtroom, those present stood up while the clerk called the court to order, and the proceedings began.

The first step was to hold what is called a "preliminary conference" – a discussion between opposing counsel and the judge immediately before a jury is empanelled to decide the issues to be covered in the trial. Soon after the conference opened, Bress submitted a lengthy proposed "findings of fact and conclusions of law," which he offered to the court as a formula by which the issues could be limited and the time the trial would take could be reduced.

Stavis was on his feet at once. "I think this is an unheard-of procedure," he protested, and pointed out that Bess hadn't even had the courtesy to show him the proposed findings, and that he was obviously trying to stop the defendants from telling their story. Glancing angrily at his opponent for a moment, Stavis turned back to the bench and said, "From the very beginning of these proceedings, Mr. Bress has had one sole objective: to prevent the McSurelys from proving on the witness stand the facts that they think are decisive to their innocence."

"You might at least read what he has," Judge Smith replied.

"Thank you, Your Honor – when?" Stavis said. "In the midst of the argument?" He asked for an immediate recess, but Judge Smith refused, and ordered him not to interrupt.

Bress read his long proposed findings, which consisted of his earlier arguments against Stavis's various points on matters of law in the case – namely, that the seizure of the McSurelys' papers was carried out by Kentucky officials under a state statute that they presumed was lawful; that the federal court's overturning of the statute was not based on the Fourth Amendment and was not retroactive; that even if the seizure violated the amendment, that did not bar a congressional committee from basing subpoenas on information received through such a seizure, since the exclusionary rule didn't apply to Congress; and that, accordingly, the subpoenas were valid. Afterward, Bress proposed the questions to be resolved by the jury – whether the subpoenas were properly served on the McSurelys, whether they refused to comply with a lawful command of Congress, and whether their refusal was willful.

Although Stavis had expected a maneuver of this sort, he was still outraged when it was made. As soon as Bress finished, Stavis rose and said, "What has happened is the following: that Mr. Bress has taken a mass of material and has said to you, 'Judge, I would like *you* to find these facts from this mass of material. And because I want *you* to find these facts, we don't really have to have a hearing about it.' "

Ordinarily, the defense in a criminal case is permitted to present all the facts in the case to a jury, and then, at the end of both sides' presentation, the judge rules on which facts are pertinent and are to be considered by the jury, which facts are irrelevant and to be ignored by the jury, and which facts amount to matters of law and are to be decided by the judge. In the McSurely case, Stavis said, the prosecution was asking the court to limit the facts that could be laid before the jury in advance of the trial. That is, the judge was being asked to rule that all the facts which would show why the McSurelys disobeyed the subpoenas were actually matters of law and couldn't be even mentioned to the jury. In the Court of Appeals' ruling that the McSurelys had a right to some form of discovery, Stavis now pointed out, Chief Judge Bazelon had said, "The McSurelys are entitled to call the witnesses necessary to develop the factual basis for their claim, either in pre-trial proceedings or at the trial." On the basis of that statement, Stavis continued, he had moved to take depositions and to inspect the subcommittee files in order to discover whether there was, as formerly claimed by the government, any independent evidence besides the Kentucky raid to support the subpoenas.

When Judge Smith denied his motion and quashed the subpoenas he had served on McClellan and his staff, Stavis went on, "We were not permitted to employ one of the two alternatives suggested by the Court [of Appeals] – namely, pre-trial proceedings. But the other alternative, Your Honor, is at the trial. By [Bress's] selective process, it is proposed, Your Honor, that we be denied that."

"In this trial, Mr. Stavis, we will try the issues here," Judge Smith told him. "We are not going into any collateral matters that are not the subject matter of this trial."

A little later, Stavis brought up the Stearns motion, and Bress jumped up and angrily retorted that if he had referred to Tennessee rather than Kentucky in his presentation to the grand jury, "it was purely typographical – purely and simply."

Stavis remarked that if the error was merely typographical it was odd that it had been made four times.

"There is no merit in that motion," Judge Smith said. "It will be denied."

Also during the preliminary conference, Stavis asked that he be allowed to put Brick on the stand and to introduce before the jury the inventory of the documents that he had copied in Pikeville and taken back to Washington, for the purpose of showing that "these intimate and personal letters were distributed throughout the Senate Permanent Subcommittee . . . and that this entire proceeding, Your Honor, has absolutely no legislative purpose but is . . . an evil design to attack a lady and persons with whom she may have been associated."

While Mrs. McSurely was willing to besmirch her reputation in public, Bress and the Judge were not.

"The government opposes it," Bress said.

Judge Smith added, "The request is denied."

Stavis knew that if he failed to get the McSurelys' story on the record by some means, not only would the jury be likely to convict his clients but he would be foreclosed from raising the issue of McClellan's role in any appeal afterward. Stavis pleaded again and again for permission to introduce the facts behind the McSurelys' refusal to comply with the subpoenas, and repeatedly cited the Silverthorne doctrine in support of his right to make these points. But Judge Smith dismissed his pleas, on the ground that in denying the supplemental motion he had already ruled that the doctrine was irrelevant. On the other hand, he permitted Bress to place in the record the entire three-hundred-and-fifty-page volume of the McClellan hearings on the Nashville disturbance, along with numerous statements made on the floor of the Senate prior to McClellan's appointment as chairman of the investigation of the riots — all of them fulsome in praise of his abilities and fairness. Then the Judge adopted Bress's proposed findings of law and fact virtually as written, and the preliminary conference ended.

"Judge Smith used the preliminary conference to take as much of the case as possible away from the jury and decide it himself," Stavis said later. "His whole design was to make sure that the case presented to the jury was as naked and sterile a case as possible — and he did a very skillful job of it. If he could deal with what he called the legal issues and force us to present our story before him instead of before the jury, and ruled on it in advance, he could strictly limit what the jury would hear. In the end, that's what happened. The main strategic problem in the trial was to break through Judge Smith's legal cofferdam and give the McSurelys their day in court before a jury, not a judge."

Mrs. McSurely was in despair after the conference. "I was sure we were going to prison then," she said. "All I could think of was how horrible it would be and what would happen to our little boy while we were away."

Her husband told the three reporters at his "press conference" that what was being done was one more demonstration of the lengths "the ruling class" would go to in order to crush its opponents, and that there had been a conspiracy to rig the trial. Judge Smith, he explained, was out to destroy the defendants *and* the Fourth Amendment.

During the selection of a jury, it turned out that one venireman had directed a government investigation of SCEF and the Appalachian Volunteers a couple of years earlier, and had received a field report on the McSurelys' activities. At the present time, the man was working for the General Accounting Office, and he said, "Incidentally, I might add, Your Honor, as you probably know, Your Honor, that our office is an agency of Congress. We do have very close relations with the various committees of Congress and particularly with Senator McClellan's Committee on Government Operations and the Permanent Subcommittee on Investigations." Of course, Stavis asked that the man be released from serving on the jury, on the basis of the defense's unlimited right to challenge prospective jurors for "cause," or the likelihood of their being biassed. Judge Smith denied the request, thereby forcing Stavis to use one of his ten peremptory challenges. Judge Smith also accepted as jurors two men who had served in the National Guard and been on duty when black rioters burned down a large part of the capital following Dr. Martin Luther King's assassination, along with a woman shopowner in Washington who had suffered business losses because of that riot. Stavis used three more peremptory challenges on them.

In an opening statement to the jury, Stavis managed to briefly mention the raid on the McSurelys in Kentucky, but he was quickly stopped from going on with that story:

STAVIS: Mr. and Mrs. McSurely turned to the federal court in Kentucky, and that federal court —

BRESS: I object, Your Honor.

JUDGE SMITH: The objection is sustained. There will be no further argument along that line.

STAVIS: It is not argument. It is proof that I intend to produce.

JUDGE SMITH: The objection is sustained. Proceed, Mr. Stavis.

STAVIS: May I approach the bench?

JUDGE SMITH: No, sir.

STAVIS: I trust the following is within your guidelines. I trust it is, Your Honor. I have asked to approach the bench.

JUDGE SMITH: You may continue.

STAVIS: I trust the following is within your guidelines. I am asking to approach the bench.

JUDGE SMITH: Come to the bench. (*At the bench*) Mr. Stavis, let me say that if there is any further disobedience of my orders you are going to be adjudged in contempt of court.

The exchange was typical of the trial, during which Stavis repeatedly tried to get some of the McSurelys' story before the jury and the Judge and Bress repeatedly stopped him. He was interrupted so many times during his opening statement that it was unlikely the jurors could have made much sense of what he was actually saying, let alone figure out what he was trying to get across. Judge Smith sustained almost all of Bress's objections, almost none of Stavis's, and again and again threatened Stavis with contempt of court.

Within the limits imposed on the trial by the Judge, the government had an airtight case – until Bress himself kicked a hole in it. To prove that the subpoenas had been properly served on the defendants, he was obliged to put Brick on the stand to testify that he had gone to Kentucky with the subpoenas under official orders of the chairman of the subcommittee, that he had delivered the subpoenas to the deputy United States marshal there, and that he had seen the marshal serve the subpoenas on both the McSurelys. That would have been sufficient to make the essential points. But then Bress asked Brick about a conversation he had with McSurely after the McSurelys' papers were returned to them and Brick handed back the copies he had made, as required by law, and checked them off an inventory:

BRICK: . . . I said, "I will have to tell you not to dispose of these documents or destroy them in any manner, because if you do so you may be liable for contempt of Congress."

BRESS: Who did you say that to?

BRICK: I said that to Alan McSurely, and Mrs. McSurely was standing by. I don't know whether she heard it or not.

BRESS: Did he reply?

BRICK: Yes, sir, he did.

BRESS: What did he say?

STAVIS: I object.
JUDGE SMITH: The objection is overruled.
STAVIS: He is not being charged with –
JUDGE SMITH: The objection was overruled.
BRICK: He said, "Contempt of Congress is something we have plenty of already."

Of course, expressing one's low opinion of Congress is one of America's most popular sports and doesn't constitute a crime, but Bress was clearly trying to demonstrate that the McSurelys had intended to defy Congress unlawfully all along. That demonstration was wholly unnecessary, since their outright refusal to obey the subpoenas at the hearing held on March 4, 1969, and their failure to deliver their papers on March 7th as ordered by McClellan were ample evidence of their intent. Apparently, though, Bress couldn't resist using the exchange between Brick and McSurely to emphasize this point. It was a foolhardy misstep, for it gave Stavis the opening he had so desperately sought and been denied.

Later, when he put McSurely on the stand, Stavis asked whether he had spent any time with Brick on the day the subpoenas were served. McSurely answered that he had been with Brick for an hour and a half, going over the inventory of the copies Brick had made and was returning. As it happened, the McSurelys had lost their copy of the inventory – an accident that made Stavis despair of ever getting it introduced in the trial record when he had his clients on the stand. However, at an early stage of the trial when Brick was testifying on matters that the Judge ruled were not to be heard by the jury, which had been sent out of the courtroom, Stavis asked the witness if the government still had its copy of the inventory, without letting on that the McSurelys no longer had theirs. Brick admitted that it did, and Stavis managed to put it in the record of the proceedings, although not in that part of the record the jury would be allowed to consider. Now Stavis picked up the inventory and asked McSurely if it was the one that Brick used when he returned the copies of the documents. McSurely said that it was.

Bress jumped up and objected to this line of questioning, and said that the inventory had "nothing at all to do with the issues in this case."

"What is the purpose?" Judge Smith asked Stavis.

Stavis knew that he had reached the crucial point in the trial, and he carefully answered, "Mr. Bress . . . over our objection, introduced evidence and a purported conversation between Mr. McSurely and Mr. Brick in which Mr. McSurely was supposed to have made some statements, which Mr. Bress had introduced for the purpose of showing the intent of Mr. McSurely and which conversation was something to the effect that Mr. McSurely had contempt for the committee. Now, in so doing Mr. Bress has opened the door, because that conversation occurred at the conclusion of Mr. McSurely's spending an hour and a half with Mr. Brick, reviewing, as you will see by all these check marks [on the inventory], reviewing every one of these items. . . . Now, since Mr. Bress has introduced testimony about the conversation, which was at the conclusion of an hour and a half's review of these documents, Mr. McSurely is entitled to testify as to what the circumstances were and what he did in fact say."

Again Bress heatedly objected. Judge Smith hesitated, said that he was "inclined to agree with the government's position" but consented to give Stavis "some latitude" on the matter, and agreed to let Stavis present the inventory as evidence. On the basis of standard trial procedure, the Judge had to allow Stavis this latitude or face a reversal on appeal. Stavis said he wanted to read to the jury the inventory of the two hundred and thirty-four documents Brick had taken back to Washington from Kentucky. Judge Smith quickly broke in to say that he could pass the document to the jury but it need not be read aloud in full. Stavis angrily complained that the prosecutor had been allowed to read huge chunks of other material to the jury, and again the Judge was obliged to give in.

In reading the inventory to the jury and questioning McSurely and later Brick about it, Stavis managed to bring up Mrs. McSurely's relationship with Pearson, to describe the columnist as one of

Senator McClellan's most hated enemies, to suggest that McClellan was more interested in Pearson's letters to his former mistress than in any connection the McSurelys may have had with radical groups or riots, and to show that the materials Brick had obtained and taken back to Washington included letters to and from friends and relatives of the McSurelys, their birth certificates and wedding license, a few political and sociological essays McSurely had written, a twenty-seven-page list of names and addresses of their friends and associates in the Movement, and even McSurely's income-tax returns — in short, that the subcommittee had confiscated personal property that could not conceivably be related to any legislative purpose. At each step of the way, though, Bress objected and the Judge upheld him, thereby preventing Stavis from giving the jurors any clear picture of the whole story. In all, Stavis later estimated, he had managed to put perhaps a tenth of it on the record, and then only in a disjointed and confusing fashion. Still, he was gratified by the opening that Bress had created, for now the trial record contained at least some basis for an appeal if the verdict went against his clients.

To explain to the jurors why the McSurelys had refused to comply with the subpoenas, Stavis offered their civil complaint against the members of the subcommittee for the record, but Judge Smith wouldn't allow the complaint to be introduced or even described. Finally, Stavis was forced to ask the McSurelys what their reasons were. Their answers justified Kunstler's fear that they would fail to explain their refusal in clear and concise legal terms. McSurely was on the stand first, and when Stavis put the question to him he launched into an impassioned tirade that must have confused and almost certainly antagonized the jurors. McSurely spoke of being "subjected to the most criminal, most sick sort of behavior on the part of the United States government in conspiracy with the coal interests in eastern Kentucky," briefly mentioned the raid on his house there, declared that members of the Senate had taken "the most personal letters of my wife and spread them all over the United States Capitol," and concluded by declaring that when the letters were finally returned he had vowed that he would "never give them back to that crooked Senate committee or those criminal sick minds that exist up here in Washington, D.C." In view of all that he had been through in the previous three years, McSurely's spluttering rage was understandable, but it probably harmed his cause more than if he hadn't answered at all.

When Mrs. McSurely took the stand, she spoke softly and calmly. At one point, Stavis asked her whether she had known at the time of the raid that her personal letters had been seized during it:

> MRS. MCSURELY: Well, I couldn't remember everything I had. I had a lot, you know. I kept a lot of things, I guess, that I should not have kept, and they were, you know, stuck back in drawers . . . like you would have a box of stuff in a closet and what not, and you just put it back in there and you forget what you all have in it. I didn't realize that I had all of this stuff. . . .
>
> STAVIS: Had you ever revealed those items to your husband?
>
> MRS. MCSURELY: Oh, no!
>
> STAVIS: Had you kept a personal diary prior to August 11, 1967 [the date of the raid]?
>
> MRS. MCSURELY: Yes, I did.
>
> STAVIS: Had that been seized on that date?
>
> MRS. MCSURELY: Yes, it was.
>
> STAVIS: Was that finally returned to you . . . ?
>
> MRS. MCSURELY: Yes.
>
> STAVIS: What was yours and Alan's reaction to Mr. Brick returning these personal letters?
>
> BRESS: I object, Your Honor. It is irrelevant.
>
> JUDGE SMITH: She may answer. The objection is overruled.
>
> MRS. MCSURELY: I was horrified.

To explain her reasons for refusing to obey the subpoena served on her, Mrs. McSurely merely stated that the civil complaint described them — an answer that was of little help to Stavis, since the contents of the complaint were unknown to the jury. "In the second place," she went on, "they took out of our house the names and addresses and letters from a lot of friends who are very important people, and I wasn't about to . . . subject our friends to the same kind of harassment that we had been getting, because if Senator McClellan got these names and addresses and published them he would turn over to the Ku Klux Klan the names of our friends in the South and in the mountains [of Appalachia], and . . . I wouldn't do that to my friends."

The trial lasted four days, and at the end of it Bress, in his summation, told the jurors that their task was a simple one — to decide whether the McSurelys had been properly served with subpoenas and had unlawfully defied them. As for the account of what had happened to them before the subcommittee hearing, he said, "The only reason I could see for bringing out these irrelevant matters is to . . . impress some jurors to think that the United States Senate had invaded the privacy of these people. Nothing could be further from the truth."

Stavis, in his summation, put together a few fragments of the McSurelys' story, but again he was prevented from presenting a coherent account. Finally, in an attempt to persuade the jury to "override" the Judge's rulings by finding the McSurelys innocent, Stavis beseeched the jurors to save "these two young people" whose only misdeed was their struggle to help the poor, for which they had become "the object of oppression and tyranny."

Then Judge Smith delivered his instructions to the jury — in precisely the manner that Bress requested — and told the jurors that none of the reasons offered by the defendants to explain their disobedience to the commands contained in the Senate subpoenas "constituted a defense."

The jury was out for a little more than two hours, and at five minutes to two on the afternoon of June 26th the jurors returned to the courtroom to announce their verdict: each of the McSurelys was guilty as charged on both counts.

Later that afternoon, Senator McClellan went to the floor of the Senate to inform his colleagues of the contempt conviction of two recalcitrant witnesses before his subcommittee. "I have found, after more than fifteen years of experience in conducting investigations . . . that there is nothing pleasant in the performance of an official duty of this kind," he said, and added, "When we really dig into some of the problems and try to get the truth for the record, and try to get information that Congress needs upon which to premise legislation, it is characteristic that we run into all kinds of obstructions. Often, witnesses . . . will talk, as in this instance, about defying Congress, and then they will hire the best attorneys they can get to try to confuse the issues, perplex the juries, and mislead them into bringing in verdicts of acquittal. That effort was made by defense counsel in this case. In my judgment, he did not try to seek the facts but simply tried to conduct a smear effort in his defense of his clients, instead of dealing with the issues. . . . No one likes to see people punished, but we are at the point in America where if we cannot enforce the law subversive elements in the country are going to defy the courts, defy Congress, and defy decent society. If we are to continue to maintain the tie that binds our society, we find that we have no alternative except to resort to our courts and hope that justice may be done."

McSurely told the reporters present at the trial that the government had purposely concealed the facts in the case and that the Judge and Bress had met "behind closed doors" to concoct this "judicial conspiracy." Actually, of course, it could be argued that the McSurelys' experiences on every level of government, from a rural sheriff's office and a county court on through the federal judiciary, the United States Senate, and the Department of Justice, demonstrated something far more appalling than a conspiracy among a handful of public officials — a national instinct for repression that did not require a collusive design to prompt disregard for the rights of citizens. A few weeks before the McSurelys' trial, the United States invaded Cambodia, anti-war protesters again went out into the streets in great numbers, National Guardsmen shot and killed four students at Kent State University, and inflamed discord swept across the country. The Nixon Administration contended, and a large majority of the public appeared to agree, that radicals were threatening the nation's existence and had to be put down by whatever means the authorities could muster. People like the McSurelys were unpopular, even detestable, in the minds of people whose fears of disorder persuaded them to support order of any kind. And yet, as Justice Frankfurter once observed, "It is a fair summary of history to say the safeguards of liberty have frequently been forged in controversy involving not very nice people."

Nearly four months lapsed between the time of the McSurelys' conviction and their sentencing, and during this period Stavis reviewed all of the papers filed by both sides, together with the trial record, to see if any important points that might be useful in an appeal had been omitted. One day while going over the various motions he had submitted before the trial, he realized that the defense team had spent so much time arguing over whether the seizure of the McSurelys' papers in Kentucky was illegal because the sedition law under which it was conducted had been ruled unconstitutional that another issue hadn't been raised — the validity or invalidity of the search warrant itself.

Over the years, the Supreme Court has laid down various rules to implement the Fourth Amendment's declaration that "no Warrants shall issue, but upon probable cause, supported by Oath or affirmation, and particularly describing the place to be searched, and the persons or things to be seized." For one thing, a court officer cannot issue a warrant to search a private dwelling unless he finds probable cause from the facts or circumstances presented to him by witnesses under oath to believe that the place contains evidence of a crime. Simple statements by witnesses expressing a belief or suspicion that such evidence exists in such a place does not constitute probable cause. And when a witness offers hearsay information about the presence of criminal evidence, the presiding magistrate must be told enough of the underlying circumstances to be persuaded that a suspect is involved in some specific illegal activity — in other words, that the witness's belief or suspicion is sufficiently believable to amount to probable cause.

The most famous statement on this subject is from a Supreme Court opinion delivered in 1948 by Justice Robert Jackson, who said:

> The point of the Fourth Amendment, which often is not grasped by zealous officers, is not that it denies law enforcement the support of the usual inferences which reasonable men draw from evidence. Its protection consists in requiring that those inferences be drawn by a neutral and detached magistrate instead of being judged by the officer engaged in the often competitive enterprise of ferreting out crime. Any assumption that evidence sufficient to support a magistrate's disinterested determination to issue a search warrant will justify the officers in making a search without a warrant would reduce the Amendment to a nullity and leave the people's homes secure only in the discretion of police officers.

When Stavis reëxamined the warrant issued by a Pikeville magistrate, he discovered that it was based solely on information contained in an affidavit sworn to by one of the McSurelys' neighbors who was described only as "a reputable citizen of Pike County" and who stated that he had "reasonable grounds to suspect and believe . . . that seditious printed matter and printing press or other machinery to print and circulate seditious matter is being kept on the premises of Alan McSurely." The basis for his belief, it turned out, was that his father, also "a reputable citizen of Pike County," had told him that he "did observe certain seditious materials, being pamphlets, films, pictures, and articles or equipment used in the teaching of sedition and printing and circulating seditious matter."

Not only were none of the things to be seized particularly described in the warrant but there was no apparent basis for probable cause to believe that a crime had been, or was being, committed other than the vague opinion of one man who had passed on this hearsay "evidence" to another. Moreover, the local court's inventory of what was seized from the McSurelys under this warrant – their books, every scrap of paper, and even a suitcase full of clothing, which an excited deputy sheriff had flung onto the pile of confiscated materials – demonstrated that their house had been not searched but ransacked under the authority of a general warrant. Accordingly, Stavis drew up a motion to dismiss the indictments on this ground, and submitted it to the District Court a week before the McSurelys were to be sentenced.

At nine-thirty on the morning of October 20th, the McSurelys and Stavis appeared before Judge Smith. Stavis asked for a ruling on the last motion, and the Judge said, "The motion will be denied. Anything further with reference to sentencing, Mr. Stavis?" There was — statements that the defendants wanted to make before their sentences were imposed. McSurely stood up and delivered a lengthy recital of the facts in the case — that is, the story that the government had kept from the jury. Then Mrs. McSurely rose and approached the bench. "Judge Smith, I hope you don't mind if I talk plain to you," she said. "You knew [that] when we were arrested in Kentucky in 1967 and our personal papers were apprehended there was a fierce struggle going on between coal operators and the people. . . . You knew our home was raided and our papers were seized under an unconstitutional state law. These papers were given to McClellan, and yet our rights were not protected in your courtroom. You knew that McClellan lied to the United States Senate when he said the subpoenas were based on outside information about our involvement in the national disorders, and then later in this courtroom the government reversed its position, and again our rights were not protected in your courtroom. You agreed to a set of rules offered by Mr. Bress, which were designed to thoroughly confuse the jury and to violate due process, and still our rights were not protected. You graduated at the top of your class at Georgetown Law School. You're a smart and experienced judge. All of us who attended the trial have no doubt that you have an understanding of the Constitution; you know the law and the facts in this case. It all boils down to whose interests you serve. . . . Each time you ruled against fair play, you taught more than a hundred of our speeches could. So when they speak of contempt or disrespect for the judicial process, remember what you taught them."

Judge Smith sentenced McSurely to a year in prison and Mrs. McSurely to three months in prison.

Stavis's appeal on behalf of the McSurelys covered a wide range of issues, but dealt at greatest length and in most detail with the Fourth Amendment questions that he had raised earlier. Bress dropped out of the case after the trial, and the government's response to Stavis's brief on appeal was handled by a team of lawyers from the Criminal Division of the Justice Department. They repeated all of Bress's contentions, including the "evidence" linking the McSurelys with the Bradens, the Bradens with Communism, the "secret meeting," and the speech Carmichael was supposed to have given on "S.N.C.C. – Black Power for Communism." But they unaccountably ignored altogether Stavis's attack on the validity of the Kentucky search warrant. Instead, the government concentrated heavily on its claim that the exclusionary rule did not apply to congressional committees – a claim that Stavis, in a reply, hotly contested, partly because he knew that it would destroy his case if the Court of Appeals accepted it, and partly because he hoped to thwart the government's efforts to get rid of the rule by way of a court decision, and thereby weaken the heart of the Fourth Amendment.

While the McSurelys waited for the Court of Appeals' decision on their case, they decided to revise their civil suit against the members and aides of the subcommittee. To conform with the theory that McClellan had engaged in a conspiracy with Commonwealth Attorney Ratliff from the start, Stavis rewrote the complaint along these lines. He eliminated all the members of the subcommittee except McClellan, added Brick and Ratliff to the two aides already cited, and eliminated the various organizations that had originally been plaintiffs in the suit. The complaint charged that the five defendants had conspired together to deprive the McSurelys of their rights under the First, Fourth, Fifth, and Fourteenth Amendments to the Constitution, and asked for fifty thousand dollars in compensatory damages and fifty thousand dollars in punitive damages from each defendant for each of the McSurelys – or a total of a million dollars.

As in the criminal case, dozens of motions, briefs, memoranda, and appeals were filed in the civil suit, and the McSurelys spent hundreds of hours working on legal papers to save the Center for Constitutional Rights, which also represented them in this case at no charge, the time and money it would otherwise have had to spend. (The cost of such a suit handled by a private law firm would run to well over a hundred thousand dollars.) Although the McSurelys didn't have high hopes that they would win this suit, they felt that it was a worthwhile cause. "It's the only way we can stop people like McClellan from doing the same kind of thing," McSurely explained. "The object lesson is important. Since we have the legal help and the knowledge to do it, and black people and poor people who suffer from similar oppression don't, we feel that it's our duty to fight on to the end."

To Stavis, the civil suit would perhaps be more significant, in the long run, than the criminal case. "I've spent most of my time in the past few years trying to find effective remedies for lawlessness by the government," he said recently. "Often the unconstitutional acts that are committed by government officials are criminal acts, but since the criminal-law process is controlled by those who break the law, the wounded citizen has little recourse. He or she can sue, but it's very, very, very rare that this approach succeeds. Even so, it's important to try, because even an occasional success will help in the long run to make the Constitution mean something real for the citizens of this country."

With support from SCEF, the McSurelys set up a McSurely Freedom Committee in the winter of 1971 to organize public support for their appeal in the criminal case. They held numerous meetings, collected a couple of thousand dollars for their defense-and-publicity fund, persuaded supporters to write letters and sign petitions to be sent to members of the Senate who might lend their voices to the couple's cause, and visited some senators they thought might be sympathetic. "They were appalled when they learned what had happened to us," McSurely said afterward. "None of them had known what they were voting on in citing us for contempt, and, of course, McClellan hadn't told them he had all that stuff on Pearson. Sam Ervin told us it was 'a dirty business,' using local cops to steal such stuff, but that it was 'handy.' He didn't like what had been done, but he wouldn't help. Neither would any of the others. I guess they were all scared of McClellan and of getting tied up with us after he had Red-baited us so."

Late in the winter of 1971, Mrs. McSurely enrolled in a practical-nursing course at Columbia Presbyterian Medical Center, in New York. A few months after she completed it, a year later, she and her husband decided that they had had enough of life in New York, so they moved back into the basement of his mother's home in Virginia. "We wanted to save money to pay off our debts, and make arrangements to have our boy taken care of if we finally went to prison," Mrs. McSurely said. "I got a job as a nurse at George Washington University Hospital, and Al went to work teaching in Washington at Antioch College's Center for the Study of Basic Human Problems. We liked being back in Washington, and both of us were very happy in our work. But we were constantly discouraged and tormented by uncertainty while waiting for the Court of Appeals to act. One day, we drove over to Alderson, West Virginia, where the federal women's prison that we figured I'd be sent to is located. When I saw the place, I was terrified."

On December 20, 1972 — two and a half years after the McSurely's trial — the Court of Appeals handed down its decision on their case. In an opinion for the three-judge panel that reviewed the case, Judge Burnita Shelton Matthews stated that the search warrant issued by a Pike County magistrate was a general warrant and clearly violated the Fourth Amendment; that Brick's examination and seizure of the McSurelys' papers also violated the Fourth Amendment; that the exclusionary rule was binding on Congress; and, accordingly, that since the Senate subpoenas were based on illegally seized evidence, they should not have been admitted at the trial. In conclusion, the Court of Appeals reversed the McSurelys' conviction and ordered the District Court to acquit them.

But the McSurelys' long ordeal was not over. Just as they had a right to appeal the District Court's conviction, the government had a right to appeal the Court of Appeals' reversal of that conviction. Under federal regulations, the Department of Justice has thirty days to submit an appeal — in this instance, to the Supreme Court. Near the end of that period following the Court of Appeals' decision, the department asked for and received a thirty-day extension from the Supreme Court to allow more time to prepare an appeal. Once again the McSurelys had to endure the painful uncertainty of a delay. If the Supreme Court accepted their case, Stavis warned them, it might be a year or more before the issue was finally settled. Far worse, he felt obliged to add, the decision there might well go against them, since the Nixon appointees and White — all of whom invariably came down on the side of the state in such cases — would make a majority.

Above all, Stavis feared that the Department of Justice might seize the opportunity presented by the McSurely case to argue before the Supreme Court that the exclusionary rule should not be binding on congressional committees. Since these committees were now rarely looked upon as the instruments of official repression that they were during the congressional witch hunts of the nineteen-fifties, he suspected that the Nixon Administration might be planning to use a relatively unobtrusive legal tactic of this sort to establish a precedent for limiting the exclusionary rule, and thus undermine the Fourth Amendment without arousing widespread public indignation. The next step, of course, would be to get rid of the amendment altogether.

Unknown to Stavis at the time, the Department of Justice was waiting for word from the Supreme Court on whether it would review another Fourth Amendment case — United States v. Calandra, in which the issue was whether illegally seized evidence could be presented before a grand jury. In view of the Calandra case's involvement with loan-sharking — that is, organized crime — it was obviously a more suitable vehicle for an appeal designed to weaken the exclusionary rule, politically speaking anyway, than the McSurely case, with its long and sordid record of official persecution and malfeasance. Another compelling factor from the government's viewpoint may have been that grand juries consider hundreds of thousands of criminal charges every year, whereas congressional committees are only occasionally concerned with such matters. And, finally, the government's use of grand juries as investigative and inquisitorial bodies had become the Nixon Administration's primary means of repression through the law. In any event, on the morning of February 20, 1973 – the day that the time for filing an appeal in the McSurely case was to expire – the Supreme Court announced that it would review Calandra. That afternoon, the Department of Justice announced that it would not pursue the McSurely case further.

McSurely was gratified by the news that the criminal case against him and his wife was at last closed, but he was also embittered by the long struggle. "It's not justice that we are finally proved right after five and a half years," he told reporters. "Justice would be that we were never arrested, or, if mistakes do happen, justice would be that the mistake was corrected fairly and quickly." In the time that has passed since the case ended, McSurely has become more convinced than ever that the American system is essentially unjust, and more determined than ever to change it. "They made a real mistake in persecuting me," he said recently. "Before all this, I was just a liberal reformer. Now I'm a real revolutionary."

Mrs. McSurely was also gratified and embittered. "I couldn't believe it at first," she said, shortly after learning the news. "Finally we were vindicated. And, of course, I was real glad we weren't going to prison. But then I realized that they could never pay us back for all the time and energy we had spent during those years. What could make up for our pain and frustration and fear and helplessness? It was true that the law had ultimately worked for us, and we could believe in the Bill of Rights again. But we had paid a terrible price. The feeling that we got run out of the mountains, that someone hated us enough to try to kill us, made us wonder about ourselves. When we had to ask our friends to send us money and to help out in all kinds of other ways, we did something that people usually don't do to their friends. It was a strain on everybody, and that made us feel bad. Our friends were really wonderful, and we never would have made it without them. But when a couple of people we knew and liked stopped coming by or calling us, we were frightened by the rejection, and wondered if we'd been wrong about what we'd done. Another hard part was learning how to fight back and still go on living a normal life. It's not a matter of spending a few days in court and getting it over with. It's a constant, long, and exhausting struggle. All that is bound to leave scars, and it has. I feel deeply wronged. We were really treated very badly, and I get mad as hell whenever I think about what was done to us. But we made a good fight, and we learned a lot. If you get treated the way we did, you have to fight back. If you don't, you're lost, because your persecutors can make you feel that you've done something wrong when you haven't. That makes you doubt yourself, and you end up believing their lies. But once you stand up and fight, you see that *they* are the wrongdoers. That makes you feel good. Some people say, 'Don't make waves and it will all go away.' But it won't. Once you accept oppression, you destroy yourself."

When the Supreme Court handed down its ruling on the Calandra case — in January, 1974 — the McSurelys saw how narrowly they had escaped the caprice of the law. If that decision had been on the books when the Court of Appeals reviewed their case, their convictions would almost certainly have been upheld, and they would have gone to prison. In the Calandra case, to recapitulate briefly, the government contended that illegally seized evidence could be used before grand juries — that is, that the exclusionary rule doesn't apply to those bodies. The decision, a muddle of judicial distortion delivered by Justice Powell, upheld the government's contention. Powell utterly ignored the basic purpose of the Court in Mapp, which applied the Fourth Amendment to the states, and he implicitly overruled Justice Holmes's famous command in Silverthorne: "The essence of a provision forbidding the acquisition of evidence in a certain way is that not merely evidence so acquired shall not be used before the court, but that it shall not be used at all." But now Powell ruled for the Court that such evidence could be used before grand juries. Since congressional committees function in much the same way as grand juries do, the Court of Appeals would probably have been obliged, under the Calandra ruling, to conclude that the illegally seized evidence on which the Senate subpoenas were based was irrelevant to the McSurelys' refusal to obey them. In the end, then, the McSurelys probably escaped imprisonment and ruin only through an accident of judicial timing. From now on, those who are haled before congressional committees under similar circumstances won't have even the slim chance the McSurelys had to preserve both privacy and freedom. And from now on those who are summoned before grand juries or are the victims of government harassment will have no chance at all to resist the most lawless intrusions upon what Brandeis called "the right to be let alone — the most comprehensive of rights and the right most valued by civilized men."

Justice Powell, in a footnote to his Calandra opinion, observed that those whose privacy is invaded "may have other remedies to redress the injury" and "may be entitled to maintain a cause of action for damages." Stavis immediately began basing his future strategy in the civil suit on this statement. "The Court said that people like the McSurelys had other remedies, so we're trying the only remedy open to us — personal damages for infringing their constitutional rights," he explained.

On October 28, 1975, the Court of Appeals for the District of Columbia Circuit, in a two-to-one vote, upheld the claim made by the Department of Justice lawyers representing McClellan and his aides that the immunity clause in the Constitution relieved them of any liability for their acts in the case — unless they could be shown to have participated in the Kentucky raid on the McSurelys' house or to have given the McSurelys' papers to anyone outside the committee.

The Court of Appeals' opinion was written by Judge Malcolm Wilkey, who delivered an astonishingly pro-government ruling on the most crucial issue in the case:

> Thus, it matters not that the true purpose behind a committee's use of its investigative power is to ridicule, harass, or punish a

> private citizen. So long as the particular investigative activity does not trench upon executive or judicial prerogatives — so long as it remains facially legislative in character — the committee and its employees are protected.

At another point, Judge Wilkey said, "Calandra makes clear that a grand jury or, we submit, a congressional committee has the right in its investigatory capacity to use the product of a past unlawful search and seizure." In other words, the courts will do nothing to protect citizens from the most vicious abuse of their rights by government. In a footnote, Wilkey added, "Courts are not the place for such controversies. Self-discipline and the voters must be the ultimate reliance for discouraging or correcting such abuses." It would be difficult to imagine anything more unlikely than self-restraint from a man like McClellan — especially if Wilkey's views are ultimately upheld and all politicians are given unlimited freedom to desecrate the people's most sacred rights.

On November 10th, Stavis filed a combined petition for a rehearing before the Court of Appeals, and asked that the entire nine-judge court hear his petition *en banc.* Despite his conviction that his case was indisputably just, he had little hope that the petition would be granted, since it is extremely rare for courts to grant such requests. But on February 10, 1976 — to Stavis's astonishment and delight — the *en-banc* hearing was granted *and* Judge Wilkey's ruling was vacated. The *en-banc* hearing was held on April 19th, but so far no decision has been handed down. That could take months, and any ruling could revise, eliminate, or reinstate Wilkey's harsh conclusions. In any event, the McSurelys' civil case could drag on for several more years — if they, and Stavis, have the stamina to go on with it. Whatever the outcome, the McSurelys will have spent at least ten years fighting for their rights as American citizens.

Part Three

Taking the Fifth

I

The informer — the Judas figure — has been an odious creature in the popular mind throughout history. Even so, governments have always used his services, and one measure of freedom in any society is the extent to which the informer flourishes. In a tyranny, the informer contributes a basic necessity to the tyrant's survival — the people's fear of him — by demonstrating that any deviant political expression or behavior may be reported to the state and then punished. In a democracy, on the other hand, the sovereignty of the people is supposed to encourage diversity of thought and allow open dissent and outright opposition to the public policies of those who are elected to run things temporarily. But even the most democratically conceived government comes to behave as if its own survival, rather than the people's welfare, is the paramount good. This happens not because democracy inevitably degenerates into tyranny through repressive leadership at the top but because the government's ordinary day-to-day operations depend on entrenched "public servants" — the bureaucracy — who are always most concerned about protecting and expanding their own power. In time, bureaucrats transform government into a kind of private institution that exists for their sake, and this makes them deeply committed to preserving the system — *their* system — as it is. The deeper their commitment, the more alarmed they are likely to be by anything that seems to threaten the system; and the more alarmed they become, the more likely they are to resort to extreme measures to meet the threat. One extreme measure that has been increasingly resorted to by government in the United States during the past few years is the official use of informers from the bottom to the top of our society.

On the local level, most police departments of any size in this country now have "intelligence units," which use electronic surveillance and undercover agents, or informers, to spy on citizens who are suspected of unlawful activity (and, all too frequently, on citizens who are not engaged in anything illegal but are up to something that might subject them to political or economic blackmail). On the national level, recent revelations about the federal government's spying on its citizens on an immense scale — by such bureaucratic institutions as the Federal Bureau of Investigation, the Central Intelligence Agency, the Army, the Secret Service, the National Security Agency, the Internal Revenue Service, the Postal Service, the Drug Enforcement Administration, and the Customs Service — raise the question of whether this undemocratic and often unlawful practice does not imperil the Republic more than did the perilous episode known as Watergate.

While informers are of little use in controlling the kind of crime that Americans are most worried about — violent street crime — informers are the chief means of dealing with the kind of crime that the government is most worried about — group crime. The given group may be organized for the purpose of financial gain through crime, in the pattern of the Mafia, or it may be organized for political purposes, such as those proclaimed by the Communist Party, the Socialist Workers Party, the Black Panthers, the Symbionese Liberation Army, or any of the various groups that loosely make up the New Left. It has often been said that half of the American Communist Party's ten thousand or so members are F.B.I. informers. That outfit is fairly easy to infiltrate, because it is a rigid bureaucratic structure of the sort that the F.B.I., itself a rigid bureaucratic structure, is familiar with. It has also often been said that the F.B.I. has failed to keep tabs on the activities of the New Left — for instance, the Bureau has been able to learn about and stop less than two per cent of the violent acts planned by left-wing radicals — because the Bureau cannot comprehend that movement's character. The New Left is anything but bureaucratic, for the groups that comprise it are generally rather formless and undisciplined, and their members drift in and out of its many factions and schisms. Nor do most of these collections of radicals have clearly formulated policies and programs, but are more likely to rely on inflammatory rhetoric than on direct action as an outlet for their social discontent. Then, too, members of the New Left often live and dress and speak in ways that the upstanding informer would find repugnantly inimitable.

Probably the clearest example of the bureaucratic inability to understand these rebels and revolutionaries is to be found in the government's grossly disproportionate reaction to the threat that they actually pose, given the size of the United States and the conservative character of its people. Those who tremble at the spectre of revolution here often cite the relatively few people who seized power in Russia during the First World War, but such a nervous comparison ignores the fact that Russian society had collapsed from internal corruption when it was taken over. Today, the principal danger from the far left in this country is that it has provided the far right with an excuse to crush it, in a manner that might be generally acceptable if the government goes on scaring the wits out of everybody about a handful of impotent left-wing radicals. And although the right wing is also diffuse and weak, there is one powerful group that could become its unifying ally at any time — the nation's thousands of police departments, which are becoming more and more paramilitary, well organized, interconnected, heavily armed, and political-minded. To an alarming extent, the only control over them is the control they maintain over themselves, and our personal freedom is largely at their sufferance.

Yet the national government has ignored this peril altogether, and has concentrated its immense firepower on the few radical left-wing outfits still in business, like the "army" of Symbionese Liberators, who apparently never numbered more than a dozen people. While the S.L.A.'s kidnapping of Patricia Hearst was surely a sensational event, her supposed conversion to active terrorism made her, legally speaking, merely another accused outlaw. But the publicity surrounding the case, the inflamed political statements issued by her and her confederates, and their embarrassing success in eluding thousands of pursuers apparently drove the F.B.I. to frenzied lengths to capture them. During the search for the Hearst woman, it was reported that the Bureau had questioned over twenty-seven thousand people about her in the San Francisco area alone. At the time, the Bureau, for all its efforts, hadn't found her, because it hadn't found anyone who would inform on her. And when it finally captured her its success was due to an informer.

Having failed to turn up any dependable informers in the Hearst case in its early stages, the F.B.I. desperately resorted to a relatively new law-enforcement technique — the use of compliant federal grand juries to help the Bureau do the job that it couldn't do on its own. Although under law grand juries are supposed to determine only whether crimes have been committed and to indict those who seem to have committed them, and are not supposed to serve as investigative tools for prosecutors or law-enforcement agencies, nowadays grand juries are frequently, and improperly, used to amass evidence against people who have already been indicted, to obtain leads on fugitives, or even to find missing persons like Jimmy Hoffa. The F.B.I. merely persuades a coöperative United States Attorney to instruct the federal grand jury he in effect runs to subpoena relatives, friends, and acquaintances of the person being sought, and then the prosecutor forces these witnesses, under threat of imprisonment for contempt of court, to divulge whatever they may know about the fugitive — or, for that matter, about anything under the sun that the prosecutor (or the F.B.I.) feels like asking, however irrelevant and personal. In short, if the government cannot find informers it creates them.

On September 23, 1970, three white men and two white women held up a branch of the State Street Bank and Trust Company, a Boston bank, and escaped with twenty-six thousand dollars in cash.

As they were making their getaway, a policeman tried to stop them, and one of the bandits cut him down with a burst from a machine gun. The policeman died, leaving a widow and nine children, and the greatest manhunt in New England history got under way. The search was led by the F.B.I., which had jurisdiction over the crime since the bank was insured by the federal government, and by that night one of the wanted men had been captured. He turned out to be an ex-convict who had been recently paroled from a Massachusetts prison, and he quickly informed on his four partners. The other men were also ex-convicts, and all three had been studying at Brandeis and Northeastern Universities, in Massachusetts, after completing a college-preparatory course in the same prison. The women subsequently indicted for the crime were both twenty years old, from respectable middle-class families, and one was a senior at Brandeis, while the other had graduated there the previous June. According to the informer's story, the five bandits had formed a radical movement of their own called the Revolutionary Action Force to protest the American involvement in Vietnam and Cambodia, and had held up the bank to finance their movement, which, the informer told the F.B.I., was designed "to break down the military structure of the country." One of the other men, who later described himself as commander-in-chief of the Revolutionary Action Force—East, said that they had held up the bank because the United States government had ignored their official declaration of war against it.

The two remaining male fugitives were captured within a few days, but there was no sign of the two young women — Susan Edith Saxe and Katherine Ann Power, who soon became known simply as Saxe and Power — and they quickly made the F.B.I.'s "most wanted" list. Posters bearing their pictures and physical descriptions were circulated through F.B.I. offices, police stations, and post offices across the country, but for more than four years the authorities were unable to find a trace of them. Then, around the beginning of January, 1975, a young man in Lexington, Kentucky, happened to see one of the "wanted" posters, and thought that the fugitives closely resembled two women he had known as Lena Paley (Saxe) and May Kelly (Power), who had lived the previous summer and fall in a lesbian community on the fringes of the University of Kentucky campus, in Lexington. He mentioned his suspicion to a woman who lived in the community, and she notified the F.B.I. field office in Cincinnati, across the Ohio River from Lexington. The fugitives' identity was quickly verified.

If the F.B.I. had difficulty understanding the New Left, it had far greater difficulty understanding a related development known as women's liberation or the women's movement, and could understand nothing at all about an outgrowth of that movement – the increasing number of women who had become, or admitted being, lesbians. In the Saxe-Power case, the Bureau's inability to cope with this particular pair of radical adversaries was illustrated at the top by its reaction to the news about the presence of Saxe and Power some months earlier in Lexington. The Bureau did not quietly send a few able women agents to the lesbian community in Lexington to see if they could unobtrusively pick up a lead on the fugitives. Instead, it dispatched droves of male agents to the area, and thereby notified Saxe and Power that the government had picked up their trail and virtually suggested to them that they would do well to stop hanging around with lesbians while the F.B.I. wasted its time investigating lesbians. And, at the bottom, the F.B.I.'s attitude was illustrated by an agent in the field who interviewed a waitress in a Lexington restaurant that was frequented by lesbians; when she told him that although she was not a lesbian she had once had a drink with one of the fugitives, the agent said, "If I went out for a drink with a homosexual man who had no interest in women, I wouldn't know what to talk about."

Saxe and Power were soon reported to have lived in several lesbian communities in the East, and the F.B.I. apparently concluded from this fact that such communities were havens for criminals of all sorts – especially left-wing political criminals. Homosexual acts are crimes in most jurisdictions in this country, even if the men and women who are homosexual are not often prosecuted for it, and their way of life is sufficiently despised by the heterosexual public to make official persecution of them generally acceptable. In short, the Bureau was free to harass homosexuals as ruthlessly as it could a nest of drug traffickers or Reds. And harass them it did. F.B.I. agents began questioning scores of people in the "gay" community in Lexington, many of whom were susceptible to pressure because they had hidden their private lives from their families and employers. F.B.I. agents went to their families, divulged their quarries' sexual habits, and forced the reluctant witnesses to talk — either because of the implicit threat that their employers would be the next to learn about them or because they were simply crushed by such revelations of their secret lives and caved in. Most of these members of the gay community had known Saxe and Power as Paley and Kelly, and some of them told the F.B.I. where the women had apparently gone after leaving Lexington — to Hartford, among other places.

Before long, though, word went around the gay community that no one was legally obliged to answer questions put by F.B.I. men or any other government officials and, in fact, that it could be extremely dangerous to talk to them at all. A little-known federal statute, Title 18, Section 1001, of the Federal Criminal Code, makes it a federal crime, punishable by up to five years in prison and a ten-thousand-dollar fine, for a citizen to lie to *any* government agency. In legal terms, of course, what is a lie and what is not is up to a jury to decide. One may believe that one is telling the truth when being questioned, only to later recall events somewhat differently; if one then tells the revised version of those events before a grand jury or a court, one can be prosecuted for having lied in the first place. Even as seemingly small an untruth as telling a goverment official that one doesn't know anything about what is being inquired into when one does know something about it is a criminal act. And while the F.B.I. ordinarily warns criminal suspects of their constitutional rights once they are taken into custody — mainly the right not to speak and the right to have a lawyer present — agents do not warn non-suspects of any rights they have or of the danger of violating Section 1001 when they are questioned about someone else who *is* a criminal suspect. In other words, most of those who are questioned by the F.B.I. or by other government officials are not given the ordinary forms of due process of law, and some lawyers would argue that the only sensibly self-protective course for anyone, guilty or innocent of wrongdoing, is to refuse to speak to *any* government agent unless a lawyer is present—at least, until Congress takes Section 1001 off the books. In any event, when inhabitants of the Lexington community learned of their right to remain silent, more and more of them refused to say anything to the F.B.I.

In midmorning on January 24, 1975, two F.B.I. agents appeared at a silverware-manufacturing plant in Meriden, Connecticut, and asked to see an executive who worked there, Mrs. Alice Grusse. They were shown to her office, identified themselves, and asked where they could find her daughter Ellen. Mrs. Grusse was alarmed, and asked what they wanted to see her for. The older of the agents, a rather grandfatherly sort of man who conducted the interview, assured her that as far as they knew her daughter hadn't done anything wrong but that she might be able to tell them something about two women fugitives who were wanted for bank robbery and murder. Mrs. Grusse was frightened by this news. She had never, to her knowledge, seen an F.B.I. man before. Also, she could not believe that her daughter, who had been a quiet, generally obedient, though sometimes stubborn, child and seemed a quiet, orderly woman, could conceivably have had anything to do with bank robbers and murderers. Nervously, Mrs. Grusse asked the agents to wait, and telephoned Ellen at her apartment in New Haven, where she had moved from Hartford a month earlier. Mrs. Grusse's voice was shaking as she told Ellen that two F.B.I. men were in her office and wanted to know where she lived, so that they could speak to her about some women fugitives.

As it happened, her daughter—a slender woman of twenty-eight with curly, light-brown hair, a thin, rather childlike face, and an intense manner—had heard about the F.B.I.'s search for Saxe and Power, and had read in the press that a number of people in Lexington had asserted their right to refuse to talk to the F.B.I. After a moment's hesitation, she told her mother that she didn't want to speak to the agents. Mrs. Grusse began to protest, saying that she *had* to talk to them, but Ellen quickly cut her short with the assurance that she didn't have to, and wouldn't, talk to them. Mrs. Grusse then asked if she should tell them where Ellen lived, and her daughter, after another pause, decided that it was her responsibility, not her mother's, to handle the matter and said yes.

When Ellen Grusse hung up the telephone, she quickly described the call to the person she lived with — Marie Theresa Turgeon, a quietly pleasant, thirty-one-year-old woman with short dark hair who was known to her friends as Terri. Both of them recalled at the same moment that a few days earlier they had overheard a woman at the New Haven Women's Liberation Center asking about where she could get some legal advice on how to deal with a landlord who insisted that she get rid of her cat. The person in charge of the center's referral service had replied that a young woman named Diane Polan handled many legal problems for women associated with the center. Now Grusse telephoned her, explained what had happened in Meriden, and asked what she should do to avoid talking to the F.B.I. agents. Polan turned out to be legal assistant to a lawyer named Michael Avery, and she transferred the call to him. Avery informed Grusse that she could not be compelled to talk to them, and said that if she wanted to discuss the situation further she could come to his office. (Avery, though only thirty years old, had already had a good bit of experience with the F.B.I., because since graduating from the Yale Law School he had represented such clients as the Black Panthers, the Communist Party of Connecticut, and various other radicals in the course of his criminal-law practice.) The two women expected the F.B.I. men to drive directly over from Meriden, some twenty miles away, and wanted to be prepared for them, so they left for Avery's office at once. He was tied up, though, and it was a couple of hours before they got in to see him.

"His advice was simply that we insist on having our lawyer present during any interview with the F.B.I.," Grusse said recently. "He didn't see the situation as being any problem, because in his experience whenever F.B.I. men hear someone say 'lawyer' they just go away."

Grusse and Turgeon got back home at a little before three

o'clock that afternoon. Five minutes later, there was a knock at the door, and Turgeon went to answer it. Two men were waiting, and one of them – the elderly man who had spoken to Mrs. Grusse at her office – asked if she was Ellen Grusse. Turgeon introduced herself, and called Grusse. When she appeared, the older man demanded, "Where have you been? We drove all the way here from Meriden and had to wait three hours for you."

Assuming that F.B.I. agents probably spent much of their time waiting for people, Grusse ignored that point and said, "As a matter of fact, I want to talk to you about that. I went to see a lawyer, and his advice is that I not talk to you unless he is present." According to Grusse, the agents were clearly taken aback. "The older one literally gasped when I said 'lawyer,' " she said later. "He started in talking about bank robbers and murderers, and said I wasn't in any trouble, so why did I want to see a lawyer? I just handed him Avery's card and told him to set up an interview. He wanted to use my phone for that, but I said no, because I figured he was just trying to get into the apartment, and I wasn't going to allow that unless he had a warrant. Finally, I asked Terri to call Avery, but he wasn't at his office. Then the agent behaved as Avery had told us he would. First he tried the good-citizen approach: I wasn't suspected of any crime, so why wouldn't I, as a good citizen, help find these bank robbers and murderers? When I still refused to talk to him, he began threatening me, saying that I could get in a lot of trouble for harboring fugitives. Before that, he had said that I wasn't in any trouble, but now it seemed that I was, or at least could be. And if I could be, then it seemed that he was trying to trap me into incriminating myself. So I said, 'I prefer to get my legal advice from a lawyer, not the F.B.I.' After that, they left."

The agents did not call on Avery. Instead, they reported Grusse's refusal to coöperate with them to the agent in charge of the search for Saxe and Power in Connecticut, and he presented the matter to an Assistant United States Attorney, William Dow III, in New Haven, who presented it, in turn, before a federal grand jury sitting there. On January 27th, three days after the two agents attempted to question Grusse, the grand jury issued subpoenas for both her and Turgeon, stating, "You are hereby commanded to appear in the United States District Court for the District of Connecticut at P.O. Bldg. 141 Church Street – Rm. 208 in the City of New Haven on the 28th of January 1975 at 10:00 o'clock A.M. to testify before the Grand Jury."

When a U.S. marshal arrived at the Grusse-Turgeon apartment on the afternoon of the twenty-seventh to serve the subpoenas, Grusse was out, working at a temporary job she had recently got, so he could serve only the subpoena for Turgeon. She telephoned Grusse and then Avery. He was surprised by the news, and unsettled by the legal problems it presented, because he was unfamiliar with grand-jury procedures and had only a few hours to prepare some kind of plea to the District Court to quash or at least delay the subpoenas' order, to gain time in which to prepare a legal defense for his clients. Avery got on the telephone at once to the National Lawyers Guild, in New York, a left-wing group he belonged to, which had prepared extensive research documents on the government's tactics in using grand juries to pursue suspects whom the F.B.I. couldn't find on its own.

Late that afternoon, Grusse and Turgeon went to Avery's office for another conference, and during it Grusse thought about whether she should try to avoid being served the subpoena by fleeing. She soon gave up the idea. "I was convinced that the only reason they subpoenaed Terri was because she lived with me," Grusse said. "When the F.B.I. came to talk to me, they didn't even know who she was. I decided that I couldn't let her go through it alone. I had to support her. Besides, I knew that I would have to face the thing sooner or later."

At six-thirty the next morning, she was awakened by a loud pounding on the door of her apartment. She went to answer, and the same marshal asked if she was Ellen Grusse. She yawned and said that she was, and he handed her the subpoena commanding her to appear before the federal grand jury three and a half hours later.

Ellen Grusse was born in Meriden, Connecticut, in June, 1946, and grew up there and in Southington, Connecticut. There were six children in the Grusse family, and although both parents worked – the father as a salesman and the mother as a private secretary – the family was often rather poorly off financially. In 1964, Ellen enrolled at the University of Connecticut at Storrs, but after a couple of years there she quit and moved to San Francisco, where she lived for three and a half years. "It was the time of the hippies and the flower children and the youth rebellion at Berkeley," she has said. "But I was very apathetic and never got involved in any of that. I wasn't interested in civil rights or the Vietnam war or the kids' fight against authority. I was very square and worked for outfits like U.S. Steel and an import-export firm, and I remained untouched by all the upheaval going on out on the West Coast at the time." In 1969, she came back East and settled in Hartford, where she got a job as a clerk with the Travelers Insurance Company. After a few years there, she was promoted to the position of budget analyst, a fairly high post that paid a decent salary and gave her a good bit of responsibility. But she was dissatisfied with her life, and decided to go back to college, at night, to study psychology. After two years of work and study, she concluded that she should do one or the other and do it properly, so she arranged to work part time and go to college full time. In December, 1972, she graduated with a degree in psychology.

"During my last year in college, I began to get interested in the women's movement," she said. "It was a big thing in college then. All the male professors were trying to be non-sexist, and the talk about women was incessant. Then, after I left college and moved back to Hartford, I met some women who called themselves feminists. I was curious about what that meant, so I joined several feminist groups." In the fall of 1973, Grusse went to work for a farmers' milk coöperative, and before long she became a computer programmer. Her boss, a young man whom she got along with comfortably, was killed in an automobile accident, and his replacement was a much older man. "He was very stern and disagreeable and a gross sexist," Grusse recalled. "He made terrible personal remarks to me, so I quit. I went on unemployment for a few months and worked at part-time jobs when I could find them. But I spent most of my time studying the women's movement, trying to find out what it was all about and where I might fit in. Up to then, I had never fit in anyplace."

Before long, Grusse became deeply absorbed by the movement. "It was something that I could identify with very strongly, in a way that I hadn't been able to with the civil-rights movement or the anti-war movement," she explained. "Those were basically political, and I'd never been interested in politics. I always got D in political science in school. But feminism was personal for me. When women talked about sexism, I could certainly identify with them, because I had been pushed around all my life – not always by men but by the human tug-of-war our social system creates. Ever since I was a teen-ager, I felt different. I wasn't interested in dating or clothes or makeup. I felt there was something the matter with me. But when I got involved in the movement, I met other women who had felt the same way once but no longer did, and I began to feel that maybe there wasn't anything wrong with me after all. I fit into the women's group very easily and naturally, and that was really good for me. I guess the biggest impact feminism has had on me began during a course I took in college called 'Women in Society.' The teacher was a woman and a Marxist. Her views – the economic and political reasons behind what had happened to women over the centuries – had never occurred to me. She presented an analysis that really made me think hard. My position had been that we should fight for equal rights for women within the system. But then she opened this door to a wider view. I didn't go through that door, though, because at the time I couldn't accept her analysis."

After Grusse graduated, there was a Marxist-feminist meeting at Storrs, and she decided to attend it. "I met some women in Hartford who were going, so I went along," she said. "The result was that I got involved in that approach for about a year, mostly from just studying and thinking about it on my own. During that time, I met a lot of women with widely differing opinions about what feminism means. At one end were those who feel that it means equal rights and equal pay for women — that is, equality with men. At the opposite end were the women who call themselves lesbian separatists and talk about building a lesbian nation. In between these extremes were women who see the basic structure of society as the problem and argue that society will allow some women to become equal with men but only at the cost of treading on other women to get that equality. To their way of thinking, the whole system has to be torn up and completely changed. Anyway, scattered between the equal-pay, equal-rights feminists and the lesbian separatists were Marxist feminists, Socialist feminists, lesbian feminists, and even feminist feminists. Some were for reform, some were for revolution. For myself, I fear even the word 'revolution.' It suggests violence, and any kind of violence freaks me right out."

Grusse finally settled for a Socialist-feminist group in Hartford, and as she attended its consciousness-raising sessions she found many of her lifelong assumptions about herself gradually changing. "At first, I talked about my background, and I insisted that I hadn't been hurt by it," she said. "I had been given a decent education, and had built the start of a decent career. There had been no pressure from my family to get married. Overall, I didn't see myself as being oppressed, and I believed I had a worthwhile future. But as we talked in the group I began to see that oppression had been there all along, and was still there. I saw it in my personal relationships with men, and then I began to see it everywhere in our institutions — in the so-called power structure. While I was in the women's group in Hartford, we mostly just sat around and talked. We wanted to act, not just to affect our own lives but to reach outside ourselves and bring about social change. But we didn't know where to start. I had deep personal fears about confronting anything or anybody. During the late sixties and early seventies, I was to the right of most of my friends, who were generally liberal. My upbringing had been very conservative, and I agreed with the people who said things like 'Sure, Socialism may be all right, but how about the individual?' or 'I'd rather have an imperfect capitalist society with some freedom than an imperfect Socialist society without freedom.' When I met women in the movement who took politics very seriously and who sincerely wanted to change society, I saw that it was a very risky business. It meant that I would have to reject my family and all that I had been taught to believe in."

Grusse put off making any decision on the choice before her, and tried to translate her feminist beliefs into action by talking to the women she worked with, most of whom, she became convinced, were treated badly by the men they worked for, and all of whom seemed to her to be manipulated and underpaid by their male employers. In time, though, Grusse realized that she, too, was abusing these women. "I used to think of men as being more perfect than women," she said. "All positives and privileges were identified with men in my mind. So I thought I had to depend on men to have identity. I got involved with a man who had an important job at one place where I worked, and I became very powerful there because of my association with him. When I suddenly realized what I was doing, I hated myself. So I left the man and the job. Using that man to get power, and then abusing the women who worked with and under me to show my power, was the worst kind of betrayal of feminism, because its most vital part is the bond between women. We really *are* all sisters."

In the fall of 1974, after Grusse quit that job, there was an anti-abortion, or "pro-life," convention in Hartford, and she and two other women in her group felt that they couldn't let it go by without opposing it in some public manner. Finally, they decided to hold a pro-abortion counterdemonstration at the convention. "That was really a terrifying prospect for me," Grusse recalled. "Making a public statement was frightening. Even doing nothing more than carrying a placard around was too much for me. But we organized a group of fifteen or twenty people, mostly women from our group and a couple of men, who came and carried placards and handed out leaflets at the convention hotel. The anti-abortion people came up to us and started to argue. They were very angry and abusive, and we tried to avoid a confrontation that would lead to violence. In the end, it was just a verbal confrontation. But I didn't participate in it. I was too scared to say anything. Finally, the anti-abortion people got the hotel management to call the police, who came and made us leave because we didn't have a permit. It was a Sunday, so we went over to St. Joseph's Cathedral and handed pro-abortion leaflets to the people coming out. I was brought up as a Catholic, and that act scared me, too. When it was all over, I realized that my efforts had been futile, and I knew that I had to plug in to something more lasting. But I still didn't know what or how. I didn't have any thought of doing anything political – the pro-abortion demonstration was the extent of my political activity. When the government came after me that day, I was still being tugged between where I was coming from and where I was going. As soon as I saw those F.B.I. men, I knew I had to make a commitment."

Terri Turgeon was born in June, 1943, in Lewiston, Maine, where her father worked in a textile mill until the business moved to the South after the Second World War. Then he became a welder and took his family – his wife and five children – to Plainville, Connecticut, and after a few years there on to Southington, Connecticut. When Terri finished high school, she went to work as a clerk in the local Grant's department store, and stayed there for two and a half years. From time to time, a travelling photographer who took baby pictures turned up at Grant's, and she decided that she would like such a job. She finally got one, and spent a couple of years travelling around New England taking baby pictures in places like Grant's. By the end of 1967, she was tired of moving around so much, and decided to settle down in Hartford, where she found work as a clerk at the Aetna Life Insurance Company. She stayed there for seven years and ended up as a senior underwriter, one of the few women to attain such a position in that company.

"By being in the right place at the right time and not being offensive to anyone, I finally got promoted to a job that had almost always been held by men," Turgeon said not long ago. "I could do the work, and did it very well – as well as any of the men there. I worked in a department with eleven men and thirty-eight other women who were all secretaries and clerks. The man in charge of the department was unbelievable. He kept making statements to the other women about my being in this high position and having privileges and responsibilities in order to suggest to the other women what they could do if they worked hard. This approach was used throughout the company then to make it look as if there were opportunities for women when there weren't. I had to put pressure on those women to make them work, and I knew full well that they couldn't go on to higher jobs in the company no matter how hard they worked. So I was forced to act like a man – except that I had to do a lot more work than the men to keep my job."

In 1974, Turgeon began to get interested in the women's movement. "I happened to meet some women who described themselves as feminists and explained to me what that meant to them," she said. "I really wanted to get involved in the movement. It would give me some dignity, I thought. These women were finally a disappointment to me personally, but I learned a lot from them. Ellen and I had met a couple of times in women's groups, and when she held the pro-abortion demonstration I joined in. I'd had strong feelings about abortion for a long time – mostly about back-alley butchers – but I'd never done anything about it. In fact, I'd never done anything about anything. The demonstration was my first political act. And I was scared. I've always been very afraid of authority. If I got a speeding ticket, I'd thank the cop for giving it to me. Anyway, I told my mother about how I wanted to get involved in these things, and she was worried I'd get sent to jail for it. I thought there was a possibility of my going to jail, like in the anti-war and civil-rights protests, but only for overnight or a day at the most. Still, I was scared. When I went along with Ellen to St. Joseph's Cathedral was when I was most afraid. I was brought up as a Catholic, and whenever my family drove past a Catholic church in our car my mother would always tell us to bow our heads."

By the fall of 1974, Turgeon had become increasingly unhappy about her job and dissatisfied with her life in general, and she decided to study the women's movement to see if it might be for her the emotional and social haven that it was for some other women. "I wanted to know what women had been through, and to really study the movement in and out, so it seemed that the best way to start was by getting out of the job where I was the token woman, the untrue example," she said. "I quit, and since then I've learned a lot about feminism and about myself. Feminism has given me a new sense of my dignity as an individual. It has let me accept myself as a person, and now I know that it's O.K. to be who I am. It has put me in touch with my personal strengths, and allows me to call them strengths for the first time. It provides a framework in which I can say 'I am a woman' without feeling there is something basically wrong with me. It's allowed me to express some weaknesses and not be completely ashamed of them, as I would have been before. It's helped me know that I can turn to someone else and expect understanding. It's allowed me to trust others, and to make myself vulnerable and not suffer for it."

After meeting in the fall of 1974, Turgeon and Grusse continued to see each other. They soon found the kind of companionship that neither of them had known before, and decided to live together. Hartford had come to seem dull to them, the women's movement there was weak, and the city reminded them of the unhappy period before they had found each other. They looked around for a more congenial place to live, and settled on New Haven, partly because Yale gave that city a feeling of great vitality and freedom, but largely because of the New Haven "women's community," which consisted of about a hundred militant feminists. It was not a community in a geographical sense, since its members were scattered through town, but they had a common bond — women's liberation, which is the most fundamental, and even revolutionary, movement going on in the United States today.

In the view of the New Haven community's members (and in the view of those in similar communities around the country), the F.B.I. was using the Saxe-Power search not merely to find two fugitives from justice but to investigate this new radical movement. "At some point during the F.B.I.'s search for Saxe and Power, the Bureau found somebody who talked about the radical feminist 'network,' as the F.B.I. calls it," Avery has said. "Anyway, when the men at the top of the F.B.I. learned more about the movement — just how radical and determined these women are — they must have said, 'Jesus, we didn't know this was going on!' Then they began using the Saxe-Power case to learn more. While they claim that this isn't a political case at all, that's obviously nonsense. There are a lot of bank robbers and murderers loose, but the F.B.I. doesn't go to these extraordinary lengths to catch *them*. Of course, the government's idea of who is a threat to society has been weird all along. Take its attempts to break up the Socialist Workers Party over the past twenty years. A glance at the party's history shows that, as decent and progressive as it has been, it was always totally ineffectual politically. But the F.B.I. spent tens of thousands of man-hours keeping it under surveillance, getting its members fired from their jobs, rifling its offices, opening and reading its members' mail. While the government has never understood the New Left, it has no comprehension at all of things like consciousness-raising — basically, an attempt to change relationships between people — which grew out of the New Left by way of feminism. The government seems to view any sizable group of people who don't want to live the way the ordinary government official thinks people should live as conspirators and revolutionaries."

Avery paused for a moment and then went on, "Anyway, when the F.B.I. learned that a couple of fugitives had hidden out in lesbian communities it went after the lesbians under the pretext of looking for the fugitives. Naturally, F.B.I. men couldn't bear anyone who was *that* different. And when they saw that a lot of people with very different ideas and life styles were collected together in these feminist communities, they concluded, as they always have, that there must be a conspiracy to bring down the government. Actually, the women's movement *is* truly revolutionary, in a way that none of the movements of the nineteen-sixties were, because in time this movement is bound to change our political system and our society radically. Even so, there is nothing remotely illegal about feminism, so the government has no right to snoop around in it. But the government was badly frightened by all the social turmoil of the past decade, and is now determined to smash people who look dangerous before they can do any harm. That's why we have to oppose the government at every step of the way. If we don't, it will smash all of us by destroying the freedom of the individual to be an individual. That's the conspiracy this country faces today."

During the Presidency of Richard Nixon, the Administration saw, or pretended to see, conspirators everywhere. To impose a tyrannical conformity on the nation, the Administration tried to destroy its political opponents by charging them with crimes, and conspiracy to commit crimes, against the state, and it prosecuted scores of people who had done little more than raise their voices in protest against the government's illicit use of its power. While the government lost almost every case that it took to court, it doubtless intimidated thousands of people who feared the same treatment if they spoke out. That result was as useful to the Administration as convictions and long prison sentences would have been, for it was conformity – subservience, in the end – that Nixon was after, so that he could do as he pleased with the nation. Although Nixon and his top confederates were run out of office, most of the hundreds of officials who carried out their orders – particularly, agents of the F.B.I., members of United States Attorneys' offices around the country, and lawyers in the Department of Justice – remain at their posts. For instance, Guy Goodwin, who headed the special-litigation section of the Internal Security Division of the Justice Department under Nixon and directed the prosecutions of the Harrisburg Seven, the Gainesville Eight, the Camden Twenty-eight, and numerous other political cases, is still at work in the Department. And most of the U.S. Attorneys who tried such cases are also still in office.

The methods used during the late sixties and early seventies to silence the opposition and the methods used in the searches for Patricia Hearst or Susan Saxe and Katherine Power are almost identical. The government claimed that in its investigation of the more militant parts of the women's movement it was solely concerned about a different kind of conspiracy — a conspiracy to conceal the whereabouts of two women charged with bank robbery and murder. Government spokesmen also contended that the women's movement used the F.B.I.'s investigation to create a smoke screen to conceal its own divisions and shortcomings, as well as to get publicity and converts. And, until recently, the government claimed that whatever it did was entirely legal, and that it had merely used, and would go on using, all the lawful means available to it in order to bring such fugitives to justice. If the only way of doing that was by questioning people about their personal lives, the government said, then it would question them, under the established legal principle that the state has a right to every person's evidence.

The primary question in the case — whether Turgeon and Grusse knew anything about Saxe and Power that might have helped the government in its search for them — can be answered only by the four women, perhaps their lawyers, and possibly some close friends. To the government, it has seemed that Grusse and Turgeon must have known something that could have been useful to the authorities. Otherwise, it has been said, the two women would undoubtedly have talked freely and demonstrated that they knew nothing of any significance. This conclusion ignores a number of possibilities. It may seem unlikely that Grusse and Turgeon had not met Saxe and Power (at least as Paley and Kelly) or known others who knew them; if they knew nothing, the two women could simply have answered no to every question asked them before a grand jury and gone on their way. But the *kind* of knowledge they may have had could go far to explain their silence. For instance, they may have unwittingly committed some kind of offense that they only later learned was a crime — say, that they had known someone who had put up two strange women for a night without knowing they were fugitives, that Grusse and Turgeon had subsequently learned who the strangers were and what they were charged with and had not informed the police about the incident, as required by law. Or they may not have known the fugitives at all but simply knew someone else who knew them, who had nothing of value to reveal, and who would be irreparably damaged in some way by being dragged into the case; in that event, the only way for the two women to avoid going to prison, even though they were wholly innocent, would have been to betray someone else who was also innocent.

Since grand-jury proceedings are not supposed to be made public – except that witnesses are free to report what was asked them and what they answered – if Grusse and Turgeon were to testify about anything, however unimportant, it might appear to outsiders that they had given the government information that ultimately led to the fugitives' capture. In other words, the only way for Grusse and Turgeon to prove that they hadn't become informers would be to go to prison to show that they had remained silent. Further, if they testified in secret before the grand jury about anything of the slightest import, no matter how innocent they were personally of any wrongdoing, they could later be compelled, by way of a grant of immunity, to testify in public at a trial of Saxe, Power, or anyone who had been culpably involved with them. Given the intense loyalty in the women's movement, any act of this kind would surely have closed all doors to the sanctuary that Grusse and Turgeon had found at last. Or they may have known the fugitives only under their aliases, may have known nothing about their past or present whereabouts, and may have felt that they had to resist official intrusion into their private lives, since it could produce nothing of use to the government and might seem like a betrayal of two friends who, as far as Grusse and Turgeon knew at the time, were simply a couple of innocent women. Finally, of course, the two women may have known the fugitives by their true identity, may have known what they were accused of, and may have helped hide them. In that case, they would have been guilty of committing serious crimes, and could scarcely be expected to be informers against themselves. One of the most ancient principles of Anglo-Saxon law is the principle that is embodied in the Fifth Amendment to the Constitution, which states, among other things, that no one "shall be compelled in any criminal case to be a witness against himself."

For their own part, Turgeon and Grusse would say only that they had done nothing wrong. Apparently, the government believed that this claim was false — at the outset, anyway — for Dow, the Assistant U.S. Attorney in charge of the case, told Avery around the time the women were subpoenaed that he felt obliged, "in all fairness," to warn him that his clients were "targets" of the grand jury; in other words, they were likely to be prosecuted, although he would not say for what crime. Avery passed this news on to the women, and explained to them that the only way they could legally refuse to testify would be by pleading their Fifth Amendment right not to speak on the ground that whatever they said might incriminate them. But even a Fifth Amendment plea would not secure their right of silence for long, Avery went on, because the Department of Justice could ask the court to grant them immunity against any future prosecution based on their testimony. Once a grant of immunity was offered them and the court ordered them to answer all questions asked by the prosecutor in the presence of the grand jury, he explained, their refusal to answer would amount to contempt of court.

If they refused to testify, it would be up to the government to decide whether to prosecute them for civil or criminal contempt. And under the law civil contempt may be more harshly punished than criminal contempt, for in criminal-contempt cases where the government asks for a sentence of more than six months defendants have a right to trial by jury, whereas in civil-contempt cases recalcitrant witnesses can be sent off to prison immediately, with no more than a judge's order, and can be kept locked up until either they agree to talk or the term of the grand jury expires. In the present case, the grand-jury term was to exire on April 1st — slightly more than two months away. Moreover, if the women refused to coöperate with the government and were found in contempt and imprisoned, once they were released they could be again subpoenaed to appear before a newly impanelled grand jury, and if they again refused to talk they could be sent back to prison for the life of the new grand jury — ordinarily eighteen months. The civil-contempt provision under current law is so unclear that conceivably the courts could rule that recalcitrant witnesses must spend the rest of their lives in prison without ever having been charged, tried, or convicted of a crime. But Avery's interpretation of the law had convinced him that his clients couldn't be imprisoned for more than eighteen months altogether, no matter how many grand juries they refused to testify before on this issue. In any event, Avery told them that Dow had warned him he meant to have them cited for contempt and jailed if they were granted immunity and refused to testify, would subpoena them again to appear before the succeeding grand jury, and would send them back to jail once more.

Grusse and Turgeon decided to take their chances. "We have an absolute moral belief that the investigation the government is engaged in will violate our basic constitutional and human rights," they stated in a press release that they put out shortly afterward to explain their reasons for refusing to testify. "We believe that the right to privacy and confidentiality in human relationships goes beyond those traditionally recognized confidences such as attorney-client, spouse-to-spouse, doctor-patient, etc. We believe that every person has the right to keep her affairs private without intervention by government agents. . . . Although we fear the complete loss of freedom and dignity that [imprisonment] holds for us, we feel strongly that it is imperative to insist on our fundamental rights and to halt the chain of invasions that is perpetuated by coöperation with government abuse of power." As absolute as their moral belief was and as just as their cause may have seemed to them, they didn't have a scrap of law on their side.

Avery and Polan worked all afternoon and evening and far into the night preparing three motions on the women's behalf. The first asked the presiding judge to quash the subpoenas. The second asked the judge to delay the witnesses' appearance before the grand jury in order to give them time to prepare a legal position on the issue. And the third asked the judge to instruct the grand jury that it "is not subservient to the United States Attorney but has its own independent responsibility for calling witnesses and issuing indictments; that witnesses have an absolute right to assert the Fifth Amendment prior to any grant of immunity to compel testimony, and the grand jurors are to draw no inference from the exercise of Fifth Amendment rights; that witnesses have the right to leave the room to consult with their attorneys, and the grand jurors are to draw no inference from such actions; [and] that the grand jury can decline to question a recalcitrant witness, and thereby not compel her to choose between violation of her conscience by testifying or sentence to jail."

Avery completed the motions just before Grusse and Turgeon arrived at nine o'clock on the morning of January 28th at his office – a small, plainly furnished suite of rooms that he shared with two partners in an old building a few blocks from the federal court. They walked with Avery to the post office – where the District Court, the U.S. Attorney's office, and the grand-jury room were situated on the second floor. He asked the women to wait in the anteroom of the U.S Attorney's office while he had a talk with Dow to see if he had changed his mind about demanding their testimony. As Avery later stated in court, when he entered Dow's office he found him with David Miller, the F.B.I. agent in charge of the Saxe-Power investigation in Connecticut. Dow immediately told Avery that he had been wrong the day before when he said that Grusse and Turgeon were targets of the grand-jury investigation, and added, "I have had a further conversation with the F.B.I. agent, and all [he] really wanted to do is talk to these women, and if they will talk to Mr. Miller – and you can even be present – that will be the end of the matter." Avery replied that his clients refused to talk to any government official about their personal lives and rejected the offer.

District Court Judge Jon O. Newman (who had served for five years as U.S. Attorney in Hartford before being appointed to the federal bench by President Nixon in 1972) agreed to hear Avery's motions and oral arguments from both sides on the issues raised. During the hearing, Judge Newman contemptuously dismissed Avery's arguments, formally denied his motions, and ordered the witnesses to be ready to testify before the grand jury at 2 P.M. It was then nearly twelve-thirty, and Avery pointed out that he had a trial before Judge Newman starting at two o'clock, and could not be both in court and outside the grand-jury room to advise his clients at the same time. The Judge brushed aside that argument, too, and ordered the trial to commence as scheduled and Grusse and Turgeon to be in the U.S. Attorney's office at two o'clock.

The only local lawyer Avery could think of to take his place outside the grand-jury room was a young man by the name of David Rosen, who was also a graduate of Yale Law School and had offices in Avery's building. As it turned out, Rosen was off on business in Bridgeport, but when Avery finally tracked him down by telephone Rosen said he would drive back to New Haven immediately. He arrived at Avery's office at one-forty-five, which gave Avery only fifteen minutes in which to brief him on the case during their walk to the post office. "That is what we call 'due process of law,' " Avery said later. At two o'clock, Grusse, Turgeon, and Rosen were waiting outside the grand-jury room, in a marble-floored hallway around the corner from the courtroom of the federal District Court.

Grusse was summoned before the grand jury first, and she entered the chamber — a large room with a T-shaped table — to find Dow seated at the head of the T and the grand jurors, twenty-three as required by federal law, seated to his right and left and down both sides of the leg of the T, as well as in chairs along two walls of the room. Grusse was directed to the witness chair, at the foot of the T, next to a court stenotypist. "The atmosphere was very intimidating," Grusse said afterward. "The room was crowded and stuffy, and when I sat down and saw the stenotypist beside me ready to take down my every word and all those grand jurors staring at me I was scared — very scared. I had been able to build up some confidence and strength before I went in there, but the whole thing was so terrifying that I lost most of my nerve right away."

To regain control of herself, Grusse began concentrating on Rosen's advice. He had warned the two women that if they answered any questions besides what their names were, they might thereby waive their Fifth Amendment right and have to answer all questions asked them. Called "opening the door" by lawyers, this kind of waiver was established by only one federal-court case, and has not been fully tested judicially, but is still accepted as a rule.

In any event, Rosen had suggested that they not refuse to answer each question on Fifth Amendment grounds as soon as it was asked but that they write down each question, appear to hesitate over whether or not they should answer it, and then ask if they might go outside to confer with their lawyer. By this means, he explained, they would have a chance to learn what Dow's purpose and the scope of the grand jury's inquiry were. If they answered all the questions by immediately "taking the Fifth," Rosen warned them, Dow would probably stop after the second or third question and excuse them.

Grusse's voice shook when she gave her name, and then Dow asked his first question – her address. Grusse wrote down the question and asked if she could consult her lawyer before answering. Dow nodded, almost imperceptibly, to the foreman of the grand jury, who gave the permission, and Grusse rose and walked outside to where Rosen and Turgeon were waiting. She handed Rosen the piece of paper she had written the question on; he glanced at it and handed her another piece of paper, on which he had written the answer. She looked at it distractedly and said, "God, it's terrible in there – terrible." Turgeon put an arm around Grusse's shoulder and murmured a few words of encouragement to her.

Returning to the grand-jury room, Grusse sat down and read the answer Rosen had prepared: "I decline to answer the question. I have been advised by my lawyer that if I answer this question I will have waived my right to refuse to answer other questions. I am basing my refusal to answer on my right not to give evidence which might tend to incriminate myself, which right is secured to me by the Fifth Amendment to the Constitution of the United States."

There was a long silence, during which Dow and most of the grand jurors stared at her. She tried to return their looks firmly, but her courage failed her, and she looked down at the table. The silence – especially the silence of the stenotype machine, above which Grusse could see the court reporter's fingers poised – was nearly unendurable, and she gulped in relief when Dow finally went on to his next question: whether she knew Susan Edith Saxe, by name or alias. Again she went outside, and came back to give the same answer. She was then asked the same question about Katherine Ann Power, and went through the same procedure. Dow asked her to identify photographs of the fugitives, which she declined to do. Then he asked whether she had ever met various women at a certain address in Hartford — women whom he identified only by their first names — and she again took the Fifth. Finally, Dow had a brief whispered conversation with the foreman, who nodded and dismissed the witness. Turgeon was asked fewer questions, and was released after spending a dozen minutes in and out of the hearing room.

In the end, Rosen and Avery concluded that the questions asked the two women were based on nothing more than suspicion — especially since Dow knew only the first names of women the witnesses may have been associated with — and that the grand jury was being improperly used as an investigative body. Even so, had either witness answered any of the questions incorrectly, she could have been prosecuted for perjury. And had she answered in the affirmative the key question put to her — whether she knew Saxe and Power — the next question undoubtedly would have been whether she knew that they were wanted for bank robbery and murder; in answering *that,* she might have implicated herself and admitted that she had committed misprision of felony in not notifying the police. Of course, many ordinary citizens are probably unaware of the law on misprision or of various other obscure laws that can be used against them when they are, as far as they know, innocent of any crime. But since grand juries are not obliged to inform witnesses what the inquiry under way consists of and whether or not the witness is a suspect and subject to indictment, even the most guiltless person who is called before a grand jury may run afoul of the law by failing to claim the Fifth Amendment right to remain silent. The legal principle stating that ignorance of the law is no excuse may be essential to the support of our criminal-law system, for without it anyone could plead that he hadn't known a given act was legally a crime and get off. But ignorance of the law clearly *is* an excuse in many circumstances, because no one can know the millions of laws on the books in this country, and if one is denied the right to have a lawyer present, then one is intentionally being kept ignorant of the law and afterward is subject to its penalties.

Afterward, Avery and Rosen (who remained in the case as co-counsel from this point on) warned Grusse and Turgeon that Dow would probably ask the Department of Justice to request immunity against prosecution for the two women in exchange for their testimony and would recall them before the grand jury. Under the so-called use-immunity law — enacted by Congress during the Nixon Administration years — once prospective witnesses are given immunity they can't be prosecuted for anything they say under oath, except for perjury if they are subsequently shown to have lied. But they can still be prosecuted for the crimes they are questioned about as long as the prosecution is wholly based on evidence obtained independently of their testimony. The most pernicious flaw in the immunity law exists when two witnesses are involved, as in the case at hand: while Grusse's testimony could not be used to incriminate Grusse and Turgeon's testimony could not be used to incriminate Turgeon, Grusse's testimony could be used to incriminate Turgeon and Turgeon's testimony could be used to incriminate Grusse — that is, if either had done anything incriminating to begin with. In other words, the lawyers explained, if the government granted the witnesses use immunity, their ordeal had only begun.

Late that afternoon, Turgeon and Grusse returned to their apartment in a state of exhaustion, bewilderment, and fear. "Everything was up in the air," Turgeon said later. "We had no idea what would happen or when it would happen. We didn't know whether the threats of immunity and contempt and jail were real or not. We didn't know anything, and had even thought we might be arrested that very day when we refused to talk. And that night, after our appearance before the grand jury, there was real terror for us. We thought maybe they'd come and drag us out of bed and throw us in jail. We were terrified. We called the lawyers, and they assured us that the government couldn't do anything like that, and promised us that they would protect our rights at each step of the way. But we still didn't know what to believe. We couldn't see that we had any rights, and the government seemed so vicious and relentless that we thought it could do anything. That was the real horror — not knowing, trying to live hour by hour, day by day, and constantly fearing what would finally come."

The two women got little sleep that night, but by the next morning they felt somewhat more relaxed. They rose early, and Grusse went to peek through the curtains to see if anyone was outside guarding the place or keeping it under surveillance. There was no sign of anyone. They had breakfast, and then began discussing a suggestion that Avery had made the day before — that they create publicity about their case in order to deter the government from behaving as capriciously as it might if no one was aware of the case, and to gain public support and perhaps some financial help. "We were very worried about what it would do to our personal lives if we went public," Grusse said. "We are both very private people. For myself, just having my name known out there really frightens me. But we wanted people to understand what was happening to us and what the issues were — the people in the women's community here first and then people throughout the country. It was a hard decision to make. Finally, we decided we had to sacrifice ourselves in order to save ourselves and maybe help some others."

Once the two women decided to make their case known to the general public, they agreed to a proposal made by some of their supporters in the women's community — that a Grand Jury Defense Committee be set up in New Haven to generate the publicity they sought, to get people to attend their court appearances as a means of discouraging the kind of high-handed official behavior that often characterizes unpublicized court proceedings, to educate local citizens about *their* rights, and to raise funds for the defense. In line with this overall strategy, Grusse and Turgeon put out their press release, which recounted the story of the F.B.I.'s search for Saxe and Power, presented the basic reasons for not talking to the F.B.I. about personal matters, accused the government of illegally invading their privacy and improperly using the grand jury as an investigative tool, and concluded:

What makes us most angry is that we have been forced into a position of playing the Man's games, the rules of which deny us our basic rights, dignity, and responsibility and control over our own lives. In reality, it is not very different from the everyday life of every woman living with the fear of rape, brutalization by men, defining herself through her "man," etc. We feel that giving information to the F.B.I. gives in to the power that they hold over us, a power that perpetuates women's position and the position of all oppressed peoples.

A couple of days later, Grusse and Turgeon distributed the release among members of the New Haven community and the press. "Before long, we were appalled by how public we had become," Grusse said later. "It had never occurred to us when we decided to go public that it would become known we were lesbians. That clearly had nothing to do with the case, and we felt that it was the worst imaginable invasion of our privacy. But within a matter of days everyone knew about us. Our lives were spread out in the papers, over radio, on television — everywhere."

At the same time that Grusse and Turgeon began trying to exert pressure on the government to leave them alone, the government began trying to exert more pressure on them to coöperate with it. Two days after the women appeared before the grand jury, an F.B.I. man turned up at the home of Turgeon's parents to question them about their daughter Terri. The elder Turgeons weren't at home, but one of their two other daughters, Madeleine, was, and once the agent learned that she was there alone he began questioning her intensively about her sister Terri. Madeleine was flustered and alarmed, and, as she later recounted in an affidavit, "The F.B.I. agent did not say what he was looking for, except that he wanted to find two women about whom my sister might have information. . . . He asked me if I was close to my sister and if we confided in each other about our personal and private lives. He later told me that my sister was now living with another woman, named Ellen Grusse, and he said he knew a great deal about their personal and private lives together, implying that my sister was a lesbian. After he revealed this detail of my sister's personal life, he said that his visit to me would not have been necessary if my sister had coöperated with him. He also encouraged me to put pressure on my sister to coöperate with his investigation, and said to me, 'It would be good for someone to get her to co-operate with us.' "

When the agent left, saying that he would come back to talk to her parents, the woman was so upset by what he had told her that she decided she had better tell her parents about Terri rather than have him spring the news on them unexpectedly. The Turgeons were hurt by the story about their daughter's life and stunned by her supposed involvement with criminals. As it happened, the F.B.I. man never returned to question the Turgeons, and the suspense of waiting for him increased their torment. Mr. Turgeon, in fact, was in such a state of anguish that he could not bear to speak to Terri about the case. Her sister telephoned her and begged her to stay out of trouble and to do whatever the government wanted. Terri promised to come over to see them in a few days to explain what had happened and why she was doing what she was. Then she asked that the family stand by her. "I need help," she said. "I need help very badly."

A few days later, the same F.B.I. man appeared at the office where Turgeon's other sister, Judy, worked in a suburb of Hartford. He asked the girl about her sister's private life, friends, acquaintances, and habits. "My co-workers were present during the course of this thirty-minute interview," she stated in an affidavit. "At several times during the interview, the F.B.I. agent said in a loud voice, 'I wouldn't have to bother you if your sister wasn't so uncoöperative.' After I answered one particular question, the agent indicated that he did not believe me, thus questioning my truthfulness in the presence of my co-workers."

F.B.I. agents also questioned two uncles of Turgeon's in Lewiston, Maine, and a cousin in Baltimore. And four agents turned up just before midnight at the North Carolina home of a man and woman who were living together and whom Grusse and Turgeon had visited some months earlier on a holiday trip to the South. The four agents — who were apparently under the impression that Grusse was Saxe, although there was no resemblance between the two women — split up into two-man teams and questioned the man and woman separately, simultaneously, and intensively for nearly an hour. "They were terrified," Grusse reported later. "It was the midnight knock on the door."

Before long, Turgeon's family rallied to her support, and stood by her throughout what was to be a long and increasingly harrowing ordeal. "My father didn't understand what was happening at first," Turgeon said. "But when our lawyer wasn't allowed into the grand-jury room to protect us, Dad thought that was unfair. After all, in America you're always supposed to have the right to a lawyer. Then my father met some of my friends, some of whom are professional people and very impressive, and he learned that long hair and beards and strange clothes don't matter. And the government's continuing persecution of me finally outraged him, and now he's radicalized by this case, just the way that I and many of my friends have been."

Grusse's family, on the other hand, were unable to understand or sympathize with her plight. "My parents didn't see the larger political picture or the basic issues involved, and they just wanted to protect me," she said. "They kept saying to me, 'Talk to the grand jury and stay out of jail.' That was a strong and constant pressure on me. It caused a temporary break in my relations with them. They tried to understand — they really wanted to help me — but they simply couldn't grasp it all. They think these things don't happen to good, honest people. And the fact that I am a lesbian was too much for them. It put them in a position where it was emotionally difficult for them to support me. Their view was that the United States government always acts in the best interests of the people. That is a view I don't share. For them, the law and the Constitution are there to protect *us,* Terri and me, and *we* are abusing both — not the other way around, as we believe. Anyway, the women's community here is also my family now. Its members have supported us strongly most of the way. At first, a few of them said to me that maybe this case — the hunt for two fugitives wanted for bank robbery and murder — wasn't the issue to take a stand on against the government. After all, they said, those are very serious crimes. I agree with that. But I answered that unfortunately I hadn't had any choice in the matter, that the government had handed me the issue. Since *I* hadn't done anything wrong, I had to stand up now, or I would never be able to stand up to anything or anybody in the future. Then they understood."

A few of Grusse and Turgeon's friends were so frightened by the F.B.I. and the publicity surrounding the case that they avoided the two women. "Some of them are terrified by the whole thing," Grusse said. "They're frightened by the stigma of being publicly known as lesbians, the way we are now, so they live very privately, even secretly, to hide their lives from their families and employers. And now they're afraid of the political stigma, too. It used to be that lesbians were thought of as merely being perverted, but now they're seen as bank robbers and murderers or, at best, as friends and abettors of bank robbers and murderers. We believe that this is the government's basic motive — to intimidate women in the movement, to create fear among us, to split us up, and finally to destroy the women's movement. The best way to do that is by making the innocent seem guilty."

On February 5, 1975, the Department of Justice formally granted the U.S. Attorney's office in Connecticut permission to apply to the court for an order giving Grusse and Turgeon immunity. The letter from the Department conveying official permission to seek the grant was received and filed in the U.S. Attorney's office in New Haven on February 10th, and at six-thirty on the morning of the twelfth the U.S. marshal reappeared at the apartment shared by Grusse and Turgeon and served them with a new set of subpoenas, which ordered them to appear before the grand jury at ten o'clock the following morning. When they telephoned Avery, he told them that Judge Newman would undoubtedly grant the immunity requested before they were questioned by the grand jury the next day, and added, "They are going to send you to jail."

Later that day, Avery went to have a talk with Dow, in the slim hope that he might persuade him to drop the case. Avery told him that as a matter of public policy the government, with its immense power, should yield to the minute power of the individual when the opposition was so passionate and principled, as it clearly was in this case. Avery had little hope that this argument would prevail, though, and said privately, "I don't think the government will do that. It won't back off until its losses exceed its gains. The people who run the government should try to relieve democratic tensions when they can in order to preserve the system. But they don't see things that way, even though it's in their own self-interest. If the government is ever toppled, it will be its own officials who bring it down."

Dow refused to listen to any suggestion that he alter his course. "A policeman was killed, and left nine kids," he said.

Grusse and Turgeon dreaded even the thought of going to prison, and kept hoping that the government would finally see that they were innocent and determined to remain silent. "Justice needn't be tempered with mercy — it should simply be fair," Grusse said. "If the government believes we are guilty of something, then it should charge us, take us to trial, and give us a chance to defend ourselves. That would be justice."

"I don't think we've done anything wrong," Turgeon added. "We haven't committed any crime. Our stand is solely a matter of principle with us. We are two innocent women, and yet we have the whole United States government against us."

II

Late in 1637, an English Puritan by the name of John Lilburne was arrested for importing seditious books from Holland into England. From the government's viewpoint, the arrest was to prove a calamitous mistake, for Lilburne, who was then a twenty-three-year-old clothier's apprentice with little formal education, turned out to be one of the most stunningly effective revolutionaries in English history. A volatile, contentious, unyielding, self-righteous, and abrasive man, of whom a contemporary said, "If John Lilburne were the last man in the world, John would fight with Lilburne and Lilburne with John," he was also, as he described himself, "an honest, true-bred, freeborn Englishman that never in his life loved a tyrant nor feared an oppressor." By the time he died, twenty years later, Lilburne had brought the British government to its knees.

After his arrest, Lilburne was turned over to the Attorney General, who assigned an aide to question him. The aide told Lilburne what he was charged with and informed him that a confederate had sworn to an affidavit against him. Lilburne replied that he had indeed visited Holland and that he had talked to some people and looked at some books there, but he claimed that he was innocent of the charge against him, and refused to say more about the affair. "I see you go about by this examination to ensnare me, for seeing [that] the things for which I am imprisoned cannot be proved against me, you will get other matter out of my examination," he said. The aide finally gave up and passed Lilburne on to the Attorney General, who had no more luck and sent him back to jail.

A couple of weeks afterward, Lilburne was taken before the Court of Star Chamber — an inquisitorial body that functioned as the sovereign's personal tribunal for trying matters of state. A clerk handed him a Bible and told him to swear by it.

"To what?" Lilburne asked.

"That you shall make true answer to all things that are asked of you," the clerk said.

"Must I so, sir? But before I swear, I will know to what I must swear."

"As soon as you have sworn, you shall, but not before."

Lilburne refused to take the oath, was sent back to prison, and a few weeks later was again brought before the Star Chamber, this time for trial, together with an alleged accomplice, an elderly bookseller named John Wharton. The Attorney General charged them with refusal to take the required oath, and then read the affidavit against them. Declaring that the charge was "a most false lie and untrue," Lilburne once more refused to take the oath, as did Wharton, and the two were returned to their cells. A week later, they were brought back for trial before the same court, and repeated their refusal to take the oath, which, Lilburne told his judges, was "both against the law of God and the law of the land." This time, the Star Chamber found them guilty of contempt, and sentenced them to fines of five hundred pounds each, punishment in the pillory, and imprisonment until they took the oath and testified as ordered; Lilburne was additionally sentenced to be whipped through the streets on the way from Fleet prison to the pillory, a distance of two miles. Tied to the back of a cart and stripped to the waist, he was lashed every few steps by an executioner wielding a three-thonged whip, and at the end the prisoner's shoulders "were swelled almost as big as a penny loaf," a contemporary reported, and the "wales on his back . . . were bigger than tobacco pipes." The streets along Lilburne's route were lined with spectators, who moaned at his agony and shouted words of encouragement. Once in the pillory, Lilburne dumbfounded everyone by proceeding, despite his pain, to deliver a stirring half-hour oration to the crowd, which was spellbound by the account of his ordeal, including his trial, which, he told them, was "absolutely against the law of God, for that law requires no man to accuse himself."

The oath that Lilburne refused to take was known as the oath ex officio, which had an ancient lineage reaching back to the thirteenth-century oath *de veritate dicenda* — swearing to speak the truth in answer to all questions. This device, an invention of the Catholic Church in 1215, had become one of the most feared instruments of the Inquisition's attempts to stamp out heresy, and was subsequently used by a long series of British clerics and British monarchs to suppress religious and political unorthodoxy. Suspects who were given the oath were not told the evidence of their misdeeds, the identity of their accusers, or the charges against them. If they refused to take the oath, they were considered guilty of the offenses being investigated; if they took the oath and lied, they were guilty of perjury, and swearing falsely was not only a grave sin against God but was taken as evidence of guilt in the offenses at issue; and, of course, if they told the truth they might condemn themselves. In short, the oath had one purpose: to trap witnesses into betraying themselves and others.

Official reliance on the oath — and the physical and mental torture often inflicted on those who resisted it — became so widespread and abusive in England that bitter opposition to it rose among members of Parliament and of the common-law bar, who saw the overweening power of royal and ecclesiastical courts as a threat to both the common law and all free Englishmen. Protests were mounted, petitions were signed, and early in the fourteenth century Parliament outlawed the oath. Both Crown and Church ignored the prohibition. Throughout the remainder of that century, opponents of the inquisitorial system fought for its replacement by the common law's accusatorial system, through which the state had to prove an accused person's guilt without his assistance and under prescribed rules. To this end, they repeatedly invoked Magna Carta, then over a century old, and contended that its command to the sovereign to obey "the law of the land" guaranteed everyone accused of any crime the right to a formal accusation and to a trial by jury under common-law procedures. There was no justification whatever for the claim, but the myth that Magna Carta spoke for the freedom of all men of the realm and not, as it clearly had, solely for the rights of the barons who forced King John to sign the document at Runnymede was to survive and ultimately to be widely accepted as fact. And, of course, history has repeatedly demonstrated that myth is a far more powerful influence in human affairs than truth.

During the sixteenth century, resistance to use of the oath in the Court of Star Chamber and its ecclesiastical equivalent, the Court of High Commission, mounted. Sir Thomas More, who as Lord Chancellor had compelled many heretics to take the oath ex officio and had sent them to their deaths for what they revealed, refused to take the oath himself and reveal why he opposed Henry VIII's claim to be head of the Church in England. More argued that he was being forced to condemn either his soul (if he lied) or his body (if he told the truth); the dilemma was resolved when the King had him beheaded and the Church made him a saint. A few years later, Mary Tudor devoted most of her five years on the throne to wiping out all traces of Protestantism by killing Protestants. Not long after her death, John Foxe wrote *The Book of Martyrs,* which recounted the history of Christian martyrdom since the eleventh century, including the fate of Bloody Mary's victims. He described how innocent people in her reign were ordered to answer on oath all questions about their beliefs and associations, were tortured if they resisted, were forced to accuse themselves and their friends and relatives of crimes that often had not been committed, and then were burned alive at the stake. *The Book of Martyrs* went through many revised and expanded editions, and it became a sort of primer of the theory that there was an inherent personal right to freedom of religious conscience, and that there were also inviolable legal rights such as the guarantee of a formal accusation and a fair trial, and the right to refuse, as Lilburne was to refuse some eighty years later, to incriminate oneself. For over a century, *The Book of Martyrs* was, after the Bible, the most popular book in the English-speaking world.

Around the time that Foxe's book was first published, Chief Justice James Dyer ruled for a unanimous Court of Common Pleas that a witness who refused to take the oath ex officio was justified by the maxim *"Nemo tenetur prodere seipsum,"* or "No man is bound to betray himself." This appears to have been the first common-law use of the principle that was to be embodied more than two centuries later in the Fifth Amendment to the United States Constitution: "No person shall be . . . compelled in any criminal case to be a witness against himself." According to Professor Leonard W. Levy's splendid book *Origins of the Fifth Amendment* (the basic work on the subject, winner of the Pulitzer Prize for history in 1969, and the source for this historical résumé), Chief Justice Dyer's ruling was apparently aimed at Queen Elizabeth, to discourage her from following Mary Tudor's oppressive example. As it turned out, Elizabeth's aims were somewhat different from her predecessor's, for under Good Queen Bess's rule subjects were persecuted for political rather than religious heresy when they persisted in clinging to religious beliefs that denied supremacy of the state in matters both mundane and religious. "Politics, rather than religion, had become the basis of government policy," Professor Levy explained, and added that while the distinction may have seemed slight to those who were executed, it contributed a small advance to the English legal system, for although they underwent inquisitorial examinations at the hands of the Star Chamber or the High Commission, at least they were later tried under the common law's accusatorial system.

More and more Catholics and Protestants responded to the Queen's determination to bring their God to his knees before the throne with the plea *"Nemo tenetur prodere seipsum,"* which by now was popularly believed to be a firm principle of Magna Carta, too. They still went to their gory deaths – not at the stake but at the gibbet, where they were hanged, cut down while alive, and disembowelled — and yet their claims that all subjects possessed a natural right against compulsory self-incrimination slowly began taking hold in the minds of lawyers and judges. Originally, resistance to forced self-betrayal had developed as an outgrowth of religious conscience, but as the use of the oath ex officio became secular so did the resistance to it, and gradually a belief emerged that to force a man to inform on himself not only violated the natural law of self-preservation but destroyed his dignity and self-respect and undermined justice itself. However, official acceptance of this view was still many years away.

Lilburne's bravery while being whipped through the streets and his dramatic speech while locked in the pillory made him famous throughout London overnight. In retaliation, the Star Chamber judges ordered that he be "laid alone with irons on his hands and legs . . . where the basest and meanest sort" of prisoners were kept, and that he be denied all books, writing materials, and visitors. His warders went further by chaining him to the bare floor, without the usual pallet, and giving him no food for ten days. Suffering from his beating and a high fever that followed it, Lilburne would probably have died if his fellow-prisoners hadn't slipped food to him through cracks in the floor. He recovered from his illness, and after four months in solitary confinement he was transferred to a more hospitable part of the prison, where he was confined for the next two and a half years. During this period, he secretly wrote and smuggled out of prison nine pamphlets attacking the Star Chamber and demanding the natural rights due every Englishman. With the appearance of each pamphlet, which the authorities were unable to suppress, Lilburne's popularity soared anew.

Charles I was on the throne, and his inept policies were bringing England closer to civil war by the day. Desperately in need of money to raise an army and defend himself, he called Parliament into session in 1640 — the first time he had allowed it to sit in eleven years — but when its members refused to appropriate funds until he agreed to their demands for reform, he dissolved the session, known as the Short Parliament, after three weeks. A little later, a Scottish force defeated a royalist army and occupied the north of England, and then a London mob of two thousand people broke into and sacked the hated Court of High Commission. A few days afterward, Charles called Parliament into session again – in the Long Parliament, which was to sit, with intermissions, for twenty years – as his only hope of getting money to save his crown. The Long Parliament was dominated by Puritans, one of whom was Oliver Cromwell, a newly elected member from Cambridge, whose maiden speech was a plea for the release of John Lilburne. A few days later, popular support forced the King to free Lilburne, who immediately began demanding an end to the Courts of Star Chamber and High Commission and abolition of the oath ex officio. Petitions in support of his stand poured into the House of Commons from around the country, and the following summer Parliament enacted a bill outlawing the two courts and the oath, which the King reluctantly signed on July 5, 1641. After four centuries of torment and bloodshed, the inquisitorial power of church and state seemed at an end.

In 1642, the outbreak of civil war – fought to determine whether England would be ruled by Parliament or the Crown – brought Lilburne into the Parliamentary army as a captain. He was fiercely devoted to the popular cause, and was as fearless a soldier as he had been a pamphleteer. During a battle, he was captured and sentenced to death for treason, but when Parliament sent word that it would execute a batch of royalist prisoners if he was harmed, Lilburne was freed. He returned to London, where immense crowds greeted him, a contemporary reported, "with public joy, as a champion that had defied the King." Lilburne turned down Parliament's offer of a high post, saying that he would "rather fight for eightpence a day, till he saw the liberties and peace of England settled, than set him down in a rich place for his own advantage." Returning to the front, he soon became a lieutenant-colonel and a confidant of Cromwell's. In time, though, Lilburne grew alarmed by the anti-libertarian spirit that was overtaking the Puritan movement, which was becoming as tyrannically repressive as any British monarch. Presbyterians controlled Parliament, and they began demanding that their faith replace the Anglican Church as the official state religion and that various other forms of Puritanism, which contained scores of factions and schisms, be suppressed.

These new demands for orthodoxy were too much for Lilburne, and after Parliament awarded itself the power to censor all publications in England, he quit the army and went back to pamphleteering. He was soon in trouble again — this time for attacking religious persecution in general and censorship in particular — and after one of his pamphlets appeared he was summoned before the House of Commons' Committee on Investigation, which found the tract "scurrilous, libellous, and seditious." According to Professor Levy, Lilburne was let off because of his great popularity and his service to the Parliamentary cause, but he refused to remain silent, and was soon arrested and dragged back before the committee for libelling the Speaker of the House in print. Determined to challenge the right of Parliament to inquire into his opinions or to force him to accuse himself, Lilburne refused to testify, and demanded that the legislature obey the rules of common-law courts. The committee rejected his demand, and when Lilburne persisted in refusing to testify and claimed "a right to all the privileges that do belong to a free man as [to] the greatest man in England," he was sent back to prison. Taking up his pen again, Lilburne wrote a furious tract accusing the committee of trying "criminal causes betwixt man and man concerning life, liberty, estate" without observing the ordinary rules of justice. The committee summoned him again, and again he refused to testify and was sent back to his cell. But the Parliamentary army considered Lilburne one of its own, and its mutinous mutterings about his treatment finally prompted Cromwell to persuade Parliament to let Lilburne go after he had served four months in jail.

The following year, Lilburne was arrested and taken before the House of Lords for criticizing one of its members in another pamphlet, and he refused to testify before that august body. He was thrown back in jail and then ordered to reappear before the

Lords to be tried for his pamphlet. Lilburne refused to go, and had to be dragged there. Once before the assemblage, he not only refused to kneel but stopped up his ears so that he couldn't hear the charges against him. He was found guilty, fined two thousand pounds (more than most Englishmen could earn in a lifetime), disqualified for life from holding any public office, and imprisoned indefinitely in the Tower of London. "By its injudicious treatment of the most popular man in England," a historian of that period observed, "Parliament was araying against itself a force which only awaited an opportunity to sweep it away." By the following spring, Cromwell's army was said to be "one Lilburne throughout," and its soldiers regarded his writings not as commentaries on the law but as the law itself. Under pressure from the army, Parliament released Lilburne in 1648, and he immediately set about attacking Cromwell himself.

After enduring the attacks for several months, Cromwell dispatched a force of two hundred armed men, who surrounded Lilburne's house, arrested him, and dragged him and three friends before the Council of State. The prosecutor asked him whether he had written the defamatory pamphlet against Cromwell. Lilburne, retorting that he was amazed after all that had happened that such a question could even be asked, declined to answer. He and his friends were taken out of the room, and Cromwell pounded on the table and shouted at his colleagues, "I tell you, sirs, you have no other way to deal with these men but to break them in pieces. . . . If you do not break them, they will break you!" Committed to the Tower on suspicion of high treason, Lilburne wrote and smuggled out one fiery pamphlet after another, and soon petitions with tens of thousands of signatures supporting him poured into Parliament, and the army threatened to revolt. In Cromwell's view, "the kingdom could never be settled so long as Lilburne was alive," and in the fall of 1649 he was charged with high treason and put on trial for his life.

The trial took place in London before an Extraordinary Commission of Oyer and Terminer, made up of eight common-law judges, four sergeants-at-law, the recorder of the city, twenty-six special judges (including some city aldermen and members of

Parliament), and the Lord Mayor. The trial was held in the great Guildhall, the streets around it were lined with troops to prevent demonstrations against the government, and Lilburne was kept under constant guard to prevent his rescue by the angry crowds that gathered throughout the city to protest what was being done to the man they knew as "Freeborn John." Although Lilburne had no legal training, he soon demonstrated to the court his forensic abilities. "His great achievement at the trial was holding at bay the judges and . . . his prosecutor while he expounded to them and to his fellow-citizens in the jury box and in the audience the fundamentals of fair criminal procedure from the time of arrest through trial," Professor Levy wrote. "He placed the right against self-incrimination in the context of what he called 'fair play,' 'fair trial,' 'the due process of the law,' and 'the good old laws of England.' "

Lilburne railed on endlessly over the smallest points of law and legal procedure. He insisted on having a copy of the indictment and a lawyer to represent him (rights that were still half a century in the future), and when he was refused both he said, "Then order me to be knocked on the head immediately in the place where I stand, without any further trial, for I must needs be destroyed if you deny me all the means of my preservation." When the presiding judge begged him to be silent and promised, "Hear me one word, and you shall have two," Lilburne retorted that since he was on trial for his life he must be free to speak, and if they would neither let him speak nor allow a lawyer to speak for him they might as well murder him and get it over with. "O Lord!" he cried, "was there ever such a pack of unjust and unrighteous judges in the world?" The chief judge sternly told him that no one had ever been tried by "so many grave judges of the law," whereupon Lilburne denounced the proceedings for being extraordinary, and asserted that he would rather have been tried by one judge in an ordinary court of law. The chief judge replied, "If you had not had this great presence of the court, you would have outtalked them, but you cannot do so here." Lilburne raised himself up indignantly and said, "Truly, sir, I am not daunted at the multitude of my judges, neither at the glittering of your scarlet robes, nor the majesty of your presence and harsh, austere deportment towards me. I bless my good God for it, who gives me courage and boldness." He defiantly refused to answer any questions about his authorship of the pamphlet at issue, on the ground that under the good old laws of England he could not be compelled to accuse himself. Then he triumphantly pointed out to the jury that his indictment was based partly on a pamphlet that had been published while he was in the Tower — that is, after his arrest — while the law making such statements as those in the pamphlet treasonous had been passed during his imprisonment, making it an illegal ex-post-facto use of the law.

When Lilburne finally rested for the defense, the audience broke out in loud shouts of "Amen! Amen!" and, a report on the event noted, these were followed by "an extraordinary great hum," which so alarmed the judges and the military commander in charge that three more companies of soldiers were dispatched to guard the hall. The chief judge then delivered a hanging charge, in which he accused Lilburne of fomenting a plot the likes of which "never . . . was seen in the world before." The jury was out for an hour and returned to find Lilburne not guilty. "The whole multitude of people in the hall, for joy of the prisoner's acquittal, gave such a loud and unanimous shout, as is believed was never heard in Guildhall, which lasted for about half an hour without intermission," the report said. When word of the verdict spread throughout the city, there were wild public celebrations and "the people caused that night abundance of bonfires to be made all up and down the streets."

In 1651, Lilburne wrote another pamphlet attacking an influential member of Parliament, was summoned before the bar of Commons, convicted without formal accusation or trial, and by means of a bill of attainder was fined seven thousand pounds, banished from England for life, and sentenced to death if he returned. Helpless this time, he fled to Holland. But a year and a half later, when Cromwell dissolved the Rump Parliament that had convicted him, Lilburne assumed that there would be a freer mood at home, and returned to England. He was clapped into

Newgate prison and again put on trial for his life. There were countless demonstrations on his behalf, and petitions circulated around the country came back to London with thousands upon thousands of signatures demanding his release and pardon. The furore led a contemporary to remark, "It is not to be imagined how much esteem he hath got, only for vindicating the laws and liberties against the usurpations of his time." This response, in turn, led Cromwell to clamp a virtual state of martial law on London.

At the trial, held in the Old Bailey, Lilburne argued that the Rump Parliament had been illegally constituted, so the bill of attainder it had enacted must be illegal, too. Then Lilburne solemnly warned the jurors that if he died on Monday, on Tuesday Parliament could pass sentence on every one of them, on their families, on all the people in London, and eventually on everyone in England. The jury found him not guilty. "Joy and acclamation" were said to have resounded for "an English mile," except among members of the Cromwellian party, whose leader was "infinitely enraged." At his direction, Parliament ordered the jurors examined on their verdict before the Council of State, but once there the jurors refused to speak, on the ground of conscience.

Defying the jury's acquittal, Cromwell had Lilburne secretly moved at night from Newgate to the Tower, rejected all writs of habeas corpus, and put the prisoner under such strict guard that he managed to write and smuggle out only one more pamphlet — his last. The government's refusal to free him after he had been found innocent provoked plots against the government and attempts on Cromwell's life. To remove the rebellious symbol from the center of unrest, Cromwell ordered Lilburne taken from the Tower and transported to a fortress on the island of Jersey. The following year, when the tumult over his case had subsided, he was moved to a house in Dover, where he was imprisoned until he died, two years later, at the age of forty-three.

"Lilburne had made the difference," wrote Professor Levy. "From his time on, the right against self-incrimination was an established, respected rule of the common law, or, more broadly, of English law generally." Of far greater importance, though, the fight that Lilburne had led sparked into a conflagration the movement that would ultimately overthrow tyranny — the people's growing belief that each of them possessed a personal right to be free under just laws that had to be obeyed by the highest as well as the lowest person in the realm. The concept of the individual as a being whose self-respect and dignity and privacy were inviolable had been born. According to the historian Margaret Atwood Judson, this movement was "the first great outburst of democratic thought in history, with John Lilburne . . . leading the way."

One of the basic causes of the American Revolution was England's failure to give colonists here the common-law rights that it professed to assure them. Although the common law was extremely reactionary in many ways — it severely restricted freedom of expression, for example, and its courts were used to punish criticisms of church and state long after the Courts of High Commission and Star Chamber were abolished — still the American colonists looked upon that legal system as a shield against official abuse of their basic rights. The slow, diverse, and uncertain growth of the legal protection of those rights under American colonial law is unclear, for, Samuel Eliot Morison has written, "Legal development is probably the least known aspect of American colonial history." Records are fragmentary, and much of the evidence that was recorded is more confusing than enlightening. By the late eighteenth century, however, the specific rights that were to be embodied in the Bill of Rights existed, in one form or another, in colonial laws. After the Declaration of Independence was issued, eight states adopted constitutions that included prohibitions against compulsory self-incrimination. When Representative James Madison, in response to popular demand, submitted a bill of rights to the First Congress, in 1789, his proposed guarantee against forced testimony stated, "No person shall be . . . compelled to be a witness against himself." As far as written records show, Madison said nothing to explain this proposal, either then or later. In order to avoid conflict with a statute setting up the federal-court system, a colleague in the House suggested that the proposal be changed to read, "No person shall be . . . compelled in any criminal case to be a witness against himself," and the alteration was adopted unanimously and, as far as the record shows, without further debate in either house. In 1791, the amendment was approved, along with the rest of the Bill of Rights, and appended to the body of the Constitution.

With this monumental event, Levy — then Earl Warren Professor of Constitutional History at Brandeis University — concluded his account of the Fifth Amendment's origins:

> With good reason the Bill of Rights showed a preoccupation with the subject of criminal justice. The Framers understood that without fair and regularized procedures to protect the criminally accused, there could be no liberty. They knew that from time immemorial, the tyrant's first step was to use the criminal law to crush his opposition. Vicious and *ad hoc* procedures had always been used to victimize nonconformists and minorities of differing religious, racial, or political persuasion. The Fifth Amendment was part and parcel of the procedures that were so crucial, in the minds of the Framers, to the survival of the most treasured rights. One's home could not be his "castle," his property be his own, his right to express his opinions or to worship his God be secure, if he could be searched, arrested, tried, or imprisoned in some arbitrary or ignoble manner. . . . The Framers of the Bill of Rights saw their injunction, that no man should be a witness against himself in a criminal case, as a central feature of the accusatory system of criminal justice. While deeply committed to perpetuating a system that minimized the possibilities of convicting the innocent, they were not less concerned about the humanity that the fundamental law should show even to the offender. Above all, the Fifth Amendment reflected their judgment that in a free society, based on respect for the individual, the determination of guilt or innocence by just procedures, in which the accused made no unwilling contribution to his conviction, was more important than punishing the guilty.

FREEDOM SPENT

In 1803, Chief Justice John Marshall delivered the Supreme Court's opinion in the case of Marbury v. Madison, which made the Court the ultimate arbiter of what the Constitution means by giving the Court the authority to overrule acts of Congress and the executive that violate the nation's fundamental law. Along the way in that case, Marshall ruled for the Court that a witness did not have to answer a question if he felt that his reply might incriminate him. Four years later, Marshall was riding the circuit, as justices then did, and presided over the trial of Aaron Burr for treason, in the Circuit Court for the District of Virginia. When a witness refused to answer a question on the ground of possible self-incrimination (or "crimination," in the usage of the time), the Chief Justice said, "If the question be of such a description that an answer to it may or may not criminate the witness . . . it must rest with himself, who alone can tell what it would be, to answer the question or not. If, in such a case, he say upon his oath that his answer would criminate himself, the court can demand no other testimony of the fact. . . . While that [fact] remains concealed within his own bosom, he is safe; but draw it from thence, and he is exposed to a prosecution. The rule which declares that no man is compellable to accuse himself would most obviously be infringed by compelling a witness to disclose a fact of this description. What testimony may be possessed, or is attainable, against any individual, the court can never know."

For half a century, Chief Justice Marshall's words were taken as the highest judicial support for a witness's absolute right to remain silent. But in 1857 Congress — in an inquiry into charges that some of its members had extorted money from special interests in exchange for favorable legislation — abrogated this right by passing an "immunity" statute that protected any witness who was compelled to testify "before either house of Congress or any committee of either house" from prosecution for "any fact or act touching which he shall have testified." The law uncovered more corruption and provided less opportunity for doing anything about it than anyone had anticipated, because members of Congress and those who had bribed them appeared before the investigating committee, confessed to innumerable crimes of all kinds that they had committed, and were automatically relieved under the new law of any liability for them. Recoiling at these "immunity baths," Congress repealed the law and replaced it in 1862 with a narrower "use immunity" statute, which provided not full immunity from prosecution for certain crimes revealed in compelled testimony before congressional committees but only immunity from use of the specific evidence thus extracted. Criminal proceedings could still be brought against witnesses who testified against themselves, as long as the prosecution based its case on other evidence. Then, in 1868, Congress expanded this law to cover federal judicial proceedings in specific categories of criminal cases, and when the Interstate Commerce Commission was set up, in 1887, Congress gave it the same power to compel testimony from witnesses who were granted use immunity. If witnesses refused to testify after being given immunity, they could be fined and imprisoned until they talked.

In November, 1890, a federal grand jury in Illinois that was looking into possible violations of the Interstate Commerce Act of 1887 summoned a grain dealer by the name of Charles Counselman and asked him about his dealings with several railroads that were suspected of giving illegally low freight rates to favored customers. Counselman, who had been granted immunity, asserted his Fifth Amendment right and refused to answer several questions; the grand jury reported his refusal to the presiding judge; he ordered Counselman to answer the questions; Counselman again refused; and the judge found him in contempt of court, fined him five hundred dollars plus the cost of the proceedings, and sent him to jail until he decided to talk. He decided, instead, to appeal the order. It was upheld by the Court of Appeals, so he took the case to the Supreme Court.

Justice Samuel Blatchford, in a unanimous opinion of that Court, declared that the Fifth Amendment "privilege is limited to criminal matters, but it is as broad as the mischief against which it seeks to guard," and that "the liberal construction which must be placed upon constitutional provisions for the protection of personal rights" obliged the Court to find the use-immunity law unconstitutional, since it didn't protect witnesses from the later use of their testimony, by way of its leads to other evidence, to prosecute them. "We are clearly of opinion that no statute which leaves the party or witness subject to prosecution after he answers the criminating question put to him can have the effect of supplanting the privilege conferred by the Constitution of the United States," the Court concluded, because the statute did not give witnesses "complete protection from all the perils against which the constitutional prohibition was designed to guard." That made it less than "a full substitute" for the amendment, and for such a law to be an adequate substitute it would have to provide "absolute immunity against future prosecution for the offense to which the question relates."

The notion that there could be a "substitute" for constitutional mandates was a curious one, since the primary purpose of the Framers in formulating a written constitution in the first place was to put its mandates beyond the reach of the national legislature. The only way in which the fundamental law of the nation could constitutionally be changed was by way of amendment, and the Framers had given Congress a limited role, which was shared with the people at large, in the amending process. Now, though, the Supreme Court's conclusion that the Fifth Amendment could be supplanted by a federal law effectively gave Congress the power to amend the Constitution on its own initiative and without public approval. Finally, since the Constitution flatly states, "No person shall be . . . compelled in any criminal case to be a witness against himself" — not that a person can be compelled to be a witness against himself as long as he isn't prosecuted for what he says — the Supreme Court failed to place even a literal, much less a liberal, construction on "constitutional provisions for the protection of personal rights." Rather than giving absolute protection to those rights, the Court actually limited them in the case of the Fifth Amendment by handing the state the power to compel what the Constitution said could not be compelled.

Congress wasted no time in rushing through the door that the Court had opened. Sixteen days after the decision in Counselman was handed down, a bill was introduced in Congress guaranteeing that after immunity was granted to witnesses before the Interstate Commerce Commission "no person shall be prosecuted or subjected to any penalty or forfeiture for or on account of any transaction, matter, or thing concerning which he may testify." The bill, which provided absolute immunity from prosecution for anything to do with specific criminal transactions, became known as transactional immunity. The proposal was soon enacted, and was judicially tested when the auditor of the Allegheny Valley Railway, a man named Brown, refused to answer questions put to him by a federal grand jury about low freight rates to good customers. Granted the new form of immunity, Brown pleaded the Fifth Amendment and remained silent, and the presiding judge found him in contempt of court, fined him five dollars, and sent him to jail until he agreed to testify. The Court of Appeals upheld this ruling, and the case – Brown v. Walker – went to the Supreme Court.

By a five-to-four vote, in 1896, the Court upheld the new immunity law. Justice Henry B. Brown delivered the majority's opinion, which was wholly based on the conclusion in Counselman that if absolute immunity was granted a prospective witness his Fifth Amendment right was fully protected. According to Justice Brown, that right could be looked at in one of two ways: it could be interpreted literally, as "authorizing the witness to refuse to disclose any fact which might tend to incriminate, disgrace, or expose him to unfavorable comments," or it could be viewed as an attempt "to secure the witness against a criminal prosecution." The Court concluded that "the clause should be construed, as it was doubtless designed, to effect a practical and beneficent purpose – not necessarily to protect witnesses against every possible detriment which might happen to them from their testimony, nor to unduly impede, hinder, or obstruct the administration of criminal justice."

There was no historical justification whatever for the conclusion that this was the purpose for which the Fifth Amendment was "doubtless designed." Indeed, since the "practical and beneficent purpose" that Justice Brown mentioned entirely served the interests of the state rather than those of the individual citizen, that alone betrayed the intent of the Framers — to protect the individual against the state. To get around this point, Brown took refuge in that ancient judicial sanctuary — the tradition that courts should not overturn congressional acts unless they are flagrantly at odds with fundamental law. Justice Brown conceded that the colonists had so feared the iniquities of the inquisitorial system of justice that they, "with one accord, made a denial of the right to question an accused person a part of their fundamental law." But then he went on to find ample justification for compelling one who was not formally accused of a crime — who was, in fact, given immunity against any such accusation — to tell of others' crimes. That power, he claimed, was "within the control of the legislature." And to contend, as the defendant had, that "he would incur personal odium and disgrace from answering these questions seems too much like an abuse of language to be worthy of serious consideration," the Justice said.

Above all, though, the Court majority relied on the needs of government to justify transactional immunity on constitutional grounds. "Every good citizen is bound to aid in the enforcement of the law, and has no right to permit himself, under the pretext of shielding his own good name, to be made the tool of others who are desirous of seeking shelter behind his privilege," Justice Brown declared, and thereby accused the defendant in the case of a crime that no one had charged him with — conspiracy to conceal a crime. (Although the Fifth Amendment says only that no one shall be compelled to testify against himself, testifying against others may involve admitting that one did not report a crime, and not reporting a crime is, of course, a crime.)

The Court majority's reliance on the principle of good citizenship was utterly untenable, for the duties of citizens are nowhere mentioned in the Constitution. The authors of the Fifth Amendment did not speak of good citizens or bad citizens, they merely said that no citizen could be forced to accuse himself. And, of course, the Bill of Rights was written not to help the government enforce its laws but to restrain it from abusing *any* citizen through unjust laws and unfair enforcement of them. But to the majority of the Court the needs of government were paramount, and since, Justice Brown stated, "enforcement of the Interstate Commerce law or other analogous acts . . . would become impossible" without compelled testimony, testimony must be compelled. In short, the Supreme Court declared that if legislative acts could not be enforced without violating the Constitution, then the Constitution would have to be violated to uphold those acts.

The four justices in the minority dissented vigorously, and at points bitterly, from the majority opinion. Justice George Shiras, Jr., for instance, pointed out that the immunity law specifically provided that a witness who was forced to testify was not given immunity from the crime of perjury when he testified, whereas if he were allowed to assert his constitutional right to remain silent he could not incur a charge of perjury for what he had not said. Beyond that, Shiras went on, "a moment's thought will show that a perfectly innocent person may expose himself to accusation, and even condemnation, by being compelled to disclose facts and circumstances known only to himself, but which, when once disclosed, he may be entirely unable to explain as consistent with innocence."

Another dissenter in the case was Justice Stephen J. Field, who used the defense counsel's arguments verbatim in describing the rule against compulsory self-incrimination as the "result of the long struggle between the opposing forces of the spirit of individual liberty on the one hand and the collective power of the state on the other." That power is absolutely limited under our form of government, he added, for "the proud sense of personal independence which is the basis of the most valued qualities of a free citizen is sustained and cultivated by the consciousness that there are limits which even the state cannot pass in tearing open the secrets of his bosom." Above all, Field argued in a long and passionate section of his dissenting opinion, there could be no assurance that the authors of the Fifth Amendment had not intended it to protect a witness against self-infamy as well as against self-incrimination. "Both the safeguard of the Constitution and the common-law rule spring alike from that sentiment of personal self-respect, liberty, independence, and dignity which has inhabited the breasts of English-speaking peoples for centuries, and to save which they have always been ready to sacrifice many governmental facilities and conveniences," the Justice said. "In scarcely anything has that sentiment been more manifest than in the abhorrence felt at the legal compulsion upon witnesses to make concessions which must cover the witness with lasting shame and leave him degraded both in his own eyes and those of others."

Legal scholarship of the time – especially on the Supreme Court – was so inadequate and slipshod that apparently Justice Field was unaware of an ancient sanction against compulsory self-infamy that strongly supported his argument. As far back as 1528, William Tyndale's *The Obedience of a Christian Man* had condemned the legal practice of forcing a man "to shame himself." By the late seventeenth century, this principle was embedded in English law, and in a notable case in 1679 a judge ruled that a witness could not be asked about his misdeeds even after being assured that he would not be prosecuted, because "neither his life nor name must suffer, and therefore such questions must not be asked him." And in 1696 Lord Chief Justice George Treby said, "Men have been asked whether they have been convicted and pardoned for felony, or whether they have been whipped for petty larceny; but they have not been obliged to answer, for though their answer in the affirmative will not make them criminal or subject them to a punishment, yet they are matters of infamy; and if it be an infamous thing, that is enough to preserve a man from being bound to answer." Sir William Blackstone's *Commentaries on the Laws of England,* which was published in the mid-eighteenth century and was considered the leading text on the law by the Framers, stated that "no man is to be examined to prove his own infamy."

Two years before the Supreme Court upheld the immunity act in Brown v. Walker, a lower federal-court judge named Peter Grosscup had rejected the statute as unconstitutional. In his opinion, delivered in 1894, he addressed himself to the issue of self-infamy, among other matters, as making up an integral part of the Framers' design when they drew up the Fifth Amendment:

Did they originate such privilege simply to safeguard themselves against the law-inflicted penalties and forfeitures? Did they take no thought of the pains of practical outlawry? The stated penalties and forfeitures of the law might be set aside; but was there no pain in disfavor and odium among neighbors, in excommunication from church or societies that might be governed by the prevailing views, in the private liabilities that the law might authorize, or in the unfathomable disgrace, not susceptible of formulation in language, which a known violation of law brings upon the offender? Then, too, if the immunity was only against the law-inflicted pains and penalties, the government could probe the secrets of every conversation, or society, by extending compulsory pardon to one of its participants, and thus turn him into an involuntary informer. Did the Framers contemplate that this privilege of silence was exchangeable always, at the will of the government, for a remission of the participant's own penalties, upon a condition of disclosure, that would bring those to whom he had plighted his faith and loyalty within the grasp of the prosecutor? I cannot think so. . . .

The oppression of crowns and principalities is unquestionably over, but the more frightful oppression of selfish, ruthless, and merciless majorities may yet constitute one of the chapters of future history. In my opinion, the privilege of silence against a criminal accusation, guaranteed by the Fifth Amendment, was meant to extend to all the consequences of disclosure.

Both the Supreme Court's narrow endorsement of transactional immunity and its rejection of the theory that the Fifth Amendment prohibited the government from forcing one to disgrace oneself were ultimately to abet the tyranny of the majority that Judge Grosscup foresaw. As a result of anti-Communist hysteria, which had spread throughout America from the time of the Bolshevik Revolution in 1917 until it burst out into a national nightmare of repression in the late nineteen-forties and early nineteen-fifties, Congress, which had created most of the hysteria in the first place, responded to it by enacting some of the most repressive laws ever to be placed on this nation's books. Armed with these laws, congressional committees and federal grand juries summoned their victims, who were forced to admit their radical political beliefs and associations and to inform on their friends or go to prison. In one of the most famous of these cases, which reached the Supreme Court in the mid-fifties — Ullmann v. United States — the Court upheld a transactional-immunity statute that Congress had passed to implement one of the more far-reaching anti-radical laws. Since the statute provided absolute immunity, Justice Frankfurter said for the seven-man majority, it was consonant with the decision in Brown v. Walker, which had "consistently and without question been treated as definitive by this Court."

Of the two dissenters, Justice Black opposed the decision on the ground that if the Constitution said, "No person shall be . . . compelled in any criminal case to be a witness against himself," that was what the Constitution meant. The other dissenter, Justice Douglas, called upon the Court to overturn the five-man majority opinion in Brown and to raise the four-man minority opinion there to the status of constitutional doctrine by ruling "that the right of silence created by the Fifth Amendment is beyond the reach of Congress." Above all, Douglas shared the concern expressed sixty-odd years earlier by Judge Grosscup and Justice Field about self-infamy, and he appealed to the Court to stand up for "conscience and human dignity and freedom of expression" by giving a person's reputation and his sense of independence and self-respect the full protection accorded it before the Supreme Court went to work on the Constitution. "The critical point is that the Constitution places the right of silence *beyond the reach of government*," he repeated. "The Fifth Amendment stands between the citizen and his government." But the Court's majority refused to listen.

After Brown v. Walker, the most important case concerning compulsory self-incrimination to be decided by the Supreme Court was Twining v. State of New Jersey, in 1908. In a state criminal trial, a judge had noted in his charge to the jury that the defendants had declined to take the stand in their own defense, and they appealed this act as a violation of their Fifth Amendment rights as interpreted by the Fourteenth Amendment. That amendment says, "No State shall make or enforce any law which shall abridge the privileges or immunities of citizens of the United States; nor shall any State deprive any person of life, liberty, or property, without due process of law; nor deny to any person within its jurisdiction the equal protection of the laws." The Fourteenth Amendment was adopted in 1868, and once again many people believed that its purpose was to make the entire Bill of Rights binding on the states. But, in 1873, five years after the amendment was adopted, the Supreme Court decided that it guaranteed citizens of the states only those rights the states said they possessed — that is, the Fourteenth Amendment was meaningless. Four members of the Court, led by Justice Field, bitterly contested the 1873 decision, for if the Fourteenth Amendment did no more than the majority held, he said, "it was a vain and idle enactment, which accomplished nothing, and most unnecessarily excited Congress and the people on its passage." In Twining v. New Jersey, the defendants reopened the argument by contending that the Fifth Amendment right against compulsory self-incrimination had been "incorporated" through the "privileges or immunities" clause of the Fourteenth Amendment to cover state criminal proceedings. But the Court rejected this view, and cited its 1873 decision as binding.

To buttress this conclusion, Justice William H. Moody, speaking for the Court in Twining, pointed out that the rights and privileges of national citizenship so far recognized by the Supreme Court were "the right to pass freely from state to state, the right to petition Congress for a redress of grievances, the right to vote for national officers, the right to enter the public lands, the right to be protected against violence while in the lawful custody of a United States marshal, and the right to inform the United States authorities of violation of its laws." The rights enumerated in the Bill of Rights — among them freedom of religion, speech, press, and assembly; the right to be secure against unreasonable searches and seizures, against indictment for felony except by grand jury, against double jeopardy, and against involuntary self-incrimination; the right to a speedy and public trial by an impartial jury, to a public accusation describing its nature and cause, to be confronted by one's accusers, to have the power to summon witnesses on one's behalf, and to have a lawyer; and the right not to be subjected to excessive bail or fines or to cruel and unusual punishment — all these fundamental rights were the privileges and immunities of citizens only when they came up against the authority of the federal government. Not one of these rights, the Court declared, was guaranteed to citizens against the authority of individual states unless specifically provided for under the laws of those states. In fact, the states could suspend or abolish any of the rights they had guaranteed their citizens, and no power, including that of the national government, could stop them. Accordingly, Justice Moody asserted, the right against compulsory self-incrimination was not a privilege or immunity of a citizen in a state criminal proceeding.

Going on to the defendants' further claim that compulsory self-incrimination also denied them due process of law, as guaranteed by both the Fifth and Fourteenth Amendments, Justice Moody stated that to constitute due process any legal principle had to be shown to be an intrinsic part of "the law of the land," as that phrase was meant by the authors of Magna Carta. He then asked rhetorically whether the prohibition against compulsory self-incrimination was "a fundamental principle of liberty and justice which inheres in the very idea of free government and is the inalienable right of a citizen of such a government." He answered that it was not, because a search through English and American history prior to the Revolution revealed "nothing to show that it was then thought to be other than a just and useful principle of law." In England, he went on, the "privilege was not dreamed of for hundreds of years after Magna Carta (1215), and could not have been implied in the 'law of the land' there secured."

The test Moody proposed was faulty. For one thing, many of the principles that had been considered fundamental at the time the American Constitution was adopted had not been dreamed of for hundreds of years after Magna Carta. Indeed, if the founding of the United States was nothing more than a repetition of that document's principles, then six centuries had passed with no political progress to be shown for them. For instance, when King John signed the Great Charter even jury trials in criminal cases were unknown in England. In addition, Magna Carta contained almost no fundamental rights of ordinary people as we understand such rights today. Those that were claimed so fervently – by men like Lilburne, among thousands of others – to be indelibly imprinted in it were actually imposed on it by myth in the centuries after it was written. The key sentence in Magna Carta that was later believed to contain the fundamental principles of democratic law reads, "No freeman shall be taken, or imprisoned, or dis-seised, or outlawed, or exiled, or any wise destroyed; nor shall we go upon him, nor send upon him, but by the lawful judgment of his peers, or by the law of the land," In thirteenth-century England, "the law of the land" meant trial by battle or by an ordeal such as being branded with a hot iron to see whether the burn healed quickly, which meant one was innocent, or became infected, which meant one was guilty, and "the lawful judgment of his peers" referred to those who umpired the battle or interpreted the reaction to the iron.

Continuing, Justice Moody pointed out that there was no reference to a guarantee against self-incrimination in the English Petition of Right, submitted to the king in 1628. Once again the Justice – that is, the Supreme Court – was wrong. As Professor Levy has pointed out, a crucial part of the Petition was designed to stop the sovereign from forcing subjects to lend money to the Crown, and from forcing those who declined to make such loans to take self-incriminatory oaths before a special royal commission. Moody also claimed that compulsory self-incrimination "was then a matter of common occurrence in all the courts of the realm." While that was true, Moody ignored the fact that beginning a few years later and for more than two centuries afterward compulsory self-incrimination under oath was not permitted in common-law courts in England; in fact, during this period defendants were not even allowed to testify under oath, either for or against themselves, in such courts of the realm until only ten years before Moody delivered the Supreme Court's opinion in Twining. Moody claimed that the English Bill of Rights of 1689 was "likewise silent, though the practice of questioning the prisoner at his trial had not then ceased." Actually, by that time the rule against allowing prisoners to be questioned under oath was already established. Moreover, the English Bill of Rights was largely a fraud, for it contained little to assure rights to the common man – aside from sanctions against excessive bail and fines and cruel and unusual punishment – but was mainly designed to protect the government's rights. One demonstration of this purpose emerged when Thomas Paine attacked that Bill of Rights in *The Rights of Man* by saying, "The act, called the Bill of Rights . . . what is it but a bargain, which the parts of the government made with each other to divide powers, profits, and privileges?" As if to prove his point, the British government charged Paine with treason, and he was convicted of committing, among other crimes, seditious libel against the Bill of Rights.

Justice Moody then moved on to America, and asserted that only four of the original thirteen states had asked that the Constitution be amended by adding a bill of rights that included the right against involuntary self-incrimination. He did mention that six of the thirteen states had such a right written into their own constitutions, but he did not mention that every state having a separate bill of rights prohibited compulsory self-incrimination. He also ignored the broadest and most pertinent document of freedom up to that time, the Virginia Declaration of Rights, written by George Mason, which had greatly influenced all the state constitutions and the national Constitution; it, too, contained a sanction against forced self-incrimination. And, finally, Justice Moody ignored the Supreme Court's own finding in Brown v. Walker that the American colonists "with one accord, made a denial of the right to question an accused person a part of their fundamental law."

In conclusion, Justice Moody dismissed the prohibition against involuntary self-incrimination as being in any way fundamental by saying that "it is nowhere observed among our own people in the search for truth outside the administration of the law" – in other words, the rule has no counterpart in ordinary society. This claim, which has repeatedly been made by such eminent jurists of today as Walter V. Schaefer, of the Illinois Supreme Court, and Henry J. Friendly, of the Court of Appeals for the Second Circuit, misses a couple of basic points. For one, "the search for truth" has nothing to do with the Fifth Amendment, which was obviously written with the express purpose of allowing people to conceal the truth. For another, the world outside the law is not like the world inside the law — most notably in the respect that in civil society one cannot be imprisoned for one's transgressions. Indeed, if the rules of civil society were the standard on which our criminal law were based, then no one would be forced to talk about others or go to prison, because scarcely anyone is regarded with more scorn in the ordinary world than the Judas figure — from the childish tattletale to the adult informer.

By the beginning of the eighteenth century, criminal-court judges in England generally concluded that compelled confessions were untrustworthy, and this realization became another reason for not allowing an accused person or a witness to be tortured. But in America the use of torture went on illegally for many years — and, in fact, still goes on. As it turned out, the Supreme Court was to have as much difficulty in facing this problem as it has had in facing the problem of coerced confessions in general.

In the mid-nineteen-thirties, three black men were arrested in Mississippi on a charge of murdering a white man. Five days after the crime, they were indicted, arraigned, given court-appointed counsel, and then were taken to trial the following morning. The trial lasted less than two days, and at its conclusion the three were found guilty and sentenced to death. Aside from their confessions, there was no evidence against them, and during the trial their story of how they had come to confess was laid before the jury. The story told how a deputy sheriff had led a mob to one of the defendants, hanged him by a rope from a tree outside the dead man's house for a time, let him down long enough to hear him proclaim his innocence, hauled him up again, let him down, heard him repeat his claim, then tied him to a tree trunk and whipped him until the mob tired of it and released him, without persuading him to confess. A couple of days later, the deputy and a colleague went to the man's house and took him to jail — by way of nearby Alabama, where they stopped and beat him some more. They vowed to go on beating him until he confessed, and finally he did, whereupon they took him to jail. The deputy then picked up two other black men who were implicated by the first suspect, took them to jail, made them strip and lie down over chairs, and whipped them with the buckle end of a leather belt until their backs were cut to pieces. In time, they confessed, too. During the trial, they displayed the fresh wounds on their backs to the jurors, and the defendant who had been hanged showed them the rope marks on his neck. The deputy sheriff readily admitted while on the stand that he had beaten one of the men, but, he said, "not too much for a Negro." The judges of the Mississippi Supreme Court read the trial record and upheld the convictions and death sentences.

Brown v. Mississippi, unlike thousands of similar cases across the country, ended up in the United States Supreme Court. In the arguments there, counsel for the State of Mississippi contended that Twining controlled the issue and that, accordingly, the federal rule against involuntary self-incrimination didn't apply to a state case. In February, 1936, the Court announced its decision, which upheld the state's contention on this point. "The question of the right of the state to withdraw the privilege against self-incrimination is not here involved," announced Chief Justice Charles Evans Hughes for the Court. What was involved, though, he went on, was that "torture to extort a confession" was so "revolting to the sense of justice" that it constituted a denial of due process, which was a right that the state could *not* withdraw. On this ground, the Court reversed the convictions.

State courts apparently couldn't believe that the Supreme Court had been serious in finding such practices illegal, and they continued to uphold convictions based on third-degree confessions. After all, there were states' rights, and none of them was more jealously guarded than the right to assert the police power at will. And, as Sir James Fitzjames Stephen, a prominent Victorian jurist, observed, "It is far pleasanter to sit comfortably in the shade rubbing red pepper into a poor devil's eyes than to go about in the sun hunting up evidence." To give the law some semblance of integrity, state courts went through what has been called "the swearing contest," in which policemen swore that defendants hadn't been beaten, defendants swore that they had, and judges and juries invariably took the word of the policemen. Time after time when such cases reached the Supreme Court, it repeated its insistence on due process and reversed the convictions. But, again, this had little effect on the states, whose law-enforcement officers seemed unmoved by such reversals.

Angered by the continuing indifference to its commands, the Supreme Court finally ruled in 1943, by way of McNabb v. United States, that in federal criminal cases any protracted detention of a suspect violated a federal statute ordering that suspects be promptly taken before magistrates, and that confessions obtained during prolonged detention were inadmissible. This rule, the Court explained, was meant to check "resort to those reprehensible practices known as the third degree." Of course, the rule was binding only on federal courts, but it was expected that their behavior would serve as an example to the states. However, judges on lower federal courts also apparently couldn't believe that the justices had been serious, and began ruling that before a defendant could claim coercion under the McNabb rule he had to demonstrate that there was a causal relationship between the length of time he had been detained and his confession. To deal with this circumvention, the Supreme Court ordered in 1957, in Mallory v. United States, that *any* unnecessary delay in taking a federal prisoner before a magistrate made a confession automatically inadmissible in court. Still, the prevailing abuse of the right against involuntary self-incrimination was the continuing use of the third degree in state cases, and the McNabb-Mallory rule didn't touch those at all.

Stymied by the intransigence of state officials, the Court went off in several different directions to stem these atrociously unjust practices. One of the chief means by which police often got evidence against suspects was by searching them without a warrant and using the evidence forcibly uncovered against them. Of course, this violated the Fourth Amendment's stricture against "unreasonable searches and seizures" and ignored the requirement that the police have "probable cause" to believe a crime had been committed before they could seize evidence or arrest a person. Moreover, this kind of practice also violated the Fifth Amendment, since it indirectly compelled a person to betray himself by giving up evidence of his culpability through force. Finally, in 1961 the Court decided in Mapp v. Ohio that the Fourth Amendment was binding on the states. In effect, this meant that state violations of the amendment could be taken into federal court. That ruling made the amendment's most effective and intrinsic element — the exclusionary rule — also binding on the states. In 1963, the Court also made the Sixth Amendment right to counsel binding on the states through Gideon v. Wainwright, and a year later expanded this ruling, in Escobedo v. Illinois, by holding that the right to have a lawyer commenced as soon as a suspect was taken to a police station. Like the Court's ruling on the Fourth Amendment, the one on the Sixth Amendment had a salutary effect on the right against compelled testimony, since the first piece of advice that any lawyer will give to a client who is suspected or accused of a crime is to say nothing at all to the police.

Law-enforcement officers who were temporarily dismayed by this limitation on them soon got around it — by torturing suspects before taking them to the station house. To prevent this recourse, the Court took the giant step of applying the Fifth Amendment to the states through Malloy v. Hogan in 1964. Then, two years later, the Court expanded its protection by ordering in Miranda v. Arizona that every suspect in a criminal case must be warned of his constitutional rights from the moment he becomes a suspect — including the right to have a lawyer present at any stage of the proceedings against him, the right to remain silent, and the right to be warned that whatever he says may be used against him. In time, this order created a new form of the old swearing contest, in which policemen swore in court that they had given the Miranda warning, defendants swore that they hadn't, and judges and juries invariably believed the policemen. Even so, the Miranda decision made a compelling point: If the highest court in the land could not prevent injustice, at least it would not condone it.

Speaking for the five-man majority in Miranda, Chief Justice Earl Warren said that "the privilege against self-incrimination — the essential mainstay of our adversary system — is founded on a complex of values." He went on to explain, "All these policies point to one overriding thought: the constitutional foundation underlying the privilege is the respect a government — state or federal — must accord to the dignity and integrity of its citizens. To maintain a fair state-individual balance, to require the government to shoulder the entire load [in proving a person's guilt], to respect the inviolability of the human personality, our accusatory system of criminal justice demands that the government seeking to punish an individual produce the evidence against him by its own independent labors, rather than by the cruel, simple expedient of compelling it from his own mouth."

On the same day that the Court applied the Fifth Amendment to state criminal cases, it also handed down its decision in Murphy et al v. Waterfront Commission of New York Harbor, which resolved a jurisdictional conflict that had previously existed among the states and between the states and the federal government in regard to grants of immunity. Before Murphy, when one state granted a witness immunity another state or the federal government could then prosecute him on the basis of his testimony, since no state could grant immunity from prosecution by another state or by the federal government. In Murphy, the Court ruled that when a person was forced to testify in one jurisdiction his testimony could not be used to prosecute him in another jurisdiction. However, to interfere as little as possible with the federal system, the decision allowed an exception to the absolute-immunity standard laid down in Counselman and upheld in Brown, Ullmann, and other Supreme Court decisions: it permitted use immunity to be employed in a dual-sovereignty situation when only one jurisdiction has any sort of immunity provision. Although the Court thereby made use immunity constitutional in narrowly circumscribed cases, the overall effect of the Murphy decision was to broaden the coverage and scope of the Fifth Amendment privilege by making it far more difficult to prosecute a person for what he testified to in *any* jurisdiction. That the Court meant to hold to the strict Counselman-Brown requirement of transactional immunity in all other circumstances was demonstrated a year after Murphy, when the Court struck down a congressionally authorized use-immunity statute. In that case, Albertson v. Subversive Activities Control Board, the Court unanimously found the statute unconstitutional, again cited the Counselman-Brown rule requiring absolute immunity in exchange for compelled testimony, and declared that any immunity statute must be measured by this standard.

Almost everything done by the Warren Court to interpret and apply the Fifth Amendment to the whole range of criminal law in America did little more than assure everyone of the rights that most people believed they had possessed all along. Even so, the indignant outcry from police, prosecutors, judges, politicians, the press, and laymen against the Court was so immediate and so clamorous that one might have thought the Bill of Rights had been scrapped altogether rather than at last restored in one small part to the purpose that its authors had meant it to serve.

To the ignorant citizen and to the stupid judge, the Fifth Amendment right seems like a refuge for the guilty. On occasion, the Supreme Court has tried to correct this attitude. In 1956, for instance, the Court said in an opinion on a Fifth Amendment case, "At the outset we must condemn the practice of imputing a sinister meaning to the exercise of a person's constitutional right under the Fifth Amendment." But the following year President Eisenhower told a press conference, "I must say I probably share the common reaction: If a man has to go to the Fifth Amendment, there must be something he doesn't want to tell." The President's failure to see that such a man might have good and innocent reasons – and the right – not to tell something led Justice Black to observe a little later, "The value of these constitutional privileges is largely destroyed if people can be penalized for relying on them."

Few aspects of American law have distinguished the right wing from the left wing as clearly as their attitudes toward the Fifth Amendment. On the right, it has long been attacked as a refuge for the guilty, who, it is said, *should* be compelled to admit their crimes and be strictly punished for them. And on the left, it has long been defended as the essential bulwark against an inquisitorial government — in Jefferson's view, *all* governments — which may condemn and punish the innocent along with the guilty. The leading spokesman for the right-wing viewpoint is Chief Justice Burger. Long before he was appointed to the Supreme Court by President Nixon, Burger publicly attacked the Fifth Amendment sanction at every opportunity. As a judge on the Court of Appeals for the District of Columbia Circuit, he often criticized his liberal colleagues there for applying the sanction too strictly in their rulings. And at a law symposium that Burger attended the year before he became Chief Justice, he questioned the validity of such fundamental principles of our legal system as the presumption of innocence, trial by jury, and the right against compulsory self-incrimination. On the last point, Burger said at the law symposium, "Certainly you have heard — and judges have said — that one should not convict a man out of his own mouth. The fact is that we establish responsibility and liability and we convict in all the areas of *civil* litigation out of the mouth of the defendant." To some legal scholars, it seemed astonishing that a man who made no distinction between the civil law and the criminal law — who failed to note, for instance, that their penalties are a loss of money on the one hand and a loss of freedom and perhaps life on the other — could have become Chief Justice of the United States.

Soon after the Nixon Administration took office, Attorney General Mitchell ordered a secret study made of the feasibility of altering the Fifth Amendment, either by drafting a law that would weaken its stricture against compelled testimony or by abolishing its privilege altogether through a constitutional amendment. Apparently, the second course seemed too long and too uncertain, so the Department of Justice concentrated on the first approach. A couple of years earlier, Congress had set up the National Commission on Reform of the Federal Criminal Laws, and it was still at work on its assignment when Nixon and Mitchell took over. Along the way in its deliberations, the Commission adopted a recommendation made by a consultant: that transactional immunity be replaced by use immunity across the board. In effect, the proposal endorsed a broader form of use immunity than the laws of the eighteen-sixties, which the Supreme Court first rejected in 1892 and again and again in later years. The use-immunity proposal stated that anyone who was compelled to testify could not be prosecuted directly on the basis of that testimony or indirectly on the basis of leads from it to other evidence, but that one could be prosecuted after being compelled to testify as long as the evidence used against one was obtained independently of, and was untainted by, the coerced testimony. Early in 1970, the use-immunity proposal was drafted in a separate bill, which was introduced in the House by three representatives who had served on the Commission and were also members of the House subcommittee having jurisdiction over such legislation. A single day was allotted for a hearing on the proposal to rewrite the Fifth Amendment. Of the six witnesses who testified on the subject, only one, a spokesman for the American Civil Liberties Union, opposed use immunity.

The Nixon Administration's principal legal defense for backing the innovation was that the Supreme Court's decision in Murphy v. Waterfront Commission — that is, the narrow technical exception allowing use immunity in circumscribed cases — had made use immunity in general wholly constitutional. The witness from the A.C.L.U. and various critics who were not heard by the subcommittee complained that such a law would have many drawbacks. Once a prosecutor could force a prospective defendant to testify about his crimes, for instance, the immense advantages that the government already had in manpower, money, and official intimidation would become gigantic, for then the prosecutor could immediately confine his search and concentrate all his resources on one person — the person who was granted use immunity and forced to testify against himself. And once the main target was sighted, a less than scrupulous prosecutor could easily fabricate a claim that the evidence used in court against the witness had been uncovered independently of the testimony elicited under compulsion. Even if a prosecutor was scrupulously fair, anyone among the many employees in large United States Attorneys' offices or in even larger metropolitan district attorneys' offices might inadvertently follow up a lead that came originally from a witness's testimony, and someone else might unwittingly offer it in court as untainted evidence.

Of course, prosecutors are often exceedingly ambitious, and the best way for them to get ahead is by building a record of crime-busting — even if that means, as it all too frequently does, using illegally acquired tips from wiretaps or bugs, covertly broadening court-imposed limits on search warrants in order to pick up unauthorized material evidence, or ignoring third-degree methods used by police to extort confessions. Since the Bill of Rights was written to control such prosecutors, critics of the use-immunity bill pointed out, it was folly to encourage such men to legally force a man to talk and then to illegally use his words against him — the course that would almost certainly be taken by the incompetent, lazy, or vicious prosecutor. Moreover, when two or more suspects were involved in a case, use immunity could be employed to force each of them to testify against the other, which, in effect, would amount to their testifying against themselves, since the testimony of one could be used as independent evidence against the other. Finally, federal immunity laws of the past had applied only to specific crimes that were difficult or impossible to solve without the help of a confession from someone who was involved. But the use-immunity proposal being considered by the House subcommittee provided that it would replace all transactional-immunity statutes and would be applicable to all crimes covered by the federal code four years after enactment by Congress.

The House subcommittee, which was controlled by a strong liberal majority, approved the use-immunity bill with only one vote being cast against it — by William Fitts Ryan, Democrat of New York, who said that it would destroy the Fifth Amendment. Afterward, the parent Judiciary Committee, which was also controlled by liberals, approved the measure with little discussion and sent it to the floor of the House as part of the Organized Crime Control Act of 1970. That act, which was perhaps the most undemocratic and repressive piece of legislation to be seriously considered by Congress in a generation, passed with little debate and almost no opposition; when the final vote was tallied up, only twenty-six members of the House had voted against it. In the Senate, only one member – Lee Metcalf, Democrat of Montana – voted against the measure. It was an election year, Nixon had made crime a basic issue of his Presidency, and, as fully expected on all sides, Congress was not of a mind to sacrifice itself on the altar of democracy.

In the legal community, though, it was widely believed that the use-immunity law was so flagrantly unconstitutional that not even a Supreme Court headed by Chief Justice Burger could uphold it. But few Court-watchers anticipated that Nixon would soon have four appointees on the Court. Their effect was rapidly made clear in at least one respect. "In no area of criminal justice was the Nixon Court's new departure so swift and veering as in cases arising under the Fifth Amendment's self-incrimination clause," wrote Professor Levy – now Mellon Professor at the Claremont Colleges, in California, in his recent book *Against the Law: The Nixon Court and Criminal Justice*. He went on, "The Court decided fourteen such cases during just the first two years of Burger's incumbency. . . . In all but one of the fourteen cases the right claimed under the Fifth Amendment lost."

Of the thirteen assaults on the Amendment that succeeded, the most destructive was the decision in the case of Harris v. New York, which was handed down in 1971. The opinion of the Court was delivered by Chief Justice Burger, whose target was the Miranda ruling that a suspect must be warned of the right to remain silent, of the right to have a lawyer, and of the right to be told that anything one says may be used against one in court. Although the Miranda rule made any statements obtained in violation of it inadmissible as evidence, Burger undercut this guarantee by announcing for the majority of the Court in Harris that self-incriminating statements taken in violation of Miranda *can* be used during a trial to test a defendant's truthfulness if he takes the stand. That is, once a suspect says something self-incriminating to the police before he is warned of his rights, his words cannot be used against him at the time of his trial as evidence of his guilt but can be used against him "to impeach his credibility." Of course, the immediate, practical, and overwhelming result of the new rule was to prevent any person who had made such an incriminating statement, no matter how trivial, from speaking in his own defense at his trial, for no defense lawyer could allow a client to swallow the judicial fiction that jurors would ignore self-incriminating remarks when it came time for them to decide about overall guilt or innocence. In effect, then, the Court wiped out under such circumstances an accused person's fundamental right to defend himself. And, perhaps worse, the decision indirectly encouraged policemen and prosecutors to ignore the Miranda rule long enough to obtain some kind of incriminating statement, even one that they knew was misleading, in order to prevent suspects from later defending themselves in court. "The opinion in Harris taught that government may commit crimes in order to secure the conviction of criminals," Professor Levy observed, and added, "It taught the odious doctrine that in the administration of the criminal law, the end justifies the means and the Constitution can be circumvented."

A few months after Congress passed the use-immunity law, several young men in California were subpoenaed by a federal grand jury investigating draft evasion in that area, and were asked questions about a dentist who was suspected of having provided them with unnecessary dental work to make them ineligible for military service. They refused to testify, were granted the newly enacted form of federal use immunity, again refused to testify, and were imprisoned for contempt of court. The case — Kastigar et al v. United States — went to the Supreme Court, which handed down its decision in the spring of 1972. To the amazement of most constitutional scholars, the Court upheld the law without qualification by a vote of five to two, with two justices not participating. The same scholars were amazed by the majority opinion's lack of craftsmanship, logic, and awareness of legal history. The opinion, written by Justice Lewis Powell, so misinterpreted the Court's own precedents, Professor Levy said, that it "left them twisted like pretzels."

Powell's basic argument was that transactional immunity was actually *too* broad — broader, in fact, than the Fifth Amendment right itself — and that use immunity was precisely "coextensive" with that right and thus a proper substitute for it. Since this view was flatly at odds with almost everything the Court had said on the subject over a period of eighty years, Powell was obliged to reject the entire line of Court rulings during that time without expressly saying so by overruling them. To this end, he began with the Counselman decision, the first of the line, and simply declared — erroneously — that it had upheld use immunity; its statement that only transactional immunity could replace the privilege itself, he said, was merely dictum and "cannot be considered binding authority." To be sure, the Counselman opinion on this point could be described as dictum (a statement that is less than intrinsic to the order of the Court in a given case, and is meant to serve more as a future guide than as a present command), but it wasn't dictum after the Court made it the central point four years later in Brown v. Walker and in a long series of decisions that subsequently reaffirmed the doctrine of absolute immunity. The only exception in that series was the Murphy decision's acceptance of use immunity in certain kinds of dual-sovereignty cases, and Powell squeezed through this loophole, even while denying that he was doing it, to justify the Court's ruling that use immunity is fully constitutional in all cases. In short, the Supreme Court wiped out the Fifth Amendment.

With the decision in Kastigar, the long struggle to stop government from forcing its way into the innermost privacy of people's thoughts, associations, and consciences largely came to an end. The right wing's final victory in this contest between the state and the individual was doubly remarkable in that the state itself had long felt restrained by tradition against using any form of immunity frivolously. The traditional reluctance of Congress, the courts, and the executive branch to wield such a potent weapon carelessly grew out of several factors — among them the fear that corrupt prosecutors would give "immunity baths" to those guilty of serious crimes; the belief that grants of immunity constitute grave invasions of citizens' privacy and should be resorted to only when all other law-enforcement methods have failed; and, finally, the knowledge that compulsory immunity turns people into informers.

The danger of ignoring these factors soon became clear. After the Court's decision in Kastigar, state legislatures enacted similar laws replacing transactional immunity, and local prosecutors began summoning thousands of witnesses before grand juries. There is no record of the number of people who have been compelled in state cases to testify against themselves and others or who have been subsequently prosecuted for what they revealed. Nor are the federal records complete. But one statistic is enough to reveal the extent of the new law's use: up to the mid-nineteen-sixties, the Department of Justice had granted immunity only a few dozen times; in the eighteen-month period following the Kastigar ruling, the Department reportedly granted immunity to thirty-five hundred witnesses. Hundreds of these grants were made in political cases prosecuted by the Nixon Administration, which devised the law chiefly for that purpose.

Although the Administration's ostensible social justification for use immunity was that it was essential to the fight against organized crime, use immunity, or any other form of immunity, is largely valueless in such cases. The Mafia's *omertà* code, which can be roughly translated as "death to informers," makes a few months in jail for contempt of court a comparative slap on the wrist. In fact, a mobster's insistence on silence in order to receive such a sentence is the best way for him to prove his loyalty, and is doubtless a means to promotion within a grateful mob hierarchy. In addition to organized racketeering, the kinds of crimes that have been said to be controllable only by way of enforced immunity laws are bribery, extortion, gambling, consumer fraud, bootlegging, and commercial larceny — all but the last of which are most often committed by organized criminals, too. For those crimes that aren't, probably the most effective and certainly the fairest kind of immunity would be voluntary immunity, which a prospective witness who wants to talk could accept as protection from prosecution; those who don't want to talk often lie anyway when they are forced to, and while they are sometimes convicted of perjury, that doesn't generate the information that immunity is supposed to produce.

In any event, before 1970 federal immunity statutes were specifically designed to be used only in those cases where little else would work. Now, with use immunity having replaced *all* federal immunity laws and covering *all* federal crimes, the government can, in Judge Grosscup's words, "probe the secrets of every conversation." Today, any person can be summoned before a grand jury, a court, or a legislative committee and forced to answer all questions that may be asked. The opportunities for political oppression that this opening provides are practically unlimited. Of course, political freedom was the primary goal of men like John Lilburne and the Framers of the Constitution, and political freedom was one of the basic reasons behind the adoption of the Fifth Amendment. But an even more fundamental goal of the amendment, like the rest of the Bill of Rights, was to preserve and nourish that fragile, necessary, and wondrous quality that gives meaning and purpose to human life — individuality.

III

"Let me assure you that as long as the F.B.I. has a legal mandate to protect the American people from terrorism we will use all the legal weapons at our command to accomplish this task," Clarence Kelley, Director of the F.B.I., told the Veterans of Foreign Wars at a convention in the early spring of 1975 – not long after agents from the Bureau tried to interrogate Ellen Grusse and Terri Turgeon about their possible association with two accused terrorists. Subsequent revelations about the F.B.I.'s widespread use of illegal surveillance, its practices of burglarizing suspects' homes and offices and of opening and reading citizens' private mail, and its harassment of people who were not accused of any misdeed other than holding unpopular political views have made it clear that the F.B.I. has not always been faithful to the rule of law. On the basis of the Bureau's own recent admissions of its lawless behavior, it appears that the arena in which it has been most culpably active is the political arena. It also appears that politics is the subject F.B.I men know least about. That is hardly surprising, for the Bureau's job is supposed to be law enforcement, and law-enforcement officers traditionally have a rather narrow, and often cynical, view of society in general. Their task is to find criminals. It has been said that a good cop sees everybody as a potential criminal, and Kelley, who is reportedly a very good cop, must keep tabs on every potential threat to society he sees if he is to be faithful to his duty as he conceives it. The difficulty lies in the fact that the Bureau has been allowed by every Administration in the past several decades to determine, almost entirely on its own, who and what are threats to society. Given the Bureau's long-standing belief in the dire peril posed by left-wing conspiracies — an obsession of J. Edgar Hoover's — it is also not surprising that F.B.I. men are inclined to view anybody whose politics don't square with the average Rotarian's as a threat to the survival of the Republic.

Since the executive and legislative branches have rarely stood in the F.B.I.'s way, only the judiciary remains as a check on the Bureau's abuses of its self-delegated authority. But the courts have done little to stop it from bending and breaking the law, because the courts cannot act fully until the agents who have broken the law are prosecuted. So far, despite reports about many hundreds of illegal acts committed by F.B.I. agents, not one of them has been tried for any of these crimes. In the end, this multiple failure of all three branches of the government has given the Bureau not merely an implicit right but implicit encouragement to go on snooping into the private affairs of anyone whose political views, expressions, or associates seem unorthodox to F.B.I. men.

Hoover repeatedly tried to persuade Congress to give the F.B.I. the power to issue subpoenas, but Congress, which gave him just about everything else he asked for, turned him down on this score. Such power, it was felt in Congress, was too great to hand over to a national police agency; even the Bureau's bureaucratic parent, the Department of Justice, was denied subpoena powers, because it was held that no executive department should possess what was essentially a judicial function. But when the Nixon Administration took over, Attorney General Mitchell soon came up with a simple way of helping Hoover over this barricade — by instructing the Justice Department's ninety-three United States Attorneys' offices around the country, most of which were headed by Nixon appointees, to coöperate with the F.B.I. The specific way in which they coöperated was by directing the federal grand juries under their control to subpoena those who refused to talk to the F.B.I.; if they persisted in remaining silent, they could be given use immunity and forced to testify or go to prison.

"Historically, [the grand jury] has been regarded as a primary security for the innocent against hasty, malicious, and oppressive prosecution," the Supreme Court declared a few years ago. Although this view has been shared by laymen, lawyers, and judges alike for more than eight centuries, it is another myth. From the time that the earliest form of the grand jury was established in England in 1164 until the system was abolished there in 1948, there were only two significant occasions when "the people's panel," as it was called in ancient days, stood up for the people against the English government. In the American Colonies, grand juries were widely admired, but only because they invariably absolved those who opposed the British (for instance, a number of colonists who burned British property, some of whom sat on the grand jury that considered their offense) and indicted those who sympathized with the British (including four innocent Tory civilians who were charged with murder after the Boston Massacre). By the time the Constitution was adopted, the myth of the grand jury as one of the individual's mightiest shields against tyranny was so embedded in the public mind that the grand-jury system was officially established under the Constitution by way of the Fifth Amendment, which states in full:

> No person shall be held to answer for a capital, or otherwise infamous crime, unless on a presentment or indictment of a Grand Jury, except in cases arising in the land or naval forces, or in the Militia, when in actual service in time of War or public danger; nor shall any person be subject for the same offence to be twice put in jeopardy of life or limb; nor shall be compelled in any criminal case to be a witness against himself, nor be deprived of life, liberty, or property without due process of law; nor shall property be taken for public use, without just compensation.

After adoption of the Bill of Rights, the grand-jury system was much honored rhetorically and endlessly abused in practice. In the late nineteenth and early twentieth centuries, state grand juries occasionally asserted themselves to root out corrupt political machines. But on the federal level grand juries have almost always been rubber stamps in criminal prosecutions and in political persecutions. During periods of national strife or popular hysteria, even the most liberal Administrations have allowed or encouraged grand juries to be used in the most nakedly oppressive ways – the Lincoln Administration to silence critics of the Union cause, the Wilson Administration to illegally imprison and deport several hundred innocent radicals to Russia after the Bolshevik Revolution, the Franklin Roosevelt Administration to harass Nazi sympathizers, and the Truman Administration to permit the anti-liberal vendetta waged by Representative Richard M. Nixon and Senator Joseph R. McCarthy. In the end, the Supreme Court's view of the grand jury as "a primary security for the innocent" is wholly unrealistic. A more accurate view was recently expressed by federal District Court Judge William Campbell, who said of the grand jury in general, "Today, it is but a convenient tool for the prosecutor. . . . Any experienced prosecutor will admit that he can indict anybody at any time for almost anything."

By the time that Grusse and Turgeon were given use immunity and again called before the federal grand jury in New Haven, Michael Avery had completed his crash study of the grand-jury system. It is, he concluded, "amazingly unjust." He went on to explain, "To begin with, it is based on the judicial fiction that grand-jury proceedings are not entirely criminal in nature until indictments are returned. The reason for this fiction appears to be that if the proceedings were criminal they would have to be governed by the ordinary due-process-of-law rules that govern trials – things like the right to confront one's accusers, to cross-examine witnesses, to summon witnesses on one's own behalf – and that would turn grand-jury hearings into miniature trials. In other words, some people would have to be tried twice – once by a grand jury when it questions prospective defendants and once by a petit jury when it tries them. That would take a lot of time, and the courts seem far more interested in improving efficiency in our grossly inefficient legal system than they are in the quality of justice. Anyway, it's absurd to claim that grand-jury proceedings are not criminal proceedings, since witnesses may be indicted for crimes that the grand jury is investigating, and since they can be imprisoned if they refuse to talk after being granted immunity. While someone who has never been tried or convicted of any crime can spend as much as eighteen months in prison for civil contempt, someone who faces a criminal-contempt charge that could lead to imprisonment for six months or more has a right to a jury trial and can never be imprisoned again for the same contempt because of the double-jeopardy clause in the Fifth Amendment. So under our grand-jury system those who have been found guilty can be treated more fairly and leniently than those who are innocent under the law."

The denial of due process that troubled Avery the most when Grusse and Turgeon were subpoenaed to appear the second time before the grand jury, on the morning of February 13, 1975, was that witnesses are not allowed to have lawyers present when they are interrogated. Usually they are permitted to have lawyers waiting outside the grand-jury room and are permitted to go out and consult with them before answering questions. But that, too, has drawbacks. "The only justification for not giving grand-jury witnesses the Sixth Amendment right to have a lawyer at their side is that the lawyer may advise them in a way that the prosecutor doesn't want them to be advised," Avery has explained. "But the basis for the right to counsel is precisely to allow the individual to have that kind of advice when confronted by all the immense powers of government." Moreover, he went on, the awkward and time-consuming practice of allowing witnesses to leave the grand-jury room to consult with their lawyers makes what should be a *right* to counsel seem to grand jurors to be a *privilege,* and if that privilege is requested very often they are bound to become annoyed and perhaps prejudiced against the witness. And, of course, a frightened and ignorant witness may not even assert the privilege when asked a seemingly innocent question that is actually a legal trap.

Among the other drawbacks he discovered in the system, Avery said, is that since a grand jury is under no obligation to tell witnesses what the subject of the inquiry is, they often don't know whether they are suspects, whether they have committed some crime that they were unaware of and now may inadvertently confess to, or whether they are being questioned about the activities of others. Under these uncertain circumstances, a witness who answers *anything* asked by a grand jury may be taking a grave risk. Ordinarily, prosecutors don't tell witnesses whether or not they are "targets" of the grand jury's investigation, that whatever they say may be used against them, that they can remain silent unless they are given immunity, or that they may be prosecuted for perjury if they testify and lie. In addition, if one answers *any* question asked by a prosecutor (or, rarely, a grand juror) before a grand jury — apart from one's name — one may automatically waive the right to refuse to answer any other question. Witnesses who go before grand juries without consulting a lawyer, as many do, are unlikely to be aware of this rule — or snare — and may end up being forced to testify against themselves without having even the slender advantage of being given use immunity beforehand.

Grand jurors are themselves rarely aware that the elementary principles of fair play — or "fundamental fairness," which the Supreme Court requires of all government practice in criminal cases — are suspended during their hearings, because when new grand juries are convened judges rarely tell the members anything about their supposed "historic function," or much of anything beyond their duty to indict those who seem guilty. Accordingly, grand jurors are usually the uninformed assistants of the prosecutor rather than members of a people's panel, and he can manipulate them more or less as he pleases. An unscrupulous prosecutor, for instance, can easily make a witness who tries to assert his exceedingly limited rights look guilty merely for asserting them. If a prosecutor asks a witness a seemingly innocuous leadoff question such as "What newspapers do you read?" or "What did you have for breakfast this morning?" and the witness refuses to answer on the ground that his response may tend to incriminate him — meaning, of course, that if he waives his right to silence by answering that harmless question he will have to answer a lot of possibly incriminating ones — the grand jurors are apt to conclude that the witness is simply obstructing justice. Also, prosecutors can easily browbeat witnesses by embarrassing them. Shortly after

Turgeon and Grusse had been questioned by the New Haven grand jury the first time, a federal grand jury in Lexington, Kentucky, which was looking into reports that the fugitives Susan Saxe and Katherine Power had hidden out in a lesbian community there, allowed the U.S. Attorney in charge to ask several women who were subpoenaed and put under oath, "What is your sexual preference?" For refusing to answer this question, among others, the women were found in contempt and sent to prison. And, as Avery had warned his clients, once they were both given immunity each of them could be forced to testify against the other, and thereby provide the government with "independent" evidence — if such existed — against both of them.

Despite the consequences facing them, Grusse and Turgeon were more determined than ever to remain silent, for they believed that it was the only way they could preserve their personal integrity — the essence of their humanity and individuality, as they saw it. But they also believed that the government was determined to make them talk or go to prison. Now that the Fifth Amendment had been effectively eliminated by the use-immunity law, they knew that the government possessed the kind of power over them that it had never before had over Americans — the power to decide what the *size* of any individual's integrity shall be.

At a little after nine o'clock on the morning of February 13th, Grusse and Turgeon appeared before Judge Newman to be officially notified that the court had granted them use immunity under a request from the Department of Justice, which had been formally submitted to the District Court by Assistant U.S. Attorney William Dow. At the time, Avery argued before the Judge that the grand jury had two improper purposes: to help the F.B.I. find the fugitives and to help the Justice Department prepare for its prosecution of them when they were captured. On these grounds, he moved that the subpoenas for the women be quashed.

Dow vehemently denied that catching fugitives was the government's purpose in subpoenaing the women or in granting them use immunity, and insisted that the grand jury was looking into the question of whether any federal crimes had been committed by Saxe and Power if they had lived for a time in Connecticut, as reported, or by others who might have known them and helped them hide out there or escape to another state. Of course, Dow's denial that his purpose was to obtain information on the whereabouts of the two fugitives was essential for the government, because harboring fugitives and failing to notify the authorities of a known felony, or misprision of felony, were the only federal crimes in the case at hand that the New Haven grand jury had jurisdiction over. Under the law, it could not investigate crimes committed in other jurisdictions than its own, which was limited to the federal judicial district encompassing Connecticut; also, it could not legally investigate crimes simply to help the government capture or build a case against someone who had already been indicted, as Saxe and Power had been back in the fall of 1970.

After hearing both sides present their arguments, Judge Newman dismissed Avery's contentions and denied his motion to quash the subpoenas. As the two women left the courtroom, Avery warned them that their situation looked nearly hopeless.

"I had never been so frightened in my life," Grusse said later. "We had brought our suitcases, because we thought we'd be taken off to prison that very day. I was sure I was going to prison, and the mere thought of it terrified me almost beyond control."

Turgeon was equally frightened. In fact, she momentarily considered fleeing. "I was near hysteria," she said later.

Afterward, the two women, accompanied by Avery and Diane Polan, his legal assistant, walked down the broad, marble-floored corridor on the second floor of the post-office building toward the grand-jury room. When they got there, Avery held Grusse and Turgeon in a huddle with his arms around their shoulders and whispered some last-minute instructions to them. He had little encouragement to offer, because he had been convinced by his study of the grand-jury system that his clients' chances of remaining both silent and free were slight. "I knew that I was legally helpless," he said afterward. "It was the most frustrating and discouraging experience I'd had so far in practicing law. It's terrible for a lawyer to have to stand there and not be able to do anything for a client — really nothing at all except go through the motions and hope that the other side will make a mistake. A lawyer shouldn't get too emotionally involved with clients, because it destroys his objectivity and effectiveness, but I couldn't help being involved with these women. I really sympathized with them."

Dow summoned Turgeon before the grand jury first, put her under oath, and asked if she understood that the grant of immunity supplanted her Fifth Amendment right to remain silent, and that if she testified and lied she might be prosecuted for perjury. Turgeon nodded, and Dow put his first question to her: Had she appeared before this same grand jury on January 28th? At first, Turgeon assumed that this was one of those seemingly inoffensive questions designed to trap her into waiving her right to silence, but then she realized that the grant of use immunity had deprived her of that right. Following the plan she and Grusse had drawn up with Avery, she wrote down the question, then asked if she could consult her lawyer. The foreman of the grand jury gave her permission — after a glance at Dow, who nodded, almost imperceptibly — and Turgeon left the room and returned in a few minutes carrying a slip of paper on which Avery had written her answer, which she read to the grand jury: "Upon the advice of counsel, I respectfully refuse to answer the question on the grounds that it and these proceedings violate my rights under the First, Third, Fourth, Fifth, Sixth, Eighth, Ninth, and Fourteenth Amendments to the United States Constitution, and under the United States Code, and for the reason that I believe I have been the object of illegal electronic and personal surveillance by the government, and for the reason that this proceeding and this question constitute an abuse of the grand-jury process."

It was a constitutional mouthful, but it was largely irrelevant, since courts have generally exempted grand-jury proceedings from ordinary constitutional protections. Still, the statement contained the two legal issues that were to end up being at the heart of the case: whether or not there had been illegal eavesdropping, and whether or not there had been abuse of the grand jury. The first point was a new one, and Avery raised it both because he and his associates in the case believed there was a strong possibility that the government had illegally kept them or their clients under surveillance and because the Supreme Court had ruled in 1972, by way of Gelbard v. United States, that when the government is asked by grand-jury witnesses about its use of illegal surveillance as a basis for the questions asked them, the failure to deny the use of such eavesdropping relieves the witnesses of all obligation to testify. (This ruling, which was opposed by all four of Nixon's appointees to the Court, was based not on constitutional grounds but on statutory grounds – that is, on the intent of Congress as expressed in a 1968 act governing electronic surveillance.)

Dow then asked Turgeon if she knew Saxe and Power. She again requested permission to see her lawyer, went outside, came back into the room, and gave the same response. Dow went on to describe the crimes that Saxe and Power had been charged with, and said, "It is believed that either or both Power and Saxe lived for a period of time in Connecticut, and that you knew them, and that you may have information as to other people who knew them who might have assisted or aided them while they were in this state, and [who] might otherwise be guilty of some criminal involvement with them. That is the purpose of this grand-jury inquiry. I'd like to know when you last saw either [of them], where that was, when that was, who they were with." After going through the same routine, Turgeon gave the same answer. This time, Dow warned her that she faced contempt-of-court charges, and then asked several more questions that were slight variations on the main question, all of which Turgeon responded to with the same answer. Finally, she was dismissed.

Dow asked Grusse somewhat different questions about Saxe, Power, and anyone who might have known them in Connecticut. Grusse gave the same answers as Turgeon had, but then added a long statement at the end: "Furthermore, I firmly believe that I have been called before the grand jury because I have chosen to exercise my right not to speak with the F.B.I. My decision not to speak to them is based on the moral belief that the investigation the government is engaged in will violate my basic constitutional and human rights. . . . I believe that every person has the right to keep her affairs private without intervention by government agents. I am also aware that the government, acting through the F.B.I. and grand juries, has used inquiries such as this to harass and gather information on political persons in recent years, and I do not care to be a party to that process. It's also true that there is no basis for investigating any criminal activity in the state of Connecticut, and that the grand-jury system and you, the jurors, are being used as tools of the F.B.I. to further their investigation. This is not a legitimate use of the grand jury, and I respectfully request that you excuse me on those grounds."

Dow asked Grusse if she intended to refuse to answer all questions. Before he could finish, though, the foreman unexpectedly broke in and said, "Could I ask one question?" Looking surprised, Dow nodded, whereupon the foreman turned to Grusse. "Do you understand the description of the reason that you are being called here, that Attorney Dow just stated?" he asked her. "Do you understand that the purpose of this grand jury is to investigate a crime that was committed in Boston in 1970, and your possible knowledge of any of – of any of the facts concerning the whereabouts of the people, the perpetrators of the crime? Do you understand that is the reason why you are being asked to be here?"

Of course, the foreman's question, or statement, about the grand jury's purpose was not only at odds with Dow's statement about that purpose, it was a clear admission that the grand jury was improperly seeking to help the government catch a couple of fugitives – unless the foreman had no understanding of what had been going on during the grand jury's investigation of the Saxe-Power case.

Dow hastily interrupted to say, "Let me amplify that to a degree, if I could, Mr. Foreman, to indicate that the scope of the inquiry goes beyond the crime itself that was committed in Boston, but activities of the individuals believed to have committed those crimes in the state of Connecticut, such as involving – such as possible assistance to those suspects by other individuals in the state. Is that your understanding?"

Although Dow's flapping syntax put the question beyond understanding, the foreman replied, "That's right."

Apparently, Dow had meant to say that the grand jury's inquiry included crimes committed in Connecticut, which put the witnesses under the jurisdiction of the grand jury. But his "amplification" did not diminish the significance of the foreman's statement, which had unmistakably made clear that in his view the purpose of the grand jury was to get information about a crime committed in another jurisdiction and about two people who had already been indicted for that crime – a doubly improper purpose. Of course, the foreman could have got this impression from only one source – Dow, who had decided what evidence was to be presented to the grand jury. And yet no one who had dealt with Dow in the case from the witnesses' side doubted his decency, sincerity, or devotion to duty.

"Dow spent several years working the other side of the street as a public defender in Washington, D.C.," one of the lawyers in the case said shortly after Grusse and Turgeon were granted use immunity. "He's an honorable fellow, and he doesn't like to think of himself as an oppressor. That's why he keeps talking about the nine kids that policeman left. He's trying to convince himself that he's behaving properly so he can uphold his liberal credentials. At the start of this case, we thought he would push it a little to satisfy his superiors and then would realize that he was doing something wrong and would drop it. But he didn't. He's pushed it all the way. His rationalization is that this is a local investigation of lawbreaking in this district, but it's clearly not that. Whatever Dow's own goal is, the Feds are obviously intent not on just finding Saxe and Power but on uncovering nationwide radical connections in the women's movement."

Dow impressed Turgeon and Grusse as being anything but vindictive or ruthless in their case. When they first appeared before the grand jury in late January, he went out of his way to warn them of various matters that he was under no obligation to reveal – that they were not targets of the grand jury's investigation, that they could still be prosecuted if they revealed any crimes they had committed, that they had the right to plead the Fifth Amendment and remain silent unless they were granted immunity, and that they could be prosecuted for perjury if they testified and lied. Of course, he must have assumed that Avery had already told his clients about these matters. Even so, the women regarded Dow with sympathy and even fondness. "He's a decent man — very personable and affable," Grusse said. "I think he really believes that what he's doing is right. But what he believes is right is that he should do everything in his power to catch a couple of people who are accused of bank robbery and murder. And to do that he will close his eyes to the real problems in this case — the political and legal issues involved and the personal rights being sacrificed. Our individual rights, our sense of our own integrity, our duty to ourselves mean nothing to him. All he can talk about is that dead policeman who left nine kids. I'm sorry about that, too, but I had nothing to do with it, and I have nothing to say now that Dow has any right to know."

Both she and Turgeon felt that although Dow was fair to them, he might as well have been unfair, since his purpose was to force them to betray themselves or go to prison. In Turgeon's view, Dow was also a victim of the F.B.I.'s frantic search for Saxe and Power. "I don't think he set out to do this to us," she explained. "In fact, I don't think the F.B.I. set out to do it, either. I think the Bureau was really embarrassed at not being able to catch two little women for all that time. The whole thing just got out of hand for the F.B.I. and in the end for Dow, too. Because we stood up to the system, they came to see us not as a couple of helpless individuals but as two tough radicals, maybe even criminals, who were nearly as bad as Saxe and Power. When the search for them began, the F.B.I. had no idea of how broad and deep the women's movement was. I don't mean the women's-libbers, the bra-burners, and the equal-pay advocates. I mean the serious revolutionaries who believe that society has to be turned upside down before there can be any true equality for women and any real justice. I think this discovery really scared the F.B.I., and then it saw the Saxe-Power investigation as a cover for finding out more about this radical 'network,' as they call it. So all we are — and maybe all Dow is — are tools in this investigation of the women's movement."

In the end, Dow's reliance on the legal but fundamentally unfair instruments of official inquisition — use immunity and the repressive power of the grand jury — to achieve the laudable goal of bringing to justice two people accused of vicious crimes again brings to mind Justice Brandeis's warning: "Experience should teach us to be most on our guard to protect liberty when the government's purposes are beneficent. Men born to freedom are naturally alert to repel invasion of their liberty by evil-minded rulers. The greatest dangers to liberty lurk in insidious encroachment by men of zeal, well-meaning but without understanding."

After Grusse and Turgeon refused to testify, Dow filed a motion with the court asking that they be ordered to answer the grand jury's questions, and Judge Newman set a hearing on the motion for the next morning. At the hearing, Dow put on the stand the court reporter assigned to the grand jury, and he read his stenographic notes of the questions asked by Dow, the witnesses' refusals to answer, the foreman's statement about the grand jury's purpose, and Dow's attempt to "amplify" it. When Avery got his turn, he bore down on the foreman's remarks to prove that the grand jury was being improperly used by the government. It was clearly the prosecutor's intention, Avery said, to turn over to the F.B.I. any evidence presented to the grand jury about Saxe and Power, which would violate the strict secrecy imposed by law on grand-jury proceedings as far as any member of the jury or any official of the government was concerned.

Judge Newman regarded both arguments with indifference, and at the end of the hearing he stated, "Essentially, when all is said and done, it seems to me as if the witnesses are really asserting what they conceive to be a constitutionally protected right of privacy. It's understandable they may have a personal preference not to assist a grand jury [in] uncovering evidence of the commission of federal crimes, but their preference must give way to the legitimate power of the grand jury to have their testimony. . . . There is no showing before me whatsoever of any harassing or unnecessarily personalized inquiry. The situation might be different if in a very extraordinary case intimate personal details were being probed for no apparent legitimate purpose. That's not this case at all." Newman then instructed Dow to write down the questions he had asked the two witnesses, and said that he would order the women to go back before the grand jury later that day and answer them or face contempt of court.

At two o'clock that afternoon, Grusse and Turgeon appeared before the grand jury and refused to answer the questions on the same grounds. Afterward, Dow filed a motion asking the court to find them in contempt, and Judge Newman set February 18th, four days later, for a hearing on that motion.

Early on the morning of the eighteenth, Avery and David Rosen, his associate in the case, filed a forty-two-page brief setting down all the legal issues that they had not had time to present to the court formally. They also filed a motion claiming "unlawful electronic surveillance" and demanding that the government deny there had been taps on any of the telephones used by the principals, their lawyers, and a few colleagues who had been involved in the case. To support this motion, Avery and Rosen filed seven affidavits indicating why they thought there had been wiretapping of certain telephones by the government.

In reply, Dow the same day filed a half-page affidavit swearing that he had checked all the names listed on the affidavits, and adding, "I hearby state that there has been no electronic surveillance or interception of wire or oral communications of those individuals named."

Just before the February 18th hearing, Avery subpoenaed an F.B.I. agent working on the Saxe-Power case in Connecticut, but at the hearing Dow opposed the subpoena, and Judge Newman asked Avery to explain his reasons for wanting the agent to testify. Avery replied that he merely wanted to ask him why he had requested that Dow summon Grusse and Turgeon before the grand jury in the first place, and to find out whether the F.B.I. already had the information that it was seeking from the two women. In other words, Avery hoped to show that the F.B.I. was more interested in harassing the witnesses than in getting their testimony. Moreover, Avery went on, he wanted to call Dow to the stand, to ask him whether he intended to pass on to the F.B.I. whatever might be learned from Grusse and Turgeon, despite the rule imposing secrecy on everyone involved in grand-jury hearings except the witnesses.

Judge Newman denied both requests. "I am satisfied that the representations concerning the inquiry of the grand jury as to possible violations of federal law in the district of Connecticut are sufficient to justify the grand jury asking the particular questions that were put to these witnesses," he said. Then he announced that he would deliver his finding on the contempt motion the following day.

In court the next day, Judge Newman informed Avery that the government had just submitted to him a sealed affidavit containing the evidence it possessed to demonstrate its reasons for asking Turgeon and Grusse the questions posed to them by Dow before the grand jury — reasons that included some evidence against Grusse and Turgeon themselves. (Although the judge in such a case can examine a sealed affidavit, neither the witnesses nor their lawyers are permitted to see it.) The government, Newman added, had promised the court that if it sought to indict the two witnesses for any crimes, the evidence it now had would be presented before a grand jury other than the one they had so far refused to testify before. Then, ruling that Dow's denial of illegal surveillance was sufficient and that there was no reason to believe that the grand jury was being improperly used or that the witnesses were being harassed by the F.B.I., the Judge found Grusse and Turgeon in contempt of court. He ordered them "remanded to the custody of the United States marshal until such time as they elect to purge their contempt by testifying, but in no event for longer than the expiration of the term of the grand jury on April 1, 1975." Finally, he delayed execution of his order for five days, to allow the women time to appeal.

"Our feeling of helplessness is just incredible," Turgeon said afterward. "In a case of this sort, it's really hard to feel at all like a person. We can't express ourselves in any way. Everything that is said in court has to be said by our lawyers. They've been wonderful, but when the values we hold dear are translated into legal language they lose all personal meaning. They become so abstract that everyone forgets there are people involved — except those people. The frustration is awful, because the truth is lost in all the legalisms. The basic truth is that we have the right to silence. The issues of grand-jury abuse, wiretapping, harassment by the F.B.I. are beside the point. But the truth doesn't matter. What matters is power, and all the power is on the other side."

On February 20th, the day after Judge Newman's decision, Avery and Rosen filed a notice of intent to appeal it and another motion for a stay in carrying out the contempt citation until the appeal was ruled on. Then Dow filed a motion asking the Court of Appeals to deny any delay, on the ground that the contempt law prohibited this if an "appeal is frivolous or taken for the purposes of delay" — both of which, Dow contended, applied to the case at hand; moreover, he said, since the law requires the Court of Appeals to rule on such an appeal in not more than thirty days, if that court took its full allotment of time there would be only eleven more days until the term of the grand jury ran out, which "would render the adjudication of contempt meaningless." On February 21st, the Court of Appeals rejected Dow's arguments, and on the twenty-fifth the court gave the two women two days to prepare their appeals for oral argument before a panel of three judges.

Since Avery was occupied with other cases in New Haven, he decided to call in a specialist in appellate and constitutional law — a young woman named Kristin Booth Glen, whom he had known for years. Glen had got her early legal training in the law offices of Leonard Boudin, one of the most accomplished legal practitioners on the political left, and then she taught at New York University Law School and worked with the National Lawyers Guild, in New York, until she went into private practice. The Guild, which Avery had contacted at the start of the case, was set up forty years ago; it had played a major role in defending victims of congressional witch hunts against the left in the early nineteen-fifties, and had responded to the Nixon Administration's misuse of the grand-jury system to persecute the President's political opponents by setting up a group to study the legal ins and outs of that system. By the time the Grusse-Turgeon case came along, the standard legal work on the subject was a thick Guild handbook, which was used by lawyers on both sides in such cases. Armed with the handbook and assisted by consultants at the Guild, Glen set up a legal command center in a friend's office in New York, and for two days and most of two nights – the extraordinarily short time allotted by the Court of Appeals – she worked on the crucial issue of electronic surveillance for her part of the appellate brief. Back in New Haven, Avery, Rosen, Polan, and a battery of students from Yale Law School worked on their part of the appeal – abuse of the grand-jury system. "It was an around-the-clock job," Polan said later. "We had to drop everything else at the office to work on the brief."

In the end, the brief ran to forty-seven pages, and ranged over a wide variety of complicated technical matters. Overall, though, it concentrated on Avery's two major points: that the government's denial of surveillance had been inadequate and that there had been flagrantly improper use of the grand-jury process. On the first issue, Glen pointed out that the government's "search" of its surveillance records had consisted of a few telephone conversations between Dow and the F.B.I. agent in charge of the Saxe-Power case in Connecticut, who had reported that his surveillance records showed no sign of any surveillance having been conducted on Grusse, Turgeon, or any of the lawyers and legal assistants in the case. Apparently, Dow had not asked the agent to check any records in the offices of the F.B.I. or other government agencies in Washington that commonly engage in electronic surveillance. Citing a 1974 decision of the same court she was appealing to – the Court of Appeals for the Second Circuit – Glen asserted that its own ruling then had required a government prosecutor who was challenged on the issue of illegal surveillance to show by affidavit each of the agencies that was checked and its specific written denials that any conversations of anyone using any of the telephones involved had been overheard. (Government wiretapping and bugging, both legal and illegal, have become so widespread that the Second Circuit often requires what is called an "eight-agency check" — of the F.B.I., the Secret Service, the Internal Revenue Service, the Customs Service, the Drug Enforcement Administration, the Postal Service, the Criminal Division of the Justice Department, and the Bureau of Alcohol, Tobacco, and Firearms. Actually, though, at least twenty-six federal agencies conduct surveillance of private citizens.)

On the issue of improper use of the grand jury, Avery quoted the foreman's statement about the New Haven grand jury's purpose, which, he said, constituted "a prima-facie case of abuse of the grand-jury function." Quoting the Second Circuit's opinion in an eleven-year-old case on this issue, he reminded the court that it had said there, "It is improper to utilize a grand jury for the sole or dominating purpose of preparing an already pending indictment for trial." Once there was such evidence of abuse as the foreman's admission, Avery argued, Judge Newman had erred in depriving Grusse and Turgeon of their right to due process of law in the contempt hearings by refusing to let them call witnesses on their behalf — that is, the F.B.I. agent and Dow — to ask why they had been subpoenaed in the first place. Further, he said, the District Court had jurisdiction over the grand jury, and Newman had also erred by failing to halt the government's use of a grand jury in one federal district to investigate crimes committed in another district, as well as by failing to prohibit the government from violating grand-jury secrecy by passing on information obtained in secret proceedings to agencies like the Department of Justice.

In reply, Dow submitted a twenty-seven-page brief, in which he declared that his affidavit denying the use of electronic surveillance was sufficient under the rules laid down in that circuit. "[The witnesses'] claim that the grand jury is preparing an already indicted case for trial, even if true, does not constitute an abuse of the grand jury," he went on. "While it is often argued that a grand jury cannot continue to hear evidence in a case in which it has already returned an indictment, the cases most often cited to support that proposition do not do so." He then analyzed the cases most often cited, and concluded that as long as a grand jury's investigation of indicted suspects was not its "sole or dominant purpose," the courts could not interfere with the process. Nor, he said, could he find a "court decision which would prohibit a grand jury from investigating the whereabouts of fugitives for the sole purpose of achieving their apprehension." And, finally, he contended that it was wholly proper for him to pass grand-jury evidence on to an agency like the F.B.I.

The issues were clearly drawn, and the Court of Appeals chose to ignore them altogether. At the end of the oral arguments, on the afternoon of February 27th, the three judges recessed for ten minutes and then reconvened to read their two-to-one decision upholding the government — a decision that had obviously been prepared before the oral arguments. In the formal opinion that was filed later, Judge William Timbers, formerly chief judge of the District Court in Connecticut and a Nixon appointee, spoke for himself and Judge J. Edward Lumbard, an ex-U.S. Attorney. The opinion was based on three points. First, Timbers said, there was "the strong public policy reflected in the statute" enacting contempt-of-court penalties for refusing to testify after being granted use immunity and in the "congressional concern over disruption of smooth and efficient operation of the grand-jury system."

Of course, "the strong public policy" was the Nixon policy of destroying his "enemies" by way of use immunity and the power of the grand jury. Federal courts traditionally examine what is known as the "intent" of Congress in interpreting its legislation, and Judge Timbers took the overwhelming congressional support for the bill that the contempt and use-immunity provisions were part of — the Organized Crime Control Act of 1970 — as evidence of Congress's firm intent. As it happened, though, neither use immunity nor any other part of that act received more than cursory attention by Congress, whose members knew that they risked defeat at the polls if they voted in an election year against anything called the Organized Crime Control Act when the public's fear of crime, which the Administration had largely created and had then relied on when it proposed the legislation, was at such a feverish height. Actually, many of the members who voted for the bill trusted that the courts would undo the effects of their cowardice by overturning the worst parts of the law, which was the most malevolently repressive piece of legislation to be approved by Congress in a generation. In short, their intent was simply to stay in office. By endorsing Congress's timidity and carelessness, Judge Timbers failed to recognize the clear intent of the Framers of the Constitution in establishing an independent, nonelected federal judiciary — to serve as a check on demagogic excesses committed by the popularly elected legislature. And his argument about Congress's concern for the efficiency of the grand-jury system betrayed an ignorance of American history, for no one had ever conceived of any of the safeguards set forth in the Bill of Rights as an attempt to make our law-enforcement system more efficient.

Timbers' second point was that his court had already dealt with the issues raised in the Grusse-Turgeon case the year before through In re Persico. In that case, a grand-jury witness had refused to answer a question based on electronic surveillance that had been approved by a court before it was undertaken and had demanded a hearing, which was denied, on whether the admitted wiretapping violated the law. In Persico, the Second Circuit had ruled that in denying Persico's request for a hearing the District Court had acted properly, in line with "the traditional notion that the functioning of the grand-jury system should not be impeded or interrupted." Now Timbers cited Persico and said that "the present case is an even more compelling one for adhering to the strong public policy of this circuit of not permitting disruption of grand-jury proceedings absent compelling reasons." He added, "We find no such compelling reasons here." He ignored Glen's contention in her appeal that Persico was "entirely inapposite" — a point firmly upheld by the dissenting judge in the Grusse-Turgeon case, James Oakes, another Nixon appointee, who has turned out to be one of the most liberal judges on the federal bench today — because there had been no evaluation of allegedly illegal wiretapping by a "neutral and detached magistrate" in the case at bar, whereas in Persico the wiretapping had been approved beforehand by a judge.

Finally, Timbers found Judge Newman's decision that Grusse and Turgeon were in contempt and must go to prison "a striking example of the balancing by a conscientious and comprehending district judge of the interests of the appellants as witnesses before the grand jury, on the one hand, and, on the other, of the public interest." Judge Newman's decision, he added, was "unassailable." There is probably no judicial device that is more assailable than the tired old balancing test, in which the interests of the state and the interests of the individual are weighed against each other. A striking example of judicial cowardice that is used by the most statist judges to justify whatever the government wants to do, the test might well be used in Russia or China today, for essentially it provides an opportunity to put a mask of fairness on tyranny. When a judge places all of society on one pan of the scales of justice and one person on the other pan, there cannot be much doubt about the outcome. In fact, the only time that the test works in favor of the individual is when there is nothing at all to put on the government's pan.

It takes four justices of the Supreme Court to grant certiorari — that is, to agree to review a case — and ordinarily it takes the Court several months to get around to deciding whether a petition for certiorari should be granted, and then several more months may pass before the Court reviews and decides a case. But when a citizen stands in danger of suffering irreparable injury by the state, the justice assigned to the judicial circuit involved can grant a stay of any prosecution or imprisonment until the full Court has had a chance to consider a petition for certiorari. To give Grusse and Turgeon an opportunity to take advantage of this rule, the Court of Appeals allowed them six more days to appeal to the justice responsible for the Second Circuit, Thurgood Marshall, and Glen prepared an emergency appeal, which Polan filed at his chambers on March 4th.

Glen's brief asking for a temporary stay was much the same as the appeal she had written, except that now she pointed out the different rulings by different circuit courts on the issue of what was an "adequate" denial of illegal surveillance by the government in such cases, and asked the Supreme Court to resolve the question once and for all. Then she came up with a balancing test of her own on behalf of her clients. "Because their loss of liberty can never be justly compensated, petitioners will be irreparably and irrevocably injured if the stay is not extended while their serious constitutional claims are being litigated," she said. "If, on the other hand, the stay is extended to avoid certain irreparable injury to the petitioners, the government will not suffer unduly." And if the government was serious in contending that its purpose in demanding testimony from the two witnesses was to uncover crimes committed in Connecticut rather than to capture two fugitives, Glen pointed out in conclusion, there was no great hurry, for "the only injury which can be justly claimed by the government is inconvenience." Justice Marshall rejected the application on the following day without comment.

At four o'clock on the afternoon of March 5th, Turgeon and Grusse turned themselves in to the U.S. marshal at his office down the hall from the grand-jury room in the New Haven post office. A matron searched the women for weapons, and then the marshal handcuffed each of them and chained them together at their waists. He apologized for the manacles, explaining that they were required by federal rules. "It's unbelievably stupid," Avery said later. "If they wanted to escape, they wouldn't have turned themselves in at all. They would have taken off when Justice Marshall turned down their application that morning. It's just another official attempt to humiliate and degrade people who stand up to the system."

When the prisoners were led out of the marshal's office, they saw heavily armed policemen in riot gear stationed along the corridor, and in the parking lot behind the post office there were several police cars and more riot police. "Obviously, they had come to view us as hardened, dangerous criminals," Grusse said. "And we were merely two women who had vowed not to discuss their personal lives with anyone."

On the way out of the building, the group passed Dow, and Grusse lifted her manacled arms to him and said, "Thanks a lot, Willie."

Dow looked stunned. "*I* didn't do it," he said. "It's not *my* fault."

The Connecticut Correctional Institution at Niantic, about fifty miles east of New Haven on the Connecticut coast, is a state prison for women that houses a few federal prisoners under contract with the U.S. Bureau of Prisons. During the ride to Niantic, the prisoners sat in the back of the marshal's car, a green sedan, while he drove and the matron sat beside him. "I was absolutely terrified," Turgeon recalled afterward. "All I knew about prison life was those old movies and the stories about Attica – bars and cells and sadistic guards and vicious criminals. There was nothing, absolutely nothing, in my past experience to prepare me for what lay ahead, and I was paralyzed by fear."

Grusse was, too. "I knew that most of the other inmates would be black and poor," she said. "That really frightened me, because I had my own stereotyped idea of what such women would be like – tough and contemptuous and ready to hurt anyone they didn't like. I feared that they would resent me because I'm white and educated – in short, privileged. And I was frightened most of all by what they might do to us when they found out that we were lesbians."

Their fears on all of these scores proved baseless. The prison turned out to be an "open facility." There was no fence around its spacious grounds, the "cellblocks" consisted of five cottages, each housing twenty to thirty inmates, and the "cells" were private rooms for each inmate; the guards were generally decent; and the other inmates, most of whom were black women convicted of prostitution or narcotics-related violations, were friendly. "They helped us learn the ropes and settle into the place," Grusse said. "And while they were curious about our being gay, they gave us no trouble about that. In fact, they gave us no trouble at all. They even supported our refusing to talk, because somebody's talking was why most of them were in prison."

Turgeon and Grusse were assigned to tutor inmates in basic mathematics during mornings and to work in the prison library during afternoons. "Although prison life wasn't anywhere near as bad as I had expected, it was terrible," Turgeon said. "Worst of all, they treat you like a bad child who has to be controlled or helped all the time. You're considered to be incapable of making a decision on your own, and if you question anything, they tell you that you just don't understand the reasons behind it. Usually there isn't any reason — just bureaucratic rules that exist for their own sake. And, craziest of all, they never tell you what the rules are until you break one. They kept telling us to act like adults, but every time someone did — by taking responsibility of one kind or another, which is what adulthood means — they would say, 'You're causing problems.' The simplicity of their idea of 'correction' is unbelievable. When we arrived, they even taught us how to take showers. They said, 'You turn on this faucet for hot water, this faucet for cold water, and then adjust them until you get the temperature you want for your shower.' I thought we'd been taken to a madhouse. And when you get angry, they simply give you tranquillizers to control it. The whole system is aimed at control, but to no purpose. And the boredom is stupefying. Each cottage has a television and a stereo set, which are always on full blast. The inmates are mostly young, and they shout and talk a lot. You can go to your room for privacy, but you can never get away from the incessant noise, except at night, and then you're sleeping. You can take a walk, but only if a guard goes along. There's a pretty little lake on the prison grounds, and I longed to go sit by it alone. They wouldn't allow that unless a guard went with me. In the end, I felt much the same at Niantic as I had in the courtroom — helpless. It's as if society's true purpose is to destroy every shred of individuality in anyone who stands up to it. And it was just that — my individuality — that had brought me there and that I was trying so hard to preserve."

On March 27th, after the women had been in prison for three weeks, Susan Saxe was captured while walking along a street in Philadelphia. Five days later, the term of the New Haven federal grand jury ran out, and that afternoon Grusse and Turgeon were released from prison. The marshal drove up from New Haven to deliver their release papers, but then, as the two women stepped out of the prison administration building into freedom, he handed each of them a subpoena to appear before a newly convened federal grand jury in New Haven on May 6th, five weeks away.

The Grand Jury Defense Committee, which had been set up in New Haven a few weeks earlier to publicize and create opposition to the government's pursuit of Grusse and Turgeon, kept public interest focussed on their case, and when they returned to New Haven they found that they had become celebrities among members of the women's community there. Once word of the new subpoenas and the threat of sixteen or seventeen months more in prison if the two again refused to testify got around, their fame spread more and more widely. The publicity made the two women uneasy, because they valued their privacy more than ever now, and they feared the damage that such publicity might do to them personally. "I had to look at myself very closely to make sure that what I was doing was for good reasons and wasn't an ego trip or the result of a desire to become a celebrity," Turgeon said. "I'd never been one to analyze myself, but this time I had to. When I thought about it, I realized that the stand I was taking had nothing to do with my ego, because being a celebrity of any kind was the last thing I wanted. I just wanted, and want, to be left alone to live in peace in my own way. I decided then that I had to do what I was doing because it was right. When I realized that I would not willingly do anything that I considered wrong, I knew that I was sincere in my decision to remain silent. Since I didn't think that anything I had done was wrong, how could I help the government prove that what I had done *was* wrong? If the government disagrees with something I've done, then it's up to the government to prove that something against me. But the government wants *me* to prove I was wrong. That is simply and fundamentally unjust."

To Grusse, the effects of being a celebrity were also distasteful. "Some people seem to see us simply as two women who refuse to talk, so we're not individuals at all," she explained. "Some others see us as superstrong celebrities. But that's not the way we see ourselves at any time. When we are invited to speak to women's groups in other cities, there are those who act as if we have perfectly formed views, clear politics, absolute strength. In other words, people try to make us into leaders. We aren't leaders, and we don't want to be. We're not allowed to be what we are — often confused and very frightened women. Also, a few people now seem to feel that they have a right to ask the kinds of personal questions that I never would have allowed anyone to ask me before. I guess that's because we're no longer private individuals. We're public figures, and people feel we belong more to them than to ourselves. The effect has two sides. On the one, I'm more willing to express myself in terms of what's happened to me, because I feel that it's urgent to let people know that this kind of thing can happen to *them*. This has opened up my private space to others. But, on the other side, my experience has made me less willing to talk about myself, because all this limelight has destroyed my privacy, and I constantly try to pull back out of the publicity in order to be myself. Besides all this, people continually come up and ask me for advice. I find that frightening, because I'm not really a different person than I was before anyone asked me for advice. They seem to think that because I'm sure of *my* course I can help *them*. All this has made it very hard for me to be me — just an ordinary person, which is what I am and what I want to be."

At nine o'clock on the morning of May 6th, an hour before Turgeon and Grusse were scheduled to appear before the grand jury, their lawyers submitted three motions to Judge Newman. The first asked him to quash the subpoenas, on the ground that the government was improperly using the grand jury. The second asked that he issue "protective orders" instructing the government to submit to the court all the evidence it had against the two women up to that day. (As it happened, Dow submitted to the court that same morning another sealed affidavit containing the government's evidence up to that point.) The purpose behind Avery's request was to make sure that the evidence the government had at that time would be separated from the evidence it might obtain if the women testified before the grand jury, so that if they were subsequently tried the defense would have a better chance of making sure that the prosecution was not using any evidence based on their coerced testimony, which would violate the use-immunity law's stipulation that trial evidence must be independent of such testimony. The protective orders that Avery asked for would also prohibit the government from seeking indictments against the witnesses by the same grand jury that they were shortly to appear before; would forbid the prosecutor to pass on any information he got from the witnesses to other government agencies, unless the government demonstrated that it was essential for the grand jury's deliberations, and then gave the witnesses a chance to oppose any transfer of such information; and would assure the witnesses of the right to have a transcript of their testimony. Avery's third motion asked Judge Newman to compel the government to disclose any surveillance. Avery contended the government should be compelled to conduct a complete search of its records on a total of forty-four telephones, and to submit to the court detailed affidavits from those who conducted searches of records in various governmental agencies showing whether or not there had been any surveillance in the Grusse-Turgeon case.

Avery also submitted to the court several affidavits sworn to by his clients, himself, Polan, Rosen, Glen, and various other lawyers directly and indirectly working on the case who claimed that their telephones had been acting strangely. The most persuasive of the affidavits was the one signed by Glen, who reported that the office in New York that she used while preparing the Grusse-Turgeon appeal had been leased by a lawyer who was subsequently notified by a judge of the New York County Supreme Court in a separate case that he had been the subject of a national-security wiretap by the federal government. "This disclosure obviously raises a very substantial likelihood that calls with regard to these witnesses and my representation of them were overheard," Glen stated in her affidavit.

Judge Newman denied the motion to quash the subpoenas, and reserved decision on the other motions.

Shortly after ten o'clock that morning, Grusse and Turgeon

went before the new grand jury. Each was asked the same list of nineteen questions – most of which pertained to what they might have known about others who might have known Saxe and Power in Connecticut – and each answered by refusing to testify, on the grounds they had cited before the previous grand jury. Prepared for this, the government asked the court for an order granting use immunity and compelling the witnesses to testify, and Judge Newman complied. The next day, May 7th, they went back before the grand jury and again refused to testify.

This time, Grusse added a new statement at the end of her final refusal: "This matter has been brought before the grand jury for the sole, dominant purpose of apprehending Katherine Power, an alleged fugitive, and of gathering evidence to use against Miss Power and against Susan Saxe in the trials of indictments which have already been issued. My subpoena is also part of a coördinated campaign by the F.B.I. to punish people who legally refuse to talk with them by exposing such people to threat of contempt of court, and to harass and intimidate people, particularly women's groups, so they will coöperate with the F.B.I. and abandon their legal rights to privacy. I decline to answer the questions for the further reason that the Assistant United States Attorney has publicly stated he will breach the secrecy of your proceedings here and will transmit any evidence which I give [you] to the F.B.I. to assist in the capture of an alleged fugitive, although this is in clear violation of the law. I decline to answer for the reason that the immunity which has been granted to me . . . is not adequate to protect my Fifth Amendment rights. I also ask members of the grand jury to take control of your own proceedings and to refuse to be a party to the abuse of your historic function that the government is insisting on here. I also ask you to order the Assistant United States Attorney to dismiss my subpoena and put an end to this violation of my rights. And if you feel that these proceedings are legitimate, I would appreciate hearing the reasons for your position. Would anyone care to answer?"

"We don't have to respond to your questions," the foreman said. "It's our duty to ask you questions. Do you refuse to talk – so you took the Fifth to protect your rights?"

"Yes," Grusse answered.

"It is our job here as an investigating group to ask questions, not to answer your questions."

"O.K.," Grusse said wearily, and with that she was dismissed.

Afterward, Avery said, "The trouble with grand-jury cases like this one — and there are more and more of them now — is that no one besides the witnesses takes the historic function of the grand jury seriously. Jurors don't take their own function seriously because usually they don't know that it exists in the way it's supposed to. They aren't even aware that they have both rights and the duty to assert them to protect the individual against the power of the state. Prosecutors don't take the grand-jury function seriously because to do so would impede their attempts to get indictments and to use grand juries as investigative tools to help them prepare for trials or to catch suspects, as in this case. And judges don't take grand juries seriously because they almost never instruct newly convened grand juries about their rights. So there is no way to get to those twenty-three people and say, 'Look, you have these definite rights, and you can assert them to save the innocent and strike a blow for freedom.' What the government fails to see in all this is that it is needlessly creating its own enemies by the methods it uses. I know that every case like this one, in which the government treats its citizens so unjustly, deepens my radical feelings. But think what it has done to these two women and their friends. These women weren't even political before, but they are now — deeply political and defiant — and their friends are, too. So in attempting to control radicals the government has mindlessly created hundreds more of them."

Judge Newman set May 12th for a hearing on why Grusse and Turgeon should not be found in contempt of court. But he also ordered the government to respond specifically to the charges of illegal wiretapping by June 3rd, which effectively postponed at least until that day any final ruling on the contempt question. At the hearing on May 12th, Avery once again tried to put an F.B.I. man — the agent in charge of the Saxe-Power case in Connecticut — on the stand in order to prove that the Bureau and the U.S. Attorney's office were using the grand jury to find Power and to prepare a case against her and Saxe. But Judge Newman refused to let him pursue this line of questioning, and said of the government, "They have filed their affidavit under seal indicating the basis on which they have reason to investigate crimes occurring in the district of Connecticut, and it's a very detailed affidavit. . . . The Court of Appeals affirmed this case the last time without even seeing that much [of] a detailed affidavit, so if they thought the case was right the last time, it's hard to see how it's any less right this time, when there is far more detail in support of the government's claim."

Avery said that he would like to look at the affidavit, but Newman refused, saying, "This is not just a nice privacy device to keep the prosecutor happy. . . . That affidavit mentioned several people's names who are potential suspects of a federal crime. I have no idea if they are guilty or innocent, but until they are properly indicted their names are not going to see the light of day, unless a higher court orders me to do it. So the rule of secrecy is not just for the benefit of the F.B.I. or the grand jury and U.S. Attorney. It's for the benefit, primarily, of those suspected of crime, but as to whom there may be no indictment and no prosecution, and we are just not going to get into names and places and dates that identify those people unless an indictment results. That's why that line of inquiry is just not going to be opened up."

While the Judge's explanation reflected the historic reasons for grand-jury secrecy, it was fundamentally misleading, and his decision was fundamentally unfair to the witnesses. Of course, "that line of inquiry" — whether or not the government was misusing the grand-jury system — was crucial to Avery's case, and it could have been opened up and closed without getting into any names and places and dates. All Judge Newman would have had to do was to allow Avery to ask the F.B.I. agent a simple yes-or-no kind of question: Did you ask Dow to subpoena Grusse and Turgeon in order to help the government catch and prepare a case against Saxe and Power? The answer would have settled the issue once and for all, and would not have jeopardized the grand jury's secrecy.

Avery went on to point out that when there are two potential defendants whose compelled testimony can be used as "independent" evidence against each other, use immunity does not protect their Fifth Amendment right against involuntary self-incrimination. Once again, this argument lay at the heart of the use-immunity issue. Under the old form of transactional, or total, immunity, a witness who was forced to testify could not be prosecuted later on for anything to do with the transaction or act he or she was questioned about. Now, though, under use immunity two witnesses who were involved in the same transaction could be forced to testify against each other, thereby providing incriminating evidence that was independent of their own admissions of criminal activity and laying each other open to prosecution. Judge Newman was not interested in the argument.

Glen again handled the issue of illegal surveillance, and pointed out that the F.B.I.'s indexing system, according to a recent account in the *Times,* was faulty, and argued that a far more complete search of the Bureau's records would be necessary. Judge Newman wasn't interested in this point, either, and said that any ruling on the surveillance issue would have to wait until the government submitted its affidavits denying or affirming impropriety on June 3rd. "It's my honest belief that most of the claims that have been made are . . . a smoke screen," he said.

On the morning of the third, the National Council of Churches, which represents thirty-one religious denominations having a total membership of more than forty million people, filed an *amicus curiae* memorandum with the District Court in New Haven appealing for leniency in punishing Grusse and Turgeon if they were found in contempt of court. The Council said, in part:

> This court has the physical power to say, "You will be put in jail and kept there until you talk." In such a situation, the greater the witness's moral commitment to silence, to confidentiality in human relations, the greater the possibility of perpetual incarceration. And because of the principled nature of the witnesses' refusal, the major purpose for imposing a jail term – that of coercing the witnesses into testifying – would appear irrelevant. Only retribution remains, and we contend that the community does not demand or require retribution in this case.

> From the point of view of the National Council of Churches — and the community at large — the prospect of protracted imprisonment for civil contempt is horrifying. It is resoundingly offensive to the generally accepted sense of fairness of our society that a person who has committed no criminal act, has not been convicted by a jury of her peers nor even charged with any crime, can because of a moral commitment be placed in jail and returned to jail by means of successive grand juries.

The support of the Council was considered by the principals in the case to be vital, for it was the culmination of all the efforts by Grusse and Turgeon, their friends, and, most of all, the Grand Jury Defense Committee to turn the spotlight on the affair as a means of discouraging the Judge from disposing of it hastily or capriciously. "It worked, too — at least to a degree," one of the lawyers in the case said that morning, after the *amicus* was filed and made public. "At the start, all the contempt here was on the court's part. Newman dismissed everything we said with utter contempt, and treated us like lepers. But as support in the community and publicity in the media increased, he got more and more judicious, and increasingly took pains to seem fair, even if he wasn't at some points. Now with this huge support from the 'straight' community, he's got to be more careful than ever."

In this lawyer's opinion, the stand taken by the Council prompted Judge Newman to make an unprecedented, and wholly unexpected, move to resolve the problem of grand-jury abuse — by summoning the grand jurors into the courtroom at the hearing that morning and formally asking them what they considered their purpose to be in the present inquiry. At a quarter past eleven, the grand jurors filed into the courtroom; nineteen of the twenty-three members were present, and they were roughly divided between the sexes and ranged in age from the early twenties to the late sixties. Once they were seated in and around the petit-jury box, Judge Newman explained that he had brought them into court so that he could describe to them the law governing their procedure. While one purpose of any grand jury was to indict the guilty, he went on, another and equally important purpose was to protect the innocent. Pointing out that it was not permissible for a grand jury in one jurisdiction to ask witnesses questions about crimes committed in another jurisdiction, or to help the prosecutor prepare a case against someone who had already been indicted, or to get information that might lead to the capture of fugitives, Judge Newman asked the grand jurors to disregard whatever they thought their proper or desired purpose was supposed to be and to express only their personal opinion of what their actual purpose was in asking the two women the nineteen questions they had refused to answer. Then he gave them the list of the questions and posed the basic issue to be resolved: "Does the grand jury seek answers to these questions from these witnesses for the purpose of investigating possible violations of federal law that may have occurred in the district of Connecticut?" He asked nothing about whether this was their dominant purpose or whether they were trying to help the F.B.I. capture Power and prepare a case against her and Saxe.

Copies of the nineteen questions and the Judge's "interrogatory" were given to the grand jurors, but as they rose to leave Avery quickly got up and asked if he could approach the bench before they went out. Newman impatiently consented, the jurors sat down again, and Avery and the other lawyers in the case went to the side of the bench away from the jury box to confer with Newman out of the jurors' hearing. Avery asked the Judge not to permit Dow to accompany the jurors, but Newman curtly dismissed the request, saying Avery knew full well that the prosecutor was always with "his" grand jury. At that, Avery said that if Dow was allowed to be with the grand jurors during their deliberations, then a lawyer from the witnesses' side should be allowed to be present, too, but Newman rejected this request as well. He didn't tell the grand jurors that they had the right to decide who would be present when they talked over their purpose in the case, that they could even fire the prosecutor and demand that a new one be appointed, or that they could refuse to take any orders from the court – in short, that they could use their broad powers as *they* deemed fit. In any event, they left the courtroom at eleven-thirty, and a recess was ordered until they returned.

When Newman left the bench, Grusse stared at the wall behind and above it where the word "Justice" was carved in relief on the oak panelling. Then she shook her head slowly and said, "This is the biggest farce I've ever seen put on. The Judge is covering himself on everything in case there's an appeal. First he explained the grand jurors' duties to them, and then he asked their opinion, their personal opinion, about what their purpose is. Of course, they're going to say that their purpose conforms to their duties to investigate crime in the district of Connecticut. What else *can* they say? If they have any doubt about what they're supposed to say, Dow is in there to help them out." She shook her head again and fell silent.

A lawyer who followed the Grusse-Turgeon case but wasn't involved in it directly, and who had occasionally tried cases before Judge Newman, said that Newman's conduct throughout the affair had been typical of his and many other federal judges' approach to the law. "Newman is a decent sort of fellow and very smart," he said. "He's known as a liberal, because he always gives the appearance of being fair, but actually he's a tough law-enforcement guy. A balancing test always goes on in his mind, and the government always wins. He's not much different from other federal judges, except that he's more intelligent than most of them. Basically, like them, he reflects the system. He has an interest in seeing it operate without such gross abuse that the people will rise up and throw it out. That's the best way to preserve the system, of course. From what I've seen of him in action, I'd say that he really tries to apply the law. He knows that while the law itself isn't against the individual, the grand jury *is* against the individual. So he can go along strictly applying the law, because he's fairly certain that the grand jury will come out for law enforcement rather than the individual every time. That way, he looks great, and the government gets its way. It seems pretty clear that there *was* abuse of the grand-jury process and that there may have been illegal surveillance in the Grusse-Turgeon case. But Newman got around all that by putting a gloss of fairness on his decision to lock up these women."

An hour after the grand jurors went out, the foreman returned alone and handed the court clerk a piece of paper. The clerk gave it to Judge Newman, who read it and announced, to no one's surprise, that the grand jurors had unanimously agreed that their purpose was to investigate federal crimes committed in Connecticut. That settled the issue of grand-jury abuse. Then the Judge gave Dow three more days in which to collect affidavits from various government agencies on the question of surveillance, and set June 6th for a hearing on that issue. He was clearly irritated by the delay, and when he left the bench Grusse said to Avery, "You know, it's incredible the way everyone acts as if it's all right to tap people, even illegally. There's a federal judge who's sore at a federal prosecutor for taking so much time, and who says, in effect, 'Haven't you got this dirty business computerized by now?' "

At ten o'clock on the morning of June 6th, Dow announced in court that the government had completed its search of surveillance records, and added, "That search was negative." Glen argued that, given the kind of radical and criminal clients she and Avery represented, it would be extremely unlikely that the two of them or people they talked to hadn't been tapped. Newman showed little interest in this argument. He had directed the government to examine its surveillance files not only in the F.B.I. office in Hartford and in the Washington offices of the various government agencies that commonly employ such surveillance but in the field offices of the F.B.I. and the Justice Department in places where Saxe and Power were believed to have lived, such as Lexington, Kentucky, and Philadelphia. Now Glen pointed out that the government had failed to examine its records in these field offices as ordered by the court, and demanded that the subpoenas be quashed on that ground. As she sat down, the audience in the back half of the courtroom — about a hundred people, most of them women in their twenties and thirties — burst into applause. The Judge threatened them with expulsion or "other penalty," and when the tumult subsided he denied Glen's motion.

Toward the end of the hearing, Newman paused for a long time, and then said that the witnesses' claims had already been largely, if not entirely, ruled on by the Court of Appeals, and that nothing new and significant had been offered to change his view of the issues. The claims about grand-jury abuse, he went on, were no different from those made in the previous contempt case, and this time he had taken the additional precaution of asking the grand jurors their personal opinion of their investigative purpose. In the end, he added, the witnesses' overall attack was not on this grand jury's procedure but on the grand-jury system itself. The President of the United States wasn't above that process, he continued, so clearly these two witnesses were not above it. (Of course, President Nixon had refused to appear before a grand jury while in office, and he had not been found in contempt.) As for the claims about wiretapping, Newman said that he was quite satisfied with the government's denials, which he found "more than adequate." Finally, he announced that he would issue a formal order later that day finding the two witnesses in contempt.

Avery got up to plead for leniency in sentencing, and suggested that the court might impose "something less than confinement" or might at least limit any confinement to a specific period. Pointing out that the women had already spent twenty-eight days in prison, and that their lives had been "held in abeyance" since they were first subpoenaed more than four months before, he asked the Judge to consider "the constant strain, the constant demands, the travail" they had endured. Their refusal to testify, he went on, had been based from the start on principle, and because of that principle they would continue to refuse to testify, whatever "coercive penalty" was meted out to them, so any coercion would actually amount to punishment, which was a violation of the law in civil-contempt cases. Finally, Avery cited the broad public support for the women, including that of the National Council of Churches. Judge Newman broke in to say that the case wasn't "a popularity contest," and that he wouldn't be influenced in any manner by publicity. At that, Grusse and Turgeon smiled at each other.

Then Rosen got up and said, "No one should be compelled to choose between perishing or betraying a friend." The women had not been charged with any crime, he continued, but were being punished for refusing to betray their belief in the right to privacy.

When Glen took her turn, she asked the Judge to allow a representative of the National Council of Churches to speak on behalf of the two women. Newman refused, saying that he had read the Council's *amicus curiae* memorandum and would leave it at that. "These witnesses are *women*," Glen said angrily. "They're here because they are women. . . . Letting me address you as a woman merely because I'm a lawyer and not letting women who represent this community, this state, this country address you is an outrage!"

She stalked off to her seat, and Newman calmly turned to Grusse and Turgeon and asked if they had anything to say. Turgeon went to the bench to speak for both of them. "We have refused to answer these questions on the basis of principle," she told the Judge. "Imprisonment is not coercion but punishment. We haven't done anything wrong, and I think we should either be charged and tried or let go."

Finally, Dow got up and said that a robbery had been committed in Massachusetts in 1970 and that a policeman who had nine children had been killed. It wasn't true, he added, that the government was using the investigation of that crime and the search for those who were accused of committing it to find out more about the women's movement.

Judge Newman gave Grusse and Turgeon four days to settle their affairs, and ordered them to be taken into custody by the U.S. marshal at noon on Tuesday, June 10th, and to be imprisoned until they volunteered to testify or until the grand-jury term ran out – in sixteen months' time.

The audience immediately began chanting, "Silence is our right, is our right, is our right! With our sisters we will fight!" The marshal, who had been standing at the door, moved toward them bellowing, "Silence!" They obeyed, except for a couple of men who cried out, "Fascist! Fascist!" Finally, they fell silent, too. Judge Newman threatened anyone who disrupted the proceedings again with contempt-of-court sentences, and then he adjourned the proceedings and left the bench.

Turgeon turned toward Grusse and shrugged helplessly. With a wan smile, Grusse nodded. Neither of them spoke until a dozen or so women and a couple of men from among the spectators came up and embraced each of them in turn. A young woman with long brown hair and gold-rimmed glasses kissed each of them, then burst into tears and hurried out.

Glen watched the group in silence. "God, I hate courtroom practice," she said. "It's so brutal."

Given the Court of Appeals' rejection of their appeal back in February, Grusse and Turgeon decided that another appeal would be a waste of everyone's time. The time already spent on the case by the three lawyers had brought them little financial return — modest government pay for Rosen and Glen, who had been appointed by the court to represent the women as indigents, plus a relatively small contribution to the defense collected by the Grand Jury Defense Committee. The lawyers split the total, which came to about a tenth of what their fees would ordinarily have been. Despite their financial sacrifice, they were prepared to continue the legal battle, but in the end they agreed with their clients that an appeal would be futile.

That evening, Turgeon and Grusse left New Haven to spend the weekend at a women's retreat being held at a nearby camp in the woods. "That was what we needed most of all," Grusse said the following Monday. "We saw all our friends, but nobody talked about the case. We discussed *women's* problems, not ours, and that was just right. They know that there are real things at stake here — our personal integrity, our individuality, our independence, our sense of being ourselves — and they gave us both love and space. I've learned a lot from them. And I've learned a lot more from our experience. It has confirmed for me what the radicals have been saying about our society all along. Still, I'd hesitate to call myself a revolutionary. That word means violence to me, and I hate and fear violence of any kind. All I know for certain now is that I don't feel responsible or accountable to the United States government, because it's not responsible or accountable to me. I don't know what the future will bring – I might finally be forced into becoming a revolutionary, just as I was forced into this resistance – but for now all I want to do is fight injustice."

Turgeon listened to her and nodded slowly. "One of the big surprises in all this for me was I found I could stand up for a principle," she said. "That brought out traits in me that I didn't know were there, both strengths and weaknesses. It showed me how much I need other people, like our friends and supporters on the retreat. I *really* need them. Without the people who stood by us, I never would have made it. Then I learned how far I will go for something I believe in and how stubborn I can be. I've also been surprised by how political this has made me. Before I got involved in this case, I wasn't interested in politics at all. But now I see that all politics are personal, because they affect each of us every minute of our lives. I've always been afraid of any kind of authority, and I'm no less intimidated by it now, but at least I know where I stand and that I can stick there if I have to for my own sake. From now on, I won't talk to anybody about anybody. What goes on between two people *belongs* to those people."

Turgeon paused thoughtfully for a few moments, then went on, "Of course, all this has had a bad side, too. I realize that my future is probably going to include some kind of government agent. The government knows who I am now, and it will probably keep an eye on me and come by and try to question me from time to time just to keep me in line. And whatever I get involved in in the future, I will always wonder in the back of my mind whether maybe the person I'm dealing with is an undercover agent. That's pretty frightening. And the threat of being watched hangs over my friends simply because they are my friends. So in a way I feel less free, and people close to me feel less free. Someone even said to me the other day that I'm not free at all, that I'm being used by others for their own political ends. The idea that this is all some sort of power game really denies who I am – an individual acting on her own. Who I am is why I had to do what I've done. If I hadn't, I could never have been myself again."

After a week of cold, overcast, and rainy weather, June 10th turned out to be a perfect day, with a clear Caribbean sky and the temperature in the low seventies. At eleven o'clock that morning, Grusse and Turgeon attended a rally on their behalf held on the New Haven Green — a spacious, well-tended park opposite the post office. About a hundred people, again mostly young women, were there, and they milled about in small groups, talking and laughing together. Avery was on hand, and he watched his clients as they stood chatting animatedly with a couple of friends. He looked off at the fresh spring green of the park and shook his head. "It's terrible for a lawyer the day a client is taken away," he said. "But to go to prison on an incredibly beautiful day like this is too much — too much." A minute later, the group formed into ranks of six, with its members placing their arms around each others' shoulders or waists, and began walking at a leisurely pace toward a First World War monument — a flagpole atop a marble-and-bronze base — a few hundred yards away, near the center of the Green. As they marched, they sang, "Some of our sisters are subpoenaed./ *Bella ciao, bella ciao, bella ciao, ciao, ciao./* Their silence makes us speak out:/ We want our revolution now."

The group stopped at the monument, where several television and newspaper reporters were waiting, and Turgeon read a brief statement. "It is not out of respect for the courts, or for the unjust treatment we have received in those courts, but out of respect for ourselves and the people who have supported us that we are here," she said, and then repeated the charges about the government's persecution and its political motives. Afterward, the group sang several women's-liberation songs, some of its members came up to say good-bye to the two women, and then the gathering formed into ranks again and headed off toward the post office. In the corridor on the second floor, the marshal looked out the window as the file moved toward and across Church Street. "I wish it had rained," he said to a deputy marshal. "Rain always keeps down the crowds." At that moment, the crowd reached the front door of the post office, and suddenly began chanting, "Silence is our right, is our right, is our right!" A couple of minutes later, the post-office elevator stopped at the second floor, the door slowly slid back, and Grusse, Turgeon, Polan, Avery, and Rosen stepped out.

"Are you ready to surrender, Mr. Avery?" the marshal asked.

Avery nodded, and the two women stepped forward. The marshal took up a position at one side of them, the deputy took the other flank, and the group walked rapidly down the hallway to the marshal's office. This time, there was no special police guard on hand, but Turgeon and Grusse were again searched for weapons, handcuffed, chained together at the waist, and driven under guard to the Connecticut Correctional Institution at Niantic.

On September 26th, after the two women had been in prison for another fifteen weeks, Avery filed a motion and a supporting brief with the District Court requesting a "revocation of order of confinement." Despite the court's decision that his clients' arguments "in defense of their silence are either legally insufficient or irrelevant," Avery wrote, "they have remained committed to the moral and ethical principles, and to their constitutional rights as they understand them, which underlie their decision not to respond to the questions of the government before the grand jury. They will continue to refuse to answer the questions of the government before the grand jury." Accordingly, he concluded, "continued incarceration of the witnesses would be punitive rather than coercive."

Seven weeks later, Judge Newman rejected the request. Speaking in general of witnesses who are found in contempt — "contemnors," in legalese — he said, "If a contemnor's own insistence that he will not answer could be used to hasten his release, the coercive purpose of the civil-contempt remedy would be turned upside down. The contemnor would secure his release as soon as he demonstrated the continuing contumacious nature of his conduct." And in response to Avery's contention that the grand-jury investigation of the case had not continued and was not "serious," Newman said, "Those who have thwarted its progress cannot realistically complain of its lack of success."

It seemed clear to the lawyers for Turgeon and Grusse that Judge Newman had no intention of releasing them before the grand jury's term expired, on September 19, 1976. In an attempt to make life somewhat easier for them in prison, Avery wrote the Judge a personal letter in November, 1975, asking him to intervene on their behalf. As it happened, they had been transferred in late summer to the Niantic prison's "honor cottage," which was reserved for prisoners who had been, Turgeon said later, "real, *real* good." The policy at the prison was to allow ordinary inmates a forty-eight-hour weekend furlough every sixty days, whereas residents of the honor cottage were allowed such furloughs, plus six extra hours, every thirty days. Grusse and Turgeon had applied for a furlough soon after moving into the honor cottage but so far had not been granted one — on the ground, the warden told them, that it had to be approved by the District Court, since they were not, like the other inmates, "sentenced" prisoners but could obtain their release anytime they decided to coöperate with the government. Now Avery asked Judge Newman to allow the two women a furlough for Christmas, and said, "Whether or not they are released for brief periods of time [for] holiday or other furloughs is hardly likely to affect their decision not to testify. Indeed, it seems to me that a brief visit outside the institution with family and friends, if it has any effect, might make long-term incarceration even more painful than it already is. In any event, it certainly will not make the lengthy confinement these women now face any less coercive." And, he added, "It would seem not only ironic but unfair if Ms. Grusse and Ms. Turgeon, who are the only women at Niantic who have not been convicted of any criminal offense, have less privileges than other prisoners."

A couple of weeks later, before Newman had replied, Rosen learned that Dow was disturbed about the Grusse-Turgeon case, and wanted to find some way of settling it other than by keeping the two women in prison indefinitely. Rosen immediately went to see Dow, who told him that he had formerly been convinced that such middle-class women as Turgeon and Grusse wouldn't be able to endure prison life, and sooner or later would agree to testify. Now, he said, he was convinced that they would never talk. While he thought their decision was foolish, he had come to accept it, but he was upset by the adverse publicity the government might get if it let them out of prison now. Rosen knew that there had been a lot of pressure on Dow — much of it generated by the Grand Jury Defense Committee — to release the women, so he quickly pointed out that the grand-jury investigation had obviously come to a standstill and couldn't proceed without the women's testimony, which would never be forthcoming. Dow heard him out, nodded, and, after a few minutes' thought, said that he would drop the case.

On December 18th, Dow wrote Judge Newman a letter outlining the facts in the case and concluding, "Although the grand jury's investigation remains incomplete, the subpoenas for Grusse and Turgeon's testimony are withdrawn at this time and need no longer be enforced by adjudication of contempt. It should be noted, however, that the investigation may develop further information which may cause the witnesses to be subpoenaed again."

The Judge had no choice but to order the two released from prison. His order was filed with the court at twelve minutes after ten o'clock on the morning of December 19th, Grusse and Turgeon were informed at ten-thirty, and they left Niantic — for good, they hoped — at a little after one-thirty that afternoon. They had served a total of seven months and one week.

The first move the two women intended to make, after enjoying the holiday festivities, was to do whatever they could to help a woman named Jill Raymond, who had been sent to jail for contempt of court, together with four other women and a man, in Lexington, Kentucky, for refusing to talk to a federal grand jury there about Saxe and Power shortly after Grusse and Turgeon had defied the District Court in New Haven back in early February. The six in Lexington remained silent for several weeks, but finally the intolerable conditions in the local jail where they were locked up persuaded all but Jill Raymond to coöperate with the authorities. When Turgeon and Grusse got out of Niantic, Raymond was still in jail — in fact, she served more than a year for her silence. Early in January of 1976, Grusse and Turgeon telephoned a friend of Raymond's in Lexington and said they wanted to visit her in jail, and perhaps attend some rallies in her support. The friend gave them detailed instructions on which highway routes to take, and on January 7th the two set out, in Turgeon's Volkswagen, for the trip to Lexington.

"We were followed all the way," Grusse said afterward. "At each state line, a different car, always with two men in it, would pick us up and keep us under surveillance. They were very obvious about it at times. One car followed us for a long while, and then it passed us very slowly, while the passenger carefully looked at both our rear and front license plates, and then he picked up a telephone and talked to someone. So we're not free even now."

In the view of one of the lawyers in the case, the authorities' continuing harassment of these women was further evidence that they were "just pawns in a great chess game being played by the government." He added, "They were never accused of any crime, yet they were treated worse than if they had been convicted felons. And, from beginning to end, their fate lay in the hands of Willie Dow. He tried to be a good man and to act justly, but he failed. In effect, *he* tried them, *he* sentenced them, and *he* let them out."

Once again, events demonstrated that ours is a government of men, not laws.

Epilogue

Too Strong for Liberty

"It has long been a grave question whether any government, not too strong for the liberties of its people, can be strong enough to maintain its own existence in great emergencies," Abraham Lincoln said in November, 1864, to a group of citizens who had come to the White House to congratulate him on his reëlection to the Presidency. Since a national election had just been held during a great civil war — an event unique in world history, he told his audience — Lincoln was satisfied that both government and personal liberty had been preserved. Today, though, this nation seems to exist in a permanent state of emergency. There is always a threat of war abroad, with the attendant peril of nuclear holocaust; there is rampant crime at home that stirs the deepest fears of the ordinary citizen; there is political terrorism; there is economic frailty; and there is constant government usurpation of our liberties. At best, it is difficult for us to endure the uncertainties and pressures of modern society, and this raises a question that is at least as grave as the one Lincoln posed: Do most Americans truly want liberty?

Freedom can be a heavy burden, because it demands the kind of mental and moral exertion that many people are not equal to. They want to be told what to do, and they seek leaders who will command them, who will provide them with the dependence and security of childhood. They are the "timid men" Jefferson spoke of who "prefer the calm of despotism to the boisterous sea of liberty." The number of such people in this country cannot even be guessed at, but there must be a lot of them to have brought our nation to its turning point — where the people allow their government to behave as though they exist for its sake.

If privacy is, as has often been said, essential to a civilized society, we may not be sufficiently civilized to demand, or accept, freedom. According to a nationwide poll taken by Roper Reports in 1974, an astonishing number of Americans are willing to have their privacy invaded by just about anyone — that is, they accept the most pervasive and destructive form of tyranny over their personal lives. When asked what they would permit a government agency that was considering them for jobs to know about them, seventy-four per cent said they would turn over their prior employment records, sixty-four per cent their medical records, sixty-six per cent their psychiatric records, and thirty-one per cent their sexual histories; and when they were asked what they would allow local police to know about them, twenty-seven per cent said they would permit examination of their employment records, twenty-five per cent their medical records, thirty-four per cent their psychiatric records, and twenty per cent their sexual histories. Taking only the last, and lowest, figure, it means that some twenty-seven million adult Americans are willing to let their local policemen know the most intimate details of their most intimate lives.

Nor do the people seem greatly perturbed about even more dangerous threats to their liberty than the Watergate episode — the widespread illegal activities of the F.B.I., the C.I.A., the I.R.S., the N.S.A., and various military "intelligence" outfits. Newspaper reports and congressional hearings have revealed, and these organizations have admitted, that government officials in the past few years have broken the law in many thousands of cases, and have violated our most sacred rights — to express ourselves freely, to be secure in our homes, and not to be forced to testify against ourselves and inform on others. Charles James, Margaret and Alan McSurely, Ellen Grusse, and Terri Turgeon are only examples of what has been happening in this country, and their cases could be duplicated by thousands of others.

The government has opened and read citizens' mail, it has tapped their telephones and planted electronic bugs in their bedrooms, it has bribed informers to concoct false evidence against them, it has written anonymous and untrue letters to their associates and employers to get them in trouble, it has turned Mafia killers against radicals, it has fomented riots, it has broken into and ransacked the homes and offices of political dissenters, it has encouraged police violence and trained policemen to break the law, it has prompted militants to murder one another, and it has tried to blackmail and drive to suicide one of the greatest leaders in American history. Moreover, it has done all this to Americans who were innocent under the law. Yet the general public doesn't seem to care. Its response to these revelations was so muted that the congressional investigations into them were cut short long before they were completed. What is more, not a single government official who broke the law has been prosecuted.

Perhaps George Orwell was right when he observed that most people don't mind tyranny as long as it is imposed on them in an acceptable form. Perhaps we have the freedom that we now possess only because a few men and women — like those in this book — have stood up to the juggernaut of government to preserve their own freedom, and have saved some measure of it for the rest of us. Perhaps, on the other hand, the great majority of the American people want to be free, and fail to fight for freedom only because the myth has persuaded them that they already have it and are secure. Of course, they are not, and unless they awaken to reality and demand their rights, one day they won't have any.

The pressures in favor of tyranny in America are immense. Most policemen, prosecutors, judges, members of Congress, and bureaucrats, together with many millions of citizens, clamor for order — for security — above all else. They have forgotten not only the lessons taught by the Founders of this nation, but now put aside all thought of the courage that it takes to be free. "Our nation at the time of the Constitutional Convention was also faced with formidable problems," Chief Justice Warren said during the tumultuous discord that tore at this country during the nineteen-sixties. "The English, the French, the Spanish, and various tribes of hostile Indians were all ready and eager to subvert or occupy the fledgling Republic. Nevertheless, in that environment our Founding Fathers conceived a Constitution and Bill of Rights replete with provisions indicating their determination to protect human rights. There was no call for a garrison state in those times of precarious peace. We should heed no such call now."

Although Americans feel powerless before their government today, they are still the ultimate repository of power in the United States, and they still have the means to regain their rights and to restore their individual liberties – if they have the will.

Our system of government was marvellously wrought by the Framers, who mistrusted every man and all power to such a degree that they designed the Constitution to strictly control those who govern in the name of the people, and to fragment every aspect of delegated power by endless checks and balances. Almost from the start, though, that system has been relentlessly perverted by Congress, by the executive, and by the courts, until it scarcely resembles its original form. Indeed, it could be said that democracy has never actually been tried in America, and that much of what has survived of the Framers' ideas are merely the symbols of democracy that make up the myth of freedom.

The erosion of democracy in America began soon after this nation was founded – in a manner that has been widely ignored by historians and that is wholly unknown to the public at large. In 1793, two years after adoption of the Bill of Rights, the Supreme Court was asked, by way of Chisholm v. Georgia, whether a citizen of one state who had been deprived of his property in another state could sue it in federal court for recovery of damages. The issue was as crucial as any ever presented to the Court, for it raised the problem of whether the states, and indirectly the federal government, could be sued for damages by individual citizens who believed their rights had been violated. By analogy, the issue was similar to the ancient doctrine called sovereign immunity — that is, the tradition in England that the king cannot be sued. Since under a republican form of government the people are sovereign, the basic question to be resolved was whether one sovereign person could sue the collective sovereign people when the power they had delegated was used to violate his legal rights. The resolution of this question has been a national and a personal calamity, for it has rendered the Bill of Rights nearly meaningless.

By the reign of Edward I, in the middle of the thirteenth century, the doctrine of sovereign immunity was taken to mean that the king could not be sued by name in his own courts. But this did not mean that a subject who had been unjustly treated by the Crown had no recourse. In modern times it has been widely believed, especially by lawyers, that the expression "the king can do no wrong" meant that he could not even be accused of wrongdoing and thus was immune. Actually, this statement meant exactly the opposite — namely, "that the king must not, was not allowed to, not entitled to do wrong." If he did, his wrong had to be righted, so that in the end he had done no wrong. Subjects had a variety of resorts to defend themselves against royal injustice — most notably, the so-called petition of right. "In theory, at least, and there is no positive evidence as far as I know that practice did not accord with theory, consent [to hear such a petition] was given not on the basis of expediency but of law," Professor Louis L. Jaffe, of the Harvard Law School, has written. "The Chancellor made certain factual inquiries and searched the petition to determine whether there was a 'right;' if he concluded that there was, he endorsed the petition that right be done." By the time of the American Revolution, Jaffe added, the "doctrine of sovereign immunity was largely an abstract idea" and didn't limit "the subject's right to relief against government illegality."

When the United States Constitution and the Bill of Rights were written, they contained nothing about either sovereign immunity or petitions of right. If state governments and the national government were sovereign entities and there was no right of petition to the executive, then Americans had sacrificed incalculably precious rights that they had possessed as Englishmen. In any event, the Supreme Court, which then consisted of six members, denied that this had happened by ruling in a four-to-one vote that Chisholm *could* sue Georgia. In the United States, Chief Justice John Jay said, the people are "sovereigns without subjects." And Justice James Wilson, one of the authors of the Constitution, rejected the concept of sovereign immunity altogether. The states are not sovereign but every man is, he said, and added, "The only reason, I believe, why a free man is bound by human laws is *that he binds himself.*"

The Court's decision was essential to a representative system of government, but members of Congress, fearing that the states they represented and whose powers they meant to preserve might be engulfed by a flood of debts left over from the Revolution if the decision was allowed to stand, immediately adopted the Eleventh Amendment: "The judicial power of the United States shall not be construed to extend to any suit in law or equity commenced or prosecuted against one of the United States by citizens of another state, or by citizens or subjects of any foreign state." In short, if one state said that a citizen of another state or country couldn't sue it, the federal courts could not intervene. Five years later, in 1798, the states ratified the amendment. Then, in 1821, the Supreme Court reversed its position in Chisholm and ruled, in Cohens v. Virginia, that citizens of the United States could *not* sue it unless it consented.

The decision, which was delivered by Chief Justice John Marshall, a vigorous defender of strong government, was remarkable mostly for its avoidance of the basic issue. Looking back on the case sixty years later, the Supreme Court observed, "The terms in which Mr. Chief Justice Marshall there gives assent to the principle [of sovereign immunity] does not add much to its force. 'The counsel for the defendant,' he says, 'has laid down the general proposition that a sovereign state is not suable except by its own consent.' This general proposition, he adds, will not be controverted. And while the exemption of the United States and of the several states from being subjected as defendants to ordinary actions in the courts had since that time been repeatedly asserted here, the principle has never been discussed or the reasons for it given, but it has always been treated as an established doctrine."

By this extraordinarily casual process, one of the most fundamental rights of a free people was cast aside, and a form of sovereign immunity that was far more restrictive and oppressive than the form that the British had imposed on the American colonists became the law of the land. In time, this legal tradition spread from the national government to the states, counties, cities, towns, and villages. With its adoption, citizens lost the most effective weapon they might have had against government tyranny. And, by this means, our government finally became too strong for the liberties of its people.

Even so, sovereign immunity is not an immutable doctrine. As a matter of fact, it has been increasingly attacked and weakened throughout this country in recent years. Since 1957, for example, twenty-five states have largely abolished their own sovereign immunity, either judicially or legislatively; seventeen states have modified the doctrine in a variety of ways; and only eight states still retain it in its feudal form. Among municipal governments, sovereign immunity is now the exception rather than the rule, and the nationwide trend is strongly toward modifying or getting rid of it. In general, the argument that has prevailed against it has been that since the citizen who has been injured by government is entitled to some sort of redress, at least payment of "money damages" should be awarded and the cost spread among the public at large as part of the inevitable expense of government administration.

But total immunity still exists on every level for judges and legislators and for executive officials who exercise a "discretionary function." This term, which has created more confusion than enlightenment, is usually interpreted by courts to mean that any official who devises or carries out a policy matter of any kind is immune for his actions. Courts fall back on this defense as a way of allowing government officials nearly total freedom to do more or less as they please; otherwise, it is argued, they would be intimidated from acting at all. The argument is specious, for they *should* be intimidated from infringing on the constitutional rights of the people. While judges probably should continue to be immune from liability for their decisions, they should not be immune for their contumacious behavior toward litigants and lawyers who appear before them — behavior that often amounts to a denial of due process of law or of other constitutional rights. And while legislators probably should continue to be immune from liability for what they do and say that is intrinsic to the process of devising legislation, they should not be immune for clearly nonlegislative conduct that violates someone's basic rights.

Despite the advances on state and local levels, on the federal level — where the machinery, the opportunity, and the will to oppress the individual are greatest — sovereign immunity remains largely intact. Although the Federal Torts Claim Act of 1946, as amended in 1974, allows citizens who are physically injured or whose rights are physically and capriciously violated by government employees in the course of their official duties to sue the government itself for money damages, the government is not liable unless its agent can be shown to have been negligent and not to have been exercising a discretionary function. Moreover, the act contains innumerable exceptions that retain official immunity, and since it covers mainly physical injury it has nothing to do, in most cases, with official violations of citizens' constitutional rights. The furthest that the Supreme Court has allowed the injured citizen to go in most constitutional cases is to sue officials as individuals but not as agents of the government. That, of course, reduces the chances of collecting enough damages to make a lawsuit worthwhile. And, finally, if the official can show that he acted in good faith — that is, he believed his act was proper and legal — no damages are awarded.

Such rulings by the Court leave us in the peculiar position of being able to sue, say, the American Telephone and Telegraph Co., which we do not control, for its employees' illegal acts, but not able to sue the American government, which we are supposed to control, for *our* employees' illegal acts. The basic justification for this curious dichotomy is that the Court has again taken a pro-state position by ruling that corporations are "persons" under the law but public entities are not. Professor Burt Neuborne recently wrote, "In private law, once an unlawful act has been established, the focus immediately shifts to the amount of harm suffered by the plaintiff without regard to the defendant's culpability. In constitutional law, once the unlawful act has been determined, the focus remains on the amount of culpability of the defendant's act. If it is not great, no compensation is awarded, no matter how seriously the plaintiff has been damaged." The unsuccessful lawsuits by those who were injured and the survivors of those who were killed by National Guardsmen at Kent State University in 1970 demonstrates the point. (Another case in point is that of Charles James, who collected both back pay and damages against local school officials probably because of their particular legal defense. If they had pleaded that their decision to dismiss him as a teacher was a discretionary function taken in good faith, James might have won reinstatement to his job, but he might not have been awarded back pay, and he almost certainly wouldn't have received payment for damages.)

Various federal-court rulings on questions of official immunity have established the principle that it can be abrogated only when an official act is sufficiently culpable to warrant punishment of the wrongdoer as a means of deterring similar officials from undertaking similar actions in the future, without unduly intimidating them in carrying out their duties. On this point, Neuborne wrote, "As it is currently applied, the law of constitutional compensation systematically subordinates the goal of compensating individual plaintiffs for injuries caused by unconstitutional actions to twin concerns of deterring future violations of law while avoiding over-deterrence of proper governmental conduct. In subordinating compensation to deterrence, the law ignores the grievance which brought the plaintiff into court and concentrates instead on enunciating appropriate norms of conduct for the future [official] while leaving the plaintiff . . . essentially unaided." Once again, then, the courts have taken a statist position on this most fundamental issue by ignoring or making secondary the citizen's constitutional rights. And these are the same courts that consider punishment the best deterrent — except when the culprit is a government official.

In all likelihood, the courts have based these decisions not on the Constitution, not on precedent, not on historical tradition, but rather on efficiency and economy in government. That, too, is essentially statist, for it makes government interests paramount to the public interest. It is a case of the United States v. the People. If government efficiency is more important than justice and personal rights, then democracy is bound to perish. Democracy is by its nature inefficient, even unmanageable at times, for its fundamental purpose — to allow the individual to flourish — inevitably creates disorder. Only despotism is efficient.

Nor should the cost of allowing citizens to sue government for violating their rights be the final, or even a major, concern. The primary concern should be that government is ultimately answerable to the people. As matters stand now, the government's violations of the Bill of Rights can be countered by the individual only through the most painful, time-consuming, expensive, and usually futile litigation. In the end, the best the citizen can hope for is that some court along the arduous way will reverse and condemn the government's unconstitutional act. But, as in the McSurely case, that leaves the citizen where he or she was before the government acted, for in almost all cases nothing is done to punish the wrongdoers or to repay the victims.

If immunity in the federal government were to be abolished or strictly limited, the financial cost of damage awards would probably be less than the costs of litigation. Any substantial increase in federal litigation would require expansion of the federal judiciary, which is already overburdened. But even a major expansion would cost comparatively little, because the entire budget of the federal judiciary is less than one-tenth of one per cent of the federal budget. In other words, if federal courts were multiplied by ten, the cost would be less than one per cent of the nation's cost of government. And that amount would still be less than one-quarter of what we now spend on the office of the Presidency alone.

While such a sum would probably be more than enough for the

expenses of judicial administration without immunity, it seems unlikely that even that much money would be needed. Most people are terrified by the thought of going to court, let alone of standing up to the government. Further, most lawyers won't take clients who can't pay them, and any lawsuit is expensive. The examples of those who fight for their rights — like the people in these pages — and who spend years of their lives and endless energy and concern would almost surely discourage most others from following their course. Assuredly, though, some people would assert the right to call the government to account, and even if they were few they would create an immensely effective symbol by demonstrating that the people are sovereign after all. And, inevitably, they would make all government officials hesitant to violate any of our rights. If the government fears they will become so afraid they won't act at all, it can simply take upon itself the costs, or most of the costs, of such lawsuits against them when they break the law, and share their burden as a co-defendant. Those are the inescapable costs not just of administering government but of preserving personal liberty.

Finally, to make sure that this right would be more than a mere symbol, it would be practical, and fair, to require the government to pay the legal costs of citizens who prove in court that their rights have been officially and illegally violated. Above all, this would encourage private lawyers to represent those who have clearly been illegally treated by government. A simple statute, demanded by the public and enacted by Congress, would fulfill both ends:

> Any citizen of the United States shall be entitled to sue the government of the United States or any state thereof for official acts by its officers which deprive the citizen of any constitutional right. Citizens who prevail in such suits shall have all reasonable legal costs reimbursed by the United States or the respective state.

Of course, such a law would not instantly give us the freedom that we have so long proclaimed. But it would be a start toward recovering our inalienable rights. It would warn government that it is the servant, not the master, of the people. And it would give all of us the encouragement and the hope that we so sorely need.

One of the gravest perils facing this nation today is the public's mistrust of government. Mistrust is readily transformed into cynicism and cynicism into despair, and a people's despair leaves them prey to tyrants. In America mistrust of government is sweeping the country, and it cannot be concealed or ignored in the hope that it will go away, any more than our belief in the myth of freedom will make us free. Watergate and the official lawlessness committed by our "intelligence community" on an unprecedented scale are merely symptoms of the disease afflicting the body politic. The disease itself is the arrogance of power — immense, overwhelming, pervasive, uncaring power — before which the individual feels utterly helpless. But we are not helpless. Richard Nixon, one of the most powerful Presidents in American history, was forced to flee from office in disgrace solely because we discovered that he had betrayed us. No leader and no democracy can survive without "the consent of the governed." If we consent to be ruled as we are now being ruled, we shall surely trade democracy for tyranny. But if we demand that *our* government be answerable to *us* — to each of us as an individual whose personal rights are beyond the reach of government — then in time we shall become free at last.

Index

Index

INDEX

Index

INDEX